THE DESERT IN MODERN LITERATURE AND PHILOSOPHY

Crosscurrents

Exploring the development of European thought through engagements with the arts, humanities, social sciences and sciences

Series Editor
Christopher Watkin, Monash University

Editorial Advisory Board
Andrew Benjamin
Martin Crowley
Simon Critchley
Frederiek Depoortere
Oliver Feltham
Patrick ffrench
Christopher Fynsk
Kevin Hart
Emma Wilson

Titles available in the series
Difficult Atheism: Post-Theological Thinking in Alain Badiou, Jean-Luc Nancy and Quentin Meillassoux
Christopher Watkin
Politics of the Gift: Exchanges in Poststructuralism
Gerald Moore
Unfinished Worlds: Hermeneutics, Aesthetics and Gadamer
Nicholas Davey
The Figure of This World: Agamben and the Question of Political Ontology
Mathew Abbott
The Becoming of the Body: Contemporary Women's Writing in French
Amaleena Damlé
Philosophy, Animality and the Life Sciences
Wahida Khandker
The Event Universe: The Revisionary Metaphysics of Alfred North Whitehead
Leemon B. McHenry
Sublime Art: Towards an Aesthetics of the Future
Stephen Zepke
Mallarmé and the Politics of Literature: Sartre, Kristeva, Badiou, Rancière
Robert Boncardo
Animal Writing: Storytelling, Selfhood and the Limits of Empathy
Danielle Sands
Music, Philosophy and Gender in Nancy, Lacoue-Labarthe, Badiou
Sarah Hickmott
The Desert in Modern Literature and Philosophy: Wasteland Aesthetics
Aidan Tynan

Forthcoming Titles
Visual Art and Projects of the Self
Katrina Mitcheson

Visit the Crosscurrents website at www.edinburghuniversitypress.com/series-crosscurrents.html

THE DESERT IN MODERN LITERATURE AND PHILOSOPHY

Wasteland Aesthetics

Aidan Tynan

EDINBURGH
University Press

Edinburgh University Press is one of the leading university presses in the UK. We publish academic books and journals in our selected subject areas across the humanities and social sciences, combining cutting-edge scholarship with high editorial and production values to produce academic works of lasting importance. For more information visit our website: edinburghuniversitypress.com

© Aidan Tynan, 2020, 2022

Edinburgh University Press Ltd
The Tun – Holyrood Road, 12(2f) Jackson's Entry, Edinburgh EH8 8PJ

First published in hardback by Edinburgh University Press 2020

Typeset in 10.5/13 Sabon by
Servis Filmsetting Ltd, Stockport, Cheshire

A CIP record for this book is available from the British Library

ISBN 978 1 4744 4335 7 (hardback)
ISBN 978 1 4744 4336 4 (paperback)
ISBN 978 1 4744 4337 1 (webready PDF)
ISBN 978 1 4744 4338 8 (epub)

The right of Aidan Tynan to be identified as the author of this work has been asserted in accordance with the Copyright, Designs and Patents Act 1988, and the Copyright and Related Rights Regulations 2003 (SI No. 2498).

Contents

Series Editor's Preface	vi
Acknowledgements	viii
Introduction	1
1. Desert Desire	6
2. Desert Immanence	52
3. Desert Refrains	94
4. Desert Islands	138
5. Desert Polemologies	177
Conclusion: Beyond the Carbon Imaginary	221
Bibliography	228
Index	248

Series Editor's Preface

Two or more currents flowing into or through each other create a turbulent crosscurrent, more powerful than its contributory flows and irreducible to them. Time and again, modern European thought creates and exploits crosscurrents in thinking, remaking itself as it flows through, across and against discourses as diverse as mathematics and film, sociology and biology, theology, literature and politics. The work of Gilles Deleuze, Jacques Derrida, Slavoj Žižek, Alain Badiou, Bernard Stiegler and Jean-Luc Nancy, among others, participates in this fundamental remaking. In each case disciplines and discursive formations are engaged, not with the aim of performing a predetermined mode of analysis yielding a 'philosophy of x', but through encounters in which thought itself can be transformed. Furthermore, these fundamental transformations do not merely seek to account for singular events in different sites of discursive or artistic production but rather to engage human existence and society as such, and as a whole. The cross-disciplinarity of this thought is therefore neither a fashion nor a prosthesis; it is simply part of what 'thought' means in this tradition.

Crosscurrents begins from the twin convictions that this remaking is integral to the legacy and potency of European thought, and that the future of thought in this tradition must defend and develop this legacy in the teeth of an academy that separates and controls the currents that flow within and through it. With this in view, the series provides an exceptional site for bold, original and opinion-changing monographs that actively engage European thought in this fundamentally cross-disciplinary manner, riding existing crosscurrents and creating new ones. Each book in the series explores the different ways in which European thought develops through its engagement with disciplines across the arts, humanities, social sciences and sciences, recognising that the community of scholars working with this thought is itself spread across diverse faculties. The object of the series is therefore nothing less than to examine and carry forward the unique legacy of European thought as an inherently and irreducibly cross-disciplinary enterprise.

Christopher Watkin
Cambridge
February 2011

Acknowledgements

Since I first conceived the idea for this project about ten years ago, a great number of people have contributed in a great number of ways towards the final product. I am especially indebted to Chris Müller, whose influence and support have been crucial to me, and who has proved a salvation on more than one occasion. In addition, I am enormously grateful to Ian Buchanan, Oliver Dawson, Tom Harman, Tim Matts, Reuben Martens, Ceri Sullivan, Caleb Sivyer, Martin Willis and all of my colleagues at Cardiff University, past and present. My parents Ted and Carmel have my respect and gratitude, now and always.

Thanks are due to Chris Watkin for carefully reading the entire manuscript and offering some key suggestions and corrections. Thanks are likewise due to Carol Macdonald at Edinburgh University Press for her exemplary editorship and advice. I would like to thank the postgraduate students who have taken my Ecotheories module over the past few years. Our classroom discussions helped shape and refine my thinking on many of the issues explored in the following pages. A period of research leave generously provided by the School of English, Communication and Philosophy at Cardiff University gave me the time necessary to complete this book.

Finally, it is with deepest love and eternal admiration that I thank Sophie, who has been a singular inspiration and an abiding light in the darkness. Without her, this book would not exist.

For Sophie

Introduction

> The desert grows: woe to him who harbors deserts!
> Friedrich Nietzsche, *Thus Spoke Zarathustra*

> 'Devastation' means for us, after all, that everything – the world, the human, and the earth – will be transformed into a desert. . . . The being of an age of devastation would then consist precisely in the abandonment of being. Such a matter is, however, difficult to think.
> Martin Heidegger, 'Evening Conversation'

> For here is the desert propagated by our world, and also the new earth.
> Gilles Deleuze and Félix Guattari, *Anti-Oedipus*

> Stay in the desert long enough, and you could apprehend the absolute. The number zero was holy.
> Margaret Atwood, 'Time Capsule Found on the Dead Planet'

It is entirely fitting that there is no simple or self-evident approach, no clear path, to the topic of the desert. We can grasp it as a natural wilderness or as a barren wasteland, as an ecology sometimes unusually rich in life and surprisingly fragile, as an idea of geographical extremity or alterity, as a sacred or accursed site, as a metaphor for nullity, as a subjective or existential terrain, or as an object of sheer aesthetic exultation. This book moves freely between these and other conceptions of the desert. I remain guided throughout, however, by a set of philosophical texts, beginning with the work of Nietzsche, in which the desert is figured principally as a speculative topology, a *place of thought* where an exhausted metaphysical tradition can imagine its self-overcoming. An immediate objection may be that this philosophical topology is not a real desert but a mere metaphor or rhetorical strategy, one concocted, furthermore, by a Western subjectivity ill equipped for life in desert places. The objection is legitimate, but my response – on which this entire project rests – is twofold.

First, it is not at all obvious where the distinction between the real and rhetorically constructed desert lies. Even scientists have noted the problem of comprehensively determining what a 'real' desert is – as one scientific text puts it, 'no single, conclusive ecological definition of the term "desert" has been accepted'.[1] In any case, all places are, to one extent or another, rhetorical or semiotic constructions. Deserts seem especially so precisely because they challenge life's ability to *make* a place for itself. They thus tend to put our conceptions of place and belonging into question. This is borne out by the analyses of literary deserts from Romanticism to the contemporary period that occupy much of this book. Second, that the Western philosophical tradition has been preoccupied with deserts itself demands investigation given the ecological crises we now find ourselves facing. Since Nietzsche, the problem of nihilism – the loss of confidence in 'higher values', in the transcendent authority of God and state – has been repeatedly explored through the figure of the desert as an ambiguous terrain of both loss and salvation, that is to say, as a risky *soteriological* terrain. That the Earth today is recognised as bearing the indelible marks of industrialised humanity is not unrelated to the fact that philosophers for the past century or more have used the desert to think through a crisis of modern subjectivity in the aftermath of the death of God.

What we find when we look at deserts and wastelands in literary texts from Percy Bysshe Shelley's sonnet 'Ozymandias' (1818) to Don DeLillo's novel *Point Omega* (2010) is that they feature as symbols and motifs for this crisis. The approach I pursue owes much to ecocriticism, inescapably, but I reject the privileging of place found in the vast majority of ecocritical work. Rather than presume the grounding role of the home or habitat (the *oikos*), I enquire into what happens when such a presumption becomes untenable, when earthly life of all kinds must come to terms – as today it must – with an attenuation of the grounding role of its territories. Simply put, ecocriticism must move beyond the ecocentricity on which it is founded in order to grasp the crises of ecology now underway. To the extent that the desert often features as a site of what Deleuze and Guattari call 'deterritorialisation' – meaning a loss or at least a loosening of the links that bind life to its territories – then an exploration of the desert in modern literature and philosophy is able to speak in important ways to our contemporary environmental condition. Rather than place and environment, then, I focus on ideas of Earth, world, territory, and space or spatiality in a manner that is best described, following Deleuze and Guattari's terminology, as geophilosophical.

Our ideas about the natural environment are connected in deep and complex ways to aesthetic pleasure and unpleasure, that is, to *desire*. Deserts have provoked a range of affective and libidinal responses occupying a wide spectrum: disgust, boredom, terror, apathy, curiosity, joy, contentment and love. By focusing on what I call 'wasteland aesthetics', I might risk overstating the negative end of that spectrum, but this is not at all my intention. Deserts can be and have often been regarded as the geographical correlate of death, places in which life's organic limits are tested. But just as death is for us such a contradictory thing, connoting both mortality and immortality, temporality and eternity, body and spirit, the desert in the literary and philosophical imagination becomes a stage on which a new awareness – a new semiosis – of life becomes possible. The desert is where the very codes by which we understand life, death and the never-living are scrambled. Western subjectivity, to be sure, often sees in the desert an image of its own exhaustion or ruin, and this is why literature from the Romantics on has often sought out such landscapes as places where death and finitude are confronted. At the same time, this literature bears witness to an urge to think beyond the impasses of an exhausted Western metaphysics of self. This distinctly modern effort at self-overcoming goes some way to explaining why the desert barely features in Western art and culture until the nineteenth century.

In his classic book *Scenes in America Deserta* (1982), the British architectural writer Peter Reyner Banham notes a link between the desert and modern aesthetics:

> the desert measurably offers immeasurable space. It is therefore an environment in which 'Modern Man' ought to feel at home – his modern painting, as in the works of Mondrian, implies a space that extends beyond the confines of the canvas; his modern architecture, as in the works of Mies van der Rohe, is a rectangular partition of a regular but infinite space; its ideal inhabitants, the sculptures of Giacometti stalking metaphysically through that space as far as it infinitely extends.[2]

While the emergence of the desert as an aesthetic category was bound to Romantic notions of sublime nature, there is little of the sublime in Banham's account here, despite the encounter with the immeasurable and the infinite that he underscores. Immeasurability amounts to a monochrome regularity, the traversal of the infinite to an interminable wandering in a disenchanted spaciousness. On the one hand, wasteland aesthetics point beyond the buoyancy of the experience of nature that animated Romantic sublimity towards the sheer inescapability of space as a brute and abstract reality. On the other hand, the desert retains the trace of everything that might populate it and thus manifests infinite possibility.

There is a duality of loss and recovery here that characterises the deployment of the desert in some of the greatest works of literary modernism. In W. B. Yeats's 'The Second Coming' (1920) and T. S. Eliot's *The Waste Land* (1922), we can detect aesthetic experiences of a world that is both falling apart and waiting to be born (to paraphrase famous lines from the former poem). While the devastations of war play a crucial role in this, other more ontological issues are at work. Within the phenomenological tradition in philosophy, concepts of world and being-in-the-world emerged around the same time as Yeats's and Eliot's poems in reaction to scientific materialism. For these philosophers, the world is not reducible to the empirical reality of the sciences but can be grasped in our relationships and attitudes to that reality. There is an uneasy sense within this tradition that to be able to philosophise about the world in this way presupposes that we are somehow at odds with it or that we don't entirely feel at home in it, that it inspires us with feelings of anxiety or dread, that it is somehow precarious, insufficient, or on the verge of disintegrating entirely. This is often how we feel about the environment today, while the desert has become central to how we imagine the world as lost and the Earth as dead. When – to give a famous example – the main characters of Cormac McCarthy's novel *The Road* (2006) carry their meagre belongings in a shopping trolley through the wasteland of a post-apocalyptic America, what comes through to the reader is not only a vision of a possible dystopian future but a certain sense of what shopping in our contemporary consumerist society really *is*. What I argue in this book is that a critique of modernity involves confronting such an uncanny feeling of being in a world that is no longer really a world. The figuration of deserts and wastelands has provided literature and philosophy with spaces in which this confrontation can take place.

The first chapter outlines the scope of the book and functions as an extended introduction in which I begin to show how the desert has featured in modern philosophy since Nietzsche and in modern literature since Romanticism. I explain how wasteland aesthetics can be used as a category by which to think certain key formulations of modern spatiality. The book's environmental and ecological framework is introduced in this chapter through a discussion of the Anthropocene, which I argue – taking my cue from Donna Haraway and Timothy Morton – forces us to confront the notion of worldlessness as a planetary condition affecting human and non-human life. In Chapter 2, I develop the central geophilosophical impetus behind many of the book's arguments and outline a post-psychoanalytic understanding of the desert as a libidinal space as well as a space of energetic crisis. While I focus on Deleuze and Guattari and what I call their 'theoretical geocentrism', I show how their work can and should be understood in relation to Nietzsche, Freud, Husserl, Heidegger and others. The problem of what Nietzsche enigmatically identified as modernity's growing desert is conceptualised here as an ambiguously soteriological space. Chapter 3 pursues a genealogy of the desert as a key topos of modern literature from Romantics such as Percy Shelley to the modernism of T. S. Eliot and D. H. Lawrence to the postmodernism of Thomas Pynchon and Paul Auster. I approach the desert in these works in terms of how modern experience tends to provoke an anxiety regarding the semiotic consistency of space. I use Deleuze and Guattari's concept of the refrain to suggest how the desert should be seen as a deterritorialising dislocation by which Western subjectivity seeks out transformative symbols of its own exhaustion. In Chapter 4, I turn to a key feature of capitalist self-mythologisation, the desert island, and suggest how the Anthropocene can be viewed as an age of shipwrecks in which the island of the Robinson Crusoe myth becomes a confrontation with worldless space. I discuss how Derrida and Deleuze understand the Robinson narrative in their different ways, before going on to analyse modern-day retellings of Defoe's story in works by Michel Tournier, J. G. Ballard, Ursula Le Guin and Kim Stanley Robinson. In the fifth and final chapter of the book, I turn to the question of violence and ask what kinds of violence are at stake in the ideas of desertification and devastation outlined in the previous chapters. I argue that in order to understand the violence of environmental damage, we need to understand how what Deleuze and Guattari call the state-form normalises its regime of violence. I explore these ideas through texts by T. E. Lawrence, Cormac McCarthy, William S. Burroughs, Angela Carter, Don DeLillo and Reza Negarestani, all of which concern themselves with the link between the desert and war. Through these desert polemologies, we find ways to combat, at the speculative and affective level, the structural violence by which environmental damage becomes difficult or impossible to signify. The desert in modern literature and philosophy can thus be understood, I conclude, as an eschatological space by which capitalism speculates on its own collapse.

NOTES

1. Olafur Arnalds, 'Desertification: An Appeal for a Broader Perspective', p. 10.
2. Banham, *Scenes in America Deserta*, pp. 61–2.

1. *Desert Desire*

POINT ZERO: THE DESERT AND MODERNITY

Scholarship across a range of disciplines has shown just how indebted our notions of the natural environment are to art and aesthetics. Work in ecocriticism over the past three decades has shown how Romanticism in particular contributed to an aestheticisation of nature that has influenced modern environmentalism in a number of decisive ways.[1] The Romantic period's conceptions of the 'picturesque' were crucial to the emergence of modern environmental consciousness.[2] Thinking critically about the environment would be an empty notion without the kinds of affective power manifest in the poems of Wordsworth.[3] Timothy Morton, in a more polemical mode, has gone as far as to claim that many environmentalist notions of nature at work today remain, often unwittingly and sometimes perniciously, entangled in their Romantic origins:

> the 'thing' we call nature becomes, in the Romantic period and afterward, a way of healing what modern society has damaged. Nature is like that other Romantic-period invention, the aesthetic. The damage done, goes the argument, has sundered subjects from objects, so that human beings are forlornly alienated from their world. Contact with nature, and with the aesthetic, will mend the bridge between subject and object.[4]

But if the environmental consciousness of the modern West has been shaped, even to a harmful extent, by an aestheticisation of nature as a unifying ideal in opposition to industrial modernity then it is also true that this same consciousness has envisioned a world bereft of life, or one in which life is reduced to bare survival, as a *correlate of this same ideal*. 'Green' or hospitable nature has been, in part at least, an ideologico-aesthetic construct of modernity, but this has frequently depended on other kinds of constructions in which nature appears inhospitable to life. This is particularly the case if we shift our perspective from the local to the global. A text such as Byron's poem 'Darkness', for example, provides us with a total view of earthly life as devastated and the world as void. In a similar way, as Kelly Oliver suggests, anxieties about nuclear war and environmental destruction in the twentieth century produced both pop cultural fantasies of global annihilation and philosophical investigations of notions of Earth and world from the likes of Heidegger and Arendt. It was 'as if we could think the whole earth only by imaging its destruction, [and] all attempts to "save" the planet require first imagining destroying it'.[5]

If nature figured as harmonious or palliative ideal plays an ideologico-aesthetic role from the Romantic period onwards, as Morton insists, then a different though similar role has been played by evocations of inhospitable environments where life and nature seem to diverge. I argue that deserts and wastelands in their various forms, evoking affects of wonder and joy or disgust and terror as the case may be, constitute a crucial but largely ignored component of our global environmental imaginary. From imperial travel writing to postmodernism, from the Old Testament to salvagepunk, the desert has been a *terrain of desire* over which the Western imagination of space and place has ranged. As our environmental and ecological crisis heads in increasingly catastrophic directions, a critique of the figure of the desert in literature, philosophy and wider culture can help us map an environmental affect that finds itself both attracted to and repelled by arid, depopulated, derelict or barren spaces of various kinds.

My approach in this book involves putting two distinct bodies of work into dialogue. On the one hand, the European philosophical tradition from Nietzsche and Heidegger to Levinas, Blanchot, Derrida, Deleuze and Guattari, Virilio, Baudrillard and others has repeatedly deployed the image of the desert in its critique of modernity. As I show in this and subsequent chapters, the desert often functions in this tradition to suggest how modern society devastates life and meaning through a homogenising disenchantment of space, but also how these devastated spaces, in their very strangeness and solitude, may offer a potential re-enchantment and revivification. The desert has come to constitute modernity's eschatological horizon for thinkers working in the aftermath of what Nietzsche described as the death of God. In this sense, the desert has been a crucial philosophical figure for thinking difference and indifference, meaning and meaninglessness, metaphysics and the death of metaphysics. On the other hand, I look at how the desert becomes a crucial topos in a range of key literary texts. T. S. Eliot's *The Waste Land* (1922), D. H. Lawrence's

The Plumed Serpent (1926) and T. E. Lawrence's *Seven Pillars of Wisdom* (1926), for example, deploy very different kinds of desert environments in the pursuit of new aesthetic and spiritual realities in the aftermath of the devastations of the First World War. The deserts of 1920s modernism give way later in the century to the shocking libidinal wastelands of William S. Burroughs, which serve as the settings for bodies subjected to new technologies of control and manipulation as well as being sites of resistance. Canonical postmodernist authors such as Thomas Pynchon, J. G. Ballard, Angela Carter, Paul Auster and Don DeLillo all deploy the desert extensively in a way that suggests a concern with the spatiality of power, war and American imperialism in late capitalism.

What this book offers, then, is very much *not* a view of the desert as a natural wilderness, nor does it pursue an ecocritical reading of the desert in any kind of traditional sense. My central premise, rather, is that the desert in literature and philosophy can tell us some important things about the experience of being modern. There is a curious link between modernity and the desert that ideas of nature and *oikos* fail to grasp, since modernity itself involves a profound transformation of what we mean by place and dwelling. As the social geographer and historian Kevin Hetherington has suggested, the project of modernity may be said to consist in a certain form of spatial ordering that gives rise to marginal or in-between places, neither utopian nor dystopian, whose precise value is hard to pin down. Hetherington has called these the 'badlands of modernity'. Places such as the Palais Royal of late eighteenth-century Paris allowed for a carnivalesque contestation of norms and intermingling of social classes, much as the famous boulevards and arcades of Baudelaire and Benjamin subsequently would. Since Foucault, social and cultural theory has shown a concern not only with the spatiality of modern capitalist society but also with the possibilities for resistance that marginal 'other' spaces, or 'heterotopia', to use Foucault's famous term, may provide.[6] Theoretically informed work on deserts in modern literature has sometimes insisted on their heterotopic quality.[7] My analysis diverges from this trend. Deserts may function as sites of resistance and alterity. But it is also true that modernity finds, and indeed must find, ways to aestheticise and thus *absorb* its limits, its uncertain borders and cutting edges. This, I claim, is what gives rise to an aesthetic fascination with the desert as a site from which modern experience comprehends the spatial alterity through which it must inevitably pass. Even if the desert can be granted a heterotopic status as a site of resistance, then, it remains central to the ideology of capitalist modernity and its environmental imaginary.

Desert Desire

In a classic book on the concept of modernity, Marshall Berman uses Goethe's *Faust* to insist upon the importance of the wasteland to industrial society's conceptions of itself as perpetual self-overcoming and renewal. For Berman, Faust is the quintessential modern hero. He observes that in acts 4 and 5 of Part II of Goethe's text,

> [Faust] and Mephistopheles find themselves alone on a jagged mountain peak staring blankly into cloudy space, going nowhere. They have taken exhausting trips through all history and mythology, explored endless experiential possibilities, and now find themselves at point zero, or even behind that point, for they feel less energetic than they were at the story's start. . . . Suddenly the landscape around him metamorphoses into a site. [Faust] outlines great reclamation projects to harness the sea for human purposes: man-made harbors and canals that can move ships full of goods and men; dams for large-scale irrigation; green fields and forests, pastures and gardens, a vast and intensive agriculture; waterpower to attract and support emerging industries; thriving settlements, new towns and cities to come – and all this to be created out of a barren wasteland where human beings have never dared to live.[8]

The aesthetics of desert spaces, in which we can include not only the desolate sublimity of natural deserts but also the anti-picturesque of urban wastelands and edgelands, relate to the ideological forms by which capitalist culture understands its internal and external limits. Capitalism is unique amongst social formations in that it must render itself obsolete, must *lay waste to itself*, in order to renew and thus sustain its habits of production and consumption. If we take seriously Deleuze and Guattari's post-psychoanalytic libidinal economics (explored in depth in the next chapter) and understand capitalism as a production of collective *desire*, then what desire wants most of all is the desert, the zero point from which it renews itself in the Faustian manner analysed by Berman. The various deserts, wastelands, junkscapes and depopulated zones that our culture so often fascinates itself with constitute the environmental aesthetics of an uneven planetary expansion that devastates the Earth in order to fashion it anew.

This is perhaps as old as capitalism itself. Shakespeare's Lear, as William Viney argues, is an obsolete king 'cast onto the moor or "common" wasteland, . . . a space as inactive as his sovereignty'.[9] An obsession with images of ruin begins in the landscape painting of the seventeenth century and carries through to Robert Smithson's photographs of the waste spaces of New Jersey in the 1960s.[10] Robinson Crusoe's island was a way of imagining the spatiality of the colonial periphery as a site for the reproduction of the centre, and in this way constitutes a privileged figure of the zero point. Even though Robinson is never really alone – his 'Island of Desolation' contains inhabitants of various kinds – it must be apprehended by him as absolutely unpopulated in order for him to constitute it as ground of the reproduction of the world. In *Concrete Island* (1974), Ballard rewrote Defoe's narrative as a struggle for survival in the wasteland created by the intersection of three London motorways, but in Ballard's text the castaway is ultimately seduced by the island and refuses the opportunity of rescue. What is unique for us today, however, is that this aesthetic obsession with the devastated underside of modernity's cutting edges has taken on an urgently epochal dimension that is reconfiguring our very notions of life.

The anthropologist Elizabeth A. Povinelli argues that the desert is crucial for understanding contemporary formations of power. She describes our current period as one in which biopower – the political management and governance of biological life – is slowly being replaced by what she calls 'geontopower', 'a set of discourses, affects, and tactics used in late liberalism to maintain or shape the coming relationship of the distinction between Life and Nonlife'.[11] She argues that the 'figure of the Desert' is key to understanding these transformations because in it and through it we see dramatised 'the gap between Life and that which is conceived as before or without Life'. This gap is a 'scarred region' of the contemporary global imaginary that informs how we think and feel about fossil fuels, extraterrestrial exploration and apocalyptic futures:

> The Desert is the affect that motivates the search for other instances of life in the universe and technologies for seeding planets with life; it colors the contemporary imaginary of North African oil fields; and it drives the fear that all places will soon be nothing more than the setting within a *Mad Max* movie. The Desert is also glimpsed in both the geological category of the fossil insofar as we consider fossils to have once been charged with life, to have lost that life, but as a form of fuel can provide the conditions for a specific form of life – contemporary, hypermodern, informationalized capital – and a new form of mass death and utter extinction; and in the calls for a capital or technological fix to anthropogenic climate change. Not surprisingly then the Desert is fodder for new theoretical, scientific, literary, artistic, and media work.[12]

The Eurocentric account of life that led to the biopolitical framework by which all systems could be thought of in terms of their organic functioning was only possible on the basis of some conception of the non-living against which life could be perceived *as* living. Biopower thus, of necessity, gives way to a confrontation with Nonlife, which may possess its own dynamisms and energies, but which a consciousness forged under the biopolitical regime – in other words, the consciousness of the capitalist West – can only recognise as an omega, a zero point or absolute stasis. The figure of the desert thus appears on the horizon of what Povinelli calls our 'Carbon Imaginary', our habit of viewing everything in terms of birth, life, death and finitude. The Carbon Imaginary must contend with 'the problem of how something emerges from nothing and returns to nothingness; how the one (1) emerges from the zero (0) and descends back into it'.[13] What Freud described in terms of the death instinct must be located on a geological and geopolitical and not just a psychosexual level. The zero retains a transformative potential, however, as we will see.

THE ANTHROPOCENE: BEING WITHOUT A WORLD

Deserts are real places, but when we look to the imaginative and speculative figuration of the desert in modern culture it is striking how frequently it is used to evoke experiences of placelessness or dislocation, or of what Deleuze and Guattari call, in their unique theoretical vocabulary, *deterritorialisation*. The desert can be said to be a place that forces us to rethink the very concept of place, to the extent that the latter has arisen as a form of sedentary or rooted being. For Derrida, for example, 'the desert [is] a paradoxical figure of the *aporia*', an impasse suggesting both the loss of a defined sense of place *and* the possibility of signifying place as such. In the desert there is

> no marked out or assured passage, no route in any case, at the very most trails that are not reliable ways, the paths are not yet cleared, unless the sand has already re-covered them. But isn't the uncleared way also the condition of *decision or event*, which consists in opening the way, in *(sur)passing*, thus in going *beyond*?[14]

The place of the impasse is where the 'event' of founding a place or a territory takes place. Since the nineteenth century, the experience of such a paradoxical relation to place has come to feature across a wide variety of work in art, literature and philosophy. Lukács, following Novalis, famously defined Romanticism as a kind of 'transcendental homelessness'.[15] Levinas, in a text written while he was a prisoner during the Second World War, argued that modern art in general aims 'to present reality as it is in itself, after the world has come to an end'.[16] Space in this worldless reality is not fixed but 'a swarming of points'.[17] Deleuze and Guattari's affirmation of nomadism emerges from this break with fixed space and the ontological certainty of being-in-the-world. Where Heidegger stressed dwelling, Levinas stresses nomadism: 'as in a desert, one can find no place to reside. From the depths of sedentary existence a nomadic memory arises. Nomadism is not an approach to the sedentary state. It is an irreducible relation to the earth: a sojourn devoid of *place*'.[18] The desert becomes important in this discourse on the precariousness of place because it provides an aesthetic resource – an affective environment, a *sensorium* – for forms of thinking and feeling that are no longer certain whether they have an environment. While for Levinas this is a matter of ethical urgency, for us today it is also a matter of ecological urgency.

The ecological relates, of course, to the idea of the *oikos*, the Greek term denoting the home, household, habitat or place of dwelling by which life is embedded in a network of interconnected relations. In this sense, ecological crisis can be understood as a *crisis of dwelling*. This is far from being simply a human issue, as it is for philosophers such as Heidegger and Levinas. Consider, to give just one of many possible examples, how the current mass extinction of parasites is causing the surviving species to migrate to new hosts, leading to all sorts of unpredictable invasions and processes of co-extinction.[19] The plight of dwelling today is coextensive with such vectors of devastation. Elizabeth Kolbert describes our present age of ecological crisis in terms of a 'remixing [of] the world's flora and fauna' produced by the kinds of mobility industrialised humanity has acquired over the past two centuries.[20] Mass extinction is one of the results of this remixing. Transcendental homelessness can be extended to include these non-human forms of homelessness, all of which can be traced to humans as the ultimate invader species. The transcendental, here, no longer relates to subject and object but to Earth and territory. This shifting of the ground of the transcendental is the central idea of what Deleuze and Guattari call geophilosophy.[21] This is why we cannot simply presume the *oikos* as a grounding principle of thought and criticism. Ecocriticism must embrace a geophilosophical concern with Earth, world, territory, ground and spatiality.[22]

In a striking irony, it is precisely the *humanisation* of the Earth that has led us and other species to feel and be not-at-home on it. Much recent work in philosophy, literary studies and critical theory has deployed the concept of the Anthropocene, a term which first emerged around 2000 by way of the atmospheric scientist Paul Crutzen but which has spread since then into non-scientific disciplines and popular discourse. In a 2002 article in *Nature* titled 'Geology of Mankind', Crutzen describes the Anthropocene as the present

> human-dominated, geological epoch, supplementing the Holocene – the warm period of the past 10–12 millennia. The Anthropocene could be said to have started in the latter part of the eighteenth century, when analyses of air trapped in polar ice showed the beginning of growing global concentra-

tions of carbon dioxide and methane. This date also happens to coincide with James Watt's design of the steam engine in 1784.[23]

More recently, scientists have suggested that the Anthropocene may be said to have begun in 1945, when the first atomic bomb tests deposited radioactive material on the Earth's surface.[24] Simon Lewis and Mark Maslin, on the other hand, suggest the year 1610 as a more accurate starting point from a stratigraphic perspective, as this is when carbon dioxide levels trapped in Arctic ice can be seen to dip briefly as a result of the deaths caused when smallpox and other European diseases wiped out more than 50 million people in the Americas. The devastation of indigenous societies in the New World meant farmland reverted to forests which absorbed enough carbon dioxide to temporarily cool the planet. This was 'the last globally cool moment before the onset of the longterm warmth of the Anthropocene'.[25] Such a view aligns with Jason Moore's contention that what he prefers to call the Capitalocene begins 'in the Atlantic world during the long sixteenth century'.[26] However we date it, the idea of the Anthropocene maintains that we are living in a new geological epoch characterised by the indelible impact of industrial, global humanity on the planet. The last time the Earth experienced a comparable epochal shift was about 12,000 years ago with the end of the last ice age and the onset of an interglacial period of global warming called the Holocene. But the environmental conditions under which human civilisation as we know it developed have changed. The biophysical changes being detected by climate scientists are leading us out of the Holocene and into a new chapter of geological history, only this time the reasons for the change have to do with the activities of humans themselves. The key point is that what we have come to regard as 'nature' is no longer to be taken for granted as a grounding principle of earthly life.

There is thus an irony in Crutzen's choice of name for this new epoch. The industrial age is the age of 'man', the Anthropos, who no longer signifies a distinct niche of planetary ecology defined by quintessentially human attributes (culture, language and technology) but a much vaster planetary condition in which man's uniqueness is both dissolved and intensified via perilous entanglements with the non-human. In one sense, the Anthropocene can be viewed, despite the ecological crises it entails, as a triumph of the project of Enlightenment reason, a Promethean liberation of man from the tyranny of nature. A 2007 article written by Crutzen, Will Steffen and John R. McNeill describes the Anthropocene in somewhat optimistic terms as 'the evolution of humans and our societies from hunter-gatherers to a global geophysical force'.²⁷ According to another reading, however, the man/nature metaphysical binary breaks down in this new epoch such that the older anthropocentric narrative of human progress is fatally undermined. We should, I insist, fully embrace the irony of the Anthropocene against the temptation of any triumphal humanism *or* celebration of the dissolution of 'man' into an interconnected whole. Neither position fully captures what we are living through. The geological inscription of humanity marks the exhaustion of man as an ideological or metaphysical entity. The transcendental homelessness once thought to be man's unique condition *passes into the biosphere* as a result of the activities of humanity as a geophysical agent. Life in the Anthropocene will increasingly be characterised not only by extinctions and biodiversity loss but by increased adaptability and hybridisation, the ability to invade and exploit new habitats and thrive as an invader species. The popular environmentalist notion of 'rewilding' (returning species to their original habitats) runs counter to the directions in which life is now evolving. In many cases, it is not even clear what an 'original' habitat would be, so any attempts to 'rewild' life takes place in the context of a collapse of distinctions between wild and domesticated.²⁸

How, then, are we to continue to imagine the Earth as the *oikos* of life (human and otherwise)? The discipline of ecology first emerged with Ernst Haeckel and Jacob von Uexküll in the late nineteenth century via concepts of home and world. As Peter van Wyck notes, such ways of thinking about the environment in the subsequent development of ecology have tended to figure the Earth as a *container* of life, that in which life is fixed or embedded.²⁹ One unexpected effect of the Anthropocene, then, is that it calls into question the quasi-phenomenological conceptions of being-in-the-world that have inflected the development of ecology. Indeed, the Anthropocene may be defined, from a geophilosophical point of view, as *the point at which Earth and world diverge*. Donna Haraway argues, following anthropologist Anna Tsing, that the point marking the Anthropocene's onset is the loss of natural refuge areas such as forests and coral reefs: 'the Holocene was the long period when refugia, places of refuge, still existed, even abounded, to sustain reworlding in rich cultural and biological diversity'.³⁰ The post-Holocene Earth no longer guarantees life the security of a refuge, a world, a territory, an *oikos*. The insecurity at issue here, however, is not merely physical but more deeply ontological. Morton, going further than Haraway and Tsing, argues that there are 'serious questions about whether there is such a thing as "world," and whether world-making ("worlding") provides a sufficient reason for protecting life forms'.³¹ World may itself be an aesthetic more than a simply physical reality, one that is now dissolving as the true interconnectedness of human and non-human life becomes apparent. Instead of world, we should be thinking this interconnectedness, Morton argues.

Some prefer to call the Anthropocene the 'Capitalocene' because the effect of capitalism has been to knit the fate of industrial humanity to that of planetary life itself. Moore, writing from an eco-Marxist position and drawing on the notion of *oikeios*, understood as dialectically combined human and non-human environment-making, argues that global capitalism should be regarded not as a social formation distinct from nature but 'a co-produced world-ecology of capital, power, and nature'.[32] Peter Sloterdijk, from a decidedly non-Marxist position, defines capitalism in similar ways to Moore as a 'world interior', 'a hothouse that has drawn inwards everything that was once on the outside'.[33] This world remains haunted by the extra-worldly, the outside it has tried to banish. What I argue, breaking with the ontological centrality given to the *oikos* or *oikeios* and related terms, is that dissolving the nature/society or nature/culture binary requires that we first think through the disjunction of Earth and world.[34] One way of doing this is to see life as increasingly threatened by worldlessness, in flight from a world that is failing to sustain or environ it. But what does it mean to say that life can be separated from an environing world in this way? How do we envision an Earth that can no longer guarantee its lifeforms the ontological security of a world? The Anthropocene has undeniable eschatological and apocalyptic dimensions. We are, however, living through the 'end of the world' not, or not only, as a physical cataclysm but also as a devastation of certain environmental aesthetic frameworks that have allowed us to picture a self-sufficient natural domain. These frameworks have often involved picturing nature as a discrete 'thing over there', separate from us but also environing and sustaining. World suggests a world *view*, a world *picture*.[35] World and nature are entirely bound up with aesthetic experience, and these are in turn bound up with our sense of place and dwelling. But the Anthropocene tells us that nature, conceived as an indifferent background of human activity, is increasingly obsolete. Bruno Latour, following Isabelle Stengers, calls this 'the intrusion of Gaia', which collapses any contemplative distance between us and the Earth.[36] All distances have become forms of nearness, Heidegger maintained, but because of this, everything seems both far and near at the same time.[37] Desert travellers have noted the same phenomenon.[38] Space itself becomes uncanny under such conditions. Following this Heideggerian inspiration, Morton writes: 'in an age of global warming, there is no background, and thus there is no foreground. It is the end of the world, since worlds depend on backgrounds and foregrounds. *World* is a fragile aesthetic effect around whose corners we are beginning to see'.[39]

Yet if there is an aesthetics of world there is also an aesthetics of 'unworlding'. The two are necessarily very closely related, since to imagine a world involves imagining what it might be like not to have one. World and what lies beyond it (i.e., interconnectedness) cannot be opposed in any simple or decisive way, which is why Morton ultimately suggests maintaining a version of Heidegger's concept of world.[40] The very aesthetics of world contain conceptions of unworldling and end-of-the-world visions which in themselves point beyond the world. Heidegger, the pre-eminent thinker of world, argued in *Being and Time* (1927) that the world as such becomes a problem for philosophy precisely because it strikes us in certain affective moments – when we feel anxious or bored, for example – as strangely oppressive, insignificant or obtrusive.[41] We are most tuned in to the world when it appears flat and lifeless. For Heidegger, the worldliness of the world can feel strange or uncanny, sensations we would be more likely to associate with the loss or impoverishment of the world than its simple presence. This coexistence of the world with its uncanny disappearance is suited to considerations of the desert, and Heidegger used the desert as a motif to describe this uncanniness, as I show below.

My theoretical approach throughout this book, then, derives from an unlikely mixture of Heidegger, who defined philosophy as homesickness, and Deleuze and Guattari, who are famous for their conceptions of nomadic thought and politics. Despite the differences between Heidegger and Deleuze and Guattari, they are alike in that they define the most fundamental activities of life in terms of dwelling and territoriality. For Deleuze and Guattari, a bird's song or spider's web are territorial markers, what they call 'refrains' or 'ritornellos', signalling the pre-human beginnings of art.[42] For Heidegger, art emerges from a deeply and uniquely human need to build and from what he calls the 'plight of dwelling'.[43] Dwelling is a plight precisely because there is no 'nature' to ground our relationship to space, but it is part of the human 'essence' to forget that fact and to naturalise our being-in-the-world. The intrusion of Gaia is beginning to make this forgetting impossible and thus challenges the human essence, behind which lies a deterritorialised Earth pulsing with refrains.

WASTELAND AESTHETICS

The Western literary tradition does not display much of an interest in the desert prior to the nineteenth century. Michael Ondaatje is only slightly exaggerating when he writes in *The English Patient* that 'there is, after Herodotus, little interest by the Western world towards the desert for hundreds of years. From 425 BCE to the beginning of the twentieth century there is an averting of eyes. Silence'.[44] It is true, as Richard Bevis has quite definitively shown in a near-encyclopaedic work, that European travellers to desert regions prior to the nineteenth century paid scant regard to the desert as an object of aesthetic value, often passing over it without comment.[45] The main aesthetic sentiment associated with deserts and wastelands in the seventeenth and eighteenth centuries was *disgust*. Deserts were understood as a form of environmental abjection.[46]

The Romantic aesthetics of nature changed all this and from the late eighteenth century onwards writers came to be inspired by the new possibilities offered by waste spaces of various kinds. This new interest in the aesthetics of deserts was made possible by a new imaginary of landscape in which affect and environment came to reflect one another. The predominance of the desert in this shift is apparent in works such as Charles Doughty's monumental *Travels in Arabia Deserta* (1888) and John C. Van Dyke's seminal work of environmental aesthetics, *The Desert: Further Studies in Natural Appearances* (1901), but we can also look to less obvious sources for the rise of a new awareness of inhospitable landscapes. Thomas Hardy's description of Egdon Heath, the fictitious setting of his novel *The Return of the Native* (1878), can be considered emblematic in this respect, as Bevis points out. Hardy describes his landscape as a 'Thule' – a polar wasteland – that may nevertheless come to be regarded as possessing the Edenic charms of a 'vale of Tempe'. The 'chastened sublimity' of a 'gaunt waste', Hardy suggests, is more in keeping with the modern mood than orthodox forms of natural beauty:

> Fair prospects wed happily with fair times; but alas, if times be not fair! Men have oftener suffered from the mockery of a place too smiling for their reason than from the oppression of surroundings oversadly tinged. Haggard Egdon appealed to a subtler and scarcer instinct, to a more recently learnt emotion, than that which responds to the sort of beauty called charming and fair.[47]

Egdon is not the sublime counterpoint to pastoral beauty but the subdued or chastened *inverse side* of sublime nature by which a prior sense of disgust is transformed into new affects.

That a devastated or barren landscape can convey a sense of what it means to be modern is not, perhaps, such a new idea any longer, and we may even claim that the mood Hardy here begins to detect is now culturally dominant. The brilliant opening scenes of Pixar's animated film *WALL-E* (2009), for example, show us an empty city reduced to a dusty, windblown wasteland. Billions of tons of rubbish are stacked high in the streets to be endlessly sorted through by the titular robot-scavenger left behind by his human makers, who have long since fled the dying Earth. These opening scenes tell us much about our contemporary condition through the affective force of their images alone, which seem to capture a sense of the epochal not through any distinctiveness in terms of their content but precisely through an erosion and obsolescence of all particularity. This could be any city and this rubbish could have been anyone's. But this generic trash, precisely because it has lost what once made it distinctive and thus desirable, tells us all the more powerfully about who and what we are, as if waste could be the expression of our species being. Our collective desires form a history that can be read in the temporality of the abandoned and the salvaged. Modernist texts from the 1920s – most famously, of course, *The Waste Land* – demonstrate the very same thing. For postmodernism and after, the desert becomes significant because it suggests, in its very timelessness, a loss of the historical sense.

W. H. Auden, in his lectures on the symbolism of the sea in Romantic poetry, observes that 'the desert is the dried-up place, i.e., the place where life has ended, the Omega of temporal existence. Its first most obvious characteristic is that nothing moves; the second is that everything is surface and exposed. No soil, no hidden spring'.[48] And yet, it is precisely the fact that the superficiality of the surface may acquire a profundity usually attributed to temporal depth that explains a large amount of the power of the desert as an aesthetic figure. The surface may be a temporal zero point, but it still has an *epochality* in which we recognise something of ourselves and our own omega. In both Hardy's heath and *WALL-E*'s junkscape, we find an epochal feeling inscribed at a surface level, at the level of erosion and exposure, rather than at the level of a depth in which something might take root, conceal itself or be buried. Edward Abbey opens *Desert Solitaire* (1968), his famous account of his sojourn in the deserts of Utah and Colorado, by admitting that 'I know nothing whatever about true underlying reality ... I am pleased enough with surfaces – in fact they alone seem to me to be of much importance.'[49] In his remarkable literary history of the Sahara, Sven Lindqvist observes, in similar fashion, that the relationship between surface and depth is, in fact, 'the fundamental experience of the desert'.[50]

Given the significance of the literary texts that feature desert environments, and given the importance of the kinds of issues they raise, it is strange that ecocriticism has largely neglected this crucial topic. Or, perhaps, it is not strange at all. When we think of literary representations of nature, we tend to think of environments of flourishing, plenitude and diversity. As Rune Graulund, one of the few critics to address the topic of the desert in any extended way, observes:

> We do not find prose praising the desert as Thoreau praised the woods or Hemingway the sea, nor do we find an Ode to Sand by Wordsworth, Keats or Shelley. Yet in a way we do. The texts are out there, floundering on the desert dunes for lack of attention. Critical opinion just never bothered to spend a lot of energy on the subject.[51]

This is not to say that critical work on the literature of the desert does not exist. Bevis details, with remarkably wide reading, an aesthetics of great and vast nature in European and American literature. Arnold's darkling plain, Eliot's wasteland and Frost's desert places, he writes, all use 'vistas of natural voids to make their point'.[52] Bevis's argument, however, proceeds largely through a painstaking enumeration of examples, with extensive quotation, and does not provide an adequate theorisation of the issues that the textual examples raise. But even the texts that he picks out have a bias towards the genres of travel writing, nature writing and memoir. This is a bias that affects most of the critical work on literary deserts. This fact is perhaps best exemplified by Gregory McNamee's *The Desert Reader: A Literary Companion* (1995), which presents a selection of desert writings ordered by continent. This expedient excludes a whole range of key speculative and other-worldly deserts as found in Frank Herbert's science fiction classic *Dune* (1965) and Kim Stanley Robinson's terraforming epic *Red Mars* (1992), to give just two examples. The literary deserts that generally gain the attention of critics are those found in the personal accounts of travellers and naturalists rather than in works of modernism, postmodernism and speculative fiction. The literary desert tends to be sought out in works such as Doughty's *Arabia Deserta*, Saint-Exupéry's *Wind, Sand and Stars* (1939), Abbey's *Desert Solitaire* (1968) and Terry Tempest Williams's *Red* (2001) rather than, say, J. G. Ballard's *The Drought* (1964) or Octavia Butler's *Parable of the Sower* (1993).

The deserts of the American southwest have received a fair bit of ecocritical attention. Patricia Nelson Limerick's *Desert Passages* (1985) and David Cassuto's *Dripping Dry* (2001) approach these desert landscapes via myths of national identity, showing how a confrontation with extremes of aridity had a determining effect on the course of American history from the mid-nineteenth century onwards. Tom Lynch's *Xerophilia* (2008) takes a bioregionalist approach inspired by the poet Gary Snyder. Gersdorf's *The Poetics and Politics of the Desert*

(2009) also focuses on the role of the desert in American mythopoetics, but avoids the simplistic bioregionalist thesis that sees alienation from nature as the central ecological problem. There are some commercial books on the deserts of the world and their inhabitants – for example, Roslynn Haynes's *Desert: Nature and Culture* (2013) and Michael Welland's *The Desert: Lands of Lost Borders* (2015) – but no book on the cultural and literary significance of the desert in general exists. Unlike the above-mentioned volumes, I tend to avoid nature writing, travel writing and memoir. These are the genres in which the vast majority of literary deserts have been sought, as if critics have needed the validation of an author's actual desert experiences before taking the desert as a critical object.

The present book is not strictly speaking a work of ecocriticism, but it has close affinities with strains of ecocriticism that attempt to go beyond the localist and bioregionalist biases that have embraced untheorised conceptions of 'nature' and uncritically favoured nature writing over other genres. The best recent examples of strong ecotheoretical research can be found in the edited volumes *Ecocritical Theory: New European Approaches* (2011) from Axel Goodbody and Kate Rigby, *Prismatic Ecology: Ecotheory Beyond Green* (2013) from Jeffrey Jerome Cohen, and *General Ecology: The New Ecological Paradigm* (2017) from Erich Hörl and James Burton. These collections signal how in the past ten years the theoretical foundations of ecocriticism have shifted beyond a conventional green awareness of nature as a domain separate from culture, politics and technology. Cohen, in his introduction to *Prismatic Ecology*, explains the limitations for ecocriticism of a purely green analysis:

> A green reading offers an environment-minded analysis of literature and culture, and is typically concerned with how nature is represented within a text and how modes of human inhabitance unfold within an imagined natural world. . . . Yet green readings have a tendency to reproduce . . . a split between nature and culture that founds a structurating antinomy even in the face of constitutive and intractable hybridities. Assuming such a split can lead to analyses stressing anthropocentric and detached concepts like stewardship, preservation, and prescriptive modes of environmental management.[53]

The desert confronts us with a number of intractable hybridities that call for non-green approaches. Even though they are often regarded as the ultimate wilderness and as sublime nature in its purest form, deserts can be found as easily outside of natural environments, in cities, suburbs, shopping malls, apocalyptic futures, utopias, dystopias, alien worlds and battlefields.

Research addressing the desert as a conceptual or theoretical category is hard to come by, but David Jasper's *The Sacred Desert* (2004) is by far the best example of work in this vein. Jasper provides a cultural history of the desert from the point of view of the Judeo-Christian tradition, drawing on a range of sources from the Desert Fathers and Thomas Altizer to Kafka, Derrida and Cormac McCarthy. Jasper's analysis suggests an important link between the early Christians and the modernist sense of spiritual exhaustion found in Yeats and Eliot:

> In the mythic imagination of the poet the desert is becoming the Waste Land, and worse. The centuries of the Christian church have awakened the nightmare, the demons that the Fathers fought, and the desert has become *us*. What is always represented in its otherness from the order of the city and society is now realized as the anarchy of that society.[54]

If the desert has functioned for thousands of years as a space of theological yearning and ordeal, as a site more spiritual than geographic, in the twentieth century it comes into its own as an environment in which exhaustion seems to coexist with forms of abundance and plenitude unique to Western capitalist society. Writers from Yeats and Eliot to Baudrillard, Carter and DeLillo privilege the desert precisely because it seems the *spatial correlate* of twentieth-century capitalism. What Jasper suggests, ultimately, is that a theology of the desert provides an important framework for understanding the spiritual and aesthetic consequences of modernity as the era of the death of God.

Nevertheless, the narrow theological frame of Jasper's work needs to be broadened to include questions of energetic as well as spiritual crisis. The fossil-energetics of environmental crisis and the fate of spirituality in secular modernity must be considered as overlapping phenomena. We live today in an age when the abundances afforded by advanced capitalism exist alongside anxieties over resource scarcity and depletion. The hallucinatory surfaces of mass consumerism have, for all their sophisticated variety, a strangely attenuated and degraded quality, as postmodernist writers and critics have long noted. What Baudrillard famously described as 'the desert of the real' would seem to be the aesthetic manifestation of a whole range of disavowed beliefs: we know God is dead, but we act as if something were nevertheless guiding our fate; we know the images of mass media are simulacra, but we act as though they were the real thing; we know fossil fuels will run out, but we act as if they were infinite, and so on. The theological sense of the desert is carried over into our secular and post-secular condition but in ways intimately connected with contemporary concerns over energy. Energy and spirit today are a lot more closely related than we might think. Clayton Crockett and Jeffrey W. Robbins's book *Religion,*

Politics, and the Earth: The New Materialism (2012) articulates a geophilosophical conception of energy as the mode by which the Earth comes to understand itself as an absolute subject:

> Earth becomes itself by thinking through its own materiality, energy forces, layered strata, atmosphere and magnetosphere, enfolded forms of life, and so on ... energy is immanent Deleuzo-Hegelian spirit (or Spirit), and energy avoids the traditional dichotomy between spirit and matter, because everything is energy transformation.[55]

Energy in this sense is the mode by which the Earth becomes subject. Entropy and the spectre of depletion, on the other hand, is the mode by which subjectivity encounters its relationship to the Earth. In order to understand energy in this way, I draw throughout this book upon Deleuze and Guattari's post-psychoanalytic conception of desire as the dynamic process that grounds us in territories but also ungrounds and deterritorialises us.

FROM THE ERĒMOS TO THE EREMOZOIC

It is always tempting to begin with problems of definition. It is particularly so for this project as there is little consensus regarding what, exactly, constitutes a desert. Throughout the twentieth century, scientists have struggled to arrive at a comprehensive definition, but today deserts are generally defined in terms of rainfall (along with temperature and humidity), even though parts of the Kalahari and Australian arid regions have a rainfall that exceeds the standard definition of 10 inches a year. Aridity – the rate at which water evaporates – is often more important than rainfall. Ultimately, scientific definitions of the desert are relative to the regions being classified. The geologist Michael Welland remarks that 'how you choose to define a desert depends very much on why you wish to do so in the first place'.[56] The word 'desert' comes from the Latin *desertum*, a translation of the Greek *erēmos*, meaning emptiness or solitude, the place of an eremite or hermit. The Desert Fathers of late antiquity – religious ascetics who retreated to the deserts of Egypt and Palestine – used the term *paneremos*, meaning 'absolute desert'. *Desertum* has an ancient Egyptian origin related to the hieroglyph pronounced 'tesert', meaning a place that has been forsaken. *Desertum* is the past participle of *dēserō*, which means literally to unbind or disconnect. 'Desolation' derives from the Latin *dēsōlō*, which means to abandon. 'Waste' was used to translate *desertus* in early English versions of the Bible and comes via Old French from the Latin *vāstus*, meaning both empty and vast or immense. *Vāstus* is cognate with the German *Wüste*, which means desert or wasteland, while the adjective *wüst* can mean wild but also vile, rude, ugly and chaotic. 'Devastate' comes from the Latin *vāstare*, meaning to lay waste. As Edward Casey observes, devastate is a 'composite word' combining the senses of *waste* with those of *vast*.[57] This etymological fact is important because it links time and space: *waste* is that which is no longer of use from the perspective of human temporality and intentionality, whereas *vast* suggests the spatiality of this temporal condition. In the desert, time in-itself as both eternity and passing-away seems to be manifest. As the legendary nineteenth-century desert traveller Isabelle Eberhardt put it, 'in this country without green, in this country of rock, something exists: time'.[58]

In the environmental sciences, meanwhile, there is much debate about 'desertification', meaning the degradation or loss of arable land due to deforestation, intensive farming, drought, climate change and other factors. Dryland researchers David Thomas and Nicholas Middleton's 1994 book *Desertification: Exploding the Myth* argues that the use of the term 'desertification' since the 1970s to talk about soil degradation, drought and the misuse of land draws on unfounded European cultural fears about the colonial periphery and non-European forms of agriculture.[59] The term itself originated in the late nineteenth century in French colonial North Africa, and the image of a 'growing desert', as we'll see, has perhaps more to do with European anxieties about the decline of its own civilisation and morality than any ecological reality in the strict sense.[60] The absence of a universal definition of what a desert is in the strict physical sense is thus particularly notable in the history and politics of the idea of desertification. The forced settlement of nomads has a long history in colonial policy, and a certain image of the desert as a place of nefarious rootlessness has accompanied this. The French sought to settle nomads not only for perceived ecological benefits but because it was part of their *mission civilisatrice*.[61] Today, it is recognised that one of the major causes of land degradation in Africa has in fact been 'the conversion of nomadic pastoral societies to sedentary lifestyles with a focus on raising cash crops instead of subsistence ones'.[62] In an excellent recent book, Hannah Holleman suggests, following climate researcher Joseph Romm, that 'dust-bowlification' is a more apposite term for the intertwined processes of drought and soil erosion that have marked the intensification of capitalist colonial agriculture since the late nineteenth century, the American Dust Bowl of the 1930s being a regional manifestation of much larger global processes affecting the viability and productivity of soil.[63] Whatever its shortcomings, however, the term 'desertification' continues to be used widely to denote problems of drought, overgrazing and deforestation, which have been acknowledged as major problems occurring on every inhabited continent, with some accounts suggesting that arable land is being lost at a rate of 12 million hectares a year.[64]

The desert as a cultural and aesthetic category, meanwhile, has displayed a remarkable flexibility and variability across a range of contexts and traditions. Vittoria di Palma, in her cultural history of the fens, marshes, swamps and other kinds of 'unimproved' common land of seventeenth- and eighteenth-century Britain, writes that 'the emptiness that is the core characteristic of the wasteland is also what gives the term its malleability, its potential for abstraction'.[65] Medieval culture was able to regard the forests of Europe as deserts in order to imitate the monastic practices of the Desert Fathers of late antiquity. Jacques Le Goff writes that for the twelfth-century French troubadours, 'an almost natural epithet for the forest was *gaste*, meaning devastated, empty, arid'.[66] Morton argues that the polar wastes of Coleridge's *Ancient Mariner* evoke 'imperialism in the abstract, the attempt to grasp the pure space, the intangible spacious*ness* of the environment'.[67] Nature as desert wilderness is here identical with an abstract sense of freedom or mobility beyond any specific immediate goal. This is demonstrated in environmentalist texts such as Abbey's *Desert Solitaire*, in which the city, the *polis*, is equated with tyranny.

Certain elements within contemporary experiences of the desert are strangely akin to the spiritual ordeals of the Desert Fathers. These early Christian monks sought out the deserts of North Africa and Palestine in order to practise an eremitic life of fasting and solitude. The opposition of desert and city that one finds here is, curiously, the inverse of Abbey's. As Jacques Lacarrière observes, for these ascetic mystics 'society is as natural to man as eating or procreation', and 'the retirement to the deserts was therefore at no time a return to any sort of "natural" or wild life but, on the contrary, was a seeking after a way of life as anti-natural as possible'.[68] For the Christian ascetics, the desert is an antidote to a nature identical with sin because it offered life the conditions of unnatural constriction. The desert environment makes possible a profoundly *artificial* life, often embodied in the paradox of a *desertum-civitas* or city in the desert.[69] Desert spirituality, through its abnegation of a society designed to gratify natural appetites, creates not only a life divergent from nature but a paradoxical *world outside of the world*. This speaks to experiences far removed from the monastic cultures of early Christianity. When renowned theorist of the postmodern condition Jean Baudrillard travelled through Las Vegas and other cities of the American southwest in the 1980s, he likewise saw a paradoxical *desertum-civitas* in radical contrast to nature:

American culture is heir to the deserts, but the deserts here are not part of a Nature defined by contrast with the town. Rather they denote the emptiness, the radical nudity that is the background to every human institution. At the same time, they designate human institutions as a metaphor of that emptiness and the work of man as the continuity of the desert, culture as a mirage and as the perpetuity of the simulacrum. The natural deserts tell me what I need to know about the deserts of the sign. They teach me to read surface and movement and geology and immobility at the same time. They create a vision expurgated of all the rest: cities, relationships, events, media. They induce in me an exalting vision of the desertification of signs and men. They form the mental frontier where the projects of civilization run into the ground.[70]

For Baudrillard, postmodern culture is manifested in the hard, inorganic surfaces of geology. The desert is not nature, here, but a vision of the empty form of the sign and the institutions built upon it. There is a strange asceticism at work in this geological theory of signs: the sensuous fullness of the referent dissipates into a denuded spaciousness where signs acquire a reality and an agency beyond mere representation, while the referent itself is annihilated in the semiotic space. This space is what Baudrillard elsewhere calls 'the desert of the real', and it is for him the terminus of all signifying activity, all history and culture, that we find in postmodern hyperreality.[71] The postmodern desert city in itself renders up a critique by dismantling those categorical oppositions – nature and culture, rural and urban – that have provided the Western *polis* with its grounding principles.

Following a similar path, the American artist Robert Smithson, famous for his monumental land art – much of it desert based – once observed how the modular suburban houses of 1960s New Jersey resembled, in their austere geometric abstraction, the barren, lunar surfaces of a stone quarry.[72] This continuity of built and natural space as seen in the formalism of the desert is suggested by Smithson's idea of 'entropic landscapes'. He defined these as 'visual [analogs] for the Second Law of Thermodynamics, which extrapolates the range of entropy by telling us energy is more easily lost than obtained, and that in the ultimate future the whole universe will burn out and be transformed into an all-encompassing sameness'.[73] That energetic exhaustion could provide an aesthetic principle is something Smithson explores in the realms of science fiction, sculpture, and architecture. In his own practice, he develops these ideas through land art, his signature piece *Spiral Jetty* (1970) being an attempt to provide an environmental representation of entropy.[74] Beyond Smithson's specific aesthetic goals, the entropic landscape provides us with a conceptual category for thinking about how the desert becomes a figure for exhaustion and depletion. In modernist and postmodernist culture, we repeatedly find the desert being used to articulate the sense of an energetic zero point.

Today, this sense cannot be dissociated from visions of environmental collapse and mass extinction. The way we think about the biosphere is increasingly determined by the thought of its decline and disappearance. The famed biologist E. O. Wilson – who coined the terms 'biophilia' and 'biodiversity' and is known to many for his controversial accounts of sociobiology – has proposed that we are not simply entering into a new geological epoch marked by the dominance of humans, but into a new *era* that he names the Eremozoic.[75] More recently, he has also used the term 'Eremocene' as a direct alternative to the Anthropocene.[76] He argues that the rate of biodiversity loss now being witnessed was last seen with the end of the Mesozoic age 65 million years ago. With the extinction of the dinosaurs the Cenozoic, the Age of Mammals, begun. Today, we may be leaving the Cenozoic and heading into a new age characterised not by the biological diversity of the past two ages but by biological impoverishment. Wilson derives the term Eremozoic from the Greek *erēmos*, meaning both solitude and desert. The Eremozoic or Eremocene is, then, the Age of Loneliness or the Age of Deserts. After the age of cold blood and warm blood comes a kind of bloodless age, an age of biological impoverishment in which man finds himself alone with a nature he has modified so thoroughly as to be an extension and reflection of himself.

Heidegger, writing near the end of the Second World War in a posthumously published text, also proposed an Age of Deserts:

> the desert is the wasteland [*die Öde*]: the deserted [*verlassene*] expanse of the abandonment [*Verlassenheit*] of all life. . . . The geographical concept of the desert [*Wüste*] is just the not yet sufficiently thought-out idea of desolation [*Verödung*], which proximally and thus mostly comes into our view only in particular circumstances and conditions of the surface of the earth. . . . May we call a historical age in which a form of 'life' still in some manner holds sway, 'the age of devastation'? . . . The being of an age of devastation [*Verwüstung*] would then consist precisely in the abandonment of being. Such a matter is, however, difficult to think.[77]

For Heidegger here, for reasons we will come back to, the age of modern technology causes being itself to withdraw, to be abandoned and for us to be abandoned by it in a double turning away. This state of abandonment is the historical condition of the modern West. In its biblical use the *erēmos* denoted a desert or wilderness, but also the place where sheep are abandoned by a shepherd: 'Which one of you, having a hundred sheep and losing one of them, does not leave the ninety-nine in the *erēmos* and go after the one that is lost until he finds it?'[78] In his 'Letter on Humanism' (1947), Heidegger wrote that 'Man is the shepherd of Being', but we should add that he is so today under the conditions of abandonment that render him and the object of his care lost to one another.[79]

The idea of an Age of Deserts has been depicted perhaps more powerfully than anywhere else in contemporary literature by Margaret Atwood's science fiction fragment 'Time Capsule Found on the Dead Planet' (2009). This brief text describes the history of a planet in four ages. The first is the age of gods, the second the age of money, and the third the age of money-as-god. But

> in the fourth age we created deserts. Our deserts were of several kinds, but they had one thing in common: nothing grew there. Some were made of cement, some were made of various poisons, some were of baked earth. We made these deserts from the desire for more money and from despair at the lack of it. Wars, plagues, and famines visited us, but we did not stop in our industrious creation of deserts. At last all wells were poisoned, all rivers ran with filth, all seas were dead; there was no land left to grow food. Some of our wise men turned to the contemplation of deserts. A stone in the sand in the setting sun could be very beautiful, they said. Deserts were tidy, because there were no weeds in them, nothing that crawled. Stay in the desert long enough and you could apprehend the absolute. The number zero was holy.[80]

Atwood is here giving us a kind of Eremozoic aesthetics in which the devastation of nature gives rise to a new desert asceticism, a new spirituality based no longer in the redemption offered by *another* world beyond human finitude but in the absolutisation of indifferent space in *this* one. Matter is spiritualised by perfect stasis. Atwood's vision is eschatological, then, but crucially does not give us an Earth without humans or an Earth returned to its wild state and reclaimed by non-human life. This is all too easily done, and has been a key ecoaesthetic strategy from Richard Jefferies's *After London* (1885) to the History Channel's *Life After People* (2009). The Eremozoic – an Earth in which life is not eliminated but reduced to a zero-intensity state – would seem a different prospect. The Eremozoic, then, may be a necessary supplement to, and not as Wilson suggests a competitor term for, the idea of the Anthropocene. It suggests not the typical apocalyptic scenarios of nature in revolt against humanity, which all too easily gratify a desire to consume nature as a spectacular object, but something more like an environmental *an*aesthetics, an environmental sensorium reduced to zero intensity in which nothing moves and nothing grows but where the aesthetic persists as contemplation of the inertia of matter in its irreducible indifference to life.

We are so used to thinking of art in terms of newness that we sometimes fail to recognise what it can tell us about indifference, inertia and exhaustion. Theories of the postmodern, of course, have for a long time drawn our attention to the fact that culture can thrive on the loss of originality and the depletion of aesthetic intensity. What if, today, we should understand this not simply in terms of the cultural superstructure of a global capitalism that sees itself at the end of history but, more radically, in terms of a planetary death instinct, an entropic self-depletion of life for which capitalism becomes the means? In *Welcome to the Desert of the Real!* (2002), a book published in the aftermath of the September 11 attacks, Slavoj Žižek argued that America had for years prior to the event been dreaming about its own destruction in the form of Hollywood disaster movies.[81] Can we say something similar about the desolate environments that characterise modern art and culture? Are these not the means by which the planet, through the resources of capitalism, imagines its own return to what Freud once called 'the quiescence of the inorganic world'?[82]

PHILOSOPHY AND THE DESERT ORDEAL FROM NIETZSCHE TO DELEUZE

If philosophers, writers and artists have been able to discover a corollary between modernity and the desert or wasteland, it is because the Western metaphysics of space already suggests a kind of impoverishment of our affective links with the environment. Key works such as Lefebvre's Marxist *The Production of Space* (1974) and Casey's phenomenological *The Fate of Place* (1997) argue that Western thought since the Renaissance has conceptualised space in increasingly abstract and homogeneous ways.[83] Foucault famously made the claim in a lecture given in the 1960s that if the nineteenth century was obsessed with time and history, then the twentieth is an 'epoch of space'. The origins of this epoch can, however, be dated to as far back as Galileo, whose chief impact was the reconstitution of space as infinite and open: 'In such a space the place of the Middle Ages turned out to be dissolved, as it were; a thing's place was no longer anything but a point in its movement, just as the stability of a thing was only its movement indefinitely slowed down. In other words, starting with Galileo and the seventeenth century, extension was substituted for localization.'[84] Place (or the local) is dissolved in favour of an abstract notion of space as infinite and indifferent extension.

Despite their methodological and ideological differences, these authors come to the same conclusion: the dominant accounts of space that Western thought and science have produced attenuate our ability to meaningfully inhabit space as place or – what is the same thing – to resist the malign effects of space as a deracinating abstraction or means of control. Quentin Meillassoux has provided a usefully concise summary of the trend that Foucault, Lefebvre and Casey describe:

> The world of Cartesian extension is a world that acquires the independence of substance, a world that we can henceforth conceive of as indifferent to everything in it that corresponds to the concrete, organic connection that we forge with it – it is this *glacial* world that is revealed to the moderns, a world in which there is no longer any up or down, centre or periphery, nor anything else that might make of it a world designed for humans. For the first time, the world manifests itself as capable of subsisting without any of those aspects that constitute its concreteness for us.[85]

Modernity produces a glacial placelessness or 'atopia', as Casey puts it, which precipitates a crisis of affective or libidinal investment in the physical environment.[86] Once space becomes exhaustively mathematisable, as it does with Copernicus and Galileo, the possibility of dwelling, of meaningfully inhabiting space, is called into question. Concepts such as world and environment thus start to emerge as objects of direct philosophical concern. As Bruno Latour puts it, 'the paradox of "the environment" is that it emerged in public parlance just when it was starting to disappear'.[87] Once we feel ourselves to be 'nowhere', to be atopian, the question of what place is comes to the fore.

The most important modern philosophical attempt to provide an alternative to the Western metaphysics of space came from Heidegger. For Heidegger, human existence equates to Dasein, meaning being *there*, being placed, being-in-the-world. It is impossible to detach from subjectivity the fact of its emplacement. But a strange corollary of this fact is that place becomes an uncanny thing. Work in the phenomenology of place has often deployed Heideggerian approaches while ignoring some of the more interesting avenues down which Heidegger's thought leads.[88] Casey, for example, writes of the need to assert the 'concrete, multiplex, experiential aspects of the place-world' in opposition to the abstractions of space.[89] The concept of world is often presented in ecophenomenology as something vaguely synonymous with the environment as a source of meaning and enriched experience. What tends to get lost in these attempts to remedy atopia by 'getting back into place', to quote the title of one of Casey's books, is that the idea of 'world' is for Heidegger fundamentally problematic in a way that prevents us from reducing it to embeddedness or locatedness in a surrounding environment. The paradox here is that to think world as a problem requires the experience of worldlessness. The world is thus encountered by way of a perturbing and irreducible *uncanniness*. One of Heidegger's examples of this from *Being and Time* is fear of the dark. In the dark, the world has both disappeared *and* come oppressively close.[90] The world is never 'where' it is supposed to be. Our sense of place is thus fully bound up with a sense of our own *displacement* and, consequently, our being-in-the-world contains some form of awareness, subsequently repressed or forgotten, of a worldlessness without which there would be no being-in-the-world at all.

Ecophenomenological attempts to naturalise the world miss this problematic aspect of it. If the world were *not* a problem for us, there would be no need to philosophise it or regard it as ontologically significant. What Heidegger and Levinas suggest is that world, place, environment and so on can only become objects of philosophical thought because of a feeling that our connection to them is frail, lacking or troubling. There is something *wrong* with the world, as revealed to us in times of trauma or disturbance. As Morton points out, Heidegger conceives the world as 'inherently lacking, inherently ragged and faulty'.[91] *World is its own loss or impoverishment*. Pursuing this idea, Levinas during his imprisonment in the Second World War attempted to go beyond Heidegger's ontology by articulating a philosophy of existential worldlessness: 'Expressions such as "a world in pieces" or "a world turned upside down," trite as they have become, nonetheless express a feeling that is authentic'.[92] In his later work, he argues for an anti-ontological conception of space as an 'outside where nothing covers anything, non-protection, the reverse of a retreat, homelessness, non-inhabitation, layout without security'.[93] Whereas for Levinas this is a distinctly human problematic (the ethical problem of the other), we can now view worldlessness as increasingly the situation of life in the Anthropocene. Heidegger distinguished humans as world-builders from animals by saying that the latter are 'poor in world', while inorganic things such as stones are worldless entirely.[94] But our contemporary condition suggests that all life on Earth is now confronting a *common precariousness of dwelling* rendering such presumptions to human uniqueness obsolete. At the same time, Heidegger's insistence that our being-in-the-world is disclosed to us in moments of boredom and anxiety suggests that we do not grasp the fact of our uniquely human being-in-the-world without the troubling feeling that we are not at home there. There is something specifically human about this paradox, to be sure, but on a humanised planet it might be said to converge with a crisis affecting *all* life.

The philosophical figure of the desert, as I deploy it in this book, begins with Nietzsche's warning in *Thus Spoke Zarathustra* (1883–5):

'the desert grows [*Die Wüste wächst*]: woe to him who harbors deserts!'[95] Nietzsche is at once describing modernity as a spiritual wasteland and insisting that the desert itself is a mode of growth or self-propagation, a highly fraught mode of becoming where the certainty of belonging is precluded. If nihilism portends the nullity of a desert, it also leads beyond itself in a self-overcoming. The most influential interpretation of Nietzsche's growing desert comes from Heidegger's lecture course *What Is Called Thinking?* (1952). Here, Heidegger argues that the *Wüste* is the terminal metaphysical landscape of modern, technological society. It is also a turning point in history that marks man's 'becoming the future master of the earth' in the form of the Overman.[96] Modern technoscientific rationality is, according to Heidegger, the self-extinguishing of a form of thinking that began with the metaphysics of ancient Greece but whose fate is played out in the societies of the capitalist West. The desert, then, denotes not just the physical devastation of the Earth by modern technology but a devastation of being itself in which the entire Western tradition culminates. At the same time, the desert marks the threshold of an epochal transformation of man's relationship with the Earth. The *Wüste* on this view is an extremely ambiguous terrain marking a pivot in human destiny with elements of what theologians call *soteriology*, a doctrine of salvation.

We can tie this philosophical tradition to the aesthetic possibilities that modern literary texts find in deserts and wastelands of various sorts. These texts do not simply display an interest in certain types of landscapes but constitute something comparable to what Blanchot has called a 'space of literature'. For Blanchot, literature exists at a remove from the world and the writer in a condition of exile or errancy. Like the land surveyor in Kafka's *The Castle* (1926), the writer is forced to inhabit a space 'where the conditions of a real dwelling lack, where one has to live in an incomprehensible separation'.[97] The separation between individual and world is where the literary imagination arises but this 'where' is an atopia, a voided position that precludes dwelling, while the individual becomes the transmitter of an anonymous expression that resonates in the void. In the desert of literary space, language loses its communicative power but gains the curious ability to make silence itself speak: 'the poet is he who hears a language which makes nothing heard'.[98] While for Heidegger dwelling and art are connected by a shared world-building activity, Blanchot seeks a different role for art in which a space distinct from the world and an aesthetic activity distinct from the 'work' of building it become available to thought and creative practice.[99] This space is not inhabited by the kinds of poetic dwelling Heidegger envisions in his well-known analyses of Hölderlin,

Trakl and Rilke but is traversed nomadically by the errancy of refrains that redraw the limits of territory towards an absolute Outside. Levinas underscores the contrast between Blanchot and Heidegger in this respect:

> Art, according to Blanchot, far from elucidating the world, exposes the desolate, lightless substratum underlying it, and restores to our sojourn its exotic essence – and, to the wonders of our architecture, their function of makeshift desert shelters. Blanchot and Heidegger agree that art does not lead (contrary to classical esthetics) to a world behind the world, an ideal world behind the real one. Art is light. Light from on high in Heidegger, making the world, founding place. In Blanchot it is a black light, a night coming from below.[100]

Art not only reveals a world but also the world's desolate underside, the point where world and unworld appear to converge. Levinas is exaggerating the difference between Heidegger and Blanchot here, however, since something of this penumbral, desertified unworld is already at work in Heidegger's account of the devastations wrought by modern technoscientific rationality. The latter have their source in representations that operate by 'enframing' the world for consciousness and pressing being into presence for the purposes of consumption. Through this process 'the "world" has become an unworld'.[101] The unworld forms the conditions under which the world becomes a problem for art and philosophy.

Representational consciousness is bound to a special kind of violence Heidegger calls 'devastation' or 'desertification' (*Verwüstung*), meaning a neutralisation of the ontological difference. The effects of this may be physically destructive – and may indeed involve desertification in the physical sense of ravaging of the Earth's surface to the point where it is rendered unfit for or hostile to life – but for Heidegger mere physical or ontic destruction is not the whole story. The problem of devastation's violence is at once more profoundly ontological and more ambiguous or uncanny (unhomely or unearthly) than that:

> Devastation [*Verwüstung*] is more than destruction [*Vernichtung*]. Devastation is more unearthly [*unheimlicher*] than destruction. Destruction only sweeps aside all that has grown up or been built up so far; but devastation blocks all future growth and prevents all building. Devastation is more unearthly than mere destruction. Mere destruction sweeps aside all things including even nothingness, while devastation on the contrary establishes and spreads everything that blocks and prevents. The African Sahara is only one kind of wasteland. The devastation of the earth can easily go hand in hand with a guaranteed supreme living standard for man, and just as easily with the organized establishment of a uniform state of happiness for all men. Devastation can be the same as both, and can haunt us everywhere in the

most unearthly way – by keeping itself hidden. Devastation does not just mean a slow sinking into the sands.[102]

The uncanniness of devastation is that we witness in it a kind of growth: there is a spreading of everything that blocks, as if life not only as actuality but as potentiality or virtuality has been anticipated by the desert. In the grips of this paradox, the world itself becomes a kind of virtual realm, increasingly automated, administered and compressed. Nature, meanwhile, becomes mere material to be demanded forth from the Earth and used in human projects. The question to be asked is not just how we can regain contact with a meaningful place-world in an age of globalised placelessness, but – more importantly – where the world's self-propagating desolation comes from and where it is leading us. Rather than following Heidegger's proto-ecocritical readings of Romantic poetry as a way of regaining a sense of place in a devastated world, we can ask instead if there is an aesthetics of unworlding that would also be an aesthetics for the Anthropocene.

There are important links between the modern desert ordeal and much older ones. It has often been noted by theologians and historians that the desert landscapes of Egypt and Mesopotamia were crucial for the development of monotheism. Such landscapes, by appearing abandoned by God, provided the semi-nomadic Hebrews with 'a concrete image of transcendence'.[103] Ernest Renan wrote in his *History of the People of Israel* (1888) that 'the desert is monotheistic'.[104] For Rudolph Otto – a key theological influence on Levinas – the desert's 'empty distances' give sensory actuality to the divinity of the 'wholly other'.[105] Yahweh's withdrawal from the world into a complete transcendence is inscribed, negatively, in the experience of a bare, apparently accursed, geography. With Nietzsche, however, empty space provokes a different kind of ordeal. In the famous section of *The Gay Science* (1882) proclaiming the death of God, Nietzsche's madman asks:

> Who gave us the sponge to wipe away the entire horizon? What were we doing when we unchained this earth from its sun? Where is it moving to now? Where are we moving to? Away from all suns? Are we not continually falling? And backwards, sidewards, forwards, in all directions? Is there still an up and a down? Aren't we straying as though through an infinite nothing? Isn't empty space breathing at us?[106]

To modern, secular experience corresponds a new kind of desert ordeal no longer anchored in divine transcendence. Derrida deploys the image of the desert to discuss the persistence of religious questions through the rationalisations and formalisations of modern knowledge. In 'Faith and Knowledge', he asks whether a discourse on religion can be dissociated from a 'discourse on salvation: which is to say, on the holy, the sacred, the safe and sound, the unscathed'. The question of salvation can only be addressed, he says, through a consideration of the forces of 'deracination', 'delocalization' and 'abstraction' that produce globalised modernity.[107] The desire for salvation is bound to an automatism that manifests itself in the machine, in technology and telecommunications. The question of religion in modern society, then, is posed on the terrain of 'a desert about which one isn't sure if it is sterile or not'.[108]

In Deleuze's solo and collaborative work, we find a concern for themes of stoicism, asceticism, spiritual ordeal, and states of physical and mental exhaustion. Some of his earliest writing was on Robinson Crusoe and the figure of the desert island, an interest he shares with Derrida.[109] Deleuze's geophilosophical framework – discussed in depth in the next chapter – is first suggested in his article on the Robinson myth. Defoe's novel suggests an imperialist and capitalist outlook: how does one construct a civilised world in the absence of civilised others? For Deleuze, subsequent rewritings of the basic narrative subvert this question by asking: how does the concept of the 'other' structure our experience to begin with? The question is tantamount to asking how one might live without a concept of world, a radical idea that has been present in philosophy since Kant.[110] Deleuze is, of course, most famous for his explosive political theory written with Guattari. In their major works of the 1970s and 1980s, they developed a theory of collective subjectivity aimed at evading contemporary modes of social control. For Deleuze and Guattari, we must remain mobile in thought and behaviour, like a nomadic group. Such a strategy is necessary to evade the political or ideological manipulations of mass desire characteristic of the modern state. The most insidious of these apparatuses is subjectivity itself. Deleuze and Guattari criticise the psychoanalytic account of psychosexual development for recognising but ultimately capitulating to this fact. They criticise Freud's 'familial' model of subject formation, accusing him of neglecting the experience of schizophrenia in order to elaborate a conception of desire modelled on the neurotic triangle of Oedipus with the tyrannical, castrating figure of the father at its apex. For psychoanalysis, desire is necessarily welded to repression because the subject finds a place in society, a *territory*, by accepting and internalising the oedipal conflict.[111]

The schizophrenic ordeal, however, offers a different model of subjectivity in which desire not only invests social reality directly, without the mediating role of the Oedipus complex and its parental imaginary, but does so in a way that ultimately escapes the territories by which social and psychical reality impose organisation on it. Territories *local-*

ise desire. But a desire modelled on the ordeal of the schizophrenic flies headlong into the desert in order to seek a new kind of consistency, a new territory that is not really a territory at all but a deterritorialised surface that Deleuze and Guattari call, using Antonin Artaud's evocative phrase, the 'body without organs':

> Everything has been said about the paucity of reality, the loss of reality, the lack of contact with life, autism and athymia. Schizophrenics themselves have said everything there is to say about this, and have been quick to slip into the expected clinical mold. Dark world, growing desert: a solitary machine hums on the beach, an atomic factory installed in the desert. But if the body without organs is indeed this desert, it is as an indivisible, nondecomposable distance over which the schizo glides in order to be everywhere something real is produced, everywhere something real has been and will be produced.[112]

The idea of the desert of the body without organs is key because it develops the critique of psychoanalysis into geophilosophy, as I show in detail in the next chapter. Geophilosophy is a mode of planetary thinking that transforms the terms by which we understand subjectivity, calling forth something like an absolute subject. The philosophical figuration of the desert relates not only to conceptions of environment and spatiality but also to aesthetics, understood as a theory of art as well as a way of thinking about subjectivity at the level of percepts and affects, sensation and feeling. Heidegger's devastation of being already suggested an exhaustion of representational consciousness; when the frames of representation fall away, the world itself is torn to pieces. What Deleuze and Guattari help us to understand is that the crisis of representation is also a libidinal and energetic one. The schizophrenic body is itself an *entropic landscape* where the codes of sensation are scrambled.

THE DESERT AND MODERN LITERATURE

In this book, I present readings of some of the most significant examples of deserts and wastelands in literature since Romanticism by drawing on the theoretical insights I have begun to outline. As I pointed out above, the desert in literature has generally been neglected by critics. At the same time, the critical appreciation of the desert that does exist has given us an unacceptably narrow view of what constitutes the desert as a literary object. In Glotfelty and Fromm's edited volume *The Ecocriticism Reader* (1996), to give a dated but still indicative example, the desert is represented primarily by Abbey's *Desert Solitaire*, read as a mid-twentieth-century *Walden* and belonging to a tradition of desert-focused nature writing featuring Joseph Wood Krutch, John C. Van

Dyke and Mary Austin. In trying to move beyond this nature writing paradigm to suggest an alternative genealogy of the desert in modern literature, we can turn to one of the foundational texts of British ecocriticism, Raymond Williams's *The Country and the City* (1973). For Williams, the countryside in the English literary canon has served a range of ideological functions, depicting rural life as alternately idyllic and backward, liberating and corrupt. The land or 'working agriculture' defined in opposition to the city is a medium that renders social relations as a set of moral and aesthetic values which appear natural but are social and historical.[113]

Williams's work on the ideologico-aesthetic construction of the English countryside may be a strange place to look for an understanding of the desert as a modern literary topos. Nevertheless, in his analysis of Oliver Goldsmith's poem 'The Deserted Village' (1769), Williams discerns the presence of an entropic landscape. Williams calls Goldsmith's text 'a baffling poem' because it presents two simultaneous yet contrasting visions of the same place.[114] 'Sweet Auburn', the fictional village of the poem, is shown as moving from the conditions predominating in 'feudal and immediately post-feudal arrangements' to a fledgling agrarian capitalism characterised by a new commercial spirit that saw the land as an object of calculation and investment.[115] This shift manifested itself in a 'crisis of values'.[116] Williams notes the predominance in the seventeenth and early eighteenth centuries of poems that look with melancholy regret on a lost pastoral tradition and a dying mode of country life.[117] Goldsmith's text begins with a retrospective nostalgia suggestive of this earlier work but immediately contrasts this with a protest against the effects of agricultural modernisation:

> Sweet smiling village, loveliest of the lawn,
> Thy sports are fled, and all thy charms withdrawn;
> Amidst thy bowers the tyrant's hand is seen,
> And desolation saddens all thy green:
> One only master grasps the whole domain,
> And half a tillage stints thy smiling plain.
> No more thy glassy brook reflects the day,
> But, choked with sedges, works its weedy way;
> Along thy glades, a solitary guest,
> The hollow-sounding bittern guards its nest;
> Amidst thy desert walks the lapwing flies,
> And tires their echoes with unvaried cries.[118]

What separates Goldsmith's text from earlier work bewailing the loss of an old rural order is the manner in which the social crisis of values brought on by economic development is manifested as an *aesthetic* crisis. What Goldsmith depicts is not only the collapse of an idealised pastoral economy but also the collapse of poetry itself as a means of depicting the natural environment as something entirely bound up with this economy. The 'one only master' is the absent, city-based landowner representative of an emerging capitalist class for whom the village is merely a source of wealth. The tyranny of capital desolates the pastoral scene. As Williams writes, the 'actual history' of the destruction of the old social relations of the village 'was accompanied by an increased use and fertility of the land'.[119] But this fertility can only be rendered poetically by Goldsmith as wasteland. The entropic landscape inserted into the pastoral scene is an imaginative response to the break-up of an old aesthetic framework for picturing nature, fertility and cultivation as bound up with a set of organic social relations: the desert 'is what the new order does to the poet, not to the land'.[120]

Williams argues that the devastation of pastoral poetics in Goldsmith marks the emergence of a new 'structure of feeling' in the form of Romantic culture's 'assertion of nature against industry'.[121] The version of nature that emerges from Sweet Auburn's desolation is one capable of being regarded as 'out there', largely separate from human society and the social relations of any community.[122] With the Romantic poets, 'there came the sense of nature as a refuge, a refuge for man; a place of healing, a solace, a retreat'.[123] Williams explains the contradiction at the heart of Romantic nature:

> When nature is separated out from the activities of men, it even ceases to be nature, in any full and effective sense. Men come to project on to nature their own unacknowledged activities and consequences. Or nature is split into unrelated parts: coal-bearing from heather-bearing; downwind from upwind. The real split, perhaps, is in men themselves: men seen, seeing themselves, as producers and consumers. The consumer wants only the intended product; all other products and by-products he must get away from, if he can. But get away – it really can't be overlooked – to treat leftover nature in much the same spirit: to consume it as scenery, landscape, image, fresh air. There is more similarity than we usually recognise between the industrial entrepreneur and the landscape gardener.[124]

Underwriting Romantic conceptions of nature as refuge, as aesthetically distanced object of a contemplative consumption, is a vision of ruin and waste. The consumption of nature cannot be separated from the by-products of this consumption. Nature as refuge is a correlate of nature consumed, used-up and exhausted. With Romanticism, then, the desert and wasteland begin to take on a new aesthetic resonance. No longer do they relate to the moral degeneracy of the uncultivated wilderness – as they did for the land improvers of the seventeenth and eighteenth centuries – but to a new set of values located precariously on the shifting boundaries between the cultural and the natural.

The desert becomes at once a denunciation of tyranny and a site in which humanity's relationship with nature can be considered anew. Auden argues that for Romantic symbolism, the desert denotes a natural wilderness but also urban decay: 'the desert may not be barren by nature but as the consequence of a historical catastrophe. The once-fertile city has become, through the malevolence of others or its own sin, the waste land'.[125] We see this clearly in Shelley's 'Ozymandias' (1818) and in his dramatic poem *Hellas* (1822) documenting the Greek War of Independence. In both, tyranny is associated with a desert landscape, and the signs of civilisation are read as signs of lack, as ruins. Civilisation is a kind of dead letter whose ecological equivalent is the desert. But the desert is also a place of regeneration, a site where empty signs become revitalised and live once more. In Shelley's *Queen Mab* (1813), the desert is depicted as the global stage on which a whole new reign of life on Earth begins:

> Those deserts of immeasurable sand,
> Whose age-collected fervors scarce allowed
> A bird to live, a blade of grass to spring,
> Where the shrill chirp of the green lizard's love
> Broke on the sultry silentness alone,
> Now teem with countless rills and shady woods,
> Corn-fields and pastures and white cottages.[126]

This is what Morton has called Shelley's 'green desert', a place of death and rebirth simultaneously.[127] Shelley is effectively arguing for a 'technohumanist' dominion of benevolent industry over nature.[128] The desert, here, becomes essential to elaborating a vision of technological humanity's stewardship over the Earth.

Deleuze and Guattari's geophilosophical framework is useful for understanding Romanticism's deployment of the desert because they discern across European Romanticism in general a new concern, breaking with classicism, for the Earth as ravaged, deserted or solitary.[129] For the Romantics, the Earth no longer presupposes our dwelling upon it via the ontological security of a divinely created world but instead poses anew the problem of dwelling. If the securities of a divinely created world begin to fall away in the eighteenth century, then it is the Earth as an ecoaesthetic object that replaces it. As Deleuze puts it in one of his lectures on Leibniz, for the Romantic artist 'it is no longer the problem of the world, but one of the earth' that is the key issue.[130] This is not because the world has ceased to be problematic but because the Earth has intruded on the problem of the world. The Romantic problem is how best to *found* a new territory on an Earth that lacks the grounding function of the world. In *A Thousand Plateaus*, Deleuze and Guattari articulate this in terms of a disjunction of Earth and territory:

> With romanticism ... the artist territorializes, enters a territorial assemblage. The seasons are now territorialized. The earth is certainly not the same thing as the territory. The earth is the intense point at the deepest level of the territory or is projected outside it like a focal point, where all the forces draw together in close embrace. ... The earth has become that close embrace of all forces, those of the earth as well as of other substances, so that the artist no longer confronts chaos, but hell and the subterranean, the groundless.[131]

The green desert of *Queen Mab* shows us this quite clearly: Shelley rediscovers the Earth as absolutely deterritorialised, as desert, but seeks a territory for it, the process of territorialisation here being both poetic and technological. As Morton puts it using Deleuze and Guattari's own terminology, 'the empty or "smooth" space of the desert has become the populated or "striated" space of agrarian cultivation'.[132] The utopian transformation of the Earth requires the desert as the terrain of absolute deterritorialisation, even when cultivation reterritorialises on it.

When we look at twentieth-century literature, we can trace a concern for the desert that passes through modernism to the Beat Generation to postmodernism and beyond. In each case, the Romantic heritage is important. After 'Ozymandias', *The Waste Land* (1922) is the most famous evocation of the desert in modern anglophone poetry. Casey views the desert of Eliot's London as a manifestation of *horror vacui*, the terror of empty places, becoming a generalised modern malaise.[133] Eliot's 'hooded hordes swarming / Over endless plains, stumbling in cracked earth' would seem a diagnosis of the mass atopia of the modern city.[134] This illness, Casey argues, goes hand in hand with 'ontomania', an obsession with rendering being present through a technoscientific worldview. Philosophy since Aristotle has found itself panic-stricken before the empty field, before 'the dark vision of no-place-at-all', and has thus wanted to 'have and know as much determinate presence as possible' in order to fill the field at any cost.[135] The epidemic of atopia as a psychosocial malady in the twentieth century may thus be read in Heideggerian fashion as a product of the Western metaphysics of space once the latter becomes concretised in the cities of industrial modernity.

But another reading of Eliot's poem is possible. For Deleuze and Guattari, modern art is post-Romantic in the sense that it takes up the problem of the Earth as deterritorialised. Our dwelling does not need to pass through a territory or a world and thus encounters nomadic inhabitations of all sorts, whose relationship to the Earth is dramatically uncertain and open. The Heideggerian ecopoetics of dwelling may be contrasted with the refrains of a nomadic or atopian deterritorialisation. A text such as Eliot's can be read in this way not necessarily as a demand for a territory but as an exploration of deterritorialised space. Whereas for Shelley the signs of both nature and civilisation take on an unusual clarity in the desert either through their rebirth or their ruin, for Eliot the 'broken images' themselves lie in a 'heap',[136] their meanings obscured, reflecting the very inter- and intratextual dynamics of the poem itself as a sifting of fragments, or what Viney has called Eliot's 'poetics of residua'.[137] The wasteland is, for Eliot, a land of *waste*, of textual redundancies, excrescences, repetitions and fragments entering into a clamorous resonance. Signs signify only as waste to be salvaged, reused and discarded. The topos of the literary text is itself thus a kind of wasteland, a vacant lot. In his early poem 'Second Caprice in North Cambridge' (1909), he suggests that empty and derelict spaces exert an uncanny attraction in defiance of aesthetic norms:

> This charm of vacant lots!
> The helpless fields that lie
> Sinister, sterile and blind –
> Entreat the eye and rack the mind,
> Demand your pity.
> With ashes and tins in piles,
> Shattered bricks and tiles
> And the débris of a city.
>
> Far from our definitions
> And our aesthetic laws
> Let us pause
> With these fields that hold and rack the brain.[138]

The charm of vacant lots is of the same order as the 'chastened sublimity' of Hardy's Egdon Heath, but Eliot extends the energetic exhaustion of such places to the textual entropy of his own poetic practice. When the debris of North Cambridge is moved to London, it becomes swept up in all the debris of Western culture itself, now regarded as so much rubbish to be sorted through on the page.

William S. Burroughs, for whom Eliot was a major influence, takes this textual strategy to its most extreme point.[139] In experimental books such as *The Soft Machine* (1961), bodies exhausted from the excesses of sex and drugs are depicted in entropic landscapes that reimagine Eliot's North Cambridge fields through a nightmarish, hallucinatory lens:

> In a green savanna stand two vast penis figures in black stone, legs and arms vestigial, slow blue smoke rings pulsing from the stone heads. A limestone

road winds through the pillars and into The City. A rack of rusty iron and concrete set in vacant lots and rubble, dotted with chemical gardens.[140]

Burroughs's landscapes are places designed to exhaust the possibilities of language itself, textual techniques such as his famous 'cut-up' and 'fold-in' methods aiming to draw on linguistic disorder as a creative principle. The desert landscapes that feature so extensively in his writing include those of North Africa, Mexico and the American southwest and are often depicted as sites of strange fertility rituals in which we see life resurgent amidst death and decay. These barren geographies are, for Burroughs, the frontiers of a war on the agents of social and psychic control, language itself being prime among these. As Kathryn Hume observes, for Burroughs 'the city is not the metropolis of high culture but embodies the gridded spaces ruled by Control society. The desert's drought enables freedom to flourish, because lack of water renders high-density plant and human population – jungle and city – impossible'.[141]

It is mainly via Burroughs that we reach the deserts and wastelands that fill the pages of canonical postmodern authors such as Pynchon, Ballard, DeLillo, Auster and Carter. As I will show in subsequent chapters, these authors consistently return to scenes of waste and desolation. The links between the desert and postmodernism have not gone entirely without critical notice. Gersdorf, for example, points to two key non-fiction texts, both works of travel writing by Europeans, that demonstrate this link: Banham's *Scenes in America Deserta* and Baudrillard's *America*. These texts are, for Gersdorf, emblematic of a new historical moment following the 'accelerated consumption' of the postwar decades, in which space 'began to reacquire connotations of openness and imperial expansion [and] re-emerged as a geopolitical, culturally transgressive category, a development that called for new, expressive images and metaphors'.[142] For the postmodern turn, then, and whatever lies beyond it, the desert seems to provide an image of space as a new site of power, a new *imperium*, a space of death and ordeal as well as global mediatised culture.

For contemporary philosophy and theory, the link between war and the desert is often explicit. This is why philosophers interested in polemology, the discourse of war, have been drawn to the desert theme. Deleuze and Guattari described resistance to global capitalism in terms of a nomadic 'war machine' and Deleuze wrote an extensive essay on Lawrence's *Seven Pillars of Wisdom*. Paul Virilio likewise makes frequent use of the desert to suggest contemporary convergences of war, power and media. Explaining the title of his book *Desert Screen* (1991), he remarks that the screen is the site of *projection of the light of images* – mirages of the geographic desert like those of the cinema. It is also the site of *projections of the force of energy* – beginning with the desert in New Mexico, the first atomic explosion at the Trinity site, and leading up to the Persian Gulf War when *the screens of the Kuwaiti and Iraqi deserts* were to be linked with the *television screens* of the entire world.[143]

The space of the contemporary image here suggests a kind of ascesis or poverty coexistent with an extreme compression of distances in an accelerated global mediascape characterised by war, mass consumption and eschatological religion. Recent works such as DeLillo's novel *Point Omega* (2010) and Reza Negarestani's remarkable blend of fiction and theory *Cyclonopedia* (2008) approach the desert in this way. In these texts, the deserts of California and Iraq respectively are used as speculative landscapes to address the 2003 war in the Persian Gulf and its aftermath. Both texts provide accounts of the intersections of geopolitics, theology and fossil fuels.

This rough sketch for a genealogy of the desert in modern literature aims to deliberately widen the parameters of what constitutes the desert as a critical object. I have also deliberately approached the desert from a global and geophilosophical rather than a local or bioregional point of view. Viewed in this way, the desert in modern literature demonstrates a concern for the Earth that breaks with the ancient idea of a (divinely created) world. While we are still within the aesthetic space of this break, the Anthropocene and the Eremozoic (or Eremocene) give it a new epochal significance. That the desert as a literary theoretical object may be able to provide an ecoaesthetic or geoaesthetic model for understanding the spatiality of the Anthropocene is one of the claims of this book, therefore. The literary authors addressed here and in subsequent chapters can be read as providing maps of this space. First, however, we need to turn our attention specifically to the question of geophilosophy.

NOTES

1. Ecocritical literary scholarship has, since Bate's seminal *Romantic Ecology: Wordsworth and the Environmental Tradition* (1991), repeatedly returned to the Romantic period in order to construct a genealogy of contemporary ecological consciousness. Bate's work is significant because it challenged a critical orthodoxy according to which the Romantic concept of 'nature' was largely a cipher for culture or ideology. This re-evaluation, which insisted on the importance of bioregionality and local geography, coincided with the emergence of ecocriticism itself as a key critical movement. The centrality of the Romantics in all of this can, to some extent at least, be explained by a concern with the present

rather than with literary history per se. As Kate Rigby writes, 'to return to romanticism from an ecological perspective might ... contribute to an archaeology of contemporary green thought and feeling' (Rigby, *Topographies of the Sacred*, p. 1). Recent work in this vein – for example, Ottum and Reno's edited volume *Wordsworth and the Green Romantics* (2016) and Nichols's *Beyond Romantic Ecocriticism* (2011) – underscores how the affects and images that characterise environmental discourse today are rooted in the work of the Romantics. Nevertheless, the question of how green the Romantics actually were, to paraphrase the title of an important 1996 article by Ralph Pite, is a hotly debated one. Pite's article is something of a rebuttal of Bate's view that also drives it into more complex and interesting territory. This trend has been developed by Morton, whose contribution in works such as *The Poetics of Spice: Romantic Consumerism and the Exotic* (2000) and *Ecology without Nature* (2007) has been to critique the naive environmentalism of some aspects of ecocriticism (localism and bioregionalism, for example) while insisting on the importance of the Romantics for theorising our contemporary ecological condition. In particular, he has insisted that we need to submit the Romantic aestheticisation of nature to a rigorous critique that sees it as both an expression of and a reaction to the development of capitalism. In this sense, aesthetic theory must join forces with environmental criticism. This is an approach scrutinised by Malcolm Miles's wide-ranging *Eco-Aesthetics* (2014).
2. Bate, *The Song of the Earth*, p. 13.
3. Ottum and Reno, 'Introduction: Recovering Ecology's Affects', in Ottum and Reno (eds), *Wordsworth and the Green Romantics*, pp. 1–2.
4. Morton, *Ecology without Nature*, p. 22.
5. Oliver, *Earth and World*, p. 11.
6. Hetherington, *Badlands of Modernity*, p. 4.
7. See, for example, Gersdorf's *The Poetics and Politics of the Desert*, p. 32, and Grumberg's *Place and Ideology in Contemporary Hebrew Literature*, p. 30.
8. Berman, *All That Is Solid Melts into Air*, pp. 61–2.
9. Viney, *Waste*, p. 16.
10. For work on the modern aesthetics of ruins, see Edensor's *Industrial Ruins* (2005) and Hell and Schönle's edited volume *Ruins of Modernity* (2010).
11. Povinelli, *Geontologies*, p. 4.
12. Ibid. p. 17.
13. Ibid. p. 183.
14. Derrida, *On the Name*, pp. 53–4.
15. Lukács, *The Theory of the Novel*, p. 41.
16. Levinas, *Existence and Existents*, p. 56.
17. Ibid. p. 59.
18. Levinas, 'On Maurice Blanchot', in *Proper Names*, p. 136. The opposition between the sedentary and the nomadic, so crucial for Deleuze and

Guattari, goes back to the question of Heidegger's anti-Semitism and his relation to Nazism. In his seminar from 1933–4, Heidegger makes the following remark, which is indicative of his notion of dwelling:

> people and space mutually belong to each other. From the specific knowledge of a people about the nature of its space, we first experience how nature is revealed in this people. For a Slavic people, the nature of our German space would definitely be revealed differently from the way it is revealed to us; to Semitic nomads, it will perhaps never be revealed at all. This way of being embedded in a people, situated in a people, this original participation in the knowledge of the people, cannot be taught; at most, it can be awakened from its slumber. (*Nature, History, State: 1933–1934*, p. 66)

Di Cesare argues that Heidegger's *Black Notebooks* make clear the extent to which he associated what he saw as the rootlessness of Jews with the desert of modernity:

> To the Jews, seen as the rootless agents of modernity, accused of machination to seize power, of the desertification of the earth, of uprooting peoples, condemned to be *weltlos* – worldless, 'without world' – Heidegger imputed the gravest guilt: the oblivion of Being. The Jew was a sign of the end of everything, impeding the rise of a new beginning. (*Heidegger and the Jews*, p. ix)

Levinas's notion of the nomad thus enters philosophical discourse both as a rebuttal of Heidegger's anti-Semitism and as a critique of his ontology of world. Nevertheless, the eschatological significance of the desert is not adequately accounted for by being-in-the-world as dwelling. Heidegger's thought seems to point beyond the world even as his politics roots itself in the world.

19. See the 2017 article, 'Parasite Biodiversity Faces Extinction and Redistribution in a Changing Climate', by Carlson et al.
20. Kolbert, *The Sixth Extinction*, p. 198.
21. Deleuze and Guattari, *What is Philosophy?*, p. 85.
22. Bernard Westphal has suggested the possibilities of what he calls geocriticism, and takes direct inspiration from Deleuze and Guattari's analysis of spatiality (*Geocriticism*, p. 24). For intriguing links between ecocriticism and geocriticism, see Tally and Battista (eds), *Ecocriticism and Geocriticism: Overlapping Territories in Environmental and Spatial Literary Studies* (2016). For examples of recent non-Deleuzian work in philosophy that can be called geophilosophical, see Gaston's *The Concept of World from Kant to Derrida* (2013) and Oliver's *Earth and World* (2015).
23. Crutzen, 'Geology of Mankind', p. 23.
24. Zalasiewicz et al., 'When did the Anthropocene begin?'.
25. Lewis and Maslin, *The Human Planet*, p. 13.

26. Moore, *Capitalism in the Web of Life*, p. 172.
27. Steffen, Crutzen and McNeill, 'The Anthropocene: Are Humans Now Overwhelming the Great Forces of Nature?', p. 614.
28. Ashton Nichols has proposed the terms 'urbanature' and 'urbanatural' to grasp the hybridity that defines our contemporary environmental condition. See his *Beyond Romantic Ecocriticism: Toward Urbanatural Roosting*.
29. Van Wyck, *Primitives in the Wilderness*, p. 53.
30. Haraway, *Staying with the Trouble*, p. 100.
31. Morton, 'Coexistence and Coexistents: Ecology without a World', p. 168.
32. Moore, *Capitalism in the Web of Life*, p. 10.
33. Sloterdijk, *In the World Interior of Capital*, p. 12.
34. This sounds paradoxical, but appears less so once we attend to Heidegger's argument that an essential part of our being-in-the-world involves the withdrawal of the world's worldhood. It is only when we feel that there is something wrong with the world that we notice it (Heidegger, *Being and Time*, p. 105). To be in a world is already to be embroiled in the paradox that the more we are in it, the more we forget that fact. Claire Colebrook critiques a certain misunderstanding of Heidegger's notion of world by contemporary theorists who attempt to restore some essential link between man and world: 'there is a necessary forgetting in any disclosure of being: to experience the world as present for me, and to begin questioning – as we must – from this already given world, relies upon a hiddenness or non-revealing that we must leave behind in living the world as our own' (*Death of the PostHuman*, pp. 14–15). To think the world itself does not mean returning us to the fullness of the man–world relationship but on the contrary to the discovery of the fundamental aspect of the withdrawnness of the world that lies at its origin. For the Heidegger of 'The Origin of the Work of Art' (1935–7), this means thinking the strife or *polemos* between Earth and World as foundational for any being-in-the-world. I discuss this in Chapters 4 and 5.
35. Morton, *Ecology without Nature*, p. 2.
36. Latour, *Facing Gaia*, p. 107. Stengers writes:

> Gaia is neither Earth 'in the concrete' and nor is it she who is named and invoked when it is a matter of affirming and of making our connection to this Earth felt, of provoking a sense of belonging where separation has been predominant, and of drawing resources for living, struggling, feeling, and thinking from this belonging. It is a matter here of thinking *intrusion, not belonging*. (*In Catastrophic Times*, pp. 43–4)

37. Heidegger, 'The Thing', in *Poetry, Language, Thought*, p. 164.
38. John C. Van Dyke, *The Desert*, p. 5.

39. Morton, *Hyperobjects*, p. 99. The need for an aesthetic theory of the Anthropocene is suggested by Davis and Turpin (eds) *Art in the Anthropocene* (2015), who write in their introduction to that volume that 'art, as the vehicle of *aesthesis*, is central to thinking with and feeling through the Anthropocene' ('Art & Death: Lives Between the Fifth Assessment & the Sixth Extinction', p. 3).
40. Morton, *Humankind*, pp. 92–3.
41. Anxiety is privileged in this respect. Heidegger writes:

    > when something threatening brings itself close, anxiety does not 'see' any definite 'here' or 'yonder' from which it comes. That in the face of which one has anxiety is characterized by the fact that what threatens is *nowhere*. Anxiety 'does not know' what that in the face of which it is anxious is. 'Nowhere', however, does not signify nothing: this is where any region lies, and there too lies any disclosedness of the world for essentially spatial Being-in. Therefore that which threatens cannot bring itself close from a definite direction within what is close by; it is already 'there', and yet nowhere; it is so close that it is oppressive and stifles one's breath, and yet it is nowhere. (*Being and Time*, p. 231)

    For Heidegger's remarks on boredom, see *The Fundamental Concepts of Metaphysics*.
42. Deleuze and Guattari, *A Thousand Plateaus*, p. 300.
43. Heidegger, 'Building Dwelling Thinking', in *Poetry, Language, Thought*, p. 159.
44. Ondaatje, *The English Patient*, p. 133.
45. Bevis, *The Road to Egdon Heath*, p. 23.
46. Ibid. p. 24; Di Palma, *Wasteland*, p. 9.
47. Hardy, *The Return of the Native*, p. 54.
48. Auden, *The Enchafèd Flood*, p. 19.
49. Abbey, *Desert Solitaire*, p. xi.
50. Lindqvist, *Desert Divers*, p. 57.
51. Graulund, 'Contrasts: A Defence of Desert Writings', p. 356.
52. Bevis, *The Road to Egdon Heath*, p. 3.
53. Cohen, 'Introduction', in *Prismatic Ecology*, p. xx.
54. Jasper, *The Sacred Desert*, p. 71.
55. Crockett and Robbins, *Religion, Politics, and the Earth*, p. xx.
56. Welland, *The Desert*, p. 17.
57. Casey, *Getting Back into Place*, p. 315.
58. Eberhardt, *In the Shadow of Islam*, p. 25.
59. Thomas and Middleton, *Desertification*, pp. 13–14.
60. For work on the origins of 'desertification' in the French colonial context, see Diana K. Davis's article, 'Desert "Wastes" of the Maghreb'.
61. Benjaminsen and Berge, 'Myths of Timbuktu', p. 52.
62. Whyte, *A Dictionary of Environmental History*, p. 143.

63. Holleman, *Dust Bowls of Empire*, p. 9. In a 2011 article for *Nature* titled 'The Next Dust Bowl', Joseph Romm writes that 'many deserts are high in biodiversity, which isn't where we're heading. "Dust-bowlification" is perhaps a more accurate and vivid term'; p. 450.
64. Gaia Vince, *Adventures in the Anthropocene*, p. 192. For a Deleuzian interpretation of desertification in African drylands, see Sian Sullivan and Katherine Homewood's article 'On Non-equilibrium and Nomadism: Knowledge, Diversity and Global Modernity in Drylands (and Beyond . . .)'.
65. Di Palma, *Wasteland*, p. 3.
66. Le Goff, *The Medieval Imagination*, p. 54.
67. Morton, *Ecology without Nature*, p. 53.
68. Lacarrière, *Men Possessed by God*, p. 27.
69. Le Goff, *The Medieval Imagination*, p. 50. In his classic book *The Body and Society: Men, Women, and Sexual Renunciation in Early Christianity*, Peter Brown writes: 'to flee "the world" was to leave a precise social structure for an equally precise and, as we shall see, an equally social alternative. The desert was a "counter-world," a place where an alternative "city" could grow'; p. 217.
70. Baudrillard, *America*, pp. 66–7.
71. Following inspiration provided by a fable from Borges, Baudrillard writes that the map precedes and produces the territory, while the territory itself is dissolved – deterritorialised – by the map:

    > The territory no longer precedes the map, nor does it survive it. It is nevertheless the map that precedes the territory – *precession of simulacra* – that engenders the territory, and if one must return to the fable, today it is the territory whose shreds slowly rot across the extent of the map. It is the real, and not the map, whose vestiges persist here and there in the deserts that are no longer those of the Empire, but ours. *The desert of the real itself.* (*Simulacra and Simulation*, p. 1)

    The Empire relates to the one in Borges's story, but it also describes, as Baudrillard points out, the imperialism of the late capitalist West. The desert of the real is thus space as *imperium*, where the inscription of the map (or signs in general) constitutes an apparatus of power. I return to these themes and to Baudrillard in Chapter 5.
72. Smithson, *The Collected Writings*, p. 8.
73. Ibid. p. 11.
74. For more on Smithson's conception of entropy, see my 2018 article 'Ballard, Smithson and the Biophilosophy of the Crystal'.
75. Wilson, *Consilience*, p. 321.
76. Wilson, *Half-Earth*, p. 20.
77. Heidegger, 'Evening Conversation', in *Country Path Conversations*, pp. 137–8. Heidegger's term *Verwüstung* is usually translated into English as 'devastation', but since it derives from *Wüste*, meaning

wasteland, it should be thought of as a general laying waste or desertification in the ontological sense by which Heidegger understands this process. An argument can be made that 'desertification' is a better translation. Di Cesare in her discussion of *Verwüstung* writes:

> one should not think of the desert that spreads, drying out and devastating everything. Desertification, which 'bursts forth' from machination, constituting its perverse, inevitable effect, is the 'installation of the desert' that enables the emptiness of the desert to expand. Thus, it is not correct to translate this term as 'drying up' or 'devastation,' not only because the reference to the 'desert' is lost, but also because it reduces the phenomenon that, if it has a political weight, nevertheless had for Heidegger ontological relevance and was inscribed within the history of Being. (*Heidegger and the Jews*, p. 99)

The English word 'desertification' is, however, synonymous with processes of soil degradation, while 'devastation' conveys the sense of non-empirical destructiveness that Heidegger intends.

78. Luke 15: 4.
79. Heidegger, 'Letter on Humanism', p. 234.
80. Atwood, 'Time Capsule Found on the Dead Planet', pp. 192–3.
81. Žižek, *Welcome to the Desert of the Real!*, p. 17. The title is, of course, a reference not only to Baudrillard but to the film *The Matrix* (1999), in which Baudrillard's phrase makes its famous cameo when the central character, having swallowed the red pill, beholds the spectacle of a post-apocalyptic world previously hidden beneath a simulated reality. One of the things Žižek's book accomplishes is to suggest – without actually mentioning him – that Baudrillard may be compatible with Lacanian theory. The hyperreal of mass consumerist society is on this view a manifestation of a 'passion for the real', the real being understood in the Lacanian sense as an excessive or violent element structurally excluded from social reality. Lacan's notion of the body as a desert, and how this relates to Deleuze and Guattari, is discussed in the next chapter.
82. Freud, 'Beyond the Pleasure Principle', in *The Standard Edition, Vol. XVIII*, p. 62.
83. The modern Western metaphysics of space might be said to begin with Descartes and his determination of space as extended substance or *res extensa*. Lefebvre writes:

> A homogeneous and utterly simultaneous space would be strictly imperceptible. It would lack the conflictual component (always resolved, but always at least suggested) of the contrast between symmetry and asymmetry. It may as well be noted at this juncture that the architectural and urbanistic space of modernity tends precisely towards this homogeneous state of affairs, towards a place of confusion and fusion between geometrical and visual which inspires a kind of physi-

cal discomfort. Everything is alike. Localization – and lateralization – are no more. Signifier and signified, marks and markers, are added after the fact – as decorations, so to speak. This reinforces, if possible, the feeling of desertedness, and adds to the malaise. This modern space has an analogical affinity with the space of the philosophical, and more specifically the Cartesian tradition. Unfortunately it is also the space of blank sheets of paper, drawing-boards, plans, sections, elevations, scale models, geometrical projections, and the like. (*The Production of Space*, p. 200)

84. Foucault, 'Of Other Spaces', p. 23.
85. Meillassoux, *After Finitude*, p. 115.
86. Casey, *Getting Back into Place*, p. x.
87. Latour, 'Love Your Monsters', p. 23.
88. See, for example, Edward Relph's *Place and Placelessness* (1976) and Casey's *Getting Back into Place* (1993) and *The Fate of Place* (1997). For work on Heidegger and place, see Jeff Malpas's *Heidegger's Topology* (2006) and *Heidegger and the Thinking of Place* (2012). For a representative range of work in ecophenomenology, see the edited volume by Charles Brown and Ted Toadvine, *Eco-Phenomenology* (2003).
89. Casey, *The Fate of Place*, p. xi. Casey contends that Heidegger's conception of place is inextricable from the *polis*, the Greek term for city-state that Heidegger understands as the place of historical Dasein. Casey is right when he maintains that this conjunction of place and *polis* is conflicted in Heidegger's work. He points, for example, to certain passages in *An Introduction to Metaphysics* where Heidegger implicitly praises Hitler as a violence-doer who leaves or transgresses the limits of the *polis* in a historical venture to become '*apolis*', a ruler without limits (*An Introduction to Metaphysics*, p. 152). In this sense, Heidegger's admiration for *deviations* from the containing nature of place and *polis* are in line with his support for Nazism. Casey argues that it is Heidegger's lack of fidelity to notions of dwelling articulated in 'The Origin of the Work of Art' and elsewhere that demonstrates how his thought was led astray by Nazism (Casey, *The Fate of Place*, pp. 261–4). But this is to ignore, first, that Heideggerian dwelling is undeniably steeped in Nazi 'blood and soil' ideology, and second, how the state necessarily oversteps its own bounds in the process of expansion. I develop these points through Deleuze and Guattari's work in Chapter 2 and Chapter 5.
90. Heidegger, *Being and Time*, p. 234.
91. Morton, *Humankind*, p. 91.
92. Levinas, *Existence and Existents*, p. 21.
93. Levinas, *Otherwise than Being*, p. 179.
94. Heidegger, *The Fundamental Concepts of Metaphysics*, p. 184.
95. Nietzsche, *Thus Spoke Zarathustra*, p. 248.
96. Heidegger, *What Is Called Thinking?*, p. 59.

97. Blanchot, *The Space of Literature*, p. 77.
98. Ibid. p. 51.
99. Ibid. p. 41.
100. Levinas, *Proper Names*, p. 137.
101. Heidegger, 'Overcoming Metaphysics', in *The End of Philosophy*, p. 104.
102. Heidegger, *What Is Called Thinking?*, pp. 29–30.
103. Schneidau, *Sacred Discontent*, p. 143.
104. Renan, quoted in Debray, *God*, p. 39.
105. Otto, *The Idea of the Holy*, p. 69.
106. Nietzsche, *The Gay Science*, p. 120.
107. Derrida, 'Faith and Knowledge', pp. 42–3.
108. Ibid. p. 76.
109. Derrida's final seminar focuses on Defoe's novel and mentions Deleuze. I address the two philosophers' different approaches to the Robinson myth in Chapter 4.
110. Gaston, *The Concept of World from Kant to Derrida*, p. 28.
111. It should be noted that the concept of territory, so central to Deleuze and Guattari's work, originates with psychoanalysis. See, for example, Lacan's discussion of the territorial behaviour of sticklebacks in his 1955–6 seminar on the psychoses (*The Seminar of Jacques Lacan: Book III*, pp. 93–4).
112. Deleuze and Guattari, *Anti-Oedipus*, pp. 86–7.
113. Williams, *The Country and the City*, p. 3.
114. Ibid. p. 74.
115. Ibid. p. 60.
116. Ibid. p. 61.
117. Ibid. p. 68.
118. Goldsmith, 'The Deserted Village', in *Poems and Plays*, lines 35–46.
119. Williams, *The Country and the City*, p. 78.
120. Ibid. p. 79.
121. Ibid. p. 79.
122. Williams, *Culture and Materialism*, p. 79.
123. Ibid. p. 80.
124. Ibid. p. 81.
125. Auden, *The Enchafèd Flood*, p. 15.
126. Shelley, *Queen Mab*, in *The Major Works*, VIII, lines 70–6.
127. Morton, *Shelley and the Revolution of Taste*, pp. 87–8.
128. Economides, *The Ecology of Wonder in Romantic and Postmodern Literature*, p. 101.
129. Deleuze and Guattari, *A Thousand Plateaus*, p. 340.
130. Deleuze, *Lectures on Leibniz*.
131. Deleuze and Guattari, *A Thousand Plateaus*, pp. 338–9.
132. Morton, *Shelley and the Revolution of Taste*, p. 87.
133. Casey, *Getting Back into Place*, p. xi.

134. Eliot, 'The Waste Land', in *The Poems of T. S. Eliot, Vol. 1*, V, lines 368–9.
135. Casey, *Getting Back into Place*, p. xi.
136. Eliot, 'The Waste Land', I, l. 22.
137. Viney, *Waste*, p. 83.
138. Eliot, 'Second Caprice in North Cambridge', in *The Poems of T. S. Eliot, Vol. 1*, lines 1–12.
139. While Burroughs stated that his friend and collaborator Brion Gysin was the one who originated the famous cut-up technique – by which he would scramble syntactic and narrative linearity by randomly rearranging his own writing along with literary and non-literary texts of various kinds – he saw Eliot as being the first major writer to have exploited the collage principle on which it was based: 'when you think of it, "The Waste Land" was the first great cut-up collage' (Burroughs and Gysin, *The Third Mind*, p. 33).
140. Burroughs, *The Soft Machine*, p. 66.
141. Hume, 'William S. Burroughs's Phantasmic Geography', p. 113.
142. Gersdorf, 'America/Deserta', p. 243.
143. Virilio, *Desert Screen*, p. 135.

2. Desert Immanence

THEORETICAL GEOCENTRISM

In his sole authored work and in his collaborations with Guattari, Deleuze frequently deployed the figure of the desert as a means to think life in relation to the territories it makes for itself. He is often seen as a vitalist thinker, a philosopher of creative life in the vein of Henri Bergson, a figure known for his concept of '*élan vital*', or vital impulse, proposed to account for evolution in nature. Deleuze and Guattari's work is thus sometimes read as a postmodern or neo-Romantic *Naturphilosophie*, in which life becomes an obscure, quasi-mystical force. While this has led to them being maligned from an ecocritical point of view,[1] their influence on contemporary theoretical research on ecological and environmental issues is undeniable.[2] Their complex theoretical system has also been mobilised to help theorise the Anthropocene.[3] Indeed, their work of the 1970s and 1980s can be said to have anticipated many questions relevant to the Anthropocene by offering a broad historical view that, even as it addresses contemporary capitalist society, does not limit itself to human temporalities or to 'history' narrowly conceived. They offer a 'political geology', as Gregg Lambert puts it, that broadens the scope of historical materialism.[4] The pioneering work of Manuel DeLanda has demonstrated how a Deleuzian approach may allow us to conceive of social phenomena such as the Industrial Revolution as part of the deep history of the Earth and of terrestrial matter, and not solely as a chapter of human social development.[5] More recent work has stressed the centrality of the geophilosophical paradigm to understanding Deleuze and Guattari's oeuvre more generally.[6] Their influence may even be said to account for a key part of what some have termed a 'geological turn' within the humanities and social sciences.[7]

As I began to suggest in the last chapter, the desert has featured in European philosophy since Nietzsche as a means to think space and spatiality in an age when ontological foundations have been undermined. In a tradition that passes from Heidegger to Derrida and Deleuze via Levinas and Blanchot, Nietzsche's idea of a growing desert of nihilism has been used to describe the devastations of capitalist modernity and the death of God. While Deleuze and Guattari are too rarely considered in relation to Heidegger,[8] what I show in this chapter is that they share with the latter a concern with modernity as an age of the desert and draw on the figure of the growing desert in ways that seem inspired by Heidegger's engagement with Nietzsche as a thinker of nihilism whose thought marks the culmination of the Western metaphysical tradition. For Deleuze and Guattari, capitalism is to be defined not only as a mode of production in the Marxist sense but as the development of a mode of representational consciousness that seeks to control and dominate space through transcendent apparatuses of power (God, the state, the super-ego, etc.). At the same time, capitalism tends to undermine transcendence through the very *immanence* of capital as a decoded and deterritorialised social body. The desert emerges within the philosophical critique of capitalist spatiality both as the topology of a crisis within this double movement *and* as a space of potential resistance and overcoming. As the foundations of transcendence collapse or threaten to collapse over the course of the long history of the West, the immanent desert grows both as a terrain of lost foundations and the site of emergence of whatever might lie beyond this loss. Like both Nietzsche and Heidegger, then, Deleuze and Guattari pursue an unabashedly eschatological critique of modernity.

A focus on the desert as a philosophical topos can help to counterbalance Deleuze and Guattari's vitalism in ways that are relevant to interrogating what life means at a time when the biopolitical foundations of the modern state seem to be giving way to new formations of power. The desert allows us to read their work in terms of a movement between life (*bios*) and non-life (*geos*), in which the boundaries between the two are redrawn. We are living in an age characterised by a transition from biopower to geopower, from a politics of life to a politics of life in relation to non-life at planetary scales. The object of governance is no longer a population in an environment but the Earth as a 'geobiophysical' system understood in terms of flows, thresholds and control variables.[9] The desert provides a conceptual topology for understanding this transition. In order to make sense of what Deleuze and Guattari mean by life, and in order not to be misled either into vitalism or scientism, we must regard life as subject to what they call 'the test of desert-desire'.[10] Living systems are organised in relation to an Earth that is fundamentally hostile to all forms of organic life. The Earth is 'glacial', a *desert body* that is stratified, coded and territorialised to produce organic and social worlds.[11] The Earth, however, never ceases to resist these stratifications and to generate impulses of deterritorialisation that devastate territories while also creating new ones.[12]

Deleuze and Guattari's terminology here is indebted to Freud, who often characterised the unconscious in geological terms, comparing dreams to rocks and memories to stratigraphic layers.[13] Geophilosophy adapts Freud's theoretical geology in order to retell the story of life, its stratification and organisation, as part of the history of the Earth. Geophilosophy is therefore theoretically, and not empirically, geocentric. The goal here is not to ground subjectivity anew but to generate an escape from Western subjectivity itself and the whole subject–object dualism at its heart. It is here that we must note the key divergence from Freud: whereas geology provided Freud's depth model of the unconscious with the ultimate goal of a recovery of lost foundations, Deleuze and Guattari provide a model of the subject as ungrounded and adrift in an open space:

> As for the schizo, continually wandering about, migrating here, there, and everywhere as best he can, he plunges further and further into the realm of deterritorialization . . . It may well be that these peregrinations are the schizo's own particular way of rediscovering the earth.[14]

This rediscovery of the Earth as a nomadic space is quite opposed to Freud's attempt, in a manner in keeping with the scientific goals of his day, to recover the lost foundations of modern consciousness through the idea of a buried prehistory. The Earth is, rather, the absolutely *ungrounded* presupposed by those stratifications which ground life in a specific domain (the organic, the social, linguistic, etc.). Theoretical geocentrism, then, is the basis for a non-foundational materialism that views the Earth as a machine for 'engineering' forces and energies that have no innate form of organisation. The desert becomes important as a way of conceptualising a form of space in which potentials are at their maximum, bordering on chaos.[15]

Geophilosophy can be traced to Nietzsche's demand in *Thus Spoke Zarathustra* that we 'remain faithful to the earth' and spurn all 'extraterrestrial hopes'.[16] Deleuze and Guattari name Nietzsche the first geophilosopher, although in truth one would have to go further back to Kant and Schelling.[17] We must begin, however, not with the Earth itself but with schizophrenia, as this is key to understanding subjectivity as a flight from territorial foundations. Deleuze and Guattari present the schizophrenic body in two apparently opposing ways: first, as undergoing a collapse that impoverishes experience and makes the body a desert; and second, as offering more enriched and encompassing modes of experience than the ones we usually have. The schizophrenic body recapitulates the double movement at the heart of capitalism as a collapse and reintegration of experience following geological lines of becoming. The schizophrenic ordeal in this sense is a revelation of the groundless Earth, while the schizophrenic's desert body provides a new *aesthesis*, a new sensibility defined by intensities produced by the shattering of representational consciousness.

THE DESERT OF THE BODY WITHOUT ORGANS

In *Anti-Oedipus*, Deleuze and Guattari follow the existential psychiatry of Karl Jaspers in arguing that schizophrenia is the quintessential modern malady, the form of psychological crisis that tells us most about the experience of living in an advanced Western society.[18] Schizophrenia in its most severe and debilitating forms involves a total devastation of meaning in which habitual codes of belief and behaviour are scrambled. In the schizophrenic universe, the question of meaning is replaced by questions of force, power, energy and function. This is why Deleuze and Guattari place the schizophrenic at the heart of their conception of desire as 'machinic' and 'productive'. While *Anti-Oedipus* is an attempt to chart a post-psychoanalytic (or 'schizoanalytic') path beyond the impasses of Freudian and Lacanian theories of subjectivity, they follow Freud's most fundamental insight in understanding the unconscious in terms of quantities of psychical energy or libido, which they identify simply as desire. Their main critique of psychoanalysis is that it has approached the unconscious as a problem of meaning or interpretation instead of a problem of use: 'the question posed by desire is not "What does it mean?" but rather "*How does it work?*" How do these machines, these desiring-machines, work – yours and mine?'.[19] Deleuze and Guattari thus diverge sharply from Lacan's influential interpretation of schizophrenia as a failure to access the symbolic realm of language. Instead, they return to a more orthodox Freudian perspective that stresses the energetics of libido.

Freud was amongst the first to recognise that schizophrenic delusions often feature apocalyptic scenarios and visions of end-of-the-world catastrophes. In his analysis of the famous case of Daniel Paul Schreber, a nineteenth-century German judge who recorded his experience of schizophrenia and confinement in a remarkable memoir,

Freud accounted for such apocalyptic visions in terms of a withdrawal of libido from the external world.[20] Withdrawal of libido becomes in Schreber's imagination the delusion of world devastation, while his body becomes an Earth on which the catastrophe plays out. The catastrophic withdrawal of libido is the main characteristic that separates the schizophrenic from the neurotic or the hysteric who, Freud tells us, 'has by no means broken off his erotic relations to people and things'.[21] The catastrophic nature of the schizophrenic break, by contrast, stems from a complete withdrawal of 'libido from people and things in the external world'.[22] The delusions of the schizophrenic are, Freud argues, an attempt at *reconstruction* in the aftermath of the catastrophe. Schreber's memoir describes a profound link between his own body and the devastation of the Earth. He describes the Earth's 'glaciation' as a result of the retreat of the sun, while signs of an apocalyptic plague became visible to him on his skin.[23] He is bombarded and tormented by 'rays' emitted from God and carrying mysterious information related both to his fate and that of all life on Earth. Freud interprets Schreber's talk of God's rays as a means of conceptualising, within the terms of his quasi-theological system, the libidinal energy that he has withdrawn from reality but which returns to attack and manipulate his body in various ways. Schreber's elaborate visions are thus, for Freud, a kind of self-analysis and even self-cure: 'Schreber's "rays of God" . . . are in reality nothing else than a concrete representation and projection outwards of libidinal cathexes; and they thus lend his delusions a striking conformity with our theory'.[24]

Schreber's body, felt by him as a kind of glacial Earth-body, thus becomes the site of struggles over power and energy. His theological system, meanwhile, is a means of conceptualising energy in its (potentially catastrophic) abstraction from the objects and persons in which it is normally invested. Eric Santner maintains that the Schreber case must be understood in the context of nineteenth-century 'fears that the demands placed on the human organism by the accelerated rates of social change, the chronic shocks of urban life, and the labor requirements of a rapidly industrializing society will deplete its reserves of energy'.[25] Libido, as psychic energy, cannot be separated from the energy systems of society more generally. Freud's libidinal explanation of schizophrenia is thus only valid if it can be widened to encompass the energetics of capitalist production. Schizophrenia has key diagnostic value in this respect, as it mimics the effects of capitalism to the extent that the latter is a force of deracination whose economic determination of social relations can involve a devastation of the codes that organise the social body.

We can define capitalism as a social formation based on abstract quantities (of money, time and energy) that are exchangeable but essentially indifferent to questions of meaning. As Marx pointed out, the worker sells not a concrete type of labour but an abstract quantity of labour power measured according to socially necessary labour time. In this sense, Deleuze and Guattari argue – following Marx – that capitalism is not merely one social formation among others but the negative image of *all* social formations: 'In a sense, capitalism has haunted all forms of society, but it haunts them as their terrifying nightmare, it is the dread they feel of a flow that would elude their codes.'[26] This, as we will see in more detail, is key to how they account for capitalism within the context of a universal or epochal history of the Earth. Capital, like schizophrenia, dissolves the traditional codes of belief and behaviour that ground us in knowable environments. When the Earth becomes an energy resource, it is *undermined as ground*. Capital accumulates a massive reservoir of energy flows in this way, but these flows are inscrutable, unpredictable, and ultimately uncontrollable quantities that escape normative social codes.

Climate change can be understood in precisely this way: the ancient energies stored in the Earth as fossil fuel are conjugated with the tendencies of decoding which rip up lifeworlds. To speak of climate is to speak of a decoded environment in which flows of life and energy have escaped from knowable territories. Climate is not the objective correlate of a subject in a world but what Morton calls a 'hyperobject'.[27] Might there be a hypersubject, not as a correlate of the hyperobject but as a specific kind of manifestation of it? This is what Deleuze and Guattari's figure of the schizophrenic suggests. The modern worker and the schizophrenic are comparable in that both find themselves subject to forces that impose on them a precarious existence; both are at the mercy of inscrutable flows. Like the worker, the schizophrenic is deterritorialised, forced into a kind of nomadism to the extent that available social codes cease to explain his or her experience, but the schizophrenic *feels* this condition intensely as a libidinal crisis and not simply as a socio-economic one. The schizophrenic body finds itself in a disjunction with respect to any existential territory or lifeworld to which a subject normally belongs.[28] But it must also struggle with an energy crisis, because the desire it has detached from the world must go somewhere, even in the absence of codes and territories. The schizophrenic body, then, to the extent that it has withdrawn investment from the outer world, is barren, impoverished and 'desert-like' while also being the place of a desire that finds itself – to an unbearable extent – liberated from the demands of social investment and social reproduction.²⁹ Understood in this way, schizophrenia denotes not simply a breakdown but also a kind of revolutionary 'breakthrough' to a point beyond the capitalistic logic of resource scarcity.³⁰ The goal of schizoanalysis is to try to transpose this breakthrough out of the schizophrenic's suffering and into the terms of a coherent theoretical project.

The attempt to traverse the difference between breakdown and breakthrough motivates Deleuze and Guattari's use of the concept of the 'body without organs', a term they take from avant-garde writer and schizophrenic Antonin Artaud. Much of Artaud's writings focus on the anguished body, which feels itself under attack not simply from external forces but from its own anatomical organisation. As he puts it in the conclusion to his 1947 radio play *To Have Done with the Judgment of God*:

> Man is sick because he is badly constructed.
> We must make up our minds to strip him bare in order to scrape off that animalcule that itches him mortally,
>
> > god,
> > and with god
> > his organs.
>
> For you can tie me up if you wish,
> but there is nothing more useless than an organ.
>
> When you will have made him a body without organs,
> then you will have delivered him from all his automatic reactions and restored him to his true freedom.³¹

The concept of the body without organs is appropriated by Deleuze and Guattari to suggest a mode of corporeality distinct from the 'organic' or organ-ised body, which for Artaud is the body subjected to the judgement of God. The organism is defined here as a functional unity of part and whole, a self-moving totality that finds its ultimate model in divine transcendence. That God is the ultimate instance of a totality discernible in organic form is an idea deeply rooted in a philosophical tradition that stretches from Plato and Aristotle to Kant and Hegel. John Protevi observes that for Aristotle, 'the highest being is pure activity, pure being-at-work, *energeia*'.³² God is the perfect organism, the perfect worker. To this biotheological transcendence Deleuze and Guattari oppose the 'glacial reality' of the body without organs, which they define in terms of a 'zero intensity' state.³³ The organs are desire's 'machines' or working parts, which both emit and consume energy flows, but the schizophrenic withdrawal of desire causes the machines to stop and fuse together in a whole without parts or totalising principle:

> Desiring-machines make us an organism; but at the very heart of this production, within the very production of this production, the body suffers from being organized in this way, from not having some other sort of organization, or no organization at all. 'An incomprehensible, absolutely rigid stasis' in the very midst of process ... The automata stop dead and set free the unorganized mass they once served to articulate. The full body without organs is the unproductive, the sterile, the unengendered, the unconsumable.[34]

By defining the schizophrenic body in this way as a 'zero', Deleuze and Guattari position themselves, however idiosyncratically, within the phenomenological tradition. For Husserl, the body is not only one object among others but is what he called the *Nullpunkt* or zero point, the background against which objects of intended actions may appear in the world: 'each individual gives his being-human a position in the space of the surrounding world as the zero-point object of the oriented surrounding world in experiential apperception'.[35] The world as a set of points in space is possible only by means of the body understood as the zero point by which the ego *intuits* space before sensing or interacting with it. The body, even though it is an object itself, constitutes an absolute 'here' that allows us to engage with a world of objects over 'there'. This constitutive role of the body must, however, fade from view in our everyday activities. If it did not, the zero point would fail to play the role of ground or condition.

Deleuze and Guattari are able to integrate Husserl's phenomenological account of the body into their geophilosophy because Husserl himself extended – in anti-Copernican or geocentric fashion – the idea of the zero point to a conception of the Earth as a static, non-empirical, intuited ground of experience:

> [the earth] is the experiential basis for all bodies in the experiential genesis of our idea of the world. This 'basis' [*Boden*] is not experienced at first as body but becomes a basis-body at higher levels of constitution of the world by virtue of experience, and that nullifies its original basis-form. It becomes the total-body: the vehicle of all bodies that, until now, could be fully (normally) experienced with empirical sufficiency on all sides ... But now the earth is a huge block on which smaller bodies exist and on the basis of which they also always have become, and could have become, for us by division into pieces or by separating them off from the whole. ... Motion occurs on or in the earth, away from it or off it. In conformity with its original idea, the earth does not move and does not rest; only in relation to it are motion and rest given as having their sense of motion and rest.[36]

This gives us a useful way to think about what Deleuze and Guattari mean by the conflict between the static body without organs and the working organism. The schizophrenic Earth-body provides a model of wholeness without unity, totality or externality; it is that which is always the basis or ground of empirical unities, but is itself non-unified. Abolishing externality also abolishes the difference between inner self and external world and produces a pure Outside, as Blanchot would say, a place without territories, refuge or cover.[37] In this sense, the body without organs is a desert, and rather than being localisable as an object in space it is a topology by which physical or extensive space is produced. The spatiality of the body without organs is thus defined as *immanent* as opposed to transcendent. Where transcendence suggests totalisation (the judgement of God, the transcendent view of the world as a totality) and a relativising of all difference to some ultimate end (as parts in a functional, organic totality), immanence suggests unlimited dispersion, a realm of pure affect by which absolute difference without a goal is made possible. It is this affective field of *virtual* differences – differences prior to their actualisation as the properties of objects – that gives us access to those 'becomings' (becoming-woman, becoming-animal, etc.) for which Deleuze and Guattari's writings are perhaps most famous.

But the body without organs is not just the place of a struggle against transcendence. Deleuze and Guattari use the body without organs to account for how social formations constitute themselves in the first place. It can serve this function because it is a field of pure potentials and thus also a neutral *surface* for the inscription of signs and power.[38] All organisms are composed on the body without organs (or plane of immanence, as Deleuze and Guattari also term it), as are all gods and signifying systems. Understood in this way, the body without organs is the desert at the limit of every possible world. As well as being a site of struggle against the forces of organ-isation, the body without organs provides access to a particular kind of space in which grounding or instituting processes generate gods, organisms, signifying systems and various other transcendent structures. The subjectivity described by Freud's Oedipus complex, for example, is one defined in relation to the transcendent figure of the castrating father and the punitive super-ego, but this is only possible on the basis of libidinal flows immanent not only to the body but to the social and interpersonal field as a whole. The immanence of desire to experience is Freud's revolutionary insight. He is able to organise his theory of sexuality around the transcendent father only because he first recognised the immanence of desire to subjectivity and intersubjective relationships as demonstrated most tangibly in the child's familial complex. Desire is thus both immanence and transcendence. The theory of sexuality only becomes problematic when it is calibrated to fit the structures of social reproduction through the concept of the Oedipus complex, which insists that 'healthy' subjectivity involves identification with the Father and a renunciation of the Mother.

The lesson of psychoanalysis is crucial because – under the right conditions of critique – it reveals that every system of power depends on some immanent field defined both as a site of struggle against power *and* as a ground power it must presuppose in order to operate and concretise itself. Every transcendent centralisation of power, whether political, libidinal or religious, emerges within a prior field of immanence, a field of dispersed differences without a principle of unity or necessary forms of actualisation. Deleuze and Guattari use the figure of the desert to *spatialise this field*, to articulate how political or religious worlds have foundations that lie beyond their limits in a geospatial real accessible to topo-philosophy.[39] Through their use of the desert as an existential category, they emphasise the devastation of experience suffered in the schizophrenic break and how subjectivity is governed by territorial organisation. The desert is thus a figure of the deterritorialised body and decoded space, but it also provides a topological surface on which power can be mapped. When they discuss the origins of the state and monotheism, they frequently invoke desert landscapes, but this is in order to suggest a connection between actual desert places and the desert as a virtual *spatium* or plane of thought.[40]

The body without organs, then, is a 'place', a topos, but it is also, and more importantly, a nomadic flight from all concrete emplacement. The transcendental ego of the Western metaphysical tradition is located in a 'no place', and as we saw in the last chapter, a thinker of place such as Edward Casey sees this atopia as being at the root of a great modern malaise. In his description of Deleuze and Guattari's theory of nomadism, Casey writes that for the nomadic subject 'place itself is everywhere' and so atopia becomes impossible.[41] But it is perhaps more accurate to say that nomadism scrambles the very opposition between concrete emplacement and the abstract geometric spaces of modernity. Space in the absolute sense is thus always present in the place I am, but as a result *I am never quite where I am*. As Heidegger puts it,

> spaces, and with them space as such – "space" – are always provided for already within the stay of mortals. . . . I am never here only, as this encapsulated body; rather, I am there, that is, I already pervade the room, and thus can I go through it.[42]

It is not a question of getting back to some lost lifeworld, although Heidegger's notion of dwelling certainly leads in that direction. The schizophrenic desert body rediscovers space through a more abstract terrain than the one of atopian modernity. Casey's emphasis on the 'lived body', then, risks obscuring Deleuze and Guattari's faith in the abstract: they insist that the 'revolutionary investment of desire' is 'desert-desire' because a superior asceticism is required in order to reach post-oedipal libido and post-capitalist subjectivity.[43] It is only through a certain *ascesis* that we reach the 'abstract machine' of a deterritorialised consciousness, and in some sense we are still 'not abstract enough'.[44] This emphasis on asceticism and abstraction may seem strange given Deleuze and Guattari's apparent celebration of the body as a means of practical experimentation, but this is only to underestimate the resources the ascetic tradition may provide. It is not that the philosopher is an ascetic, but that he or she may use the ascetic virtues in the pursuit of 'extraordinary ends that are not very ascetic at all'.[45] Thus, the desert experience as it has featured in the history of religion plays a key role: as a topology or *spatium* it provides a conceptual environment in which thought may go beyond the limits of the world as the *extensio* of everyday physical space.

GEOPHILOSOPHY I: THE COGITO AND THE GRAND CANYON

Understood in this sense, the desert is not primarily a kind of physical landscape but a conceptual figure that describes the spatial conditions of immanence as the field of potentials by which any kind of concrete emplacement becomes possible. At the same time, we can insist that one encounters the field of immanence only in an embodied way through some kind of ordeal, and not merely as a concept or principle in a disembodied ego. The desert is a means of understanding how absolute space may be encountered locally; it is where absolute space is manifest in place through the nomad or schizophrenic as hypersubject. This has important political dimensions to the degree that all politics involves an assertion of some right to space. But we can also insist that the schizophrenic body is a desert in a *literal* sense because it is 'sterile' and 'unproductive', a ground in which the desiring-machines that compose the organised totality of the organism fail to take root but on which another kind of consciousness may be established. The differences between the schizophrenic body's working parts are dissolved on a great amorphous surface that allows a richer set of differences to be experienced beyond organic or physical limits.[46]

Likewise, a sojourn in the desert dissolves the coordinates by which we usually situate ourselves in the environment, allowing a different set of spatio-temporal conditions to become possible. Paul Bowles, in one of his descriptions of entering the Sahara, evokes this as a simultaneous loss and reintegration of subjectivity in what he calls a solitude without loneliness:

> You leave the gate of the fort or the town behind, pass the camels lying outside, go up into the dunes, or out onto the hard, stony plain and stand awhile, alone. Presently, you will either shiver and hurry back inside the walls, or you will go on standing there and let something very peculiar happen to you, something that everyone who lives there has undergone and which the French call *le baptême de la solitude*. It is a unique sensation, and it has nothing to do with loneliness, for loneliness presupposes memory. Here, in this wholly mineral landscape alighted by stars like flares, even memory disappears; nothing is left but your own breathing and the sound of your heart beating. A strange, and by no means pleasant, process of reintegration begins inside you.[47]

The desert ordeal mirrors the process of breakdown and breakthrough described by Deleuze and Guattari's account of schizophrenia. It is no accident that references to books on the desert tradition in Christianity by authors such as Jacques Lacarrière and Jean Steinmann are scattered throughout the pages of *Anti-Oedipus* and *A Thousand Plateaus*. The schizophrenic is offered as a new kind of desert saint, a revolutionary ascetic whose solitude calls forth a collective subjectivity, for this is 'an extremely populous solitude, like the desert itself, a solitude already intertwined with a people to come, one that invokes and awaits that people, existing only through it'.[48]

While Deleuze and Guattari's use of the term 'desert' is not primarily intended to describe actual landscapes such as Bowles's Sahara, it *is* intended to suggest that our emplacement in actual landscapes is grounded in a virtual but no less real spatial continuum that shares qualities with actual desert environments. Mystics, nomads and schizophrenics have grasped, in their very different ways, something of this *spatium* through various flights from the world, through a scrambling of the territorial coordinates of space, time and memory. It is the schizophrenic who experiences this most intimately as a libidinal and affective rupture with the lifeworld, however. The desert ordeal – the peregrination in nomadic space, the flight to the very limits of social and psychic territory – is 'the schizo's way of rediscovering the earth'.[49] We are led in this way from questions of life, libido and desire to the Earth, from *bios* to *geos*. Thus, in *What is Philosophy?*, their final collaboration, Deleuze and Guattari articulate the philosophical paradigm that they call geophilosophy. The concept first appears at the very end of their collaboration but it can be regarded as an attempt to account for why their work had always given such prominence to ideas of space and territory. Geophilosophy is an attempt to reorient philosophy away from the relationship between subject and object and towards one between territories and the Earth.[50]

This reorientation has two distinct aspects. First, they maintain that philosophy is essentially Greek, that its emergence was dependent on the commercial networks of the Greek coastline, which they describe as a 'fractal' structure.[51] Their position here retraces certain arguments of Nietzsche and Heidegger as well as historians such as Jean-Pierre Vernant. The latter argued that Greek city-states fostered an agonism or public contest of ideas in which philosophical discourse was able to flourish in a way inconceivable in an imperial society. The role played by poor soil in the development and relative stability of ancient Greek culture has often been noted. Gregory Flaxman, for example, suggests that, since the arid climate made habitation of arable regions more difficult, the Attic peninsula was forced into a relationship of trade and exchange with the world beyond its shores: 'Attica is an arid land, a pebble without history, but if this general circumstance discourages its enemies, it also demands of its people an engagement with the outside.'[52] Athens was uniquely capable of accepting 'strangers in flight' from the empires of the East and 'the borderlands of the Greek world', but aridity (the problem of grounding and roots) was a central component of this.[53] As a result, the figure of the stranger (*xenos*) begins to feature in philosophy from Plato onwards as a means of thinking the relationship between the same and the other, inside and outside, identity and difference, and so on.[54]

Second, Deleuze and Guattari suggest that philosophical thinking begins with the effort to think the physical ground of territories alongside the metaphysical ground of concepts. A preoccupation with grounds and grounding can be traced back to a seminar Deleuze taught in 1956–7 called *Qu'est-ce que fonder?* (*What is Grounding?*). The contents of this early seminar demonstrate that a concern with *Grund* in the post-Kantian, Nietzschean and Heideggerian senses of this term was present from the beginnings of Deleuze's career. This suggests that Deleuze, like Heidegger, was essentially a thinker of constitutive finitude, that is, someone for whom thinking is legitimated in the subject's self-grounding relation with itself. Thought is philosophical only once it engages in the circularity by which it grounds its own legitimacy immanently, rather than searching for legitimation outside itself. Christian Kerslake sums up the concluding message of the seminar in the following way:

> the act of grounding a constitutive system of finitude necessarily involves an encounter with an unconscious that is presupposed by the very act of grounding. In order properly to ground a self-differentiating system, the thinker must genuinely become other to themselves.[55]

The act of grounding is a *self*-grounding that involves a differentiating relation of ground and grounded. The Cogito, the self-constituting thinking subject of modern consciousness, is necessarily split by a difference from itself by which it loses its identity *through* that very identity. Deleuze goes on, in his first major work, *Difference and Repetition*, to describe this as 'ungrounding' (*effondement*):

> Ideas, therefore, are related not to a Cogito which functions as ground or as a proposition of consciousness, but to the fractured I of a dissolved Cogito; in other words, to the universal *ungrounding* which characterises thought as a faculty in its transcendental exercise.⁵⁶

The paradoxical identity of ground and grounded implied in the self-grounding act produces difference through the fractured and fracturing 'unground'. This may sound scandalously similar to Hegel's insistence on the identity of identity and difference.⁵⁷ Hegelianism's subordination of difference to identity is what Deleuze's entire conceptual assemblage is pitted against. For Deleuze, however, identity results only as a kind of misprision of difference or from an inability to *represent* a difference that nevertheless persists beneath our representational consciousness. Grasping this minimal or imperceptible degree of difference involves a dismantling of the consciousness that represents difference in terms of identity. What is needed is not a more encompassing mode of representation but a 'catastrophic' dissolution of the differences secured by representational thinking itself.⁵⁸ Deleuze regards difference as fundamentally resistant to conceptualisation, which is why he argues that the philosophy of difference from Aristotle to Hegel has consistently subordinated difference to the identity of the concept.⁵⁹

Difference, then, has less to do with the concepts by which we represent the world than with the ground presupposed by representation. The ground must be caused to rise up seismically into the world of representations, fracturing them along with the putative unity they grant consciousness. This process is the genesis of thought itself, but it can only happen by way of a subject, an I, that has become unrecognisable to itself, that has become indistinguishable from the ground it is said to stand upon: 'this ground rises by means of the I, penetrating deeply into the possibility of thought and constituting the unrecognised in every recognition'.⁶⁰ It is as if, in certain moments, we fail to be differentiated from the primordial conditions of our existence, from the abyss on which everything rests. The petrified, 'inorganic' body of the catatonic schizophrenic is one figure Deleuze and Guattari give us for such a catastrophic loss of difference and rupture with the world of representation. The catatonic body, having cast off the organs clinging to its surface, is an embodiment of the unground, the Earth-body that has risen up to shatter the world. In *The Logic of Sense,* Deleuze provides a geological image for this by quoting from a famous text by F. Scott Fitzgerald: 'it's much better to say that it's not you that's cracked – it's the Grand Canyon'.[61] The I is split but bears this more as a geological scar than a psychological duality.

It is this link between grounding, ungrounding and the Earth that Deleuze and Guattari wish to underscore with their notion of geophilosophy. Deleuze's interest in grounding was, in fact, never restricted to the history of philosophy. *What is Grounding?* opens with references to mythological founding acts, to Moses and Odysseus. The body without organs is, as we have seen, the desert or zero intensity state on which a new libidinal and sensory reality may be established. If a social formation is a working machine, a unity of parts within a whole, then every society possesses a kind of body without organs or a patch of the plane of immanence, a collective intuition of a non-unified whole that the parts must presuppose before they can even begin to work in unison. Mythologies, religions and the quasi-divine figure of the despot or monarch have provided societies with such fields of immanence, even if they then impose on these a transcendent perspective from which they can be regulated. A primitive society may relate everything back to a mythical conception of the Earth as a matrix of all being. A feudal or barbarian society may find a principle of unity in the body of the king or despot. The socio-political problem of *instituting* is thus connected to the philosophical problem of grounding as well as to geological and geographical conditions. Grounding, then, is more than a mere methodological issue but is the part of the philosophical enterprise in which the pre-philosophical and the non-philosophical become absolutely necessary.

Philosophy, Deleuze and Guattari insist, is the creation of concepts: 'So long as there is a time and a place for creating concepts, the operation that undertakes this will always be called philosophy, or will be indistinguishable from philosophy even if it is called something else.'[62] This insistence on the primacy of creation has led some to mischaracterise them as equating being with creativity rather than with the world as it already is in actuality.[63] Such a critique would amount to a charge of apoliticism and an almost aristocratic lack of concern for the real conditions of existence. However, Deleuze and Guattari are very careful to distinguish the act of creating from the act of grounding or instituting. Concepts must have a place that cannot be granted through philosophical creation. This place is the plane of immanence, which cannot be created, only 'laid out' (*tracé*):

If philosophy begins with the creation of concepts, then the plane of immanence must be regarded as prephilosophical. It is presupposed not in the way that one concept may refer to others but in the way that concepts themselves refer to a nonconceptual understanding.[64]

The plane of immanence 'constitutes the absolute ground of philosophy, its earth or deterritorialisation'.[65] Concepts come to 'populate' territories or regions on the plane of immanence, but the plane itself remains an undivided continuum, indifferent to the regions marked out by the concept. Deleuze and Guattari deploy the figure of the desert to describe this space:

> Concepts pave, occupy, or populate the plane bit by bit, whereas the plane itself is the indivisible milieu in which concepts are distributed without breaking up its continuity or integrity: they occupy it without measuring it out ... or are distributed without splitting it up. The plane is like a desert that concepts populate without dividing up. The only regions of the plane are concepts themselves, but the plane is all that holds them together.[66]

Concepts are nomads, their habitat a smooth, undivided, continuous surface. The production of philosophical concepts, then, involves problems of dwelling, population and geographical distribution as well as socio-political problems of institution. The relationship between territories and the Earth is reproduced in the relationship between concepts and the way they populate a plane of immanence. The concept is distinct from the plane it occupies just as territories are distinct from the Earth on which they are formed. The Earth is not a prior territory but an *absolutely* deterritorialised body grounding every territorial phenomenon, just as the plane of immanence is a non-conceptual space in which concepts are created. The Earth, as this desert body, is thus *common to territorial and philosophical creation* but is itself 'uncreated'.

Furthermore, the plane of immanence is laid out or instituted through means that are entirely non-philosophical and non-rational, through a 'non-conceptual understanding'. Dreams, esotericism, intoxication and pathology can thus belong to philosophical method without the latter losing its rigour or specificity as concept creation.[67] This is only possible, however, within certain socio-political and geographical environments where the disjunction between territory and Earth already plays a decisive role, where a certain degree of *relative* deterritorialisation has been reached. The geography and economy of ancient Greece facilitated this but so too did Greek myth. The myth of autochthony – the idea that one is born of the Earth – was important not because it suggested a natal link between the Earth and Greek society but, on the contrary, because it suggested a deterritorialising disjunction between them. The autochthonous citizen, like the nomad, is not tied to any region but can reterritorialise anywhere, even on the sea, as in the example of the Delian League.[68] Flaxman explains how the myth of autochthony in Hesiod split the Earth into two lineages: *ge* or *gaia*, and *kthon*:

> *gaia* emerges from chaos and, in conjunction with *eros*, sows the seeds of gods and men; *gaia* gives rise to generation, but what is generated grows apart from *gaia*, on a different ground. . . . The primordial earth (*ge*) denotes a cosmic being to which even 'those who live on the earth' (*epikhthonioi*) have no claim; human relations, which we ascribe to families and familial lineages, belong to *kthon*.[69]

This split in the unity of the Earth as matrix entered into Greek thought via mythology but it clears a path for philosophical self-grounding in the concept's relation to the plane of immanence. Philosophy emerges when the ground gives way to an unground beneath it. Flaxman continues: 'at the heart of autochthony, the Greek myth of having been born of the earth (*kthon*), there remains the distance that separates humans from the "other" earth'.[70] It is this becoming other of the Earth in relation to the territory that forces thought to engage with the ground as an ungrounding that disturbs our sense of dwelling. Nietzsche identified the Heraclitian intuition of flux or becoming with such a sense of the ungrounded: 'Its impact on men can most nearly be likened to the sensation during an earthquake when one loses one's familiar confidence in a firmly grounded earth.'[71] For philosophy to access the absolute, the Earth must emerge into thought seismically as a desertified expanse, a continuum that can be populated and mapped but never claimed by the roots that facilitate growth, generation and family. The ground can only be grasped as unground. The Earth is then regarded as a speculative object, an absolutely deterritorialised body that 'passes into the pure plane of immanence of a Being-thought, of a Nature-thought'.[72]

GEOPHILOSOPHY II: DEMONOLOGY

Modern philosophy resituates the Greek problem of grounding in a new environment marked by the emergence of industrial society. The task of German philosophy from the eighteenth century was to 'reconquer the Greek plane of immanence, the unknown earth that it now feels as its own *barbarism*, its own *anarchy* abandoned to the *nomads*'.[73] For Kant, the history of metaphysics was a war over contested ground, a conflict between the despotism of dogmatists and the anarchy of sceptics, the latter being 'a kind of nomads who abhor all permanent cultivation of the soil'.[74] But Kant's critique revealed that war was ultimately being fought over an irreal world populated by entities whose relation to actual experience is hard or impossible to determine. Metaphysical entities such as God and the soul appeared detached from any possible experience we might be said to have. It became necessary to interrogate the legitimate domains of reason's activities in order to lead philosophy back to terra firma:

> It is the land of truth (a charming name), surrounded by a broad and stormy ocean, the true seat of illusion, where many a fog bank and rapidly melting iceberg pretend to be new lands and, ceaselessly deceiving with empty hopes the voyager looking around for new discoveries, entwine him in adventures from which he can never escape and yet also never bring to an end.[75]

With Kant, philosophy becomes concerned in an unprecedented way with geographical orientation. Philosophical critique becomes the delimitation of boundaries and fields, and the limits of cognition are the limits of a territory to which metaphysics may lay a rightful claim.[76] In other words, with Kant, philosophy begins to understand itself as geo-philosophy, a process which will continue through Nietzsche, Husserl and Heidegger to Deleuze and Guattari.

The geophilosophical paradigm, then, emerges from a sense of the crisis of grounding that animates modern thought. Deleuze and Guattari tell us that 'we moderns possess the concept but have lost sight of the plane of immanence'.[77] Capitalist modernity robs philosophy of its ontological certainties, which is why Kant sought to ground reason anew on synthetic subjectivity and possible experience. Capitalism instigates a process of deterritorialisation unprecedented in human history, such that power becomes less and less dependent upon the transcendence of God and the state. Religion and state sovereignty of course persist but as *archaisms*, points on which the deracinating movement of capital can reterritorialise when the social formations that sustain it and furnish it with energy threaten to fall apart. The Kantian account of subjectivity as the capacity for *a priori* synthetic judgement is a response to this situation. The Kantian subject seeks to become capable of providing the immanent criteria by which it can evaluate its own experience. Unlike the Cartesian *cogito*, the Kantian subject does not revolve around a 'necessary' metaphysical object such as God. This is what Kant called his Copernican Revolution, which reverses the traditional coordinates of philosophical thinking: to be intelligible, Kant claimed, the objective world must somehow conform to our representations of it and the criteria of our own cognition, not the other way around.

It is, however, the unintended consequences of Kant's search for a principle of self-grounding cognition that makes him so important for Deleuze, who places great importance on the break between Descartes and Kant. With the latter, something intervenes between 'I think' and 'I am' in the form of the paradox of an intelligence that is not identical with itself:

> the spontaneity of which I am conscious in the 'I think' cannot be understood as the attribute of a substantial and spontaneous being, but only as the affection of a passive self which experiences its own thought – its own intelligence, that by virtue of which it can say *I* – being exercised in it and upon it but not by it. Here begins a long and inexhaustible story: *I is an other*, or the paradox of inner sense.[78]

This intermezzo between the two moments of a self-grounding *cogito* (thinking and being) is difference in itself, difference as pure potentiality or virtuality suspended between the asymmetrical halves of the I. Kant insists on 'the speculative death of God' in this way by recognising a temporal fracture in the subject's self-constitution.[79] It is only through this fracture that the subject thinks – temporality is the only subjectivity. This temporality, however, is not internal to the subject, it is *not an organic time*. The time in which the *cogito*'s self-affection takes place – the time of becoming – corresponds to a geological or volcanic depth that fractures any organic unity basing itself on 'resemblance' to a divine ideal.[80] The role of the geological for Deleuze is to invoke a sense of demonological becoming, an eternal return as opposed to divine eternity. The faculties of cognition are arranged 'along a volcanic line which allows one to ignite the other'.[81] Thought is more a seismic or magmatic eruption than a manifestation of 'good sense'.[82]

Kant attempts to save his system from the volcanic immanence to which his search for a self-grounding thought led him. Representational consciousness is the means by which he segregates the transcendental ego from the unknown material forces – the melting icebergs and stormy oceans – that menace the tranquillity of the island of truth. Representation retrieves a principle of unity for self-grounding subjectivity, a means for the subject to recognise itself in its cognitions, so that the relationship between subject and object is like a reflection.[83] In this way, the Kantian subject reterritorialises on the very archaisms denounced as metaphysical dogmas. In the *Critique of Pure Reason*, God survives, for example, as a pure Idea beyond any possible experience but capable of serving as a regulative principle giving systematic unity to the diversity of empirical appearances.[84] In the *Critique of Judgment*, Kant considers a purely physical teleology, that is, a conception of the purposiveness of Earthly matter absent the moral guidance furnished by the Idea of God, to be a 'demonology'.[85] Without the moral purpose through which man grounds it, the Earth would be a wasteland: 'without man all of creation would be a mere wasteland

[*Wüste*], gratuitous and without a final purpose'.⁸⁶ What Deleuze shows, however, is that Kantian self-grounding cannot avoid the demonology of the Earth and of geological depths.⁸⁷

Nevertheless, it is not simply a matter of plunging headlong into the abyss. The process of laying out a plane of immanence involves grasping depth as a surface effect, and thus of overcoming the entire surface–depth opposition that drives Kantian thought to the refuge of its island:

> Something of the ground rises to the surface, without assuming any form but, rather, insinuating itself between the forms; a formless base, an autonomous and faceless existence. This ground which is now on the surface is called depth or groundlessness.⁸⁸

The shattering of representational form takes place in a non-representational space or *spatium* that Deleuze extracts from the Kantian and post-Kantian problem of grounding: thought ceases to rely on transcendence when the ground of all forms is regarded as not lying beneath but *between* them, in a demonic interval by which their harmony becomes disharmony. Everything is based on a discord or chaos whose symbol in poetry is the inferno. It is what so troubled the Tennyson of *In Memoriam* (1850) on learning about the true age of the Earth from Hutton and Lyell:

> The solid earth whereon we tread
> In tracts of fluent heat began,
> And grew to seeming-random forms,
> The seeming prey of cyclic storms,
> Till at the last arose the man.⁸⁹

For Tennyson, the geological depths through which life must pass in its slow emergence are only redeemable by industry (in particular, *mining*): 'life is not as idle ore, / But iron dug from central gloom / . . . To shape and use'.⁹⁰ Man's dominion over the Earth is re-established through a surface–depth opposition, in which depth is redeemed as a ground for use by industrial humanity. Deleuze is charging Kant with something similar: the notion of grounding is useful only for orienting humanity's position as surface dweller. But just as we can reread Tennyson in the light of the Anthropocene such that man's apparent triumph is called into question, so too Deleuze proposes that a kind of revenge of the depths works its way through Kantian and post-Kantian philosophy. The Earth of the philosophers ceases to be terra firma but demands to be thought in and of itself. Such a risen ground promises not only a new topology but new forms of sensation, a new aesthetics beyond representation.

In this way, Deleuze develops his political critique of capitalism with Guattari. What Deleuze and Guattari describe as a 'geology of morals' suggests that the political resignation betokened by Freud's theory of the Oedipus complex, in which desire becomes conceptualised only in relation to a law that prohibits it, fits into a much wider epochal and planetary problematic.[91] The desert of the body without organs unties the knots in which Freud had to tie desire in order to make the latter fit the logic of social reproduction. For Freud as for Lacan, the social investment of desire is conceivable only on the basis of a castrating Law or 'Father-function' along with a transcendent phallus. For psychoanalysis, that is to say, the organism can only embody desire on the basis of a knotting together of desire and repression. The body without organs dissolves this transcendence by presenting desire as an immanent field of pure potentiality, difference in itself. The link between repression and desire is still in effect, but what is now repressed is the organism itself as structural totality, while the body of desire becomes something non-organic, a whole without principle of unification. The model that Deleuze and Guattari give us for this body is the Earth as desertified or glacial. The glacial Earth persists beneath all territories and all forms of organisation (or stratification) as their simultaneous ground and unground. The desert is a form of depth that has risen to the surface, a figure of the *spatium* as absolute deterritorialisation.

CAPITALIST SPATIALITY

Deleuze and Guattari aim to retell the history of life on Earth not from the point of view of particular organisms or societies but from the point of view of the energies and forces out of which organisms, societies and all other systems construct themselves. They admit that their retelling is only possible within the context of capitalism because this is the only social formation sufficiently deterritorialised to allow us to attain to such a universal history.[92] Capitalism presents philosophical thought with a plane of immanence that can be stripped of all the various forms that may occupy and territorialise it. Capitalist modernity confronts us with groundlessness in various ways: it erodes the dogmas of metaphysics, just as it decodes traditional behaviours and beliefs, but it also literally delves into the depths of the Earth in search of the resources it needs to reproduce itself.

The metaphysical, social and geological thus come together in the plane of immanence. Modern philosophy can repeat the 'Greek miracle' by connecting the relative social and political deterritorialisation necessary for capitalism to the absolute deterritorialisation of speculative thought. Their analysis is thus premised on establishing relations between the spatiality of capitalism and the *spatium* of the plane of immanence. The ancient Greeks were able to institute a plane of immanence because their society already suggested to them how territories were capable of being deterritorialised, how the social and political plane could be stripped and instituted anew. Philosophy only became possible with the autochthonous citizen capable of reterritorialising anywhere. But capitalism, more than any prior social formation, works through rendering territories absolutely provisional. Capitalist spatiality is increasingly defined by what architect Rem Koolhaas has famously termed 'junkspace', a type of terminal disposability and modularisation of the built environment typified by shopping malls and airports, whose post-historical sheen suggests a convergence of the obsolete and the new.[93] Why, given this provisionality of territories, do Deleuze and Guattari say that modern philosophy loses sight of the plane of immanence? It is because philosophy *reacts against* social deterritorialisation and searches for some permanent ground, an island of truth or a buried foundation of experience. There emerges a certain mania for grounding that leads philosophers such as Hegel and Heidegger to align thought with the state or with the soil of a homeland. How can this be avoided?

Capital as an economic process deterritorialises but as a social form it reterritorialises on the state. We can account for this double movement in terms of a distinction between two types of space, which Deleuze and Guattari call striated and smooth.[94] Striated space is segmented, geometric and representational. It is the space of the city, the *polis*.[95] From a certain point of view, the story of the modern age is one in which the Earth is gradually transformed into what Peter Sloterdijk, in his remarkable history of globalisation, calls a 'system for localizing any point in a homogeneous, arbitrarily divisible representational space'.[96] At the same time, the Western metaphysics of space has always had to encounter *smooth* spaces that are non-metric and non-locational and that cannot serve the purpose of representing bodies in a coordinate space. Smooth spaces resist both homogenisation and segmentation: they are defined by intensities rather than by demarcations or divisions. The desert, the steppe and the sea typify smooth space: in such spaces, the representation of position that a city grid or agricultural enclosure make possible breaks down and a different awareness of space emerges by which one occupies without counting. Deleuze and Guattari define smooth spaces through the concept of the *nomos*, an ancient Greek term relating to the inhabitation of areas peripheral to the city: '[the *nomos*] stands in opposition to the law or the *polis*, as the backcountry, a mountainside, or the vague expanse around a city'.[97] This is not a question of the urban versus the rural, since one can have striated agricultural spaces. Indeed, agriculture itself is striation: '*it is the town that invents agriculture:* it is through the actions of the town that the farmers and their striated space are superposed upon the cultivators operating in a still smooth space'.[98]

At the heart of Western conceptions of space, then, there are two opposing models, but the key point is that contemporary capitalism is defined by an unprecedented entanglement of them. A prime example of this can be discerned in what urban designer Alan Berger calls 'drosscape'. Drosscape is the idea that the waste areas of cities, which are normally not included in the design process, can be 'scaped', repurposed for use and economic viability.[99] The concept of drosscape represents an attempt to engage with the fact that the urbanising process produces spaces which fall outside the framework of striation. Drosscape and junkspace, then, are *smooth spaces* of different kinds, infinitely plastic and flexible. Drosscapes are often waste spaces, but the vast interiors of shopping malls may be said to resemble deserts; we often tend to traverse them nomadically or intensively. Urban wastelands, ruins or slums often lie beyond police surveillance. Yet, such smooth spaces are *set into* the larger striated spaces of the city or *polis* and ultimately of the state, and for this reason by no means necessarily offer more freedom. In fact, power may come to operate all the more effectively in a smooth space.

Deleuze and Guattari emphasise how such entanglements of smooth and striated space should be seen on a global, geopolitical scale. Capitalist power, especially in its contemporary imperialist forms, *exceeds* the striated spaces of the state, even if it ultimately depends upon these:

> one no longer goes from one point to another, but rather holds space beginning from any point: instead of striating space, one occupies it with a vector of deterritorialization in perpetual motion. This modern strategy was communicated from the sea to the air, as the new smooth space, but also to the entire Earth considered as desert or sea. As converter and capturer, the State does not just relativize movement, it reimparts absolute movement. It does not just go from the smooth to the striated, it reconstitutes smooth space; it reimparts smooth in the wake of the striated. It is true that this new nomadism accompanies a worldwide war machine whose organization exceeds the State apparatuses and passes into energy, military-industrial, and multinational complexes.[100]

As capitalism exceeds the limits of the *polis* and striation, the state must itself become nomadic and operate through the smooth spaces that it 'reimparts' through war, technology, international trade, control and surveillance, and other means. One of the reasons the West gained global hegemony was because it needed to striate the smooth spaces of the sea, but in doing so also reimpart a militarised smooth space, as I show in some detail in Chapter 5.[101] It is not a question, then, of a simple opposition between smooth and striated but of a worldwide production of smooth space that state power must find ways to manage. This conception of the spatiality of capitalism suggests a kind of desert theopolitics of the modern state. Deleuze and Guattari observe that religions have so often taken root in the desert because they need an 'encompassing element' to oppose to a 'center': 'the entire history of the desert concerns the possibility of its becoming the encompassing element, and also of being repelled, rejected by the center, as though in an inversion of movement'.[102] The desert provides a geography in which transcendence is continually reclaimed within an expanding immanence. Thus, 'the great imperial religions need a smooth space like the desert, but only in order to give it a law that is opposed to the *nomos* in every way, and converts the absolute'.[103] Capitalist imperialism is a chapter in the history of desert immanence.

Deleuze and Guattari's critique of the Western metaphysics of space is developed not only in environmental but in botanical, horticultural and agricultural terms. The metaphysics of grounding cannot ultimately be separated from how life is materially cultivated and grounded in the Earth. If 'the tree has dominated Western reality and all of Western thought', they argue, then this is because Western culture has generally adopted the form of the 'root-foundation: *Grund, racine, fondement*'.[104] The metaphysics of grounding and the physics of cultivation are implicated in one another: 'the West has a special relation to the forest, and deforestation: the fields carved from the forest are populated with seed plants produced by cultivation based on species lineages of the arborescent type'.[105] Famously, Deleuze and Guattari see the 'rhizome' as an alternative to the dominant arborescent model.[106] But we should not let this dualism of models cause us to overlook how the Western obsession with roots has from the very first coexisted with forms of cultivation that draw close to the desert. An awareness of the desert fringe was decisive to the development of Western culture. Environmental philosopher Paul Shepard maintains that 'the dry landscapes of Egypt, Sumer, Assyria, Palestine, and the Eastern European and Eurasian borders of the Mediterranean Sea fashioned many of the concepts that define Occidental civilization'.[107] Bible scholar Herbert Schneidau argues that ideas of transcendence and immanence emerged from different ways of experiencing the desert landscape:

to Bedouin, as to Don Juan in Mexico, the desert is full of immanent 'power spots,' the landscape is mythologized, and is neither lifeless nor terrifying. But to the seminomad who must live next to it yet could not flourish on it, the desert's formlessness could suggest . . . the 'Wholly Other.' Ultimately, it is the discontinuity of the desert with the usual forms of life that could give the paradox of a concrete image of transcendence.[108]

The desert can connote either the sense of *continuity* of animate and inanimate matter, mind and nature, spirit and body, or it can suggest a world from which some vital presence has withdrawn into the heavens, leaving the landscape bereft and *discontinuous* with the creator-God. Such would be the difference between pagan immanence and monotheistic transcendence.

If the desert can be said to have been decisive for religion and metaphysics, what can it tell us about secular modernity? Drosscape and junkspace certainly suggest that contemporary capitalism has its own deserts, but the ground of capitalism itself, its body without organs or plane of immanence, can be said to consist of a form of growth without life, a strangely *ramifying barrenness*. It is as if capitalism were the attempt to synthesise the opposing metaphysics of landscapes Schneidau describes:

> Capital is indeed the body without organs of the capitalist, or rather of the capitalist being. But as such, it is not only the fluid and petrified substance of money, for it will give to the sterility of money the form whereby money produces money. It produces surplus value, just as the body without organs reproduces itself, puts forth shoots, and branches out to the farthest corners of the universe.[109]

Money, as 'fluid and petrified' capital, is the immanent milieu that provides consistency to capitalist society, even if the pre-capitalist archaisms of a mythical mother Earth and a sovereign state constantly intervene to secure the stability of capitalist social formations. Certainly, capitalism could not function without a conception of the Earth as life giver and container of resources or the state as regulator and guardian – fantasies which pervade the oedipal unconscious – but the essence of capitalism is nevertheless a paradoxically *arborescent desert* that devastates territories and topples transcendences. Oedipus, the fallen despot who must submit to his own castrative self-condemnation before wandering in the desert of exile, is the perfect symbol for the maintenance of transcendence within an ever-widening field of immanence: 'The earth is dead, the desert is growing: the old father is dead, the territorial father, and the son too, the despot Oedipus. We are alone with our bad conscience and our boredom, our life where nothing happens.'[110] Such is the modern condition.

THE DESERT GROWS

When Nietzsche, in part 4 of *Thus Spoke Zarathustra*, deploys the image of the growing desert, he provides a spatial figure for the central crisis afflicting the modern age. The desert is a conceptual topology for thinking what he called nihilism and the ascetic ideal, the latter being the set of life-denying attitudes and beliefs that have characterised Western culture since the birth of metaphysics in ancient Greece and especially since the establishment of Christianity in Europe. Secular European culture is defined by the religious traditions out of which it emerged. The problem of nihilism is thus recognised as the inability to move beyond the death of God: while we might still live according to Christian morality, God as foundation or essential truth is lacking and so we search in vain for other foundations in philosophy, art and science while still deploying the same principle of truth. In this way, the problem of nihilism comes to define culture itself. Under such conditions, Nietzsche writes, 'the highest values devaluate themselves'.[111]

How is this related to capitalism and universal history? In his first book on Nietzsche, Deleuze argues that the problem of nihilism transforms how we understand history. Nihilism is not something that takes place *in* history, not 'a historical event but rather the element of history as such, the motor of universal history, the famous "historical meaning" or "meaning of history" which at one time found its most adequate manifestation in Christianity'.[112] The inspiration for Deleuze and Guattari's subsequent form of universal history as capitalist decoding is thus clear: what Nietzsche calls nihilism, the ascetic ideal and Christianity, they call repression, Oedipus and capitalism. Nihilism, then, is a way of seeing history in the most universal terms as a history of life on Earth and the manner in which life has been taught to repress itself. The devalued codes of morality become the decoded flows of capital. But decoding is also a flight from the meanings that burden life. In Nietzsche's symbolism, nihilism manifests itself as a burden, the weight of an unbearable reality. It is what drives the spirit into the desert in search of freedom:

> To the spirit there is much that is heavy; to the strong, carrying spirit imbued with reverence. Its strength demands what is heavy and heaviest. . . . All of these heaviest things the carrying spirit takes upon itself, like a loaded camel that hurries into the desert, thus it hurries into its desert.[113]

The idea of the desert as a site of spiritual ordeal is, of course, a major theme of Judaism and Christianity, and Nietzsche plunders the Bible's apocalyptic imagery for his own symbols and allegories. *Thus Spoke*

Zarathustra can be read as Nietzsche's attempt to grasp modernity as an age of spiritual crisis in which exhausted values extinguish themselves and usher in a new era. The spirit, having been turned into a kind of beast of burden by life-denying morality and religion, is subject to another metamorphosis: 'in the loneliest desert the second metamorphosis occurs. Here the spirit becomes lion, it wants to hunt down its freedom and be master in its own desert'.[114] Once it has hunted down and destroyed the Western tradition, which Nietzsche portrays apocalyptically as a 'great dragon', it undergoes a third and final metamorphosis and becomes a child, a symbol of the affirmative existence and newfound innocence of the Overman.

The desert promises a (profoundly anti-Christian) soteriology in this sense. There is a Dionysiac, life-affirming aspect to the desert by which it becomes a site of overcoming and transformation. This is suggested by the fact that the apocalyptic-sounding phrase 'the desert grows' is given to us in the form of a song or dithyramb with sexual overtones:

> As a moral lion
> Before daughters of the desert, roar! –
> For the howling of virtue,
> My most lovely lady friends,
> Is more than all
> European fervor, European voraciousness!
> And here I stand already,
> As a European,
> I cannot do otherwise, God help me!
> Amen!
>
> *The desert grows: woe to him who harbors deserts!*[115]

Nietzsche's song of the desert owes much to Goethe's *West–Eastern Divan* which, contrary to British and French orientalism, can be seen as an attempt to break down the divide between Orient and Occident by regarding the East as a space in which Western values can be critiqued. Furthermore, Nietzsche's poem inverts the traditional association of the desert with masculine asceticism: the desert is now regarded as a feminine space where European morality, in particular sexual morality, is rebuked and a libidinal transformation might be attained.

Why, however, does the warning refrain of 'woe to him' open and close the poem, and why does it end on a strangely Christian note? Philip Grundlehner suggests the refrain echoes the closing line from another poem by Nietzsche written around the same time: '"*Weh dem, der keine Heimat hat*" ("Woe to him who has no homeland")'.[116] The difficulty of becoming properly homeless, of embracing desert immanence and dissolving the burden of inherited values, is underscored as the central problem. Salvation may be experienced more as an ordeal than a liberation. Even the lion with all its vitality cannot prevent becoming 'moral' once again: the moral lion's closing words 'I cannot do otherwise, God help me!' repeat Luther's declaration at the Diet of Worms.[117] The desert sojourn, then, can cause us to cling to the most austere morality out of fear of a complete deterritorialisation or complete nomadism. As Yirmiyahu Yovel has put it, 'man has nothing constant to hold on to in Nietzsche's world; his experience of immanence is that of a metaphysical desert, a yoke, the everlasting undoing of all transitory forms and the constant slipping of Being from under his feet'.[118] The prospect of a groundless existence, a pure immanence, may ultimately lead to a reterritorialisation on the very exhausted values from which liberty was initially sought. Transcendence may then be re-established within immanence. The opposition of asceticism and hedonism thus leads into an intractable problem. In *On the Genealogy of Morality* Nietzsche attempts to address this intractability in a more systematic manner. There he argues that asceticism originates in the *horror vacui* induced by the will's essential lack of aims and meanings. He claims that it is a fundamental fact of life that the will would rather will nothingness than will its sheer contingency. Indeed, the latter would be tantamount to not willing at all since the will always needs an aim in order to exist.[119] What this suggests is that life is opposed less to the repressiveness of asceticism than the sense that it does not have an innate *telos* directing it. Asceticism provides goals: not only religion, but philosophy, science and art arise as ascetic ideals. Asceticism thus sustains life via culture, but only at the cost of life denial. In this sense, the history of Western humanity is the history of nihilism.

The problem is one that Freud will take up in different ways. His theory of the death instinct approaches what Nietzsche meant by ascetic ideals. The death instinct states that the law of the pleasure principle is limited not by another principle but by itself alone. There is no 'beyond' the pleasure principle, no *other* principle by which the fact of pleasure's wanting what it wants can be explained. Desire grounds itself on itself, in other words, but this means that life is essentially entropic and capable of regulating itself only through a tendency towards homeostatic equilibrium. The dissolution of the various sensory excitations causing tension in the organic body is the source of all pleasure, but this means that any excess of pleasure is greeted as an unpleasurable disturbance to be eliminated. Lacan, synthesising Nietzsche and Freud, maintains that the body must become a '*désert de la jouissance*', jouissance being excessive pleasure, pleasure that causes suffering in the way it disturbs organic equilibrium.[120] Desire makes deserts of us all, in some sense. As

Nietzsche writes: 'Do not forget – Man, who quenched his lust: / You – are stone, desert, and death'.[121]

The only way out of the quandary is to assert that there is a superior asceticism capable of subsuming hedonism. We saw how the schizophrenic opens a path to this: the schizophrenic's desert body extracts from capitalism's growing desert a plane of immanence for theoretical geocentrism. Such libidinal geology is necessarily apocalyptic because desire cannot tolerate codes, territories or worlds: 'the body without organs is the deterritorialized socius, the wilderness where the decoded flows run free, the end of the world, the apocalypse'.[122] This apocalypse promises the end of history as nihilism, or, putting it differently, the end of history as the history of human consciousness. Deterritorialised desire in this way shatters the forms of representational consciousness that segregate human experience from its geological constitution. This amounts to an aesthetic apocalypse, a devastation of world as an aesthetic frame, that opens onto a new Earth.[123]

AESTHETICS FOR A NEW EARTH

Deleuze and Guattari's history of desire takes up the central ambiguity of the Nietzschean and Heideggerian desert – that it is a place of both great danger and potential salvation – through the conceptual persona of the schizophrenic, whose breakdown clears a path for a breakthrough into new forms of subjectivity. The schizophrenic's desert body brings about what we might call an aesthetic devastation: the norms or codes of sensation and feeling are dissolved in an experience of world loss that suspends the meaningfulness and purpose that normally characterise everyday life. The psychologist Louis Sass suggests that the schizophrenic break with reality is comparable to what Heidegger calls 'unworlding'.[124] For Heidegger's epochal history, the planet itself becomes an unworld in the age of modern technology and the Earth becomes a *Wüste* marked by monotony and uniformity, or indifference. Techno-capitalist production destroys or, more accurately, devastates difference: 'this lack of differentiation bears witness to the already guaranteed constancy of the unworld of the abandonment of Being. The earth appears as the unworld of erring'.[125] Erring, here, relates both to error and the errancy of wandering. But if we translate these terms into the schizophrenic experience of world loss, it becomes possible to relate the metaphysical desert to forms of aesthetic experience that are very different from Heidegger's conceptions of art as a mode of essential dwelling. While accepting the notion of the desert that emerges from Nietzsche and Heidegger, then, we can insist on an environmental aesthetics not tied to any notion of the dwelling place, homeland, lifeworld or *oikos*.

Sass argues that much of modernist art was inspired by the schizophrenic experience of unworlding. The painter Giorgio de Chirico, famous for his early canvases of deserted streets, gives us what we may regard as a first-hand account of unworlding in a diary entry describing the genesis of one of his compositions:

> One bright winter afternoon I found myself in the courtyard of the palace at Versailles. Everything looked at me with a strange and questioning glance. I saw then that every angle of the palace, every column, every window had a soul that was an enigma. ... I had a presentiment that this was the way it must be, that it could not be different. An invisible link ties things together, and at that moment it seemed to me that I had already seen this palace, or that this palace had once, somewhere, already existed. Why are these round windows an enigma? ... And then more than ever I felt that everything was inevitably there, but for no reason and without any meaning.[126]

There is, here, the combined sense of a loss of reality and an excess reality, of mystery and no mystery at all. Sass insists that this duality is common in schizophrenic experience. Everything about the landscape Chirico describes seems to withhold some mysterious revelation. At the same time, the revelation seems to be nothing other than the sheer meaningless surfaces of objects, their inevitable and silent insistence in space. This is the aesthetic revelation that there is no essential dwelling place, that the Earth is fundamentally both inscrutable and accessible.

Deleuze and Guattari's description of the breakthrough to the universe of desiring production follows a similar path of unworlding and the loss of meaning evoked by Chirico. They describe a schizophrenic on a hypothetical stroll through a mountain range:

> Everything is a machine. Celestial machines, the stars or rainbows in the sky, alpine machines – all of them connected to those of his body. The continual whirr of machines ... There is no such thing as either man or nature now, only a process that produces the one within the other and couples the machines together. Producing-machines, desiring-machines everywhere, schizophrenic machines, all of species life: the self and the non-self, outside and inside, no longer have any meaning whatsoever.[127]

Schizophrenic sensation as depicted here does not go by way of self and other, inside and outside, consciousness and its representations of the world, but by way of energy flows registered as intensities on the surface of the body without organs. These flows are not more meaningful but, in fact, resist meaning altogether: 'The unconscious poses no problem of meaning, solely problems of use. The question posed by desire is not "What does it mean?" but rather "How does it work?".'[128] This of course does not entail prescribing the existential ordeal of schizophrenia but to maintain that a transformative process can be extracted from this ordeal, one capable of leading us towards a non-representational consciousness and an *aesthetics of intensities* in which sensations are treated not as the components of a meaningful whole but as degrees of energetic increase or decrease in relation to a zero-degree state.

One example of such an aesthetics that Deleuze and Guattari provide is Turner, artist of the age of steam, whose paintings proceed from depictions of 'end-of-the-world catastrophes, avalanches, and storms' to a catastrophism of line and colour in which the 'canvas turns in on itself, ... is pierced by a hole, a lake, a flame, a tornado, an explosion ... is truly broken, sundered by what penetrates it. All that remains is a background of gold and fog, intense, intensive'.[129] Turner moves from classical depictions of apocalypse to a technique that shatters the framework of representational painting. John Berger describes this trajectory when he observes that 'at the age of twenty Turner planned to paint a subject from the Apocalypse entitled: *The Water Turned to Blood*. He never painted it. But visually, by way of sunsets and fires, it became the subject of thousands of his later works and studies'.[130] Turner's vision was a thermodynamic apocalypse of steam (heat death) that rendered visible the energetic and entropic forces of the Industrial Revolution.

We can relate the idea of an aesthetic breakthrough to the idea of the growing desert through the ways in which Heidegger's reading of Nietzsche underscores the relationship between modern technology and representation. Heidegger's influential reading of Nietzsche is generally distinguished from the readings exemplified by Deleuze, Bataille and Klossowski. Heidegger reads Nietzsche as a thinker who reveals the history of Western metaphysics to inhere in will, power and domination, allowing us to draw the necessary links between metaphysics and technology. The history of metaphysics terminates in Nietzsche for this reason. The growing desert, then, is the outcome of Western metaphysics but also a sign of its exhaustion. This is what gives the idea of overcoming metaphysics its eschatological dimensions. Deleuze reads him as a philosopher of life and of overcoming as a vital process. On this view, metaphysics does not end with Nietzsche but rather forms a *continuity* with life such that thought itself is living. Deleuze and Guattari's concepts of desiring production and desiring-machine appear to assimilate the question of technics into a form of life philosophy, however, while the task of attaining a non-representational consciousness suggests important links with the Heideggerian Nietzsche. For Heidegger, the modern frameworks for representing the world in language and science collapse Being as such into the being of objects to be measured and calculated according to the technoscientific worldview. This, in short, is the abandonment of Being.

Modernity thus compels us to think the world as unworlded and the planet as desertified or devastated but also to question the ontological ground of subjectivity. When Heidegger remarks that Nietzsche's refrain 'the desert grows' is 'a curiously contradictory turn of phrase', the contradiction he means is that what modernity drives away (i.e., Being) returns at the heart of our experience as an urgent question.[131] To the extent that we ourselves are thinking beings, it is not simply a physical desertification that is at stake but one that also progresses within thought and subjectivity, which may be said to 'harbour' their own deserts. We confront a desert, but articulate ourselves as internally desertified. This is how the problem of nihilism should be understood. The will – stricken with revulsion for its own fundamental aimlessness, its subjection to temporal flux and contingency – becomes caught within the instrumental logic of representation, just as Nietzsche had argued that it becomes caught by ascetic ideals. Heidegger writes: 'Hence the will is the sphere of representational ideas [*Vorstellen*] which basically pursue and set upon everything that comes and goes and exists, in order to depose, reduce it in its stature, and ultimately decompose it.'[132]

The growing desert, then, is the necessary terrain of a critique of representation. But Heidegger insists that the mode by which this critique is prosecuted cannot be a simple denunciatory statement about the modern world. 'The desert grows' is not, or not simply, a description of an external reality we confront – otherwise it would be subsumed into the very logic of representation it denounces:

> And so the words 'The wasteland grows . . .' become a word on the way. This means: the tale that these words tell does not just throw light on the stretch of the way and its surroundings. The tale itself traces and clears the way. The words are never a mere statement about the modern age.[133]

The refrain of the desert charts a path through it. Heidegger insists that language suffers and spreads 'desolation' (*Verödung*) by its instrumentalisation at the hands of what he calls 'Occidental "logic" and "grammar"'.[134] While he opposes this instrumentalised language to the language of poetry, and in this way suggests poetry is a way of recovering a more authentic dwelling, we can observe that there is likewise *a poetry to be extracted from the desert* in the sense that Nietzsche's refrain both describes the desolation and creates a desolate path through it. The idea of the desert refrain will be explored in the next chapter, but it should be noted here that where Deleuze and Guattari diverge from Heidegger is on the issue of where this path leads. For the latter, art can teach us ways to overcome our modern forgetting of what it means to dwell essentially upon the Earth. To dwell means first of all to cultivate and make grow, 'to cherish and protect, to preserve and care for, specifically to till the soil, to cultivate the vine'.[135] For Deleuze and Guattari, on the other hand, it is precisely the stubbornly rooted or sedentary nature of our thought and behaviour, so characteristic of the Western metaphysical tradition, that is the chief problem to be overcome if we are to be capable of thinking the devastation of the Earth. Thinking devastation is necessary for art to extract from capitalism's growing desert an entirely new sensibility, nomadic distributions of sensation capable of resisting capitalism on its very own terrain.

As we have already seen, Deleuze and Guattari's critique of the Western metaphysics of space leads them to a conception of capitalism's spatiality as a duality of smooth and striated spaces. We cannot, however, identify these spaces exclusively with physical space, just as we cannot identify devastation with physical deserts. One of Deleuze's central arguments in *Difference and Repetition* is that the way we represent space to ourselves as physically extended matter is only part of the story of space. He draws inspiration from mathematics and thermodynamics in order to argue that the properties by which we normally perceive space as extensive – length, area, volume – exist not only as measurable physical quantities but as immeasurable, purely 'ideal' or intensive differences: distance in itself, size in itself, and so on. These *intensive quantities* are the material out of which our perception of extensive space is produced. But this production is always a 'cancellation' or 'annulment' of difference, a kind of entropic dissipation of energy in which the intensive becomes the extensive. The genesis of our perception of extended space is precisely this cancellation:

> We know only forms of energy which are already localised and distributed in extensity, or extensities already qualified by forms of energy. Energetics defined a particular energy by the combination of two factors, one *intensive* and one *extensive* ... It turns out that, in experience, *intensio* (intension) is inseparable from an *extensio* (extension) which relates it to the *extensum* (extensity). In these conditions, intensity itself is subordinated to the qualities which fill extensity ... In short, we know intensity only as already developed within an extensity, and as covered over by qualities. ... Intensity is difference, but this difference tends to deny or to cancel itself out in extensity and underneath quality. ... It is true that qualities are signs which flash across the interval of a difference. In so doing, however, they measure the time of an equalization – in other words, the time taken by the difference to cancel itself out (*s'annuler*) in the extensity in which it is distributed.[136]

The representation of space as measurable and geometric (as striated space) is premised on an annulment of difference as difference in intensity. Thus, the differences by which striation divides up space is a homogenising, entropic or nihilating process. But this cancellation of intensive difference for the sake of extensive difference also tends to undermine striated space. Striated space produces forms of indifference that collapse extension, and are driven to do so for energetic reasons.

This is the paradox of an entropy that *subverts its own tendency towards zero*, something recognised by non-equilibrium thermodynamics in contemporary science.[137] Entropy, the tendency to reach equilibrium through the annulment of difference, can thereby be productive of new differences at 'far-from-equilibrium' states. The Earth can be regarded as a 'dissipative system' in this sense.[138] There is, here, a complex interplay of difference and indifference that Heidegger's desert, opposed as it is to cultivation, fails to fully grasp. Striated or geometric space is produced by divisions which break up smooth space, but these divisions are homogenising with respect to a primary intensive difference. Deleuze here is indebted to modern mathematics and topology which move away from traditional Euclidean geometry; DeLanda, for one, has shown that as we move from Euclidean to other geometries and finally to topological surfaces, space becomes less differentiated in the sense that the physical characteristics of shapes are dissolved. While in Euclidean space a circle and a triangle are distinct forms, on a topological plane any shape can be distorted into any other. DeLanda suggests that we can think of this progression through geometries as a way of conceptualising the genesis of extensive space, 'as if the metric space which we inhabit and that physicists study and measure was born from a nonmetric, topological continuum as the latter differentiated and acquired structure'.[139] The intensive space or *spatium* swarming with potential energy can also be considered a topology of thought. Because it exists at a greater degree of abstraction than the abstractions of geometry, it is an ascetic space, a kind of desert, but one that frees sensation from the organic body. The wasteland aesthetics of modernist and postmodernist writing likewise emerge from this paradoxical ascetic space, as we will see in the chapters to come.

In the desert, we find a contrast between the limited capacities of human sensation and something too great to sense. Paul Shepard writes that the desert is a 'powerful, unique sensorium . . . at once a place of sensory deprivation and awesome overload – too little life, too much heat, too little water, too much sky'.[140] This strange ambiguity of deprivation and overload suggests something of what Deleuze means by the distinction between intensive and extensive difference. He argues that it is only by encountering their limits, by encountering something imperceptible, that sensation and perception realise their true capacity: 'Sensibility, in the presence of that which can only be sensed (and is at the same time imperceptible) finds itself before its own limit, the sign, and raises itself to the level of a transcendental exercise: to the "nth" power.'[141] What Kant called the transcendental aesthetic, the set of conditions of sensation and perception, is thus generated by an encounter with a limit. Sensations, affects and percepts – the components of *aísthēsis* – are produced by the ordeal of confronting their bodily limits, and this is why life cannot be identified with organic form. This ordeal marks the point at which we discern something absolute: intensive quantities, differences in their pure form – distance in itself, size in itself, colour in itself – which cause a 'catastrophe' to overwhelm the organic order of our representations.[142]

We have seen that the Earth, as desertified or glacial, is a kind of groundless ground conditioning every territorial formation but ultimately hostile to organic life. If desire is productive, what it produces is territory, but territories develop along vectors of deterritorialisation. The semiotic mode of this process of deterritorialisation is what Deleuze and Guattari call the *ritornello* or refrain, a concept I explain in the next chapter. The task of art should not be territorial but geological. Art should not be in the business of imagining either a different world or new territorialities, but *a new Earth*. The environmental, here, does not just relate to the physical environment but to the virtual conditions, the transcendental aesthetics, by which physical space is produced. The Earth as desert is an eschatological idea but it is also the condition of rethinking and reimagining the Earth as life's ground.

Deleuze and Guattari argue that with Romanticism art comes to be located at the disjunction between territory and Earth. Whereas classicism assigned to art a creative purpose modelled on divine creation, the Romantic artist

> identifies ... with the ground or foundation [*fondation*], the foundation has become creative. The artist is no longer God but the Hero who defies God: Found, Found, instead of Create. Faust, especially the second Faust, is impelled by this tendency. Criticism, the Protestantism of the earth, replaces dogmatism, the Catholicism of the milieus (code). ... And this disjunction [between territories and the Earth] is precisely what determines the status of the romantic artist.[143]

The Romantic concern with grounding or founding has often been noted.[144] In the aftermath of the death of God, Romantic art takes on the mythopoetic role of founding a new community. It is thus only when art becomes concerned with the Earth that it becomes political in the properly modern sense. This can be understood in terms of what Latour describes as the 'new climatic regime' under which the Terrestrial becomes, for the first time, a political actor.[145] It is the Earth itself, and not the artist as creator-genius, that is the creative agency. Heidegger in 'The Origin of the Work of Art' described art in terms of a 'strife' between Earth and world in which the former allows the latter to ground itself. The Earth, here, is the unground or abyssal *Abgrund*, but it allows the world to ground itself by way of people whose historical destiny it is to dwell in it. The growing desert signals a loss of the essential strife or disjunction between Earth and world that allows us to dwell. Art in this sense becomes a reclamation of dwelling for a people as opposed to 'nomads' who know no kind of meaningful dwelling.[146] For Deleuze and Guattari, on the other hand, the Earth *must* be desertified and glacial for a modern and post-Romantic aesthetics that seizes upon it as agent of nomadic distributions of intensity. But how do we move beyond the categories of dwelling and *oikos* towards a semiotics of the environment as deterritorialisation and decoding? To begin answering this, we must move now to a consideration of the desert in literature since Romanticism.

NOTES

1. Morton, *Ecology without Nature*, p. 53.
2. For some key examples, see Mark Halsey's *Deleuze and Environmental Damage*, Bernd Herzogenrath's edited volumes *An [Un]Likely Alliance* and *Deleuze/Guattari & Ecology*, Joseph Dodds's *Psychoanalysis and Ecology at the Edge of Chaos*, Rosi Braidotti and Simone Bignall's edited volume, *Posthuman Ecologies*, and Thomas Jellis, Joe Gerlach and J. D. Dewsbury's edited volume *Why Guattari?*
3. Saldanha and Stark, *Deleuze and Guattari in the Anthropocene*.
4. Lambert, *Who's Afraid of Deleuze and Guattari?*, p. 114.
5. Delanda, *A Thousand Years of Nonlinear History*, p. 34.
6. See Gregory Flaxman's *Gilles Deleuze and the Fabulation of Philosophy* and Rodolphe Gasché's *Geophilosophy*.
7. Bonneuil, 'The Geological Turn'.
8. Key exceptions are Gavin Rae's *Ontology in Heidegger and Deleuze* and Janae Sholtz's *The Invention of a People*.
9. Biermann, *Earth System Governance*, p. 30; Steffen et al., 'The Anthropocene: Conceptual and Historical Perspectives', p. 860.
10. Deleuze and Guattari, *A Thousand Plateaus*, p. 37.
11. Ibid. p. 40.
12. As Matthew Fuller and Olga Goriunova argue, devastation can be regarded as both a failure to actualise a potentiality but also the actualisation of 'a potentiality that is wounded in a way that makes it implode, that makes it actualize a devastating becoming' ('Devastation', p. 324).

13. Freud, 'The Dream-Work', in *The Standard Edition, Vol. XV*, pp. 181–2; Breuer and Freud, 'Studies on Hysteria', p. 289.
14. Deleuze and Guattari, *Anti-Oedipus*, p. 35.
15. John Beck, in an article about the deserts of the American southwest, provides a description of the Earth that is entirely Deleuzian in this respect:

> To announce that the earth is without form and void, then, is not to claim an absolute void of nonpresence but to make a more qualified assertion about the shapelessness of the earth before the creation. So, the abyssal chaos, which is also an arid wilderness, is far from being the vacuum of worthlessness it is often read as being. It is, instead, the ground of potentiality, the necessary generative stuff of creation. ('Without Form and Void', p. 63)

16. Nietzsche, *Thus Spoke Zarathustra*, p. 6.
17. Deleuze and Guattari, *What is Philosophy?*, p. 102.
18. Deleuze and Guattari, *Anti-Oedipus*, pp. 33–4.
19. Ibid. p. 109.
20. Freud, 'Psycho-analytic Notes on an Autobiographical Account of a Case of Paranoia (Dementia Paranoides)', in *The Standard Edition, Vol. XII*, pp. 69–70.
21. Freud, 'On Narcissism', in *The Standard Edition, Vol. XIV*, p. 74.
22. Ibid. p. 74.
23. Schreber, *Memoirs of My Nervous Illness*, pp. 88, 94.
24. Freud, 'Psycho-analytic Notes on an Autobiographical Account of a Case of Paranoia (Dementia Paranoides)', in *The Standard Edition, Vol. XII*, p. 78.
25. Santner, *My Own Private Germany*, p. 7.
26. Deleuze and Guattari, *Anti-Oedipus*, p. 140.
27. Morton suggests that 'climate', far from being a synonym for world, environment, nature and so forth, relates to a disruption of our being in the world: 'I can think and compute climate in this sense, but I can't directly see or touch it. The gap between phenomenon and thing yawns open, disturbing my sense of presence and being in the world' (*Hyperobjects*, p. 12).
28. It is not, however, a matter of returning the schizophrenic to a lifeworld, or of understanding the lifeworld of his or her suffering. This is where Deleuze and Guattari break with the existential psychiatry of Jaspers, Binswanger and Laing.
29. Deleuze and Guattari, *Anti-Oedipus*, p. 136.
30. Ibid. p. 131.
31. Artaud, 'To Have Done with the Judgement of God', in *Selected Writings*, pp. 570–1.
32. Protevi, 'The Organism as the Judgement of God', p. 32.
33. Deleuze and Guattari, *A Thousand Plateaus*, p. 176; *Anti-Oedipus*, p. 329.

34. Deleuze and Guattari, *Anti-Oedipus*, p. 8.
35. Husserl, *The Crisis of European Sciences and Transcendental Phenomenology*, p. 332.
36. Husserl, 'Foundational Investigations of the Phenomenological Origin of the Spatiality of Nature', p. 223. For Derrida's analysis of Husserl's conception of the Earth as a zero point, see his *Edmund Husserl's Origin of Geometry*, p. 85. For an account of the 'transcendental Earth' in both Husserl and Heidegger, see Andrew Tyler Johnson's 'A Critique of the Husserlian and Heideggerian Concepts of Earth'. Johnson regards the transcendental Earth, as conceived by both philosophers, as the very opposite of the lived fullness of nature often described in ecophenomenology:

> while the positing of such a transcendental earth is significant insofar as it serves to open up a logical space for thinking an earth that would constitute the phenomenal field of lived life – again, an earth which is not an object of experience so much as a site or 'clearing' of possible experience, something like an earth-horizon which would be the end result of the performance of a specific kind of reduction – nevertheless both Husserl and Heidegger end up situating this earth, each in his own way, on a plane that is so rarefied and abstract that it becomes virtually unrecognizable as an earth. (p. 222)

Johnson intends this observation as a critique, but it seems to me absolutely necessary to posit the transcendental Earth as 'rarefied and abstract' in order to conceive it as an ontological ground of empirical life. In other words, it is necessary that the transcendental and the empirical do not resemble or mirror one another as if they were two halves of a living whole. Alain Beaulieu's opposition of Husserl's 'geostatic' and Deleuze and Guattari's 'geodynamic' Earth is likewise misconceived ('Deleuze and Guattari's Geodynamism and Husserl's Geostatism'). Deleuze and Guattari acknowledge that Husserl's Earth does not move, while theirs is identical with the dynamism of deterritorialisation. But they assert that this is a deterritorialisation 'on the spot', such that the Earth's transcendental immobility in the Husserlian sense is of a piece with their conception of the dynamism specific to deterritorialisation (*What is Philosophy?*, p. 85).

37. As Blanchot puts it in *The Book to Come*,

> The desert is still not time, or space, but a space without place and a time without production. There one can only wander, and the time that passes leaves nothing behind; it is a time without past, without present, time of a promise that is real only in the emptiness of the sky and the sterility of a bare land where man is never there but always outside. The desert is this outside, where one cannot remain, since to be there is to be always already outside. (p. 80)

38. Deleuze and Guattari, *Anti-Oedipus*, p. 11.
39. For an account of Deleuze in relation to topology, see Plotnitsky, 'Manifolds'.
40. Deleuze and Guattari, *Anti-Oedipus*, pp. 192–4.
41. Casey, *The Fate of Place*, p. 305.
42. Heidegger, 'Building Dwelling Thinking', in *Poetry, Language, Thought*, pp. 154–5.
43. Deleuze and Guattari, *Anti-Oedipus*, p. 378.
44. Deleuze and Guattari, *A Thousand Plateaus*, p. 140.
45. Deleuze, *Spinoza*, p. 3.
46. Deleuze and Guattari, *Anti-Oedipus*, p. 7.
47. Bowles, *Travels*, p. 76.
48. Deleuze and Guattari, *A Thousand Plateaus*, p. 377.
49. Deleuze and Guattari, *Anti-Oedipus*, p. 35.
50. Deleuze and Guattari, *What is Philosophy?*, p. 85.
51. Ibid. p. 87.
52. Flaxman, *Gilles Deleuze and the Fabulation of Philosophy*, p. 98.
53. Deleuze and Guattari, *What is Philosophy?*, p. 87.
54. Gasché, *Geophilosophy*, pp. 86–7.
55. Kerslake, *Immanence and the Vertigo of Philosophy*, p. 41.
56. Deleuze, *Difference and Repetition*, p. 194.
57. For a slightly different take on this point, see Henry Somers-Hall's *Hegel, Deleuze, and the Critique of Representation*, p. 242.
58. Deleuze, *Difference and Repetition*, p. 35.
59. Ibid. p. 288.
60. Ibid. p. 152.
61. Deleuze, *The Logic of Sense*, p. 155.
62. Deleuze and Guattari, *What is Philosophy?*, p. 9.
63. Peter Hallward, *Out of This World*.
64. Deleuze and Guattari, *What is Philosophy?*, p. 40.
65. Ibid. p. 41.
66. Ibid. p. 36.
67. Ibid. p. 41.
68. Ibid. pp. 86–7.
69. Flaxman, *Gilles Deleuze and the Fabulation of Philosophy*, p. 81.
70. Ibid. p. 81.
71. Nietzsche, *Philosophy in the Tragic Age of the Greeks*, p. 54.
72. Deleuze and Guattari, *What is Philosophy?*, p. 88.
73. Ibid. p. 104.
74. Kant, *Critique of Pure Reason*, p. 99.
75. Ibid. pp. 338–9.
76. Paul Hinlicky and Brent Adkins point out how Kant's *Critique of Judgment* proceeds as a geographical enterprise concerned with distinguishing 'the field (*Feld*), territory (*Boden*), domain (*Gebiet*), and residence (*Aufenthalt*) of concepts' (*Rethinking Philosophy and Theology*

with Deleuze, p. 16). Kantian critique in general is fundamentally legal and geographical, since it is about the legitimacy by which boundaries are drawn and a right to space asserted. Heidegger's concern with ground and worldview stems from a similar concern with boundaries and their legitimacy. The Heideggerian *Gestell* or frame of representation draws a boundary by which the world of things appears to consciousness, but the question is precisely what legitimates the drawing of such boundaries and thus how the world might appear differently (p. 45).

77. Deleuze and Guattari, *What is Philosophy?*, p. 104.
78. Deleuze, *Difference and Repetition*, p. 86.
79. Ibid. p. 87.
80. Ibid. pp. 127–8.
81. Ibid. p. 227.
82. Iain Hamilton Grant has shown how Deleuze's notion of the volcanic line is indebted to Schelling, but also how Deleuze's transcendental geology differs from Schelling's (*Philosophies of Nature After Schelling*, p. 200).
83. Deleuze, *Difference and Repetition*, p. 133.
84. Kant, *Critique of Pure Reason*, p. 608.
85. Kant, *Critique of Judgment*, p. 333.
86. Ibid. p. 331.
87. See Hamilton Grant's '"At the Mountains of Madness"' for a full account of Deleuze's demonology.
88. Deleuze, *Difference and Repetition*, p. 275.
89. Tennyson, 'In Memoriam', in *Tennyson: A Selected Edition*, CXVIII, lines 8–12.
90. Ibid. lines 20–5.
91. Deleuze and Guattari, *A Thousand Plateaus*, p. 39.
92. Deleuze and Guattari, *Anti-Oedipus*, pp. 139–40.
93. Koolhaas describes Junkspace as the endgame of modern spatiality. It is, for him, what Deleuze and Guattari call 'smooth space':

> Continuity is the essence of Junkspace; it exploits any invention that enables expansion, deploys the infrastructure of seamlessness: escalator, air-conditioning, sprinkler, fire shutter, hot-air curtain ... It is always interior, so extensive that you rarely perceive limits; it promotes disorientation by any means (mirror, polish, echo) ... Junkspace sealed, held together not by structure but by skin, like a bubble. ('Junkspace', pp. 175–6)

94. This is a distinction they take from Pierre Boulez.
95. Deleuze and Guattari, *A Thousand Plateaus*, p. 223.
96. Sloterdijk, *In the World Interior of Capital*, p. 27.
97. Deleuze and Guattari, *A Thousand Plateaus*, p. 380. I discuss this concept, and its links to the work of Carl Schmitt, in more detail in Chapter 5. Interestingly, Heidegger discusses the *nomos* and the *polis* in *An Introduction to Metaphysics*, p. 131.

98. Deleuze and Guattari, *Anti-Oedipus*, p. 481.
99. Berger, *Drosscape*, p. 12.
100. Deleuze and Guattari, *A Thousand Plateaus*, p. 387.
101. Ibid. p. 387.
102. Ibid. p. 574.
103. Ibid. p. 495.
104. Ibid. p. 18.
105. Ibid. p. 18.
106. Ibid. p. 3.
107. Shepard, *Nature and Madness*, p. 47.
108. Schneidau, *Sacred Discontent*, p. 143.
109. Deleuze and Guattari, *Anti-Oedipus*, p. 10.
110. Ibid. p. 308.
111. Nietzsche, *The Will to Power*, p. 9.
112. Deleuze, *Nietzsche and Philosophy*, p. 34.
113. Nietzsche, *Thus Spoke Zarathustra*, p. 16.
114. Ibid. p. 16.
115. Ibid. p. 252.
116. Nietzsche, 'Farewell', in Grundlehner, *The Poetry of Friedrich Nietzsche*, p. 239.
117. Ibid. p. 247.
118. Yovel, 'Nietzsche and Spinoza', p. 196.
119. Nietzsche, *On the Genealogy of Morality*, p. 68.
120. Lacan, 'De la psychanalyse dans ses rapports avec la réalité', in *Autres écrits*, p. 358.
121. Nietzsche, 'The Desert Grows, Woe to Whom the Desert Shelters . . .', in *The Peacock and the Buffalo*, p. 267.
122. Deleuze and Guattari, *Anti-Oedipus*, p. 176.
123. What Latour has recently called the 'new climatic regime' involves regarding the Earth itself as a new kind of political agent: '*another ground*, another earth, another soil has begun to stir, to quake, to be moved', *Down to Earth*, p. 17.
124. Sass, *Madness and Modernism*, p. 32.
125. Heidegger, 'Overcoming Metaphysics', in *The End of Philosophy*, pp. 108–9.
126. Giorgio de Chirico, quoted in Sass, *Madness and Modernism*, p. 44.
127. Deleuze and Guattari, *Anti-Oedipus*, p. 2.
128. Ibid. p. 109.
129. Ibid. p. 132.
130. Berger, *About Looking*, p. 143.
131. Heidegger, *What Is Called Thinking?*, p. 64.
132. Ibid. p. 93.
133. Ibid. p. 46.
134. Heidegger, 'Letter on Humanism', pp. 218–22. For a discussion of

Heidegger's notion of desolation in relation to desertification and devastation, see Müller, 'Style and Arrogance', pp. 142–3.
135. Heidegger, 'Building Dwelling Thinking', in *Poetry, Language, Thought*, p. 145.
136. Deleuze, *Difference and Repetition*, p. 223.
137. Crockett and Robbins, *Religion, Politics, and the Earth*, p. 147.
138. See Schellnhuber, '"Earth System" Analysis and the Second Copernican Revolution'.
139. DeLanda, *Intensive Science and Virtual Philosophy*, p. 26.
140. Shepard, *Nature and Madness*, p. 47.
141. Deleuze, *Difference and Repetition*, p. 140.
142. Ibid. p. 35.
143. Deleuze and Guattari, *A Thousand Plateaus*, p. 339.
144. See, for example, Nancy, *The Inoperative Community*, p. 45; Murphy and Roberts, *Dialectic of Romanticism*, pp. 74–5.
145. 'What is changing is that, henceforth, "geo" designates an agent that participates fully in public life'; Latour, *Down to Earth*, p. 41. From Latour's perspective, the new Earth arrives as the political agency of the Terrestrial at the endpoint of the process known as 'globalisation'.
146. Heidegger, *Nature, History, State*, pp. 55–6.

3. Desert Refrains

THE CLAMOUR OF THE EARTH: ECOPOETICS AND THE REFRAIN

This chapter examines several different literary motifs of the desert, from the Romantic period onwards, in a way that brackets notions of *oikos* and dwelling in favour of a semiotics of deterritorialisation. The *oikos* is not a foundational concept but conditional upon vectors of deterritorialisation that subject it to various degrees of ungrounding. I suggest in this way that we can read the desert as a literary and conceptual topos that calls our notions of place and our aesthetics of world into question. The philosophical deployment of the desert analysed thus far has emphasised how modernity devastates the experience of the local through the production of abstract spatiality. Rather than trying to reclaim a sense of place, however, we need to concern ourselves with *the force of devastation itself* since the displacement of life from the *oikos* is an ineliminable part of the modern experience of space. The genealogy of the desert in Romantic, modernist and postmodernist literature that I offer below – although I acknowledge it is only one possible genealogy – should be seen in these terms. The desert begins to appear as an aesthetic concern in Western art and literature from the end of the eighteenth century because it resonates with a modern sense of dislocation that is inseparable from a consciousness of the planetary.[1]

We have seen how Heidegger, from whom ecocriticism has taken some of its key conceptual coordinates, maintains that a tension between the desert and dwelling is central to understanding the modern experience of space as 'unworlded'. The uncanniness of modern spatiality, in which near and distant collapse into one another, comes from the paradox of living under conditions in which the resources for authentic dwelling have been stripped away. He defines language as 'the house of the truth of Being', but under the sway of technoscientific reason language undergoes and spreads a 'desolation' (*Verödung*) as it becomes a mere means of scientific or political instrumentality.[2] Heidegger insists that poetry is a way of counteracting this desolating instrumentalisation of language. In famous analyses of poetry by Trakl, Rilke and Hölderlin, he argues that poetic language 'calls' into being a world very different from the representational 'world picture' of the sciences. Poetic language allows the world to world and thus allows us to dwell by calling or singing things into our proximity as opposed to representing them to consciousness: '[Poets'] song over the land hallows. Their singing hails the integrity of the globe of Being'.[3] While technology and poetry – *technē* and *poiēsis* – are for Heidegger both forms of world disclosure, poetry allows us to step out of representational frameworks. As Jonathan Bate puts it in his landmark ecocritical text *The Song of the Earth* (2000), 'poetry is the original admission of dwelling because it is a presencing not a representation, a form of being not of mapping'.[4]

Heidegger's immense influence on the development of ecocriticism and ecophilosophy has been the subject of critique on the grounds that his sensitivity to place had links to Nazi 'blood and soil' ideology and *Volkish* notions of rootedness.[5] Bate is well aware that Heideggerian ecopoetics is tainted by the philosopher's association with National Socialism but insists that – since politics are part of the enframing by which language becomes representational and instrumental – ecopoetics is and should be seen as essentially *pre*political.[6] However, if we accept Tsing and Haraway's argument that 'the Holocene was the long period when refugia, places of refuge, still existed, even abounded, to sustain reworlding in rich cultural and biological diversity' and that the Anthropocene is the epoch in which worlding can no longer be assumed as life's prepolitical ground, then such a defence is not in any way tenable.[7] The fascism inherent in Heideggerian notions of dwelling can no longer be evaded through appeals to a prepolitical *oikos* that is assumed to be foundational. Ecopoetics, then, can and should be rethought according to the geophilosophical problematic of deterritorialisation. The Earth, as the absolutely deterritorialised, functions as a ground for life's territories *only by resisting them*. The question of dwelling forms at a disjunction between the glacial Earth and its shifting territories.

Yet simple opposition between Heidegger's ecopoetics and Deleuze and Guattari's is neither possible nor desirable. Like Heidegger, Deleuze and Guattari take particular inspiration from Estonian biologist Jakob von Uexküll, for whom there were musical laws of nature, with different species serving as motifs and counterpoints for one another.[8] Like

Heidegger, they recognise that the activity by which life forms a meaningful world is connected to art. Unlike Heidegger, though, they discern the origins of this activity in animal life, insisting – crucially – that 'art is not the privilege of human beings'.[9] For Heidegger, the animal is not only 'poor in world' (*Weltarm*) but is so precisely because it is utterly captivated by its world. This captivation *is* its impoverishment. Only humans can be aware of the opening to the world that is the condition of forming or disclosing one. But the end of the Holocene, that period of refugia for life, may well be marked by a dissolving of the ontological distinctions by which such an anthropocentric view is possible. Does Heidegger himself not recognise something like this when he speaks of an age of deserts or devastation? There is a strange inversion of the human and animal conditions implied in his critique of modernity: modern humanity is so captivated by its technoscientific, capitalist world – what Sloterdijk calls the 'world interior of capital' – that it fails to realise it no longer really lives in a world at all.[10] Non-human life, meanwhile, must adapt to and evolve on an Earth where it can no longer assume the ontological stability of a world to be captivated by. We are thus compelled to think space, and the semiotic activity by which it takes on meaning as territory, beyond the framework of the *oikos*, dwelling place or world, all of which presuppose forms of ontological embeddedness that the Anthropocene renders obsolete. It should be said that this does not mean getting rid of the *oikos* altogether, but simply seeing it as something assembled and disassembled by forces that belong to no *oikos*, forces that are themselves errant on a deterritorialised Earth.

The desert comes to take on importance in anglophone literature around the late eighteenth century, with the aesthetics of the Romantic period, as an awareness of a fundamental dislocation within the Western environmental imaginary. As Timothy Morton has argued across several of his books, it is not just that the Romantic aesthetics of nature were crucial for the emergence of what we have come to call environmental consciousness but that this emergence indicates a *contradiction* inherent in the very aestheticisation of nature: in seeking to make nature an object of aesthetic intimacy or connection, we 'frame' it as an object of contemplation or consumption and thus distance ourselves from it.[11] At the same time, we assemble the frame in order to step through it, to get closer to what we have framed, as the Romantics stepped through the frame of picturesque nature.[12] Romantic nature, then, is a symptom of the uncanniness that Heidegger saw at the heart of the modern experience of space. This is why the Heideggerian ecopoetics of dwelling need to be regarded in terms of the broader *crisis of dwelling* that provoked them as a response. Kate Rigby puts it well when she writes that 'it is in the context of the loss of a sense of belonging that the Romantic reaffirmation of dwelling needs to be situated if we are to uncover its continuing relevance to an age of increasingly universal dislocation'.[13] Romantic topographies often expose us to 'the elemental, the uninhabitable, and the incomprehensible' and not just to environments to which we can comfortably belong.[14]

The desert's role in modern literature, then, should be seen not only in terms of an aesthetic awareness of landscape and environment – a particular kind of *oikos* – but also, and more crucially, in terms of an awareness of dislocation as a fundamental part of the modern spatial condition. It is precisely for this reason that deserts and wastelands become a major concern of modernists such as T. S. Eliot and D. H. Lawrence, both of whom, in works from the 1920s, deploy desert landscapes of various kinds to suggest the devastation of the world and its potential rebirth or salvation. As in the philosophical tradition since Nietzsche, the desert became an eschatological and soteriological space. For postmodernists such as Thomas Pynchon, the desert comes to play the role of an entropic landscape in which a consistent meaning or semiotic pattern is sought, often in vain, amid chaotic signals and squandered energies. Paul Auster's postmodernist texts, reacting against the maximalism of Pynchon, see writing itself as the signification of devastation. Across several key twentieth-century literary texts, then, varieties of wasteland aesthetics function to articulate anxieties over the loss of the semiotic consistency of space.

Deleuze and Guattari's concept of the refrain (*la ritournelle*) allows us to grasp the relationship between sign and environment without making the *oikos* ontologically absolute. By refrain they mean a rhythmic 'block' capable of producing territorial marks, 'a crystal of space-time' by which life can ground its activity in sign-making.[15] The refrain has three main elements: rhythm extracts a consistency from non-localisable chaos, establishing a point of stability; an 'abode or home', a point in dimensional space, is thus established; finally, 'the point launches out of itself, impelled by wandering centrifugal forces that fan out to the sphere of the cosmos'.[16] The refrain constitutes the *oikos* but precedes and exceeds it; it is chaos, *oikos* and cosmos at once, assembling but also breaking apart territories; it is 'a patterning of spacetime always open to an outside', as geographer Derek McCormack puts it.[17] Deleuze and Guattari's main examples are ethological and musical, but their arguments have a more general significance because their aim is to show that territories don't pre-exist the semiotic activity that composes them. A bird's song, for example, signals but also *creates* the bird's territory which in turn organises the bird's lifeworld. Territories of all kinds, from animal habitats to nations, are created by such rhythmic and melodic phrasings of sign elements by which matter becomes expressive and thus capable of coding a territory's limits in relation to others.[18]

The key point is that all refrains are parasitic on one another. This makes any final delimitation of territories impossible. The semiosis of territories *implies their decoding* because refrains work only by taking on the codes of other refrains. *All* refrains are thus necessarily impure mixtures of codes. Ecologies of plant and animal life feature points of 'viral' decoding by which one kind of refrain picks up elements of another: 'It has often been noted that the spider web implies that there are sequences of the fly's own code in the spider's code; it is as though the spider had a fly in its head, a fly "motif," a fly "refrain".'[19] The patterns of a spider's web are informed by the rhythms of the fly's movements because the spider's movements are already animated by an intuition (not a representation) of the fly as a rhythmic or melodic block of spacetime. As Uexküll writes: '[a spider] weaves its web before it has ever met a physical fly. The web can therefore not be a representation of a physical fly, but rather, it represents the primal image [*Urbild*] of the fly, which is physically not at all present'.[20] He continues:

> the spider's web is configured in a fly-like way, because the spider is also fly-like. To be fly-like means that the spider has taken up certain elements of the fly in its constitution: not from a particular fly but from the primal image of the fly. Better expressed, the fly-likeness of the spider means that it has taken up certain motifs of the fly melody in its bodily composition.[21]

No territory can ever be prior to the occupation of it by life: to 'mark' a territory with signs is also to assemble it, as long as we understand that sign activity is both expressive *and* functional – the web catches flies. But territories likewise are formed only by decoding each other across species lines – the spider and fly are motifs *and motives* for each other. The song of the Earth is a counterpoint of territorial decoding that opens, ultimately, onto the cosmos. This offers us a semiotic definition of life, an ecopoesis in which decoding and deterritorialisation are primary factors. The impulses by which territories are formed imply transversal forces of attraction across territories that cause them to exceed their own limits and become deterritorialised. This entails a *processual* understanding of the sign as something that both acquires and loses meaning in relation to an absolutely deterritorialised Earth. We can thus maintain that the Earth is defined by a primary nomadism conditioning all dwelling; we dwell only because we are nomadic, as Levinas and Blanchot maintained against Heidegger.[22]

Deleuze and Guattari use the refrain to understand a fundamental shift in the experience of space and place that occurred with European Romanticism. They argue that with Romantic art the refrain comes to serve the dual purpose of founding new territories and deterritorialising existing ones. Mahler's song-symphony *The Song of the Earth* (1908) and Berg's opera *Wozzeck* (1914–22) are offered as musical examples of this:

> at the end of *Das Lied von der Erde* (The song of the Earth) there are two coexistent motifs, one melodic, evoking the assemblages of the bird, the other rhythmic, evoking the deep, eternal breathing of the earth. ... By the end of *Wozzeck*, the lullaby refrain, military refrain, drinking refrain, hunting refrain, child's refrain are so many admirable assemblages swept up by the powerful earth machine and its cutting edges ... It is owing to this disjunction, this decoding, that the romantic artist experiences the territory; but he or she experiences it as necessarily lost, and experiences him- or herself as an exile, a voyager, as deterritorialized.[23]

Dwelling only becomes possible on condition of a prior homelessness or sense of a lost or inaccessible Earth as primal territory: 'The territory is haunted by a solitary voice; the voice of the earth resonates with it and provides it percussion rather than answering it.'[24] With Romanticism, this ambiguity is developed in simultaneously aesthetic and political ways. The one who dwells is essentially a wanderer, while the native territory or homeland is an extraterritorial 'intense center' whose force of attraction is felt as a song of the Earth, as a grand refrain or clamour that leads beyond all territories but also sweeps them up in a single movement of deterritorialisation.[25] There is an ultimate discord, *a howling of the elements* that functions as an attractor for all the territorial refrains. As Blanchot puts it in relation to Odysseus and the Sirens, it is 'as if the motherland of music were the only place completely deprived of music, a place of aridity and dryness where silence, like noise, burned, in one who once had the disposition for it, all passageways to song'.[26] The Romantic experience of territory thus opens up the modern political space inhabited by fascism and the state, but by the very same gesture it also opens up the space of an anti-fascist, anti-state politics of nomadism. In the genealogy of the desert as a literary topos from Romanticism to modernism and postmodernism suggested below, the desert thus emerges as a paradoxical space in which these opposing tendencies approach one another.

CHASTENED SUBLIMITY

The Romantic concern with the desert demonstrates a sensitivity to links between meaning, signification and the physical environment, the extents to which we find meaning in a place or project meaning onto it. The desert is also the site of meaning's disappearance and precarity, the loss of significance to asignifying spatial and temporal immensity. In his book on sublime landscapes Cian Duffy notes that, somewhat surprisingly, the desert does not feature prominently as an example of the natural sublime either within Romantic writing itself or within the philosophical aesthetics of the period.[27] In fact, what we find in the Romantic engagement with deserts and wastelands is the emergence of a strange aesthetic category that Hardy in his description of Egdon Heath termed a 'chastened sublimity', where feelings of sublime exultation are intermixed with and tempered by feelings of depression and abjection.

When dealing with Romantic-period writings on the desert, we can distinguish between the 'cultured' deserts of Egypt and the Middle East, in which are found the ruins of ancient civilisations, and 'pure' desert, often typified by the Sahara, described in the travel writing of the time in terms of terrifying emptiness and uniformity.[28] Shelley's sonnet 'Ozymandias' evokes a desert of the first kind. The ruined statue of the pharaoh enables a brief but decisive statement on the ephemeral nature of political tyranny, and while the setting is the 'antique land' of Egypt, its chief target is a revolutionary Europe in which the old regimes are crumbling. Central to the poem's political sentiment is the aesthetic effect achieved by the 'boundless and bare' desert stretching off behind the ruins and leading onto a silence far more awesome than the declaration on the pedestal: 'My name is Ozymandias, king of kings, / Look on my works, ye mighty, and despair!'.[29] The irony here is that the signs of civilisation and political power only signify against an asignifying backdrop that confers on them both definition and fragility. A likely source for Shelley's poem is the explorer Richard Pococke's *Description of the East and Some Other Countries* (1745), but we can note that amid the descriptions of ruined statues that feature in this text the desert landscape is conspicuous by its absence. Bevis writes that Pococke 'imparts reams of historical and anthropological information, but has almost nothing to say about the desert, or his response to it'.[30] This absent landscape appears as the central irony of Shelley's poem. Precisely *as* absence, the desert suggests a revolutionary threat to inscriptions of political and cultural authority. As Morton observes,

> the desert sands perform the operation which should have been enacted by leveling movements of social reform. But Shelleyan reform, far from producing the smooth space of a desert, produces the striated space of an agricultural state, an oasis culture.[31]

We see in Shelley's *Queen Mab* the emergence of a new agricultural world built on the desert. The central politico-aesthetic strategy of 'Ozymandias', though, is to take the opposition of culture and desert, the striated and the smooth, and make it internal to the poem itself. Smooth space is not the political goal, as Morton observes, but it *is* where tyranny can be exposed, its significations overwhelmed.[32]

The confrontation of asignifying smooth space with the striated spaces of European culture and agriculture features in responses to the desert, especially in treatments of the 'pure' deserts of the Sahara and Southern Africa. European explorers of the late eighteenth and early nineteenth century regarded the overriding characteristic of such landscapes in terms of a monotonous uniformity alongside profound geographical alterity and physical peril. John Barrow describes his experience of crossing South Africa's Great Karoo, in an expedition begun in 1797, in terms of both hostility to life and a harrowing aesthetic uniformity:

> The eye wandered in vain to seek relief by a diversity of objects. No huge rocks confusedly scattered on the plain, or piled into mountains, no hills clothed with verdure, no traces of cultivation, not a tree nor a tall shrub, appeared to break the uniformity of the surface, nor bird nor beast to enliven the dreary waste.[33]

The usual significations of landscape (mountains and trees) are missing here, and thus the eye is culturally and not only geographically adrift in a smooth space whose aesthetic deprivations rival physical suffering. Part of the suffering here, it must be said, relates to thwarted colonial ambitions. The romantic explorer often approaches the desert expecting to find not just riches to exploit and new scientific discoveries to bring home but the *aesthetic* gratifications that a sublime natural landscape can provide. The desert *should* provide an unparalleled experience in this regard but often fails to do so. In his expeditions of the 1780s, François Le Vaillant found in the Kalahari only suffering and 'the dreary picture of dead and inanimate nature', the 'horror' of which 'was still increased by the silence which prevailed around'.[34] In Mungo Park's *Travels to the Interior of Africa* (1799) we find the same disappointed desire for sublime landscape: 'the disconsolate wanderer, wherever he turns, sees nothing around him but a vast interminable expanse of sand and sky – a gloomy and barren void, where the eye finds no particular object to rest upon'.[35]

These explorers are not so much denied the sublime as granted a strangely deadening form of it. We can note from these descriptions the references to uniformity as a primary characteristic. Edmund Burke in his famous aesthetic treatise of 1757 included uniformity among the components of the sublime, but also sought to explain why a 'long bare wall' does not therefore arouse the sublime sensations of, for example, a colonnade's uniform arrangement of pillars:

> When we look at a naked wall, from the evenness of the object, the eye runs along its whole space, and arrives quickly at its termination; the eye meets nothing which may interrupt its progress; but then it meets nothing which may detain it a proper time to produce a very great and lasting effect. The view of the bare wall, if it be of a great height and length, is undoubtedly grand; but this is only *one* idea, and not a *repetition* of *similar* ideas: it is therefore great, not so much upon the principle of *infinity*, as upon that of *vastness*.[36]

The uniformity of the desert grants vastness without infinity, oneness without the stimulating repetition that prevents sensation merging with the material objects of the senses. The desert thus strikes travellers such as Barrow, Le Vaillant and Park as sublimity without infinity and thus without the support of ideas (or *signifiers*).

Presented with this threat to the cultural signification of built and natural environments, European subjectivity in its confrontation with the deserts of Africa and the Middle East fell back on its most cherished and well-known literary deserts: those of the Bible. Barrow at one point describes the desert as a 'land of desolation',[37] echoing certain famous passages from the Old Testament, such as the one detailing God's destruction of Jerusalem: 'Then shall they know that I *am* the LORD, when I have laid the land most desolate because of all their abominations which they have committed.'[38] An ecotheological aesthetics of desolation emerges from a disappointed desire for sublime nature giving way to a religiously sanctified chastening of this same desire. The *an*aesthetic or asignifying threat of pure desert is thereby countered by strategies forged in the contemplation of the ruins of the cultured desert, in which the signifiers of culture provide definition and certainty. We find this quite explicitly in a passage from Chateaubriand's *Itinéraire de Paris à Jérusalem*, the record of his travels to the Holy Land in 1806:

> When one travels in Judea, at first a great ennui grips the heart; but when, passing from one solitary place to another, space stretches out without limits before you, slowly the ennui dissipates, and one feels a secret terror, which, far from depressing the soul, gives it courage and elevates one's native genius. Extraordinary things are disclosed from all parts of an earth worked over by miracles: the burning sun, the impetuous eagle, the sterile fig tree; all of poetry, all the scenes from Scripture are present there.[39]

Sublimity is rescued, but only through the intervention of Christianity. The desert stages a confrontation between significance and insignificance, exaltation and depression, but this is ultimately to the benefit of a European subjectivity finding its religious and moral inscriptions confirmed in the encounter with vast inertial matter. Said, commenting on this passage, remarks that

> the barren landscape stands forth like an illuminated text presenting itself to the scrutiny of a very strong, refortified ego. Chateaubriand has transcended the abject, if frightening, reality of the contemporary Orient so that he may stand in an original and creative relationship to it.[40]

A great number of Europeans would follow the same route as Chateaubriand, travelling through the Mediterranean, Greece and Constantinople to Jerusalem and Egypt. Said explains this desire for desert experience more in terms of a refortification of the European ego than of any interest in these regions themselves, their cultures and peoples, which European travellers often described as 'arid', and as unaffected by history as the desert itself.[41]

As I show in more detail in relation to T. E. Lawrence in Chapter 5, this description of the Arab world and its peoples as desert-like is an outward projection of something European subjectivity detected within itself. What we see from the Romantic period is an exhausted Western metaphysics of self looking towards the East for transformative or redemptive symbols of its own ruination. The deserts of Goethe and Nietzsche, though not orientalist in the same way as those of British and French writers, follow a similar path. The regeneration of Europe by the East was, Said argues, 'a very influential Romantic idea' because an Eastern inspiration was felt to offer solutions for the crises afflicting the secularising West.[42] For Shelley in 'Ozymandias' but also in works such as *Queen Mab* and *Hellas* (1822), the desert is a place where tyranny is recognised and overcome, and where a new utopian age may commence. In *Hellas* – a verse drama set in Constantinople and written in support of the Greek struggle for independence – we find lines which recast the imagery of ruin from 'Ozymandias':

> Let the tyrants rule the desert they have made;
> Let the free possess the paradise they claim;
> Be the fortune of our fierce oppressors weighed
> With our ruin, our resistance, and our name![43]

It is now the ruination suffered as part of a struggle against tyranny that signifies the paradise to come, while tyranny itself is presented as a propagator of deserts.

The desert thus often features in Romantic writing as part of a regenerative apocalyptic process, as it does in Nietzsche. In Book V of *The Prelude*, Wordsworth describes an 'Arab of the Bedouin tribes', a guide through the waste and an Arabian Quixote, holding a stone under one arm and a shell under the other.[44] Auden clarifies the significance of these objects in terms of an epochal clash between instinct and imagination, aridity and deluge:

> As symbolic object, the stone is related to the desert, which like the Ancient Mariner's situation is a becalmed state when the distress is caused by lack of passion, good or bad, and the shell is related to the sea, to powers, that is, which, though preferable to aridity, are nevertheless more dangerous; the shell is a consolation yet what it says is a prophecy of destruction by the weltering flood; and only a sublime soul can ride the storm.[45]

As the nineteenth century goes on, we find aesthetic attitudes to the desert changing quite profoundly. Within the space of about 50 years, the repeated complaints of uniformity and aesthetic indifference are replaced by a subtler appreciation of the possibilities the desert has to offer an eye that knows how to recognise them. Eugène Fromentin, the French novelist and painter of the Orientalist school who wrote extensively about his travels in the Sahara, offered an aesthetic theory of landscape that would come to dominate much subsequent desert writing by Europeans and Americans. Sven Lindqvist maintains that Fromentin was 'the first of a long line of writers and artists to experience the desert with an aesthetic eye'.[46] This claim is debateable, but we do find in Fromentin an important break with prior aesthetic estimations of pure desert in that he does not rely on religious or political categories in order to extract something valuable from it. In a passage from a journal written in 1853, Fromentin reflects on his journey through the Sahara and what the desert means for landscape painting, writing that

> [the Orient] upsets the harmonies that landscape has lived with for centuries. I'm not speaking here of a fictitious Orient that preceded the recent studies that have been made on the spot; I'm talking about a country of chalky dust that as it takes on color becomes a little garish and yet is a little sad when no strong colors enliven it. It appears uniform yet hides under that apparent unity of hues an infinite number of nuances and tonalities broken down; it has rigid forms that are more often placed horizontally rather than vertically, very well-defined, with no haze, no attenuation, almost without any appreciable atmosphere and no depth of distance.[47]

What Fromentin suggests in this passage is the aesthetic potential of pure desert as a smooth space by which subtle tonal differences are extracted from an apparent uniformity of colour. Horizontal features replace trees and mountains as the main formal elements. What we see here is a *decoding* of the terms of landscape in a way that responds to modern European aesthetics.

This kind of highly aestheticised description of the desert will be echoed by many twentieth-century writers, beginning with the American art historian John C. Van Dyke, whose book *The Desert: Further Studies in Natural Appearances* (1901) turns the Ruskinian notion of the picturesque to an appreciation of the Colorado, Arizona and Sonoran deserts, regions which had hitherto been regarded in mostly negative terms.[48] Van Dyke retains Fromentin's attention to colour. When riding through the mesas of Arizona, he says, 'all the glory of the old shall be as nothing to the gold and purple and burning crimson of this new world'.[49] And yet this is a new aesthetic awareness which only those cultivated by the old world can hope to grasp:

> It is sometimes assumed that humanity had naturally a sense and a feeling for the beautiful because the primitives decorated pottery and carved war-clubs and totem-posts. Again perhaps; but from war-clubs and totem-posts to sunsets and mountain shadows – the love of the beautiful in nature – is a very long hark. The peons and Indians in Sonora cannot see the pinks and purples in the mountain shadows at sunset. They are astonished at your question for they see nothing but mountains. And you may vainly exhaust ingenuity trying to make a Pagago see the silvery sheen of the mesquite when the low sun is streaming across its tops. He sees only mesquite – the same dull mesquite through which he has chased rabbits from infancy.[50]

With Van Dyke, the aestheticisation of the desert as exalted natural wilderness, and thus as a space of freedom from civilisation, comes fully into being. It is a gesture repeated by environmentalist appreciations of the desert by Edward Abbey and others. But such an environmentalist appreciation is predicated upon a 'primitive accumulation' of the desert's natural beauty from its original inhabitants, for whom the desert is nothing but the dull uniformity that repelled the old world eyes of Barrow, Le Vaillant and Park. Van Dyke worries that the aesthetic cultivation needed to appreciate the desert is 'indicative of some physical degeneration, some decline in bone and muscle, some abnormal development of the emotional nature'.[51] Sensitivity to the desert's beauty is itself a sign of the degeneration of the Western subject. That 'the red man does not see a colored shadow' is probably to his benefit.[52] The civilisation that grants such a sensitive vision is the same one that, through the systems of transport and irrigation constructed in the nineteenth century, finally made the deserts of the American west a place where European settlers could comfortably live.[53] The despoliation of nature that has, through mining and deforestation, 'stripped the land of its robes of beauty' is ultimately part of the same capitalist modernity that facilitates the appreciation of nature's beauty.[54] This contradiction will be largely forgotten by Abbey and Van Dyke's other environmentalist descendants.

WASTELAND THEOLOGY

Distinctions between wild, waste and cultivated land changed dramatically in eighteenth- and nineteenth-century Europe. Important studies such as John Barrell's *The Idea of Landscape and the Sense of Place, 1730–1840* (1972) and Raymond Williams's *The Country and the City* (1973) have linked the socio-economic changes brought about by land enclosures in Britain and their accompanying moral ideology of 'improvement' to the emergence of landscape as an aesthetic category. The key point here is that landscape as an object of aesthetic appreciation came into being around the same time that land came to be a commodity bought and sold according to abstract estimations of its value in a nakedly economic sense. There thus arose a tension between two forms of abstraction. On the one hand, land had to be seen at a certain remove or from a transcendent vantage point in order for it to become an aesthetically gratifying landscape, while on the other a different type of remove – one mediated by money and the market – became necessary for land to become a commodity in the capitalist sense. Rigby notes an 'uneasy oscillation' between land as aesthetic and as economic object in new determinations of wild versus cultivated landscapes in eighteenth-century aesthetics.[55] This oscillation entailed new distributions of smooth and striated space. The enclosures of common lands that drove the poet John Clare from his home in rural Northamptonshire were part of a process that had its roots in moral and religious convictions that reclaiming land from uncultivated wilderness or 'wastes' was a path to salvation. Striation was, in other words, divinely sanctioned. Enclosure and improvement resulted in a new striated topography that appealed to eighteenth-century notions of land as something that could be reshaped, designed and ordered. Rigby describes the process that drove Clare from Helpston in 1832 in the following way: 'Landholdings that had previously existed as series of strips (lands) scattered across the three large open fields of the parish were consolidated into square parcels divided by fences and hedges.'[56] Older systems of collective use of the land gave way to a system of individual ownership. Common lands comprising woods, heaths, wetlands and meadows to which the poor had once been allowed access were turned over to private use. All of this amounted to the disappearance in the eighteenth century of the peasantry in any classical sense and the replacement of it by an agrarian capitalist relationship between landowners, tenant farmers and wage labourers.[57]

Central to this process was a definition of wasteland as not only economically unproductive and aesthetically disgusting but also as fallen and immoral. The theology of the desert that allowed European travellers to refortify themselves by contact with geographical alterity in the Middle East was first deployed in the capitalist transformation of the European countryside. Vittoria Di Palma's history of wasteland in seventeenth- and eighteenth-century Britain shows the extent to which these transformations were rooted in Christian soteriology.[58] She suggests how John Bunyan's novel *The Pilgrim's Progress* (1678) can be read as a theological allegory of salvation narrating a journey from the City of Destruction to the Celestial City by way of, amongst other places of physical and spiritual ordeal, the Valley of the Shadow of Death. Bunyan describes the latter in terms of a biblical wasteland through which Christian needs to pass

> because the way to the Cœlestial City lay through the midst of it: Now this Valley is a very solitary place. The Prophet *Jeremiah* thus describes it, *A Wilderness, a Land of desarts, and of Pits, a Land of drought, and of the shadow of death, a Land that no Man* (but a Christian) *passeth through, and where no man dwelt.*[59]

Bunyan's allegory of a heavenly city in the wilderness resonates with subsequent American myths of manifest destiny. But the notion that the path to salvation involves a journey through landscapes of desolation is deeply rooted in various Christian and Jewish traditions. For the biblical Hebrews, a period of exile in the desert was not only of symbolic significance but part of their real experience. Adam in the garden was an agriculturalist, but fallen humanity's fate meant exile and wandering. Cain was a tiller of the soil but Abel was a shepherd, a pastoralist. As Régis Debray writes, for the Hebrews 'salvation will come by way of the nomad, the messiah of the borderlands'.[60] While Judaism emphasises the wasteland as a site of punishment and place of redemption, for the Christian tradition it is the passage *through and out of* the wasteland that becomes specifically redemptive. As Di Palma explains, this distinction can be related to the way in which the Old English *west* – the root of *westen* or wilderness – was supplanted, at the beginning of the thirteenth century, by the Anglo-Norman *wast*, which comes from the Old French *gaster*, meaning to devastate and ravage but also to spend or squander.[61] The new term 'wasteland' came to carry an economic and moral significance that *westen* did not have. The use of this term in the King James Bible of 1611 was decisive in suggesting that 'it is possible to transform a ruined and desolate place into a verdant one' and that 'such a transformation is proof of redemption'.[62]

For the proponents of improvement in seventeenth- and eighteenth-century Britain, the recognition of certain places as unproductive land meant heeding the imperative to 'build the old waste places'.[63] While

Bunyan may have seen such 'wastes' as the marshes and fens of his native Bedfordshire as aspects of a fallen landscape and thus as symbolic of sin, he was nonetheless profoundly opposed to the enclosure of common lands. *The Pilgrim's Progress* can be read as an anti-enclosure allegory.[64] For Bunyan's brand of dissenting Puritanism, the peasantry and landless poor, not the landed gentry, were on the side of 'Abel and his generation'.[65] That the same theology of wasteland could be used to justify such distinct forms of land ownership and political organisation demonstrates the instability of distinctions between waste, wild and cultivated. Di Palma writes that 'Bunyan's translation of his familiar surroundings into a universal moral landscape makes the point that wasteland can be located anywhere, as its seat is really in the soul of the individual'.[66]

As the eighteenth century went on, these instabilities made themselves felt in ways that intersect with the development of Romantic aesthetics. The striated, ordered topographies of improved land – the result of reclaiming, draining and clearing – came to be rejected by a new taste for wild nature and sublime landscape. It is in this context that we should understand Williams's reading of Goldsmith's *The Deserted Village* (1769), discussed briefly in the first chapter. The poem and Williams's analysis of it are important because they suggest how the Romantic conception of nature was premised on a prior devastation of nature as a social order. Williams underscores how Goldsmith's poem can be read not only in terms of nostalgia for an idealised pastoral past but as discerning a desert in the midst of newly productive enclosed land. The once idyllic village of Sweet Auburn, now enclosed, has no other purpose than to produce wealth for its sole owner, but this new, capitalist fertility is described in terms of its opposite: 'desolation saddens all thy green: / One only master grasps the whole domain'.[67] For all the poet's appeals to direct observation of a simple village life now lost, he is aware that the transformations taking place around him lie beyond his imaginative frame of reference in an abstract network of global economic relations:

> Around the world each needful product flies,
> For all the luxuries the world supplies.
> While thus the land adorned for pleasure all
> In barren splendour feebly waits the fall.[68]

Goldsmith thus sees, in the midst of a new capitalist productivity, a growing barrenness or fructifying death: 'The country blooms – a garden, and a grave'.[69] The desert interrupts the directness and specificity of the pastoral scene to provide an imaginative rendering of the poet's own fate in a society that dispossesses him as much as it does the peasantry. As Williams observes: 'the social condition of poetry – it is as far as Goldsmith gets – is the idealised pastoral economy. The destruction of one is, or is made to stand for, the destruction of the other'.[70] Williams insists that the Romantic 'assertion of nature against industry and of poetry against trade' is prefigured in Goldsmith's depiction of poetry exiled from the social order.[71]

Bate observes that in the nineteenth century 'the word "environment" began to be applied to social contexts exactly because of the feeling of the alienation of city-dwelling which was identified by Wordsworth and others'.[72] Concepts of environment, ecology, *Lebenswelt*, *Umwelt* and so on come into being in the Romantic period because these things *could no longer be taken for granted*, and were felt to be somehow strange, threatening or precarious. Goldsmith, in Williams's reading, apprehends the emergence of a new environmental consciousness in terms of a deterritorialisation of poetry from the pastoral lifeworld. The desert's 'barren splendour' portrays an awareness of global decoded space encroaching upon the coded village world. The concept of the environment, then, provides a sense of world but does so in the midst of forms of social disintegration where the feeling of being in a world is disappearing. The sense of threat and uncanniness that we feel today when we think of climate change and species extinction shows the extent to which the environment for us is a frighteningly decoded thing. Capital decodes space. The growing concern with the desert in European and American literature from the end of the eighteenth century is an imaginative response to this condition. In this way, the desert comes to play the role of a body without organs for Western literature's signification of the possibility or impossibility of life, growth, order and energy in an increasingly technological society. With this in mind, we can turn now to the most famous desert in modern anglophone literature.

VACANT LOTS: T. S. ELIOT AND JUNK TIME

Like James Thomson's long poem *The City of Dreadful Night* (1874), which had an important impact on the young Eliot, *The Waste Land* (1922) casts the modern urban experience as a desert ordeal. Whereas for Thomson the city-desert is where faith has been extinguished, for Eliot it is where extinguished faith may discover the possibility of rebirth. In this sense, Eliot takes from the Romantics the idea of the desert as a soteriological space. It is all too easy to regard the poem as an exemplification of the modern deterritorialised or atopian psyche in the aftermath of the First World War, but a consideration of what it might tell us about the malaise of urban atopia must be balanced against an attentiveness to how it performs a *redundancy of signification*. That is to say, *The Waste Land* draws on vast cultural resources in order to articulate culture itself as so much waste or textual noise. It is a text made of refrains, blocks of spacetime that operate to decode the very foundations on which it stands. Its fragments belong to a historical experience apprehending itself as entropy.[73] Like Nietzsche's refrain of the growing wasteland, Eliot's refrains do not simply *represent* a world in ruins. Rather, they map a depletion of the resources of literary utterance, displaying in this way what Deleuze and Guattari call a 'surplus value of code'.[74]

The poem's opening images evoke physical and spiritual aridity:

> What are the roots that clutch, what branches grow
> Out of this stony rubbish? Son of man,
> You cannot say, or guess, for you know only
> A heap of broken images, where the sun beats,
> And the dead tree gives no shelter, the cricket no relief,
> And the dry stone no sound of water.[75]

As the poem progresses, we enter the more clearly urban deserts of Eliot's London, but they are all part of the same territory. Temporality here is repetition rather than progression. Consider the reappearance of 'clutch' in these lines from the opening of section III:

> The river's tent is broken: the last fingers of leaf
> Clutch and sink into the wet bank. The wind
> Crosses the brown land, unheard. The nymphs are departed.
> Sweet Thames, run softly, till I end my song.
> The river bears no empty bottles, sandwich papers,
> Silk handkerchiefs, cardboard boxes, cigarette ends
> Or other testimony of summer nights. The nymphs are departed.[76]

Detritus has replaced the nymphs of pastoral convention. This is the song of *junk time*, in which history succumbs to an inundating redundancy of signs. We are no longer dealing with that asignifying blankness by which Shelley could imagine the ruin of tyrants but with the ruination of signification itself, as if signs have now become the very rubbish they here name.

Of course, Eliot was not the only major modernist figure to deploy the desert, which features in Yeats's apocalyptic reflection on the First World War in 'The Second Coming' (1920): 'a vast image out of *Spiritus Mundi* / Troubles my sight: a waste of desert sand'.[77] The desert is found, too, as we will see below, in D. H. Lawrence's later novels, as well as in Carlos Williams's *The Desert Music* (1954). Modernism used the desert to articulate not only feelings of placelessness and displacement, but of physical and spiritual torments that tend to evade direct representation. While appreciating how the desert is implicated in the modernist crisis of representation, however, we should also bear in mind how, in a lineage stretching from Goldsmith and Shelley to Thomson and Eliot, it has been a topos by which poetry views itself in relation to and in exile from history and the social world. It is too simplistic to assert, as Michael H. Whitworth does, that the modernist desert emerges in opposition to the verdant landscapes of the Romantics.[78] If Romanticism's 'green language' arises from the ruin of Sweet Auburn's pastoral economy, then Eliot's wasteland can be seen as the ground revealed when Romantic nature recedes in turn.

In his 1939 essay 'The Idea of a Christian Society', Eliot offers an account of religion that draws close to Romantic conceptions of nature:

> religion ... implies a life in conformity with nature. It may be observed that the natural life and the supernatural life have a conformity to each other which neither has with the mechanistic life ... We are being made aware that the organisation of society on the principle of private profit, as well as public destruction, is leading both to the deformation of humanity by unregulated industrialism, and to the exhaustion of natural resources, and that a good deal of our material progress is a progress for which succeeding generations may have to pay dearly. I need only mention, as an instance, now very much before the public eye, the results of 'soil-erosion' – the exploitation of the earth, on a vast scale for two generations, for commercial profit: immediate benefits leading to dearth and desert.[79]

A passage such as this supports Craig Raine's insistence that Eliot – influenced by works such as the pro-Nazi Gerard Wallop's *Famine in England* (1938) – possessed an ecological awareness of 'dust bowls, deserts, and deforestation caused by the mismanagement of the land', and thus that 'the waste land was not merely an emblem of spiritual aridity'.[80] Raine writes that, prior to the 1930s, 'the American Eliot was aware of the soil erosion caused by the Homestead Acts of 1862 and 1909'.[81] Settlers were encouraged to farm poor land by pseudoscientific claims that cultivation of the soil conserves moisture. The Dust Bowl of the 1930s was the catastrophic result. While Raine tries to distance Eliot from blood-and-soil politics through an emphasis on his ecological awareness, it is clear that the ecological is for Eliot already political. In *After Strange God*, his lectures delivered in Virginia in 1933, Eliot expressed his admiration for the agrarian movement of the American south and his hostility to the deleterious effects of industrial modernity, not least of which is the loss of traditional rural culture.[82]

To attempt a green ecocritical reading of Eliot that ignores his politics, or that frames his work only in terms of a contemporary liberal environmentalist politics, is entirely inadequate.[83]

How, then, should we understand Eliot's wasteland aesthetics? We can note that the wasteland motif first appears in Eliot's work neither as environmental warning nor as spiritual diagnostic but as sheer aesthetic epiphany. 'Second Caprice in North Cambridge', dated 1909 in Eliot's notebook but not published until 1996, celebrates a scene of urban and/or suburban desolation:

> This charm of vacant lots!
> The helpless fields that lie
> Sinister, sterile and blind –
> Entreat the eye and rack the mind,
> Demand your pity.
> With ashes and tins in piles,
> Shattered bricks and tiles
> And the débris of a city.
>
> Far from our definitions
> And our aesthetic laws
> Let us pause
> With these fields that hold and rack the brain.[84]

These lines, inspired by Eliot's youthful prowling of Boston's slums and seedier districts, suggest that the modern city may hold as-yet unexplored aesthetic pleasures far beyond anything his Harvard education could prepare him for. As Lyndall Gordon writes:

> in St. Louis the darker and grimmer aspects of the city had passed him by; in Boston, for the first time, he conceived a horror of the commercial city, its cluster and the sordid patience of its dwellers. . . . He was both horrified and, in a way, engaged.[85]

The vacant lot motif recurs in Eliot a number of times. He uses it to open and close 'Preludes', written in 1910–11, and it features in his 1930 translation of Saint-John Perse's long poem *Anabase* (1924). The vacant lots by which the young Eliot felt both charmed and repelled suggest an experience of place that is both aesthetically and conceptually vacant, an empty or uncertain terrain to be explored and mapped out by new poetic forms and new affects. It is Eliot's equivalent of Laforgue's 'terrain vague' from poems such as 'Complainte sur certains ennuis' and 'Pierrots': a vague or anexact space rather than a knowable location or territory.

For Eliot, the wasteland was primarily an object of fraught aesthetic impulses that his later work channelled into social, religious and environmental concerns. Through the influence of Jessie L. Weston's studies of the Grail legend and their treatment of the wasteland in medieval literature, the city-desert becomes the scene of damaged sexuality symbolic of life in need of revivification through ritual. The theme of sterility is in this way carried over from the vacant lots of his juvenilia. In his response to *The Waste Land* in 1932, F. R. Leavis wrote of Eliot's London that: 'sex here is sterile, breeding not life and fulfillment but disgust, accidia, and unanswerable questions'.[86] Leavis's reading is part of an initial critical reception that saw the poem's symbolism of fertility and infertility as key to the entire text. His use of the term 'accidia' – a Latin form of the Greek *akēdeia*, meaning boredom, apathy or indifference and identified by the Desert Fathers with the deadly sin of sloth – positions Eliot as a kind of modern-day ascetic saint. For Leavis and others, Eliot's adaptation of the Thebaid of St Anthony and the 'waste londe' or 'terre gaste' of Arthurian romance to the twentieth-century city amounted to a total moral judgement on modernity that had great spiritual and cultural authority attached to it. Subsequent critics have argued that the symbolism of infertility may be related to Eliot's putative homosexuality while others have maintained that it demonstrates a concern with eugenics, suggesting that the poem's central anxiety is not over infertility per se but forms of life that are dangerously fertile.[87] The modern city may destroy life *or* breed it in the wrong forms. Eliot's city-desert is, like Goldsmith's deserted village, a topos where death and decay may coexist various kinds of unwholesome, excessive or unwanted life.

Despite the disgust it manifests for the damaged life of the 'Unreal City' – its polluted river and deadening routines, its squalor and neuroses – *The Waste Land* nevertheless displays a remarkable textual exuberance and playfulness, particularly in its use of incantation, song and the Poundian musical phrase. This is often intermixed with Eliot's fascination for seediness and filth of all kinds. In section III, Mrs Porter and her daughter, who 'wash their feet in soda water', are figures from a ribald song about a Cairo brothel renowned for causing an outbreak of venereal disease among Australian troops on their way to Gallipoli during the First World War.[88] Pound, in a manifesto for Imagist poetry from 1912, famously insisted on the importance for modern poets of '[composing] in the sequence of the musical phrase, not in sequence of a metronome', in order to break the stranglehold of iambic pentameter.[89] In *The Waste Land*, however, the musical phrase becomes important for other reasons also: it becomes the *temporal form* by which the fragments of ancient and modern, high and low culture are sifted and salvaged like pieces of rubbish. The aesthetic fascination for the vacant lot that characterised Eliot's earliest poetry becomes a fascination for textual waste. As Tim Armstrong observes in relation to the poem's collaborative composition, Eliot 'takes pleasure in the production of waste', while Pound's excisions in the drafting process removed much material that the latter found 'fascinatingly excremental'.[90] The key point is how the refrains of the poem manage to hold everything together in an impersonal, deterritorialised consciousness. The poem's many motifs, ditties and jingles – from nursery rhymes and Wager's *Ring* to the closing Sanskrit mantra of 'Shantih shantih shantih' – mark out temporalities of ruination and retrieval. In September 1921, Eliot wrote of how Stravinsky's ballet *The Rite of Spring* brought together ancient and modern experience:

> [the music] did seem to transform the rhythm of the steppes into the scream of the motor horn, the rattle of machinery, the grind of wheels, the beating of iron and steel, the roar of the underground railway, and the other barbaric cries of modern life; and to transform these despairing noises into music.[91]

The transformation of noise into music, of the rattle and grind of mechanised life into the rhythms of poetry, is the modern version of the ancient vegetation ceremonies and fertility rituals that are the basis of both Stravinsky's ballet and Eliot's poem.[92]

But while Eliot's complex system of intertextuality might attempt to use the Western canon to revitalise modern culture, this strategy also tends to question, if not undermine, any notion of the readability or usability of texts. Eliot acknowledges how his poem is composed of 'fragments I have shored against my ruins', but these fragments are themselves the products of a historical process of ruination against which the poem would shore them, ruins shored against ruin.[93] Eliot's 'broken images' occupy a waste-time – or 'junk time', as William S. Burroughs would term it – not a use-time, and thus all of literature becomes readable only by being itself a wasteland of redundant signification. *Noise is what renders the signal intelligible*, an idea Pynchon will take up in grand historical style. William Viney argues that the very temporal problem of waste, the ways in which waste suggests a squandering or exhaustion of usable time, is central both to Eliot's poem and what it does to our understanding of literature more generally:

> The waste the poem describes can be made to operate as a synecdoche for a wider interpretative problem, one that brings us beyond the specificity of *The Waste Land* and to the temporality of reading and engaging with literature at a more general level ... Whilst ... a phone book, an instruction manual, a newspaper report ... might be read under the denotative temporal conditions of use, in which expectations are driven by specific temporal ends, *The Waste Land* and its powers to contain multiple times, texts, places

and voices, to invite repeated readings none of which will bring the work of interpretation to a determinate end, means it is a text which withstands the organizational promise of use-time.[94]

Eliot's mass of intertextual fragments, given consistency through the refrain, are not so much shored against ruination as against the use-time that would submit them to a determinate readability. The poem thus stages a precarious redundancy of meaning by which the distinction between 'useful' signification and asignifying 'noise' must constantly be negotiated and renegotiated, and remains a shifting boundary. The poem often wilfully succumbs to a sheer musicality that draws close to the very 'despairing noise' it seeks to transform. The arrival of Sweeney, Eliot's crude, animalistic Irishman, at Mrs Porter's brothel is announced by 'The sound of horns and motors'.[95] Eliot's Sweeney may have been inspired by the Sweeney of the Middle Irish romance *Buile Suibhne*, which relates the story of a king transformed by a curse into a bird. Following a line from Verlaine's 'Parsifal', Eliot produces a stanza of apparent nonsense that references the Greek myth of Tereus:

Twit twit twit
Jug jug jug jug jug jug
So rudely forc'd.
Tereu[96]

In Ovid's *Metamorphoses*, Tereus raped his wife's sister Philomela and cut out her tongue. The gods subsequently turned Philomela into a nightingale, a migratory bird whose song Eliot now has us hear as the refrains of destructive sexuality and tormented speechlessness. The mechanised song of the modern primitive Sweeney blends, almost imperceptibly, with classical mythology. The lines echo parts from 'A Game of Chess', the previous section of the poem:

             the nightingale
Filled all the desert with inviolable voice
And still she cried, and still the world pursues,
"Jug Jug" to dirty ears.
And other withered stumps of time
Were told upon the walls; staring forms
Leaned out, leaning, hushing the room enclosed.
Footsteps shuffled on the stair.
Under the firelight, under the brush, her hair
Spread out in fiery points
Glowed into words, then would be savagely still.[97]

What the poem's refrains make heard, ultimately, is the silence of words burning out, being undone by their own use. What Eliot seems to decry as waste is, in fact, inextricable from the desert desire which initially charmed him via the sinister sterility of vacant lots and which, in his most famous poem, regards the whole Western canon from the vantage point of redundant signification.

LIBIDINAL GEOLOGY: D. H. LAWRENCE'S DESERT PHALLUS

In D. H. Lawrence's late novel *The Plumed Serpent* (1926), the arid landscapes of Mexico facilitate a mythopoetics of sexuality as a geological and cosmic force. The novel has been derided for its authoritarian politics, and even Lawrence's most ardent defenders have struggled with it. Nevertheless, it is the culmination of his search, begun in response to the First World War, for a vision of socio-political and libidinal renewal. My analysis here can be considered part of ongoing critical reappraisals of the book.[98] As with *The Waste Land*, the novel condenses concerns for place, placelessness, tradition and deracination into a confrontation with the desert as a spiritual terrain. While a lot of work has been done to excavate the sources of the novel's mix of pagan and Christian ideas,[99] what interests me here is how Lawrence's Blakean vision of apocalyptic sexuality is tied to the same kind of desert ordeal that so occupied Nietzsche and Eliot. Written during a phase of Lawrence's career that manifested a deep disillusionment with Europe, the novel sees the American continent as the site of rebirth. It was the New World, and Mexico in particular, that suggested to him his notion of the 'spirit of place', the idea that there existed a deep connection between the constitution of a people – or 'blood consciousness' to use the proper Lawrentian term – and their material environment.[100] If the spirit of the American continent is 'demonic', it is in large part because of the 'unappeased ghosts of the dead Indians' that haunt the restless consciousness of white America.[101] The desert dramatises a clash between rootedness and deracination, or place and placelessness. It is precisely the spirit of place – the connection to a homeland, an *oikos* – that modernity devastates, but it is notable that in *The Plumed Serpent* the desert comes to serve both as a symbol of this loss and as the terrain of a process of recovery.

Lawrence suggests a connection between the Earth and the libidinal energy of renewal. We may thus speak of a Lawrentian *libidinal geology* in which exhaustion and malaise intermix with fertility and virility. Lawrence's work in general is closely linked to Eliot's, who nevertheless – and probably out of a discomfort the proximity caused him – described Lawrence as 'a very sick man indeed'.[102] Both writers were deeply sceptical of the value of progress and other liberal beliefs and were key exponents of literary primitivism. Eliot, however, dismissed Lawrence's depictions of 'capering redskins' in the latter's travel book *Mornings in Mexico* (1927) as themselves symptomatic of modernity's spiritual degeneration.[103] Eliot's Sweeney is portrayed as bestial in order to suggest how close the average modern city dweller is to 'primitive man'. The primitive is, in other words, the symptom and not the cure of the modern sexual malaise. In his discussion of Eliot's unfinished verse drama *Sweeney Agonistes* (1926–7), Robert Crawford remarks that

> for Lawrence, the savage world was authentic and admirable. For Eliot in 1925 it was horribly inescapable. Primitive sexual rituals pursue Sweeney and Doris into the heart of London, pursue them like Furies. What, for Lawrence, was to be embraced, was for Eliot a torment. But it was a torment which had to be seen and analysed. As Lawrence witch-doctored to the century's ills, Eliot too had his 'craving for ritual'.[104]

Lawrence recognised, every bit as much as Eliot did, that the only possible response to the twentieth-century wasteland and the devastations of war was a religious transformation of life. But while Eliot's craving for ritual led him from *The Golden Bough* to the rites of Anglicanism, for Lawrence the religious was inseparable from sexuality and its geocosmic depths. Life and sexuality, for Lawrence, come from the Earth. In *The Plumed Serpent*, this provides a temporal perspective beyond modernity and its specific dilemmas of place and placelessness. There is a strange unity of the organic, the architectural and the geological in the novel's landscapes of 'black, porous, absorptive lava rock' and decaying Spanish buildings.[105] The text's crude discussions of race and blood stem primarily from a concern to rediscover a living connection to place, although Lawrence is frequently dismayed by his own constructions of primitive rootedness. This also lies behind the novel's authoritarian vision of social and political order. Lawrence wishes to establish a mode of phallocratic rule in the desert as an answer to the European wasteland, but his relish for ritual, for the *refrains* of the desert ordeal, tends to undermine his own project.

Kate Leslie, Lawrence's protagonist, is a middle-aged Anglo-Irish woman of aristocratic stock who views the native Mexicans she encounters largely in terms of race, place and animality. She sees the indigenous Don Cipriano, one of the political leaders with whom she becomes sexually involved, as a creature born of the landscape itself:

> There was something undeveloped and intense in him, the intensity and the crudity of the semi-savage. She could well understand the potency of the snake upon the Aztec and Maya imagination. Something smooth, undeveloped, yet vital in this man suggested the heavy-ebbing blood of reptiles in

his veins. That was what it was, the heavy-ebbing blood of powerful reptiles, the dragon of Mexico.[106]

Kate becomes engaged in the authoritarian political movement led by Cipriano and the racially European Don Ramón, who uses the country's pre-colonial and pre-Christian past to organise a revolt against the government and the church. The narrative culminates in her marriage to Cipriano – who comes to represent 'the ancient phallic mystery, the ancient god-devil of the male Pan'[107] – according to Ramón's vision of a racial and sexual trinity in which the opposites of man and woman, coloniser and colonised meet in the mythic symbol of Quetzalcoatl.

For all her racism and aristocratic haughtiness, Kate is fascinated by what she sees as the cruelty and coldly unsentimental nature of her surroundings and their violent colonial past. She is gradually drawn into a sympathy with the landscape and its people:

> Those pale-faced Mexicans of the Capital, politicians, artists, professionals, and business people, they did not interest her. Neither did the hacendados and the ranch-owners, in their tight trousers and weak, soft sensuality, pale victims of their own emotional undiscipline. Mexico still meant the mass of silent peons, to her. And she thought of them again, these silent, stiff-backed men, driving their strings of asses along the country roads, in the dust of Mexico's infinite dryness, past broken walls, broken houses, broken *haciendas*, along the endless desolation left by the revolutions.[108]

Everywhere she goes, Kate feels the spaces about her, whether natural or manmade, as deserted, worn-out and penetrated with an uncanny emptiness: 'The street was stony, uneven, vacuous, sterile. The stones seemed dead, the town seemed made of dead stone.'[109] But she also brings the European wasteland with her: 'Never had she been so alone, and so inert, and so utterly without desire; plunged in a wan indifference, like death. Never had she passed her days so blindly, so unknowingly, in stretches of nothingness.'[110] Kate's inner wasteland merges and becomes continuous with the Mexican landscape. The narrative thus stages *a meeting of deserts*, and this is how Lawrence locates the possibility of renewal through an elaborate ritual symbolism drawn from the Toltec and Aztec gods of pre-Columbian Mexico.

The native populace, the 'silent peons', are portrayed in terms of a geolibidinal potency, a 'blood consciousness' expressive of the dynamisms of life and death and connected to the land's volcanic history. The novel's repeated references to 'the old, heavy, resistant Indian blood' and the 'lava-rock Indian nature' of the country's agricultural poor is suggestive less of colonialism or racism than of Lawrence's attempts to elaborate a Nietzschean geophilosophy. *Zarathustra* described the 'spirit of gravity' as the heaviness of nihilism. Nietzsche's symbolism linked this to the beast of burden that is driven into the desert in search of freedom.[111] Lawrence suggests that America may be 'the great death-continent', the place of a great downward-pulling drift towards automatism, repetition and Godlessness.[112] But Lawrence's desert, like Nietzsche's, is a place of oppositions. It is one of the abiding curiosities of the novel that Mexico appears, at one and the same time, a place of deep roots – as Ramón puts it, 'all that matters to me are the roots that reach down beyond all destruction'[113] – and extreme rootlessness. The book manifests an anxiety with modern placelessness that is played out as an anxiety over industrialised masses:

> Wherever the iron rails run, and passengers are hauled back and forth in railway coaches, there the spirit of rootlessness, of transitoriness, of first and second class in separate compartments, of envy and malice, and of iron and demonish panting engines, seems to bring forth the logical children of materialism, the bolshevists.[114]

The masses suggest both an ancient, geological and deeply rooted heaviness *and* a modern, mechanised deterritorialisation.

Lawrence's desert is where the people appear unformed or half-formed, not yet a constituency but a force that is part animal, part geological. Kate's late husband, we should note, was a leader in the Irish War of Independence: 'in England, in Ireland, during the war and the revolution she had known *spiritual* fear. The ghastly fear of the rabble'.[115] As Ramón reminds her, 'Mexico is another Ireland'.[116] Ultimately, however, and despite his anxieties over the masses, Lawrence emphasises the notion of *people* over notions of race or nationality, but this is precisely a *people to come*, a virtual potentiality of the desert as a smooth space. 'People' remains an ambiguous category because it expresses something less than race, nation, class or culture, but also something more fundamental than these. Kate sees the Mexican peasantry not as a people in the modern constitutional sense but as a 'people not quite created', as manifesting a hostility or 'insolence' to all created things and even a diabolical hostility to creation itself.[117] The sense of an unrealised or dormant potentiality within this people to come both attracts and horrifies her.

The militaristic dictatorship of the Quetzalcoatl movement, as led by Ramón and Cipriano, is Lawrence's attempt to answer the problems of colonialism and of Western society more generally. *The Plumed Serpent* is the most controversial of what are often called Lawrence's late 'leadership' novels, in which he grappled with social and political questions through fantasies of masculine power. These novels have led to Lawrence being branded a fascist, despite his recorded opposition to the regimes of Mussolini and Hitler.[118] Kate Millett's *Sexual Politics* (1970) famously scorned the book for its phallocentrism: '*The Plumed Serpent* records that moment when Lawrence was led to the ultimate ingenuity of inventing a religion, even a liturgy, of male supremacy. . . . his totemic penis is alpha and omega, the word improved into flesh.'[119] Such condemnation oversimplifies what is, in truth, an ambiguous and complex text. Its undeniable phallocentrism is counterbalanced throughout by the female narrative focus. Kate offers a consistently dissenting voice to the male characters' overblown and often absurd rhetoric, and the novel ends without making it clear whether she does ultimately submit to her marriage with Cipriano or to her role within the Quetzalcoatl trinity.

His inability to resolve these ambiguities is what led Lawrence to cast doubt on the novel's success. But to understand the text's complexities it is necessary for us to go beyond his ostensible aims. Deleuze's analysis of Lawrence can us help us here, even if he does not focus on *The Plumed Serpent* specifically. He argues that Lawrence's last major work, *Apocalypse* (1931), a study of the Book of Revelation and its links to pre-Christian traditions, demonstrates a Nietzschean suspicion of the 'collective soul' crying out for vengeance and judgement.[120] Lawrence's first encounter with the 'rabble' was, by his own account, during his Nonconformist upbringing in the coal-mining town of Eastwood, Nottinghamshire: 'the huge denunciation of kings and Rulers, and of the whore that sitteth on the waters, is entirely sympathetic to a Tuesday evening congregation of colliers and colliers' wives, on a black winter night, in the great barn-like Pentecost chapel'.[121] Lawrence, drawing on the work of the occultist Frederick Carter, suggests that the Revelation of John synthesised a very ancient (Assyrian and Chaldean) paganism with the Judaic conception of a chosen people and that this appealed to a working-class desire for justice and recompense: 'from being bottom dogs they are going to be top dogs: in Heaven'.[122] The spirit of revenge, hatred of power and sense of a final setting to rights is, he says, found nowhere else in the Gospels and it is primarily Revelation that furnishes Christianity with its nihilistic exaltation of the weak and poor. Deleuze argues that if Lawrence remained fascinated by John's Apocalypse right up until the end of his life, it is because of the power of its symbols – its horsemen, coruscating dragon, and cosmic woman clothed in the sun – even if these are overlaid by Judeo-Christian ideas. Christianity reactivates the pagan symbolic cosmos only to suppress it once and for all through an allegory of divine judgement. It is this symbolism, surviving into the Christian spirit of nihilism, that Deleuze rightly identifies as Lawrence's real interest:

> The symbol is a concrete cosmic force [*puissance*]. Popular consciousness, even in the Apocalypse, retains a certain sense of the symbol while adoring brute Power [*pouvoir*]. ... The symbol is the thought of flows, in contrast to the intellectual and linear process of allegorical thought.[123]

There is a vitalism or processual force to symbols that Lawrence recognises in pagan cosmology.

What struck the young Lawrence in particular in those barn-like chapels were the rhythms and sounds, far more than the meaning, of the clergymen's speech:

> the sound of Revelation had registered in me early, and I was as used to "I was in the Spirit on the Lord's day, and heard behind me a great voice, as of a trumpet, saying: I am the Alpha and the Omega" – as I was to a nursery rhyme like Little Bo-Peep![124]

In *The Plumed Serpent*, Lawrence has Don Ramón, much like the preachers of his childhood, evoke the potency of the Quetzalcoatl religion less through meaning or allegory than through the rhythms of its dances, liturgies and hymns as witnessed by Kate in scenes that take up many pages of the text. The Quetzalcoatl movement spreads through the country as a series of performances, recitals and refrains that suggest a pagan overcoming of Christianity:

> Jesus the Crucified
> Sleeps in the healing waters
> The long sleep.
> Sleep, sleep, my brother, sleep.
>
> My bride between the seas
> Is combing her dark hair,
> Saying to herself: Quetzalcoatl.[125]

One character tells Kate, early in the narrative: 'Ah, the *names* of the gods! Don't you think the *names* are like seeds, so full of magic, of the unexplored magic? *Huitzilopochtli!* – how wonderful! And *Tlaloc!* . . . I believe in the fertility of sound.'.[126] It is Lawrence's desert refrains that ultimately inspire Kate with a sense of life rekindled and thus convince her to stay in Mexico. But Lawrence also suggests a renewal is only possible through a prior exhaustion of Christian ritual. As Kate at one point thinks to herself: 'Curious, the old gentle ceremonials of Europe, how trashy they seem in Mexico, just a cheap sort of charade.'[127] The religion of the colonisers discovers in Mexico an exhaustion that purges it of its allegorical meaning, that renders it so much waste, before being transformed by a new rhythm that marks out the path of its overcoming.

How, then, do we explain the novel's hesitations, the sense that Lawrence is appalled by his own vision of a people to come? His accounts of Native American culture can be compared to the work of Mary Austin, an author renowned for her writings on the desert of the southwest. *The American Rhythm* (1923), a translation – or what she called a 'reexpression' – of Native American songs and chants was a likely source for Lawrence since he met Austin in New Mexico in 1924, the year he started work on *The Plumed Serpent*. It is interesting to note the difference between their respective accounts. In the essays collected in *Mornings in Mexico*, he described the native rituals he observed – such as the Spring corn dance of the Pueblo Indians and the Hopi snake dance – with a mixture of fascination, reverence and repulsion, rather like his heroine. What fascinates Lawrence is the ritual genesis of creative energy in a landscape of 'pale, dry, baked earth'.[128] But while he is transfixed by how the corn dance articulates links between word, gesture and life, he is aware that when such performances become entertainment for curious white audiences, a fatal intersection of 'white man' and 'Indian' has been reached.[129] While watching the performances, his scepticism of the collective soul, first felt in the religious services of his childhood, emerges. What really perturbs him is the *collective* nature of the ritual songs: 'the real Indian song is nonindividual, and without melody. Strange, clapping, crowing, gurgling sounds, in an unseizable subtle rhythm'.[130] His conception of phallic masculinity, on the other hand, is resolutely individual and heroic, and so cannot tolerate the pre-individual sources of the rhythmic potencies it draws on. In the pagan universe 'there is no One Spirit. There is no One God. There is no Creator. There is strictly no God at all: because all is alive'.[131] But without a Godhead there can be no model for phallic individualism to follow or overcome. The pagan universe is thus curiously listless, for Lawrence.

We can compare this to Austin's account of Native American ritual, which gives us an irreducibly collective notion of the refrain. She argues that rhythm governs organic behaviours and that consciousness itself is the product of rhythm:

> If we think of consciousness as Philosophy gives us increasing leave to do, as energetic in its nature, we have a concept of wave-like motion as the normal procedure, possibly the very mode of being itself. Moreover, the chemical changes which, as we now understand, mark the successive stages by which the emotions take possession of the organism, have each their own recognizable rhythmic modes.[132]

Affect and poetry, then, are inextricable from the environmental and ecological context in which rhythms come to operate upon the organism. Her notion of the 'landscape line' suggests a deep connection between organic demands, the social function of poetry, and the environment.¹³³ The work of Whitman and Sandburg forms a continuity with Native song and ritual, expressing a common American rhythm or territorial refrain. Crucially, rhythm has pre-human and collective origins:

> man first danced as the buck dances, and the pelican, from the recurrent seasonal urge, the intoxication of the sun coming up from the south and the new growth in the forest ... Thus he discovered that, by the making of rhythmic movements and noises, power comes. ... Man learned to resort to the dance when he felt helpless or fragmentary, when he felt dislocated in his universe ... Though there must have been a first singer, the first song, the earliest remembered and reiterated pattern of thumps and vocables was communal.¹³⁴

Lawrence can find no way to reconcile the communal and animal origins of the refrain with his commitment to a phallic masculinity which, for all its paganism, remains tied to conceptions of the One God as fertile creator. *The Plumed Serpent*, then, effectively reproduces what Lawrence denounces in *Apocalypse*. On the one hand, the novel suggests that the vital, libidinal, energetic and cosmic aspects of the symbol lost to modern consciousness may be retrieved through the territorial rhythms of ritual language, and that all attempts to impose meaning, interpretation or allegory on this symbolism are ultimately a life-denying intellectualisation. On the other hand, however, Lawrence overlays his fascination for pre-Christian life with his conception of a post-Christian one, and in this sense he allegorises his symbols according to a phallocratic political vision. He likewise identifies the vital power of the symbol with his conception of the people as an autochthonous potential energy, but this is counteracted by his suspicion of the 'rabble', which leads him to the authoritarianism of Ramón and Cipriano, for whom the Quetzalcoatl myth is an allegory of dictatorship.

ENTROPIC LANDSCAPES: PYNCHON, AUSTER AND THE IMMANENT ESCHATON

The wasteland aesthetics of 1920s modernism articulated anxieties about the semiotic constitution of space in an age dominated by the deterritorialising effects of war, technology and social upheaval. In Eliot and Lawrence's deployment of the desert, signs come to have a regenerative force that ties us to space in ways that are irreducibly political. Postmodernism breaks with modernist reterritorialisation and its various conceptions of rootedness and rebirth, and instead confronts space in terms of specifically late twentieth-century forms of devastation, deracination and eschatology. Catrin Gersdorf argues that the American desert has become a key figure of postmodernism in this way. European writers such as Banham and Baudrillard have seen in it a monument to the end of history, 'a vanishing point of European cultural, literary, and aesthetic traditions'.[135] If Europeans have seen the exhaustion of history and culture played out in American deserts, then American writers after the Second World War have used deserts and wastelands to come to terms with the historical legacies of European colonialism, war and genocide.

Thomas Pynchon's novel V. (1963) can be read as revisiting some of the problems of history that occupied Eliot and Lawrence but in ways that present the idea of some ultimate historical meaning or salvation in terms of a paranoiac's obsession with signs, codes and patterns. The search for order amid disorder becomes the fear of an inscrutable 'master cabal' operating beneath the surfaces of social and historical reality.[136] The novel charts Herbert Stencil's obsession with the initial 'V.', which recurs in his late father's files in connection to a mysterious woman who takes on difference guises throughout the narrative. While Stencil sometimes fears that his search for V. may be nothing more than a scholarly exercise, 'an adventure of the mind, in the tradition of *The Golden Bough* or *The White Goddess*', he also feels it to be 'an obsolete, or bizarre, or forbidden form of sexual delight'.[137] Stencil compares himself with the American historian Henry Adams, referring to himself throughout in the third person as the latter does in his famous autobiography. Stencil's search for V. provides us with a chronology of events stretching from 1898 to 1943, often reconstructed by Stencil from unreliable second- and third-hand accounts. The narrative's central anxiety is over whether the repeating semiotic patterns, those refrains by which history and our sense of the world are composed, are anything more than desires or projections, stencilled like signs on the surface of an indifferent reality.

While the novel presents everything through the obsession with V., Pynchon's protagonist is not Stencil but Benny Profane, a discharged sailor and self-proclaimed 'human yo-yo' whose picaresque drift through a landscape of bars, jazz clubs, slums and bohemian apartments eventually intersects with Stencil's quest in New York in 1957. The book's presiding image is the street as an abstract topos, a nomadic continuum traversed by Profane and portrayed in the book's opening pages as 'receding in an asymmetric V to the east where it's dark and there are no more bars'.[138] It is thus through Profane the human yoyo and not Stencil the historiographer that we first glimpse the mysterious V-structure. Stencil's search leads him through a number of diverse geographies, but V. is generally linked to wastelands of various kinds: the 'twin wastes' of the Libyan and Arabian deserts as seen through the eyes of a Cairo cab driver; the barren coastline of southwest Africa during its bloody German colonisation; the devastated streets of Second World War Malta; the New York sewers where Profane hunts albino alligators; and a mythical subterranean land called Vheissu located in the South Pole which, beneath its iridescent surface, conceals a terrifying void. Wherever V. goes there is an associated voiding of meaningful space.

Tony Tanner suggests that Pynchon shares with Burroughs, Norman Mailer and other American writers of his day a fear of life's entropic descent into uniformity and malleability, into something 'more like plastic than the Nature we know', as Mailer once put it.[139] This is demonstrated in Pynchon's novel by the fact that the woman known as the Lady V. – encountered variously as Victoria Wren, Veronica Manganese and Vera Meroving – succumbs to a process of gradual mechanisation, her body parts replaced with mechanical limbs and organs. In the guise of a character named 'the Bad Priest' she is eventually disassembled by children in a ruined street. But the inanimate is something that Pynchon consistently associates with landscapes more than anything else. Profane is haunted by the environmental uncanny of a stone quarry, the empty deck of a ship, an ocean covered in snow: 'Profane was afraid of land or seascapes like this, where nothing else lived but himself. It seemed he was always walking into one: turn a corner in the street, open a door to a weather-deck and there he'd be, in alien country'.[140] The fear of alien country is, of course, something deeply embedded in the American colonial experience, but Pynchon combines this with a postwar fear of entropy. The encroachment of the inanimate should not be identified solely with a critique of mechanisation or technology of the kind we have already seen in Eliot and Lawrence. For Pynchon, technology is only the expression of a tendency *already in life*. As Stencil himself half-admits, the V-structure symbolises a libidinal energy projected outward into a space that we attempt to render meaningful and habitable, to *territorialise*. The inanimate landscapes haunting Profane are the persistence of deterritorialised space. V., then, is a deterritorialising refrain, a vector of semiotic entropy.

Pynchon's most important entropic landscapes in *V.* are the deserts of colonial Africa. In one of the historical scenes that Stencil conjures up from his father's journals, a cab driver named Gebrail in *fin de siècle* Egypt describes his struggle against a growing desert: 'Not a fellah, but he does own some land. Did own. From a boy, he has repaired the wall, mortared, carried stone heavy as he, lifted, set in place. Still the desert comes. ... Soon, nothing. Soon only the desert.'[141] Bitterly, he observes that he shares his name with the angel who dictated the Koran to Mohammed and that it sounds like 'gebel', an Arabic word meaning desert. The Logos amounts to eschatology without salvation: 'the desert's angel had hidden all the trumpets beneath the sand. The desert was prophecy enough of the Last Day'.[142] In another section, a German scientist named Mondaugen studying atmospheric radio disturbances in the Kalahari becomes part of a European enclave, led by Foppl, holding out against the Herero uprising of 1922. Foppl's plantation becomes host to a 'siege party', 'a seemingly eternal Fasching' or hedonistic carnival lasting several months.[143] Mondaugen is approached by another German, named Weissmann, who asks him if he has ever heard about D'Annunzio, Mussolini or Hitler. Hugh Godolphin, the English explorer who 'discovered' the mythical Vheissu, is also at Foppl's, as is a mysterious woman named Vera Meroving who tells Godolphin: 'this siege. It's Vheissu. It's finally happened'.[144] This section of the book is important because it draws together different kinds of entropy: the atmospheric disturbances picked up by Mondaugen's radio antennae as 'whistlers' and other kinds of noise from the Earth's magnetic field, the Kalahari wastelands that surround Foppl's plantation, the fatalistic debauchery of the party itself, and the sense of a consuming void unleashed upon the world by the forces of twentieth-century history.

The section recounts some of Foppl's memories of his role in the extermination of the Herero and other native populations of German Südwest Africa: 'the barren islets off Luderitzbucht were natural concentration camps. Walking among huddled forms in the evening, distributing blankets, food and occasional kisses from the sjambok, you felt like the father colonial policy wanted you to be'.[145] Pynchon here suggests that German colonialism was a precursor of the Holocaust, but he would also have us read German actions in Africa as representative of a more general tendency of European expansion. In a letter to his editor from 1969 Pynchon writes:

> the number done on the Herero head by the Germans is the same number done on the American Indian head by our own colonists ... the imposition of a culture valuing analysis and differentiation on a culture that valued unity and integration. ... Contrast the shape of a Herero village with the Cartesian grid system layout in Windhoek or Swakopmund, read Lewis Mumford or talk to someone in the city planning department here. The physical shape of a city is an infallible due to where the people who built it are at. It has to do with our deepest responses to change, death, being human. ... What went on back in Südwest is archtypical [sic] of every clash between the west and non-west.[146]

The V-structure, then, is a way of understanding the formation of the modern world in terms of a violent globalisation of the Western mind, especially the Western metaphysics of space. Striation as a means of controlling and ordering space as *polis* culminates in a devastation that ties animate and inanimate together into a shared destiny whose precise nature remains an inscrutable pattern in the noise of history.

The significance of the letter V. can be traced to *The Education of Henry Adams* (1907), in particular a chapter titled 'The Dynamo and the Virgin' in which Adams, standing awestruck in a room full of dynamos at the Great Exhibition of 1900, described sexuality, religion and technology as key forces of history:

> the force of the Virgin was still felt at Lourdes, and seemed to be as potent as X-rays; but in America neither Venus nor Virgin ever had value as force – at most as sentiment. No American had ever been truly afraid of either ... In any previous age, sex was strength. Neither art nor beauty was needed. Everyone, even among the Puritans, knew that neither Diana of Ephesians nor any of the Oriental goddesses was worshipped for her beauty. She was goddess because of her force; she was the animated dynamo; she was reproduction – the greatest and most mysterious of all energies; all she needed was to be fecund.[147]

Adams portrays the historian as one whose business it is 'to follow the track of the energy'.[148] But if history is energy, then it is always menaced by entropy, disorder and noise. Elsewhere, Adams urges on historians an awareness of the second law of thermodynamics: 'If the entire universe, in every variety of active energy, organic and inorganic, human or divine, is to be treated as clock-work that is running down, society can hardly go on ignoring the fact forever.'[149] The twentieth century ushers in an age whose driver is nothing transcendent, neither Venus nor Virgin, but the dissipation of energy immanent to all force.

Pynchon combines Adams's pessimism with the work of Norbert Wiener, founder of cybernetics, who suggested that entropy affects communications systems.[150] If matter tends universally towards disorder, chaos and sameness, then something similar happens with respect to the signal-to-noise ratio in communications circuits. This is the key concern of Pynchon's second novel *The Crying of Lot 49* (1965), but a humorous episode from his short story 'Entropy' (1960) illustrates the point:

> 'Noise screws up your signal, makes for disorganization in the circuit.'
> Meatball shuffled around. 'Well, now, Saul,' he muttered, 'you're sort of, I don't know, expecting a lot from people. I mean, you know. What it is is, most of the things we say, I guess, are mostly noise.'
> 'Ha! Half of what you just said, for example.'[151]

The party at which this conversation takes place features an experimental jazz quartet that attempts to play a form of music without sound, while in a neighbouring apartment a couple named Callisto and Aubade maintain a jungle hothouse as a hermetically sealed 'enclave of regularity in the city's chaos'.[152] Aubade perceives everything about her in terms of music and discordancy, 'that precious signal-to-noise ratio, whose delicate balance required every calorie of her strength'.[153] For Pynchon's characters, entropic decline is an existential ordeal in which communication is often futile, while small pockets of order are often manifested by music. Pynchon intersperses his narratives with bawdy songs and verses from sea shanties to rock lyrics and nursery rhymes, as if to suggest that even noise, like Mondaugen's whistling radio disturbances, can be regarded as refrains. The influence of Eliot, meanwhile, is sometimes quite consciously demonstrated, especially in Pynchon's early stories. Levine in 'The Small Rain' is a US army communications officer and self-described 'Wandering Jew' who joins an operation to retrieve dead bodies from a swamp in Louisiana following a hurricane. In the closing lines of the story, after stating his intention to leave the military, Levine quotes from *The Waste Land*: '"Rain is pretty weird that way," he said. "It can stir dull roots; it can rip them up, wash them away".'[154] The reference suggests how modernist aesthetics of wasteland are transformed decisively in the postwar context. Whereas for Eliot deracination signals decline, for Pynchon it creates demand for new nomadic subject positions. While entropy suggests a descent into the plastic uniformity of late capitalism, it also demands new subjective modes capable of negotiating decoded, smooth spaces of all kinds.

Paul Auster, whose minimalism contrasts sharply with the maximalism of Pynchon, likewise uses deserts and wastelands to understand questions of writing and history. His work frequently touches on Jewish identity, often by combining writing with evocations of aleatory or errant movement. While most famous for his novels, Auster's poetry, written early in his career, demonstrates the major concerns of his subsequent work. In his extraordinary prose poem *White Spaces* (1979) – a key text for understanding his transition from poetry to fiction – he develops a conception of writing as conduct in an attenuated gestural space:

> I want these words to vanish, so to speak, into the silence they came from, and for nothing to remain but a memory of their presence, a token of the fact that they were once here and are no longer and that during their brief life they seemed not so much to be saying any particular thing as to be the thing that was happening at the same time a certain body was moving in a certain space.[155]

Writing is the trace of a moving body, an 'alphabet of desire'.[156] The space of writing is a blank or white space, a desert into which everything disappears, including the words that transcribe this disappearance. And yet this abyss of silence, emptiness and contingent corporeality in which language fails indicates something redemptive: 'it is sometimes necessary not to name the thing we are talking about. The invisible God of the Hebrews, for example, had an unpronounceable name'.[157] As Josh Cohen explains, in Judaic mystic traditions a 'textual dynamic' emerged 'wherein the word's impoverishment, its failure to make present its object, is also the very source of plenitude, its availability to ceaseless interpretation and reinterpretation'.[158] The Jewish biblical scholar and philosopher André Neher writes that the Logos of Genesis cannot ultimately be detached from the 'pro-Logos', the silence before creation and before the Word. Language is joined to silence, then, as being is to nothingness.[159] Whereas Pynchon's characters often find themselves trapped in a web of signs without transcendent meaning, like Stencil, or confronting entropy in asignifying immanence, like Profane, Auster is here suggesting an *immanent failure of signification* to reach transcendence. This failure indicates a devastated ground of words and gestures. With the Holocaust, the failure of language to grasp the indescribable becomes a theological question and a historical one, but in the process, writing becomes a break with history and with the world. Jewish writing after the Holocaust is what Cohen calls a 'deserted writing – a writing of the errancy of the desert, of the desertion of God and of meaning'.[160]

It is important to note the crucial influence on Auster of not only Beckett and Kafka but also Blanchot (whose work Auster has translated into English) and the Egyptian Jewish writer Edmond Jabès, author of uncategorisable works of prose poetry combining fiction and commentary in which the desert features as a way of articulating the links between writing, exile and Judaism.[161] In an interview conducted by Auster, Jabès explains the fragmentary nature of his own work in terms of the white spaces of the page: 'Our reading takes place in the very whiteness between the words, for this whiteness reminds us of the much greater space in which the word evolves.'[162] The written word implies a space of errant movement to which writing commits us. For Auster, the central question of Jabès's work is 'how to speak about what cannot be spoken. The question is the Jewish Holocaust, but it is also the question of literature itself'.[163]

Auster's second novel, *In the Country of Last Things* (1987), is written in the form of a letter telling the story of a journalist named Anna Blume and her experiences in an unnamed devastated city. The narrative initially reads like a science fiction dystopia but is suggestive of the bombed cities of the Second World War, the Warsaw Ghetto and the concentration camps: 'There are people so thin, she wrote, they are sometimes blown away. ... It is also possible to be so good at not eating that eventually you can eat nothing at all.'[164] The urban wasteland becomes a matter of sheer survival, but Anna's letter also intimates that devastation may contain some elements of a liberating exiguousness:

> you can survive only if nothing is necessary to you. Without warning, you must be able to change, to drop what you are doing, to reverse. ... The essential thing is not to become inured. For habits are deadly. Even if it is for the hundredth time, you must encounter each thing as if you have never known it before. No matter how many times, it must always be the first time.[165]

The narrative suggests an overcoming of the logic of scarcity through a heightened consciousness of things and their potentialities: 'utter despair can exist side by side with the most dazzling invention; entropy and efflorescence merge. ... Scarcity bends your mind towards novel solutions'.[166] Out of the entropic tendency comes a principle of newness:

> At a certain point, things disintegrate into muck, or dust, or scraps, and what you have is something new, some particle or agglomeration of matter that cannot be identified. It is a clump, a mote, a fragment of the world that has no place: a cipher of it-ness.[167]

The it-ness of a thing is revealed when it has no place. In this way, entropy seems to overcome itself through self-signification. Anna's struggle to survive becomes indistinguishable from her struggle to write: 'the words come only when I think I won't be able to find them anymore, at the moment I despair of ever bringing them out again'.[168] The devastation of language provides an opening to language. As the narrative progresses, the identity of writing and silence is linked explicitly to Judaism. Anna finds herself at a library where a man named Sam Farr is writing a book documenting the experiences and memories of the few remaining Jews in the city. The eschatological tenor of the novel's title is underscored when a rabbi at the library tells Anna: 'every Jew ... believes that he belongs to the last generation of Jews. We are always at the end, always standing on the brink of the last moment, and why should we expect things to be any different now?'.[169] To record the experience of the Jews is to record history itself as that which is always coming to an end but always renewing itself by resisting the closure of an end. The eschaton is thus an end *immanent to historical experience*, not a transcendent termination.

Nevertheless, the immanent eschaton still suggests a break with the world and with the sense of continuity normally attributed to history. As I argue in the next chapter, capitalist modernity involves a historical process by which a worldless space is encountered as the ground of a beginning-again. To this extent, the temporality of modernity as such is eschatological since it is always 'the last moment', but this is a moment modernity must absorb as part of its own ongoing self-narration. The theme of the desert island comes to play a central role in how capitalism, as world-system or world-interior, reckons with spatial alterity. A particular form of wasteland aesthetics – the island as bare, wild, solitary, isolated or worldless – becomes a central component of global capitalism's environmental imaginary.

NOTES

1. On the relationship between the local and global, I take the position articulated by Ursula K. Heise:

    the environmentalist emphasis on restoring individuals' sense of place, while it might function as one useful tool among others for environmentally oriented arguments, becomes a visionary dead end if it is understood as a founding ideological principle or a principal didactic means of guiding individuals and communities back to nature. Rather than focusing on the recuperation of a sense of place, environmentalism needs to foster an understanding of how a wide variety of both natural and cultural places and processes are connected and shape each other around the world, and how human impact affects and changes this connectedness. (*Sense of Place and Sense of Planet*, p. 21)

    The sense of place is not abolished, but does not figure as a founding principle. Povinelli likewise writes that an emphasis on the 'here' of the local must be balanced against flows and disruptions of global extent:

    The global nature of climate change, capital, toxicity, and discursivity immediately demands we look elsewhere than where we are standing. We have to follow the flows of the toxic industries whose by-products seep into foods, forests, and aquifers, and visit the viral transit lounges that join species through disease vectors. As we stretch the local across these seeping transits we need not scale up to the Human or the global, but we cannot remain in the local. We can only remain *hereish*. (*Geontologies*, p. 13)

    To think devastation, Povinelli seems to be saying, requires that we think the dislocation from the 'here' that the global entails. At the same time, we should take seriously Latour's contention that the poles of local and

global as we have understood them are now obsolete and need to be rethought entirely (*Down to Earth*, p. 33).
2. Heidegger, 'Letter on Humanism', pp. 222–3.
3. Heidegger, 'What are Poets For?', in *Poetry, Language, Thought*, p. 138.
4. Bate, *The Song of the Earth*, p. 262.
5. On the links between Heidegger, National Socialism and ecology, see Bambach, *Heidegger's Roots*. For a polemical argument against Heidegger's role for ecocriticism, see Greg Garrard's article, 'Heidegger Nazism Ecocriticism'.
6. Bate, *The Song of the Earth*, p. 268.
7. Haraway, *Staying with the Trouble*, p. 100.
8. For an analysis of Deleuze and Heidegger's relationship to Uexküll, see Brett Buchanan, *Onto-Ethologies*.
9. Deleuze and Guattari, *A Thousand Plateaus*, p. 316.
10. Sloterdijk, *In the World Interior of Capital*, p. 12.
11. Morton, *Ecology without Nature*, pp. 31–2.
12. Morton, *Being Ecological*, p. 25.
13. Rigby, *Topographies of the Sacred*, p. 12
14. Ibid. p. 12.
15. Deleuze and Guattari, *A Thousand Plateaus*, p. 348. Gaston Bachelard's concept of rhythm (itself based on the work of Lúcio Alberto Pinheiro dos Santos) from *The Dialectic of Duration* informs the one Deleuze and Guattari are using in their concept of the refrain. Bachelard writes:

> Matter is not spread out in space and indifferent to time; it does not remain totally constant and totally inert in a uniform duration. Nor indeed does it live there like something that wears away and is dispersed. It is not just sensitive to rhythms but it exists, in the fullest sense of the term, on the level of rhythm. (p. 137)

16. Deleuze and Guattari, *A Thousand Plateaus*, p. 312.
17. McCormack, *Refrains for Moving Bodies*, p. 83.
18. Kleinherenbrink argues that, despite the examples Deleuze and Guattari give, the refrain is not primarily an aesthetic but a social and political category. He rightly points out that any engagement with the concept of territory that ignores the refrain is inadequate ('Territory and Ritornello', p. 209).
19. Deleuze and Guattari, *A Thousand Plateaus*, p. 314.
20. Uexküll, *A Foray into the Worlds of Animals and Humans*, p. 159.
21. Ibid. pp. 190–1.
22. Levinas, 'On Maurice Blanchot', in *Proper Names*, p. 136.
23. Deleuze and Guattari, *A Thousand Plateaus*, p. 339.
24. Ibid. p. 340.
25. Ibid. p. 325.
26. Blanchot, *The Book to Come*, p. 4.
27. Duffy, *Landscapes of the Sublime*, p. 135.

28. Ibid. p. 136.
29. Shelley, 'Ozymandias', in *The Major Works*, lines 10–11.
30. Bevis, *The Road to Egdon Heath*, p. 91.
31. Morton, *Shelley and the Revolution of Taste*, p. 225.
32. Gerry Canavan has observed similarities between 'Ozymandias' and Atwood's 'Time Capsule Found on the Dead Planet'. Both pieces use the desert to present a future that is also somehow a memory:

    > Atwood's blighted vision of a ruined world recalls – and transforms – Percy Bysshe Shelley's 1818 poem "Ozymandias" as an anticipatory memory of Earth's barren future. ... The apocalypse is ... transformed into a memory, an event that is yet to come but which has also somehow, paradoxically, already happened. ('Introduction: If This Goes On', pp. 11–12)

33. Barrow, *Travels into the Interior of Southern Africa*, Vol. 1, p. 37.
34. Le Vaillant, quoted in Duffy, *Landscapes of the Sublime*, p. 142.
35. Park, *Travels in the Interior of Africa*, pp. 130–1.
36. Burke, *A Philosophical Enquiry into the Origin of Our Ideas of the Sublime and Beautiful*, p. 114.
37. Duffy, *Landscapes of the Sublime*, p. 144.
38. Ezekiel 33: 29.
39. Chateaubriand, quoted in Said, *Orientalism*, p. 173.
40. Said, *Orientalism*, p. 173.
41. Ibid. pp. 193, 230.
42. Ibid. p. 115.
43. Shelley, *Hellas*, in *The Major Works*, lines 1008–11.
44. Wordsworth, *The Prelude*, in *William Wordsworth: The Major Works*, V, l. 78.
45. Auden, *The Enchafèd Flood*, pp. 40–1.
46. Lindqvist, *Desert Divers*, p. 49.
47. Fromentin, *Between Sea and Sahara*, pp. 146–7.
48. For a discussion of Ruskin's influence on Van Dyke, see Gersdorf, *The Poetics and Politics of the Desert*, p. 142.
49. Van Dyke, *The Desert*, p. xx.
50. Ibid. pp. 12–13.
51. Ibid. p. 13.
52. Ibid. p. 13.
53. As Peter Wild points out, Van Dyke's work marked an aesthetic transition in American writing about the desert. What had once been a backdrop to 'frightening theatre' became, following the defeat of the Apaches in the 1880s and the expansion of the railroads, a place suffused with a sense of the romantic. A lot of this was driven by dreams of wealth, but some of it was driven by the boredom that came with modern comforts. Where once it signified nothing but death and terror, the desert wilderness suddenly offered itself as a refuge from civilisation, a romantic

'balm' (*Desert Literature*, p. 10). We find this in writers from Van Dyke to Abbey to Terry Tempest Williams, but it is itself a product of the great Progressive Era project of 'reclamation' that rendered the American west and southwest habitable for European settlers. For an overview of the reclamation project, see Cassuto, *Dripping Dry*, pp. 9–28 and Marc Reisner's classic book *Cadillac Desert*.

54. Van Dyke, *The Desert*, p. 61.
55. Rigby, *Topographies of the Sacred*, p. 68.
56. Ibid. p. 65.
57. Williams, *The Country and the City*, p. 60.
58. Di Palma, *Wasteland*, p. 19.
59. Bunyan, *The Pilgrim's Progress*, pp. 61–2.
60. Debray, *God*, p. 44. For Debray, the desert plays a central role in Judaism and Christianity: 'God has the history of man begin in a verdant space, and He ends it in a holy city, Jerusalem. Between the two, He placed the desert, lest we lose track of Him' (p. 38).
61. Di Palma, *Wasteland*, pp. 16–17.
62. Ibid. p. 18.
63. Isaiah 58: 12.
64. Di Palma, *Wasteland*, pp. 21–2.
65. Bunyan, quoted in Hill, *The World Turned Upside Down*, p. 146.
66. Di Palma, *Wasteland*, p. 22.
67. Goldsmith, 'The Deserted Village', in *Poems and Plays*, lines 39–40.
68. Ibid. lines 283–6.
69. Ibid. line 302.
70. Williams, *The Country and the City*, p. 78.
71. Ibid. p. 79.
72. Bate, *The Song of the Earth*, p. 13.
73. Eliot became friends with Norbert Wiener, founder of the discipline of cybernetics, while a student at Oxford in 1914. Wiener's *The Human Use of Human Beings* (1950) was a key source for Pynchon's conceptions of entropy.
74. Deleuze and Guattari, *A Thousand Plateaus*, p. 10. As they explain in *Anti-Oedipus*:

> Desiring-machines are the following: formative machines, whose very misfirings are functional, and whose functioning is indiscernible from their formation; chronogeneous machines engaged in their own assembly (*montage*), operating by nonlocalizable intercommunications and dispersed localizations, bringing into play processes of temporalization, fragmented formations, and detached parts, with a surplus value of code, and where the whole is itself produced alongside the parts, as a part apart. (pp. 285–6)

In *A Thousand Plateaus*, they develop the concept in terms of the rhizome and inter-species becomings:

> Wasp and orchid, as heterogeneous elements, form a rhizome. It could be said that the orchid imitates the wasp, reproducing its image in a signifying fashion (mimesis, mimicry, lure, etc.). But this is true only on the level of the strata – a parallelism between two strata such that a plant organization on one imitates an animal organization on the other. At the same time, something else entirely is going on: not imitation at all but a capture of code, surplus value of code, an increase in valence, a veritable becoming, a becoming-wasp of the orchid and a becoming-orchid of the wasp. Each of these becomings brings about the deterritorialization of one term and the reterritorialization of the other; the two becomings interlink and form relays in a circulation of intensities pushing the deterritorialization ever further. (p. 10)

75. Eliot, *The Waste Land*, in *The Poems of T. S. Eliot, Volume 1*, I, lines 19–24.
76. Ibid. III, lines 173–9.
77. Yeats, 'The Second Coming', lines 12–13. I quote here from the original version of the poem Yeats published in *The Dial* in 1920 and which is reproduced in Rainey (ed.), *Modernism*, p. 308.
78. Whitworth, *Reading Modernist Poetry*, p. 39.
79. Eliot, 'The Idea of a Christian Society', in *Christianity and Culture*, pp. 48–9.
80. Raine, *T. S. Eliot*, p. 162.
81. Ibid. pp. 85–6.
82. Eliot, *After Strange Gods*, pp. 17–18.
83. For an example of this kind of approach, see Terblanche's book *T. S. Eliot, Poetry, and the Earth*.
84. Eliot, 'Second Caprice in North Cambridge', in *The Poems of T. S. Eliot, Volume 1*, lines 1–12.
85. Lyndall Gordon, quoted in Marsh, 'Hired Men and Hired Women', p. 131.
86. Leavis, *New Bearings in English Poetry*, p. 79.
87. Childs, *Modernism and Eugenics*, p. 123.
88. Ibid. p. 126.
89. Pound, 'A Retrospect', p. 3.
90. Armstrong, *Modernism, Technology, and the Body*, pp. 69–70.
91. Eliot, 'London Letter', p. 370.
92. Pound wrote in 1924 that 'music is the art most fit to express the fine quality of machines. Machines are now a part of life, it is proper that men should feel something about them; there would be something weak about art if it couldn't deal with this new content' (*Antheil and the Treatise on Harmony*, p. 53).
93. Eliot, *The Waste Land*, V, line 430.
94. Viney, *Waste*, p. 93.
95. Eliot, *The Waste Land*, III, line 198.

96. Ibid. III, lines 203–6.
97. Ibid. II, lines 100–10.
98. See for example Oh, *D. H. Lawrence's Border Crossing*.
99. See Vickery, '*The Plumed Serpent* and the Reviving God' and Humma, *Metaphor and Meaning in D.H. Lawrence's Later Novels*.
100. Lawrence, *Classic Studies in American Literature*, p. 17.
101. Ibid. pp. 42–3.
102. Eliot, *After Strange Gods*, p. 61.
103. Ibid. p. 60.
104. Crawford, *The Savage and the City in the Work of T. S. Eliot*, p. 178.
105. Lawrence, *The Plumed Serpent*, p. 27.
106. Ibid. p. 63.
107. Ibid. p. 309.
108. Ibid. p. 71.
109. Ibid. p. 84.
110. Ibid. pp. 304–5.
111. Nietzsche, *Thus Spoke Zarathustra*, p. 16.
112. Lawrence, *The Plumed Serpent*, p. 73.
113. Ibid. p. 76.
114. Ibid. p. 109.
115. Ibid. p. 133.
116. Ibid. p. 69.
117. Ibid. p. 73.
118. Frost, *Sex Drives*, p. 38.
119. Millett, *Sexual Politics*, p. 283.
120. Deleuze, *Essays Critical and Clinical*, p. 38.
121. Lawrence, *Apocalypse*, p. 62.
122. Ibid. p. 63.
123. Deleuze, *Essays Critical and Clinical*, pp. 48–9.
124. Lawrence, *Apocalypse*, p. 55.
125. Lawrence, *The Plumed Serpent*, p. 117.
126. Ibid. p. 57.
127. Ibid. p. 275.
128. Lawrence, *Mornings in Mexico*, p. 121.
129. Ibid. p. 102.
130. Ibid. p. 105.
131. Ibid. p. 140.
132. Austin, *The American Rhythm*, p. 5.
133. Ibid. p. 54.
134. Ibid. pp. 26–7.
135. Gersdorf, 'America/Deserta', p. 242.
136. Pynchon, *V.*, p. 226.
137. Ibid. p. 61.
138. Ibid. p. 10.
139. Mailer, quoted in Tanner, *City of Words*, p. 142.

140. Pynchon, *V.*, pp. 20–1.
141. Ibid. p. 82.
142. Ibid. p. 84.
143. Ibid. p. 231.
144. Ibid. p. 248.
145. Ibid. p. 267.
146. Pynchon, quoted in Seed, *The Fictional Labyrinths of Thomas Pynchon*, pp. 241–2.
147. Adams, *The Education of Henry Adams*, pp. 320–1.
148. Ibid. p. 325.
149. Adams, *The Degradation of the Democratic Dogma*, p. 261.
150. Weiner, *The Human Use of Human Beings*, p. 21.
151. Pynchon, 'Entropy', in *Slow Learner*, p. 91.
152. Ibid. p. 83.
153. Ibid. p. 92.
154. Pynchon, 'The Small Rain', in *Slow Learner*, p. 51.
155. Auster, 'White Spaces', in *Collected Poems*, p. 155.
156. Ibid. p. 156.
157. Ibid. p. 157.
158. Cohen, 'Desertions', pp. 94–5.
159. Neher, *The Exile of the Word*, pp. 61–3.
160. Cohen, 'Desertions', p. 96.
161. On Blanchot, Levinas and Jabès, see Mole, *Lévinas, Blanchot, Jabès*. For Auster's relationship to Blanchot specifically, see Arce, *Paul Auster and the Influence of Maurice Blanchot*.
162. Auster, *The Art of Hunger*, p. 163.
163. Ibid. p. 107.
164. Auster, *In the Country of Last Things*, p. 3.
165. Ibid. pp. 6–7.
166. Ibid. p. 29.
167. Ibid. pp. 35–6.
168. Ibid. p. 38.
169. Ibid. p. 112.

4. Desert Islands

THE NAUFRAGOCENE

Renaissance scholar Steve Mentz suggests that shipwreck narratives can be used to understand the historical break involved in the emergence of capitalist modernity as a global phenomenon or world-system with profound ecological ramifications:

> Shipwreck lurks at the metaphorical heart of the ecology of salt-water globalization. The global maritime networks of early modern European expansion have ancient roots but radically expanded after the fifteenth century. As worldwide blue-water trade routes became essential to European economies, the cultural resonance of voyaging changed.[1]

The breaking of ship against land comes to play a key role in how modernity narrates its own breaks and discontinuities as components of a *continuous* process of reproduction, rebeginning and rediscovery. One of the alternative names Mentz suggests for the Anthropocene is the 'Naufragocene', the Age of Shipwrecks.[2] But why should the shipwreck be given such prominence, and how did it change after the fifteenth century? The philosopher Hans Blumenberg compares ancient and modern figurations of shipwreck. In Hesiod, Lucretius and others, he writes, 'there is a frivolous, if not blasphemous, moment inherent in all human seafaring, on a par with an offense against the invulnerability of the earth, the law of *terra inviolata*'.[3] For the ancients, seafaring drives humanity to go beyond its natural needs, to transgress organic limits in a way that invites shipwreck as a moment of divine punishment. 'In complete contrast to this,' Blumenberg argues with reference to works by Voltaire and Fontenelle, 'it will be one of the fundamental ideas of the Enlightenment that shipwreck is the price that must be paid in order to avoid that complete calming of the sea winds that would make all worldly commerce impossible.'[4] The myth of Fortuna, goddess of the turbulent seas, drives the adventurer into the risky domain of commerce and becomes, on the island of Robinson Crusoe and those who followed him, the spirit of the Puritan work ethic, the modern secular myth par excellence.[5]

The desert island of the Robinson myth is a desert in the sense that it is the site both of a loss of the world and the production of various possible new ones. It is the geographical form by which catastrophe converges with possibility. Deleuze's utopian and eschatological notion of a people to come is a potentiality – a 'populous solitude' – embodied in the desert island as a zero point.[6] The desert island may be deserted or depopulated, but it poses the question of filling or populating space as an immediate and urgent problem for the castaway. This involves not just matters of social organisation and survival but aesthetic matters too, since the linking of body and environment is to a large extent aesthetic, a question of sensation and perception.[7] In this chapter, I look to the figure of the desert island as a component of the modern imaginary of space as zero point. The zero is not a distant origin but an immanent condition of modernity's historicity.[8] Modernity confronts its own spatiality as a potential catastrophe in which everything is reduced to a zero-intensity state, but by the same stroke, space becomes *absolutely accessible* to consciousness. Defoe's *Robinson Crusoe* (1719) is the text where ancient and early modern accounts of shipwreck give way to a new economic realism that is uniquely capitalist.[9] Robinson is the first great cultural figure to submit the risks of seafaring to a calculus of profit and loss. His 'Island of Desolation' comes to function as a body without organs on which the world and its striations are both lost and remade. To survive on his island, Robinson must calculate every expenditure of energy against every act of consumption in order to maintain what he calls his 'comfort', a distinctly bourgeois category.[10] The desert island is thus a privileged site for the emergence of a modern economic and ecological consciousness of energy, but this also entails an aesthetic awareness of space as deserted – as bare, uninhabited, uncultivated, unworlded. It is only through such a wasteland aesthetics that space can become the correlate of a solitary consciousness capable of mastering it.

In one of Deleuze's earliest texts, the 1953 essay 'Causes et raisons des îles désertes', translated as 'Desert Islands', we see the first intimations of his geophilosophical project. This piece focuses on the figure of the desert island and the mythological aspects of the Robinson Crusoe narrative. Deleuze begins by observing that scientists traditionally classify an island as either continental or oceanic. The former is connected to a continent from which it has separated by erosion or subsidence while the latter are created by coral reefs or, more usually, volcanic activity, as in the case of the Galápagos Archipelago. Darwin in *The Origin of Species* was the first to draw attention to the zoogeographic importance of oceanic islands by noting that they lacked indigenous terrestrial mammals and amphibians.[11] Deleuze's text follows from this Darwinian insight but argues that apart from its scientific significances the distinction between these two classes of islands 'is valuable because it confirms what the imagination already knew'.[12] In a condensed and enigmatic way, he explains that the two island classes suggest two ways of negotiating the 'profound opposition' or elemental 'strife' (*combat*) between the land and the sea. In the case of continental islands, we are reminded that the sea is on top of the land, that a deluge is always possible. Oceanic islands, on the contrary, demonstrate that all land has its genesis in an unfathomable depth deeper than the deepest ocean, a *volcanic* depth that is capable of surging upwards to create new land. Both types of island arrange a kind of *détente* between land and sea that is suggestive of the different ways in which terrestrial life negotiates the Earth's dynamisms of depth and surface. Consciousness may itself be seen as a negotiation of these dimensions, which is not only an evolutionary fact but something to which myth and literature often testify.

Coleridge once remarked of *Robinson Crusoe* and Robert Patlock's robinsonade *Peter Wilkins* (1751) that 'no continentalist' could have written them. These texts manifest what Coleridge called a 'desert island feeling'.[13] Robinson's loneliness, often felt by him to be divine punishment, is expressed by Coleridge's Ancient Mariner in terms of an environment bereft of God's presence: 'Alone on a wide wide sea: / So lonely 'twas, that God himself / Scarce seemed there to be'.[14] The desert island feeling suggests how space in its material, finite vastness remains haunted by a religious sense of desolation, of abandonment by God. Oceanic islands suggest something similar. Coming as they do from a volcanic depth inimical to life, they remind us that the Earth's elemental strife is fundamentally indifferent to the security of life's territories. As Deleuze wryly observes, we find nothing in this 'to reassure us'. Nevertheless – and this is his key point – 'that an island is deserted must appear *philosophically* normal to us'.[15] In other words, the creativity of philosophical thought has more in common with the creative dynamisms of the Earth than with those life forms – such as humans – who, for the sake of their own security, 'must persuade themselves' that the Earth's elemental combat 'does not exist, or that it has somehow ended'.[16] The figure of the desert island stimulates our imagination precisely because it puts the lie to the very presumptions humanity must make in order to dwell together on land: 'that England is populated will always come as a surprise; humans can live on an island only by forgetting what an island represents. Islands are either from before or for after humankind'.[17] The desert island feeling, in this sense, confronts us with the inhuman materiality of the Earth.

The cultural fascination with desert islands suggests an affinity between the speculative imagination and the geological dynamisms from which islands themselves spring:

> The *elan* that draws humans toward islands extends the double movement that produces islands in themselves. Dreaming of islands – whether with joy or in fear, it doesn't matter – is dreaming of pulling away, of being already separate, far from any continent, of being lost and alone – or it is dreaming of starting from scratch, recreating, beginning anew.[18]

Following the shipwreck, Robinson both loses the world and creates the world anew on his island; he both separates off from a larger mass of society, like a continental island separated from its parent continent, and discovers a new origin, producing for himself a new ground of life, like an oceanic island punching through the water. The islands of our imagination may thus be said to re-enact the same movement that produces islands themselves, but the two movements – in the Robinson myth, at any rate – are strangely out of sync, existing in an inverse relationship to one another: Robinson discovers his island, his new beginning, by leaving civilisation, but having found this new beginning his acts of creation culminate in *reproducing* the world from which he has separated, creating for himself a miniature version of seventeenth-century England, complete with pets and manservant.

Deleuze goes on to make the extraordinary claim that 'an island doesn't stop being deserted simply because it is inhabited'.[19] He means that since the geological dynamisms of separation and creation are fundamental to the imagination also, our consciousness of the island is capable of extending and joining with it in ways that collapse the barrier between real and imaginary. This is the island's utopianism. Rather than colonising or territorialising the island we can become part of the deterritorialising movement that produced it, embodying the dynamisms of separation and creation, providing that we ourselves are sufficiently separate and creative, thereby giving to the island a consciousness of itself *as* deserted. Consciousness may thus extend and perfect the island's desertedness instead of putting an end to it.[20] The island's desertedness is more a thing of fantasy or desire than an actuality, a longing to unite space and thought in a single genesis. Deleuze admits that such a unity is 'not actual, only imaginary' – or, we might say, virtual. There is, then, a virtual production of space as unity of consciousness and matter preceding the actualisation of space as physical extensity occupied or inhabited by bodies.

This virtual or imaginary unity of consciousness and depopulated space infuses not only the robinsonade and its dreams of the island but much of mythology and religion, Deleuze claims. The reproduction of the world on a deserted island goes back to the biblical myth of the flood:

> the ark sets down on the one place on earth that remains uncovered by water, a circular and sacred place, from which the world begins anew . . . Here we see original creation caught in a re-creation, which is concentrated in a holy land in the middle of the ocean. This second origin of the world is more important than the first: it is a sacred island.[21]

With the idea of the second origin, which Deleuze argues is found throughout mythology, something of the origin survives a catastrophe in order to repeat the origin in a new context. The origin is sacralised by a repetition that distils its creative or genetic force. To begin is to begin again: 'The second moment does not succeed the first: it is the reappearance of the first . . . it gives us the law of repetition, the law of the series, whose first origin gave us only moments.'[22] The metaphysics of difference and repetition that Deleuze will develop years later are already present here in highly condensed form. Notable also is the mythological figure of the 'cosmic egg' that he introduces.[23] In *Anti-Oedipus* and *A Thousand Plateaus*, Deleuze will return to this by way of the mythology of the Dogon people of Mali, for whom the cosmic egg describes a second creation of the universe following the failure of the first.[24] Deleuze and Guattari use the egg alongside the desert to describe the body without organs since the latter is, as we saw in Chapter 2, a rebeginning or second origin following a catastrophic 'freezing' or collapse of the organic body that sets free an inorganic one which, like the Dogon egg, contains the whole universe as a set of intensive forces diagrammed by signs.[25]

There is, of course, a crucial difference between a piece of literature such as *Robinson Crusoe* and its mythico-religious precursors, but it is precisely this difference that interests Deleuze for whom Defoe's novel 'develops the failure and death of mythology in Puritanism'.[26] Certainly, *Robinson Crusoe* has often been read, and influentially so, as a kind of modern myth for an age of bourgeois individualism in which the Puritan work ethic provides the spiritual conditions for global capitalist expansion.[27] James Joyce described Robinson as 'the true prototype of the British colonist just as Friday (the faithful savage who arrives one ill-starred day) is the symbol of the subject race. All the Anglo-Saxon soul is in Crusoe'.[28] Robinson's narrative, mythic as it is, lies on the very borders between fiction, history, and moral and religious instruction. Rousseau's aversion to books in general was suspended in the case of *Robinson Crusoe* because he saw it as presenting a model of the independent spirit of 'natural man' and thus as the ideal children's book.[29] Marx in the *Grundrisse*, on the other hand, denounced the widespread use of the story by political economy, describing it as a utopian fantasy of self-sufficiency that only comes into being with the highly developed interdependencies of modern civil society: 'In this society of free competition, the individual appears detached from the natural bonds etc. which in earlier historical periods make him the accessory of a definite and limited human conglomerate.'[30] The conception of such an individual as humankind's natural or original state is in fact the outcome of a long historical process – described by Deleuze and Guattari in terms of deterritorialisation and decoding – but is posited by classical economists such as Smith and Ricardo 'as history's point of departure'.[31] There is likewise an important post-colonial perspective on the Robinson myth that intersects with the Marxist one. Derek Walcott, for example, identifies the condition of the colonised writer not with Friday but with Robinson himself, who 'is Adam because he is the first inhabitant of a second paradise'.[32] In his poem 'Crusoe's Journal', Walcott describes Robinson's labours on his island as 'a profane Genesis'.[33]

Read through the Marxist and post-colonial traditions, then, *Robinson Crusoe* may be said to have furnished capitalist modernity with its own version of the mythic second origin. But whereas for Marx this is illusory, functioning only to naturalise capitalism's social and historical development by way of an ideologically convenient fiction, for Deleuze, and indeed for Walcott, it is much more. We have seen how capitalism involves an eschatological collapse of the transcendence that held the pre-capitalist world together. Heidegger conceives modernity as an age of devastation in which Being is abandoned and the world no longer worlds. Transcendence survives, that is to say, but as lost or destroyed, as *wrecked*. This is less modernity's tragic fate than a structural condition of capitalist expansion. Capitalism inspires the 'dread' of decoded flows in the heart of all social organisation because its mode of production constantly requires new points of departure, new origins, new sites of primitive accumulation where it can begin again from zero, unshackled from its old ties and kinship structures.[34] Capital is a force of devastation in this precise sense and brings about end-of-the-world visions of all kinds. The capacity to view space in abstract terms as decoded, purged of meanings and territorial attachments, is linked to the cultural fascination for the desolate, the remote and the unpeopled but also to the European exploitation of the New World. Anthony Giddens evokes the imperial atmosphere of robinsonades in his account of the emergence of modern conceptions of space as abstract and empty:

> The development of 'empty space' is linked above all to two sets of factors: those allowing for the representation of space without reference to a privileged locale which forms a distinct vantage-point; and those making possible the substitutability of different spatial units. The 'discovery' of 'remote' regions of the world by Western travelers and explorers was the necessary basis of both of these. The progressive charting of the globe that led to the creation of universal maps, in which perspective played little part in the representation of geographical position and form, established space as 'independent' of any particular place or region.[35]

The desertedness of the desert island may never be real in actuality – that is, there is invariably someone or something on the island. But in the geographical imaginary of modernity, it comes to constitute a figure that allows us to conceive of space as essentially empty and awaiting discovery.

Robinson Crusoe is not a myth per se but a privileged instance of the *forgetting* of myth. Deleuze provides us with a remarkable definition of literature on these grounds: 'literature is the attempt to interpret, in an ingenious way, the myths we no longer understand, at the moment we no longer understand them'.[36] Defoe's novel and subsequent robinsonades such as Giraudoux's *Suzanne and the Pacific* (1921) show us how 'mythology fails and dies'.[37] It is significant that *Robinson Crusoe* is generally regarded as the first English novel since it suggests that the emergence of the novel as modernity's quintessential literary form is coextensive with the death of mythological traditions and the rise of a secular realist consciousness. Such a consciousness is embodied in Robinson as *Homo economicus*: Robinson is a calculator of costs and labour time. One of his first acts upon landing on his island is to make a balance sheet contrasting his good fortune (e.g., the fact he is alive) against his bad.[38] Practically every task he undertakes is calculated in terms of energy expenditure. Robinson's island functions as a zero-intensity body on which increases and decreases of energy can be abstracted from their extensive actuality. The island, like the Dogon egg, contains the entire universe *in potentia* as a series of becomings, thresholds and intensive states: 'The egg is the milieu of pure intensity, spatium not extension, Zero intensity as principle of production.'[39]

But Robinson produces only to *master his island* with a view ultimately to getting off it and resuming his former life as a slave owner and colonial adventurer. The island as intensive *spatium*, as mythical unity of consciousness and matter, then, is subordinated to the striations, fences and other architectural and agricultural improvements through which Robinson, with the help of his Bible, reterritorialises the Earth. Manuel Schonhorn observes that of all the marooned men stories of Defoe's day, 'none fenced, or hedged, or walled ... their "Little Kingdom" the way Crusoe did'.[40] The mythical beginning anew is crushed by the painstaking reproduction of the heavily striated and regimented world that has been lost. Deleuze says of Defoe's book that 'one can hardly imagine a more boring novel' and that it is sad to think of children still reading it today.[41] He maintains that it is nevertheless preferable to Giraudoux's whimsical version, in which mythology 'dies the prettiest death'.[42] Suzanne's island is little more than a temporary relief from the tedium of her Parisian existence – she is shipwrecked after having won a contest for writing a response to the question: what can remedy boredom? For all its crushing tedium, or perhaps because of it, Defoe's text is the more valuable.

THE ROBINSON PARADOX I: DERRIDA AND THE DESERT OF ABSTRACTION

In the second half of his final seminar *The Beast and the Sovereign* (2002–3), Derrida embarked on a reading of *Robinson Crusoe* via Heidegger's 1929–30 seminar *The Fundamental Concepts of Metaphysics: World, Finitude, Solitude*. The pairing of Defoe and Heidegger is surprising but ultimately fitting as both concern themselves with the problem of world by considering worldlessness. Derrida focuses in particular on Heidegger's argument that only humans have a world properly speaking, whereas animals are what he calls 'poor in world' (*Weltarm*) and inanimate things such as stones are altogether worldless (*Weltlos*). Heidegger's position, with all its apparent anthropocentrism, is both borne out and challenged by Defoe's narrative. Throughout his ordeal, Robinson strives to retain his humanity and his connection to the world while confronting the threat of becoming a worldless creature. His reproduction of the world, his transformation of the island from a space of desolation into a kingdom, not only required technological ingenuity but a primordial, 'ultra-political sovereignty that is the prize of solitude'.[43] The paradox here is that such an absolute sovereignty, combining ruler and people in the same subject, is both political and prior to politics, and even prior to society, which is why Robinson's island must be deserted. But in order to assume this sovereignty Robinson must approach something like an animal condition since animals are, like sovereigns, beyond or apart from the law.[44]

The act that founds a world cannot belong to it without inviting in the spectre of paradox.

Derrida draws our attention to how the language of sovereignty in Defoe's text overlaps with notions of animality, as in the following scene where Robinson sits down to dine with Poll, his talking parrot, and other pets:

> how like a King I din'd too all alone, attended by my Servants; *Poll*, as if he had been my Favourite, was the only Person permitted to talk to me. My Dog who was now grown very old and crazy, and had found no Species to multiply his Kind upon, sat always at my Right Hand, and two Cats, one on one Side the Table, and one on the other, expecting now and then a Bit from my Hand, as a Mark of special Favour.[45]

Robinson manages his solitude by turning it into sovereignty but, as Derrida points out, this requires a banishment of otherness, or involves rather the 'phantasm' of such a banishment.[46] When Friday finally appears, he is not an other per se but a component part of this phantasmatic world without others. Derrida also observes that the elimination of sexual difference, of woman as other, is central to the fascination the story has exerted: 'Until the last pages of the book it is a world without women and without sex.'[47] We may even suggest that Robinson's endless toil stems from the fact that, as Franco Moretti puts it, he is 'working for himself, *as if he were another*'.[48] All that time sacrificed to work is for the benefit of some other who never enjoys the products of Robinson's industry. But Robinson nevertheless remains haunted by this banished other, whose traces seem to mark the island despite his every effort to dominate it.

Shortly after he first witnesses the cannibals, Robinson discovers, in one of the book's most famous scenes, a footprint in the sand. He becomes terrified by the idea that some demonic other has arrived to torment him, though he also considers that the footprint may be his own. Derrida argues that the footprint is disturbing, ultimately, because it signifies a trace of otherness that Robinson cannot rid from himself and the insular world he has constructed: 'the bare footprint is the more *unheimlich*, uncanny, for being quite possibly his own'.[49] In this moment of terror, Robinson fails to distinguish self and other, and this suggests to Derrida that Robinson's oft-repeated fear of being eaten alive (by wild beasts but, more terrifyingly and uncannily, by other humans) conceals a more primordial desire to be swallowed up completely by the other.[50] Robinson's fantasy of sovereignty, his banishment of the other, and his fear of being absorbed by the other *are all parts of the same desire*, which Derrida understands, broadly, as a kind of self-destructive drive acting against law, reason and better judgement.[51] Robinson is driven by something self-destructive, automatic and mechanical, like the automatism of a potter's wheel.[52] As Robinson himself observes early in his narrative, there is a self-destructive and irrational force at work in him:

> my ill Fate push'd me on now with an Obstinacy that nothing could resist; and tho' I had several times loud Calls from my Reason and my more composed Judgment to go home, yet I had no Power to do it. I know not what to call this, nor will I urge, that it is a secret over-ruling Decree that hurries us on to be the Instruments of our own Destruction, even tho' it be before us, and that we rush upon it with our Eyes open.[53]

This self-destructive impulse relates to Robinson's 'autoimmune' compulsion to rid himself of all traces of his own otherness, a compulsion ultimately indistinguishable from a desire to be swallowed up by the other.

As I will show in a moment, this reading of the novel as fundamentally concerned with otherness and desire is shared by Deleuze's comparative analysis of Defoe and Michel Tournier. But we should pause here to consider Derrida's arguments in relation to the historical significance of the Robinson myth. Modernity, the imperial globalisation of capital, and the Anthropocene all suggest a world haunted by a banished otherness. As Mentz has argued, part of what we call the Anthropocene involves a 'Homogenocene', a growing sameness 'in which every ocean in the world ends up another Mediterranean sea, enclosed by human culture and labors'.[54] Modernity transforms the different oceans of the world into a single world ocean. As capitalism globalises, the Earth as a site of alterity becomes subordinate to the capitalist world system or, in Jason Moore's terms, the 'capitalist world-ecology'.[55] Sloterdijk describes globalisation as a simultaneous recognition and rejection of the outside:

> Every globe adorning the libraries, studies and salons of educated Europe embodied the new doctrine of the precedence of the outside. Europeans advanced into this outside as discoverers, merchants and tourists, but they saved their souls by simultaneously withdrawing into their wallpapered interiors. What is a salon but the place where one chats about distant monstrosities?[56]

What is the Anthropocene if not a recognition that the Earth as ground of our collective life bears our own traces, that the ground itself is produced, derived and manmade, a by-product or trace, like Robinson's own footprint in the sand?[57] In 'The Origin of the Work of Art', as I explain in more depth in the next chapter, Heidegger maintained that it is only by means of an 'essential strife' or *polemos* between the world as revelation and Earth as concealment that a world as openness to being can come to exist.[58] A world can exist only because the Earth refuses us, confronts us with a fundamental otherness that resists our technologies of disclosure. Deleuze's notion of a strife between Earth and sea is no doubt evidence of his early engagement with Heideggerian geophilosophy. But the age of modern technology threatens us with the *cessation* of this polemic between Earth and world. This is why Robinson's great fear is not the presence of some other on his island but that he himself *is* this other.

In this sense, the Anthropocene causes us all to become embroiled in the paradox of Robinson's situation: we approach a condition of world-poverty or even world loss precisely through the need to build and maintain the world through ever more technologically sophisticated means. Robinson's island is where modernity loses religion and mythology but regains them as a trace of transcendence, as the dead-alive God of capitalism's Puritan spirit. It is also where we lose the world but regain it through technology, which itself has to be regained no longer as tool or instrument but as a self-moving, *industrial* force. Derrida thus restates, in his own way, the core argument of Deleuze's early essay on desert islands. With respect to both God and the world, Robinson's acts of creation are

> a repetition, a reinvention, on the island, a second origin, a second genesis of the world itself, and of technology. But in both cases we would also be dealing with an autonomization, an automatization in which the pure spontaneity of movement can no longer be distinguished from a mechanization. ... Everything happens as though, on this fictional island, Robinson Crusoe were reinventing sovereignty, technology, tools, the machine, the becoming-machine of the tool, and prayer, God, true religion.[59]

Robinson's creation of a world according to his needs appears spontaneous but is modelled on the world and the technologies he already knows. His only genuine invention is the mechanism he makes to turn his grindstone, 'a Wheel with a String, to turn it with my Foot, that I might have both my Hands at Liberty', but even this he assures us was subsequently developed in his native country: 'I had never seen any such thing in *England*, or at least not to take Notice how it was done, tho' since I have observ'd it is very common there'.[60] The tool becomes a machine, automatic and self-moving by way of the second origin. His rediscovery of God following the irreligion of his seafaring youth is likewise a kind of automatism, Derrida argues. He cries out to God during an earthquake, in terror of being swallowed up or buried alive by the Earth, but this 'is a cry that is almost automatic, irrepressible, machinelike, mechanical'.[61] Robinson eventually becomes devout through an attention to prayer and scripture inspired by the earthquake, but Derrida's point is that true faith begins with automatism.

This link between faith and automatism was drawn in Derrida's landmark piece on religion, 'Faith and Knowledge' (1996), a paper written for a 1994 conference on the Italian island of Capri, in which he deploys the image of a 'desert' of abstraction in order to think religion 'at the limits of reason alone'.[62] It is necessary, Derrida maintains, to abstract from the social and historical content of religions in order to reach the point of their rational universality and thus to conceive of a faith free of all dogma. To accomplish this, thinking requires a desert-like topology. The desert, like an island, is an aporetic place, a place with no escape routes: 'to play the card of abstraction, and the aporia of the *no-way-out*, perhaps one must first withdraw to a desert, or even isolate oneself on an island'.[63] Derrida draws on the Platonic term chora (or *khōra*), meaning 'place' or 'locality', to conceptualise this aporetic topos. He defines chora as 'an abstract spacing' by means of which all historical, onto-theological or anthropological being is revealed.[64] By being the place of barred paths, paradoxically, the place of abstraction is identical with the spacing that founds place in the concrete sense: 'The abstraction of the desert can thereby open the way to everything from which it withdraws.'[65] Chora, like the body without organs, is thus the *condition* of place and of all world-disclosure in the Heideggerian sense. In this way Derrida, following Kant's argument in *Religion Within the Limits of Reason Alone* (1793), argues that the task of conceiving a moral (i.e., universal, non-dogmatic) religion compatible with reason involves thinking religion's relationship to radical evil, or, as Derrida puts it, radical abstraction:

> we would therefore like to link the question of religion to that of the evil of abstraction. To radical abstraction. Not to the abstract figure of death, of evil or of the sickness of death, but to the forms of evil that are traditionally tied to *radical extirpation* and therefore to the deracination of abstraction, passing by way ... of those sites of abstraction that are the machine, technics, technoscience and above all the transcendence of tele-technology.[66]

In linking religion and technoscientific reason via the aporetic terrain of the desert, Derrida is urging us to reconsider the relationship between faith and knowledge. When Robinson on his island utters his first prayers, it is not out of faith or piety but out of a fear that triggers in him a mechanical recitation. As Michael Naas puts it, 'even the most heartfelt and seemingly spontaneous language – even the most rudimentary prayer – involves the possibility of abstraction, deracination, and thus, a movement that tends already toward repetition, translation, and universalization'.[67] Derrida suggests that without this element of abstraction that links it to technoscientific discourse, religion could not aspire to universality or globality. This is all the more important to bear in mind with respect to Robinson, who at several points ponders the universality of Christianity.

For Derrida, then, Robinson's paradox is that his very solitude confronts him with otherness, and ultimately God as other, in a particularly uncanny way that suggests a curious solidarity with the world-poverty and worldlessness of non-human beings. Derrida repeats a refrain from Paul Celan's poem 'Vast, Glowing Vault': '*Die Welt ist fort, ich muss dich tragen*' (the world is gone, I must carry you).[68] Our sense of the world is haunted by its loss or absence. In 'Rams', a paper delivered in 2003 in memory of Hans-Georg Gadamer, Derrida discusses Celan's poem and links the end of the world with the death of the other:

> the survivor, then, remains alone. Beyond the world of the other, he is also in some fashion beyond or before the world itself. . . . He feels solely responsible, assigned to carry both the other and his world, the other and the world that have disappeared, responsible without world (*weltlos*).[69]

The solitude of the survivor must carry the loss of the world along with the death of the other as an *ethical* demand.[70] While the survivor Robinson reacts to this through the construction of a world without others, Derrida also suggests, toward the very end of *The Beast and the Sovereign*, that Robinson's ordeal may lead onto a form of terrestrial cohabitation with animal others despite the gulf that separates human and animal in Heidegger's account. Cohabitation with animal others points to a breakdown of the philosophical concept of *the* world in favour of a disseminated multiplicity of possible worlds: 'Not only a multiplicity and an equivocality of the world . . . but a dissemination without a common semantic horizon.'[71] But this is a multiplicity with unity, Derrida insists: 'there really must be a certain *presumed, anticipated* unity of the world even in order discursively to sustain within it multiplicity, untranslatable and un-gatherable, the dissemination of possible worlds'.[72] Derrida seems to want to retain the concept of the world as discursive possibility while simultaneously insisting that 'the world' is semantically void. It is precisely the gulf of untranslatability between the possible worlds of humans and non-humans that unites them in their dispersion on an Earth that no longer grounds. Heidegger's apparent anthropocentrism may thus be used for non-anthropocentric purposes. Humanity in its world-building sovereignty is drawn uncannily into world-poverty and worldlessness in a cohabitation that must 'carry' the absence of the world as its unifying but non-totalising element.

THE ROBINSON PARADOX II: DELEUZE, TOURNIER AND THE ISLAND AS LIBIDINAL FRONTIER

Deleuze's early interest in *Robinson Crusoe* reappears thirteen years later in *The Logic of Sense* (1969). Written just prior to Deleuze's first collaboration with Guattari, the book is concerned with logical and linguistic paradoxes in the vein of Lewis Carroll. Behind Deleuze's fascination with the Carrollian play of sense and nonsense lies a concern for how structure, understood as a virtual or incorporeal entity, comes to dominate our lives. He thus devotes much of this book to the intellectual legacies of structuralism, arguing that the work of Lacan and Lévi-Strauss in particular can be linked to a fundamental paradox: 'two series being given, one signifying and the other signified, the first presents an excess and the latter a lack. By means of this excess and this lack, the series refer to each other in eternal disequilibrium and in perpetual displacement'.[73] Signs are in excess of what we actually know about the objects to which they correspond. For this reason, there is a signification prior to any knowledge of *what* is signified. The paradox lies in the fact that this imbalance fuels totalising systems such as the paranoias of schizophrenia as well as logical, linguistic and scientific systems. In an article titled 'How Do We Recognize Structuralism?' written in 1967 Deleuze maintains that what allows any symbolic system to totalise is characterised by structuralism as an 'empty' or 'floating' signifier, a signifier with 'a zero symbolic value'.[74] This is an 'empty square', as Deleuze calls it, a transcendental 'object = x' that 'is always displaced in relation to itself' but which thereby grants the structure order and stability despite its inherent contradiction: 'No structuralism is possible without this degree zero.'[75] Lévi-Strauss's concept of 'mana' and Lacan's concept of the phallus are the best-known examples of this.[76]

Deleuze suggests that the structuralist paradox can also be called 'Robinson's paradox':

> It is obvious that Robinson, on his desert island, could reconstruct an analogue of society only by giving himself, all at once, all the rules and laws which are reciprocally implicated, even when they still have no objects. The conquest of nature is, on the contrary, progressive, partial, and advances step by step. Any society whatsoever has all of its rules at once. ... But the conquest of nature, without which it would no longer be a society, is achieved progressively, from one source of energy to another, from one object to another.[77]

Having lost the world, Robinson on his island acts *as if* he has a world, a kingdom with its totality of laws and symbolic values, even though his mastery of nature is incomplete and accomplished by degrees of energy consumption and expenditure. The paradox of the world recognised by Derrida is thus posed here by Deleuze as the problem of the coexistence of the partial with the total. Robinson's existential ordeal of solitude and survival is lived as a series of energetic fluctuations on the island as zero-intensity body. In this way, he *lives* the abstract problem of language as identified by the structuralists, which Deleuze glosses as follows:

> the elements of language must have been given all together, all at once, since they do not exist independently of their possible differential relations. But the signified in general is of the order of the known, though the known is subject to the law of a progressive movement which proceeds from one part to another – *partes extra partes*. And whatever totalizations knowledge may perform, they remain asymptotic to the virtual totality of langue or language.[78]

As we saw in Chapter 2, the concept of the body without organs is meant to suggest a virtual coexistence of a non-totalised whole with the parts that function as desiring-machines. The religious and mythological idea of deserted space, of a space depopulated by a catastrophe and assigned the role of a second genesis, features throughout Deleuze and Guattari's description of the body without organs as the terrain of a new beginning that ruptures the domination of totalities and totalising systems. The body without organs is indeed a desert, a degree zero of life, but it comes to play quite a different role than the structuralist degree zero: instead of totalising the system it instead liberates the parts as a non-totalised whole, a multiplicity of co-habitation in unworlded space. Robinson's solitude can thus be seen as a libidinal investment of space as a *zero-intensity whole* distinct from the world as totality, but – crucially – he does this only to *reproduce* the world he has lost. This is why the arrival of Friday does not disturb anything but, on the contrary, fits completely into Robinson's labour of reproduction. Contrary to what Levinas has argued, then, the encounter with Friday is not an ethical encounter with the Other, since Robinson had already contended with the problem of otherness through his solitary encounter with the island itself as a site in which self and other merge.[79] The question that leads on from the Robinson paradox, then, is how things might have gone differently had Robinson not submitted all of his efforts to the labour of reproduction.

In an article included as an appendix to *The Logic of Sense*, Deleuze presents a reading of Michel Tournier's novel *Friday, or, The Other Island*, originally published in 1967 as *Vendredi ou les Limbes du Pacifique*, in which Robinson is torn between the sovereign reproduction of the world and the genesis of an entirely new form of life. Deleuze is attracted to Tournier's novel because it takes the path not taken in Defoe's original narrative. Instead of crushing the mythology of the island with the Puritanism of the capitalist spirit, Tournier's Robinson, a Quaker, acknowledges the transformative and genuinely utopian potentials of the second origin through the figure of a Friday who this time resists the role of slave. Tournier ends the novel with Robinson refusing the opportunity of rescue that Friday takes. He remains on the island with a kitchen boy who seeks it out as refuge from the brutality of his crewmates. He and the boy begin a new life on the island – no longer named Desolation but Speranza, meaning hope. Robinson, prior to Friday's arrival, had striated the landscape and established himself as governor, writing a charter and a penal code with which to discipline himself. Such strictures of moral order appear as Robinson's only alternative to the descent into sheer animality, embodied in a literal pig wallow, that his despair initially prompts.[80] Robinson drags himself out of the wallow to crown himself governor of Speranza and subsequently documents the strange phenomenology of his world without others:

> the presence of other people is a powerful element of distraction, not only because they constantly break into our activities and interrupt our train of thought, but because the mere possibility of their doing so illumines a world of concerns situated at the edge of consciousness but capable at any moment of becoming its center. That marginal and almost ghostly presence of things with which he was immediately concerned had gradually disappeared from Robinson's mind.[81]

The loss of the other confronts Tournier's Robinson with the threat of madness: 'Optical illusions, mirages, hallucinations, waking dreams, imagined sounds, fantasy and delirium ... against these aberrations the surest guard is our brother, our neighbor, our friend, or our enemy – anyway, God save us, *someone*.'[82] Faced with this threat, Robinson constructs a replica of the world he has lost, complete with penal code, charter and palace of justice, and recognises that 'the paradox of his situation' is precisely the imbalance between the practical inadequacy and the symbolic or moral importance of the structures he has built.[83] By imposing his moral order on the island, Robinson considers himself to be bringing its hidden and potentially malignant depths to the surface. He thus regards as a prejudice the general estimation, manifested in ideas such as 'deep love', of depth over surface, suggesting that it should be the inverse:

> I measure my love for a woman by the fact that I love indiscriminately her hands, her eyes, her carriage, the clothes she wears, the commonplace things she merely touches, the place where she dwells, the sea in which she bathes

... All this, it seems to me, is decidedly on the surface! Whereas a lesser love aims directly – *in depth* – at sex.[84]

Edward Abbey, Robinson Crusoe of the American deserts, makes a similar point in *Desert Solitaire* when he studies a juniper tree: 'the essence of the juniper continues to elude me unless, as I presently suspect, its surface is also the essence'.[85] In unworlded space, the surface is itself the revelation, not the concealer, of depths.

This realisation marks the point in Tournier's text at which the element of sexuality, so scrupulously suppressed by Defoe, begins to make itself felt, and from here on we can read the narrative as a story of desire. The world as constituted by our awareness of others is complicit in identifying desire with the depths of the libidinal body. But in the absence of others, and of the world as proceeding from the other, desire is liberated from the ultimate aim of sex. Robinson feels within him the upsurge of liberated desire: 'To say that my sexual desire is no longer directed toward the perpetuation of the species is not enough. It no longer knows what its purpose is!'[86] Desire unchained from its sexual aim becomes, with the transformative intervention of Friday, a way of liberating the elemental life of the island and of creating a new mythic reality. Friday, who is 15 in Tournier's version, is a creature of surfaces and the Aeolian elements. He kills a 'great goat' in a ritual manner and out of its remains fashions a kite and Aeolian harp that produces 'music that was truly of the elements, inhuman music'.[87]

The theme of elemental strife suggested in Deleuze's 'Desert Islands' reappears in his comments on Tournier's novel: 'There is a struggle [*combat*] between earth and sky, with the imprisonment or liberation of all four elements at stake. The isle is the frontier or field of this struggle.'[88] Tournier's novel allows Deleuze to consider what he calls Robinson's 'desert sexuality', 'the coming together of the libido and the free elements'.[89] He argues that Robinson's desire is perverse in the precise psychoanalytic sense of this term. Perversion, for Freud, was the diverting of the sexual aim from its object, but Deleuze expands on this through Lacanian theory. Lacan famously defined desire in terms of 'the other', a structure of exterior recognition that we internalise in order to give our desires meaning. As Lacan puts it: 'desire finds its meaning in the desire of the other, not so much because the other holds the key to the object desired, as because the first object of desire is to be recognized by the other'.[90] We desire the other not only or primarily because we want them or what they can give us but because we imagine ourselves as wanted *by* the other, as being able to give them what they lack. Of course, this lack can never be filled – as this would cause them to cease being other, in some sense – which is what propels the dialectic of desire, for Lacan. Desire, then, is not simply directed towards others but is fundamentally organised by a structure of mutual recognition (and misrecognition) that grants it social and intersubjective reality as an economy.

But if sexual life is so prone to disorders it is because the other is fundamentally *lacking*, the site of a constitutive and infinite debt, its demands inscrutable or impossible to realise. There is a fundamental enigma inherent in the question of what the 'Other' – capitalised to suggest the structurally necessary component of intersubjectivity – ultimately wants from us. This can be used to explain the various kinds of disorders – hysteria, phobia, obsession, perversion – traditionally studied by psychoanalysis in a way that foregrounds the structuring functions of the Other. Perversion is the libidinal formation that attempts to overcome the enigmatic lack in the Other by identifying totally with the object thought to correspond to what the Other wants. As Tom Eyers writes, 'the pervert projects him or herself as the object that can satisfy the drive, that can both incite and placate the desire of the Other'.[91] The pervert solves the problem of subjectivity and intersubjectivity at one stroke by becoming a mere object of the Other's enjoyment. The masochist, for example, becomes an *instrument* for the Other to use, and ensures this condition with all the binding certainty of a legal contract. The masochist in this way attempts to put an end to the anxious play of recognition and misrecognition that characterises desire's social life. The rituals and scripted scenarios of sadism have the same effect as the masochist's contract. For both the masochist and the sadist, *the possible is exhausted* in favour of strict necessity. For this reason, an air of iciness, claustrophobia and sterility tends to hang over the scenes of perverse fantasies. A similar air hangs over Tournier's island. The pervert seeks to suspend the Other as structure entirely and thus to inhabit a world without others, a world in which the intersubjective economy of desire is frozen. The lack in the Other, once disavowed in this way, becomes an intensity = o, a 'zero point' that perverse desire invests.[92]

This is how we should understand Deleuze's bizarre-sounding claim that 'the only Robinsonade possible is perversion itself'.[93] Without the Other as structure of possibility (which Deleuze names, in Lacanian fashion, the 'structure-Other'), the world as intersubjective economy collapses. But this is paradoxically liberating. Indeed, it is properly utopian, because it dissolves the dialectical deadlock of recognition and misrecognition and the corresponding role of lack, or infinite debt, in desire's economy. Without the intersubjective dimension tying desire to the social order, desire is able to able to invest *space in itself* beyond the intersubjective world, becoming one with its elemental dynamisms. In this way, Deleuze focuses our attention on the libidinal economics of Tournier's Speranza:

> In the Other's absence, consciousness and its object are one ... Robinson is but the consciousness of the island, but the consciousness of the island is the consciousness the island has of itself – it is the island in itself. We understand thus the paradox of the desert isle: the one who is shipwrecked, if he is alone, if he has lost the structure-Other, disturbs nothing of the desert isle; rather he consecrates it.[94]

We find restated here the argument already put forward in 'Desert Islands' fourteen years earlier. But Tournier's novel now provides Deleuze with an account of the mythic re-beginning that is crushed in Defoe's narrative. Tournier's Robinson initially follows the path of his predecessor but comes to sense *'another island* behind the one where he has labored so long in solitude'.[95] For some of the text, Robinson enters into a sexual relationship with this other island, which he also regards for a time as maternal and the site of potential rebirth. But this oedipal path fails, and it is only with the arrival of Friday that an alternative appears. It is not that Friday restores the structure-Other with his arrival but that he allows Robinson to realise a new economy beyond the merely interpersonal or intersubjective dialectic of recognition. For this reason, then, Friday is absolutely central to the becoming-elemental of desire. Robinson regards him in terms of a simultaneously erotic and religious force, a new Venus emerging from the sea: 'Friday, if I am not mistaken, is in its ancient meaning the day of Venus. To Christians it is the day of the death of Christ.'[96] He names the kitchen boy, who joins him at the end of the text, Sunday, the day of resurrection. In this way, Tournier's novel points towards a post-Christian mythology of the Earth and its elemental energies.

TERMINAL ISLANDS: BALLARD'S ROBINSONADES

Of all the twentieth-century authors who have turned the robinsonade to their own purposes, it is J. G. Ballard who has done so in a way that most reflects its significance for understanding the psychical and libidinal dimensions of our contemporary spatial condition. His robinsonades explore the built environment of the latter half of the twentieth century as a projection of destructive and pathological forms of desire. It is the unity of desire and space that constitutes Ballard's utopianism as well as his dystopianism. His urban and suburban spaces are uncanny because they constitute, even in their very quotidian English drabness, great architectures of violence. Built space is for Ballard a kind of *formalisation* of the death instinct in which only a violent, sometimes spectacular, dissolution of social codes can come to satisfy the drives. As William S. Burroughs observed, Ballard is able to evoke an erotic atmosphere without any sexual content or even people simply through his descriptions of objects and spaces.[97] In the precise sense outlined above, Ballard's writings are perverse. While there is in almost all of his work a fascination, inspired to a large degree by the surrealist landscapes of Dali, Tanguy and Ernst, for deserts, wastelands, abandoned buildings and empty spaces of all kinds, it is in his reworking of the Robinson myth that a critique of the spatiality of late modernity reveals itself most persuasively as emerging from this fascination.[98]

Ballard's most self-conscious robinsonade is his novel *Concrete Island* (1974), in which Robert Maitland, a London architect, crashes his Jaguar onto a patch of waste ground beneath three converging motorways. As he struggles and fails to secure help from the speeding rush-hour traffic, he quickly realises the nature of his predicament: 'Maitland, poor man, you're marooned here like Crusoe – If you don't look out you'll be beached here for ever.'[99] The central irony of the narrative is that the sovereign domination of the environment that Robinson needed in order to survive has become the very context of Maitland's ordeal. Maitland's profession is thus pertinent in this respect. In his introduction to the novel, Ballard points to the technological transformation and domination of the landscape as the core of the Robinson myth:

> there is the need to dominate the island, and transform its anonymous terrain into an extension of our minds. The mysterious peak veiled by cloud, the deceptively calm lagoon, the rotting mangroves and the secret spring of pure water together become out-stations of the psyche.[100]

The essence of the Robinson myth is the transformation of the outer world into a manifestation of our inner psychic life and the needs of the human nervous system, but what the late twentieth century reveals is that we have ended up castaways on landscapes that are all the more alien and dangerous for having become humanised in this way, as Maitland learns.

In a sense, Ballard's entire oeuvre can be regarded as an extended robinsonade. From his early ecoapocalyptic fictions to his later visions of urban and suburban social disintegration, his concern has frequently been with small groups of people in environments cut off from the wider world. While he approaches them with the detached eye of a scientist, a key Ballardian theme is the way his landscapes meld the technological and the natural into a strange third term imposing itself on our perception. Rather than explore the ethical and political issues surrounding humanity's environmental impact, Ballard instead regards the transformative potential of technology as an elemental force of devastation beyond our control. The environmental disasters that so often provide him with his scenarios are sometimes manmade and sometimes not, but there is very rarely any moral or political lesson to be learnt from the ordeals of his survivors except for the one the ordeal has already made obvious: that our power over the environment, our ability to sculpt and shape it according to our desires and anxieties, has taken on a life as independent from us as nature itself. *The Drought* (1965), for example, tells the story of a world in which industrial waste has formed a polymer film over the oceans, preventing precipitation. As water becomes ever scarcer, Ballard's narrative presents the ecological catastrophe in terms of a *derealisation of time*, a draining away of time into ideality. The sand dunes and dry riverbeds reveal 'a world of volitional time where the images of the past were reflected free of the demands of memory and nostalgia, free of the pressures even of thirst and hunger'.[101] Cars half-covered in sand 'were like idealized images of themselves, the essences of their own geometry, the smooth curvatures like the eddies flowing out of some platonic future'.[102] The desert covering the Earth reveals a deathly convergence of technology with eternity that also liberates a desire to go beyond organic life. The apocalyptic geographies of ruined suburbs and abandoned cinemas that fill his avant-garde text *The Atrocity Exhibition* (1970) emerge from this alliance of death, the mass media image and the irresistible lure of technology.

With Ballard, the desert island becomes the narrative site of dangerous and apocalyptic forces rather than the painstaking fortification and domestication that occupies Defoe's Robinson. Ballard's engagement with desert island narratives begins with his 1964 story 'The Terminal Beach', which documents the experiences of an American H-bomber pilot named Traven who maroons himself on an abandoned nuclear test site located on the Pacific atoll Eniwetok. The text occupies an important place in Ballard's work for a number of reasons. It is written as a series of short sections condensed together in a manner that foreshadows *The Atrocity Exhibition*, his most experimental work and one whose concerns with car crashes, 1960s pop culture and psychological disintegration mark his most well-known text, the infamous novel *Crash* (1973). 'The Terminal Beach' thus represents Ballard's attempts from the mid-1960s to move science fiction into more experimental territory, but, like Vonnegut's *Cat's Cradle* (1963) – another island narrative – it also shows how science fiction writers were uniquely equipped to explore the bizarre and frightening realities of the Cold War era. Traven's experiences on Eniwetok reveal a terrifying continuity between military spaces of devastation and the everyday landscapes of motorways and urban infrastructure. He is fascinated with the modular blockhouses near the test site because they resemble, at once, the megaliths of a primitive people and the disenchanted concrete blocks of modern cities. This futuristic primitivism suggests to him a key to understanding the nuclear age.

The figure of the island has featured prominently in the British tradition in science fiction. Thomas More's *Utopia* (1516) located the ideal society on an island 'crescent-shaped, like a new moon'.[103] The shape suggests an atoll, or volcanic island. More's text, along with *The Tempest*, *Robinson Crusoe* and *The Origin of Species*, belongs to a lineage of writing that gives rise at the end of the nineteenth century to the scientific romances of H. G. Wells. The importance of the island theme for Wells is most obvious in texts such as the comic robinsonade 'Æpyornis Island' (1894) and the Darwinian fable *The Island of Doctor Moreau* (1896). The closest link to Ballard, however, is found near the end of *The Time Machine* (1898) when the Time Traveller, in search of the Earth's eventual fate, finds himself on a 'desolate beach' in a depopulated future England covered with lichen and large crab-like creatures.[104] Britain here becomes an island at the end of time, a terminal island. Ballard's Eniwetok is a similarly eschatological site, even if it also emphatically belongs to our present. Nicholas Ruddick describes it as 'a devastated Island of Desire, a concretized Waste Land with no likelihood of a regenerating thunder-shower'.[105] What is revealed there is the thanatropic underside of Robinson's desire for sovereignty. It is a landscape formed by the destructive power of technology. This is made manifest to Traven by the island's very surfaces:

> Traven stumbled into a set of tracks left years earlier by a large caterpillar vehicle. The heat released by the weapons tests had fused the sand, and the double line of fossil imprints, uncovered by the evening air, wound its serpentine way among the hollows like the footfalls of an ancient saurian.[106]

Traven arrives on Eniwetok on a small motorboat whose hull is 'torn by the sharp coral'.[107] Having marooned himself, he wanders amongst the island's irradiated bunkers and concrete blockhouses, gradually approaching the ground zero at the centre of the test site. Eniwetok functions as an eschatological present to which deep past and deep future have become fused. The only disruptions to Traven's world without others are the occasional visits of a scientist whose offers of rescue he refuses, the apparition of his dead wife and son, and the corpse of a

Japanese serviceman, a kind of Friday figure with whom Traven has an imaginary dialogue at the close of the story. The island itself he regards as non-living, exoskeletal, a fossil, but one that inverts geology's usual temporal coordinates and magnitudes: 'Here, the key to the present lay in the future. This island was a fossil of future time.'[108] This fusion of an eschatological deep future to the surface layers of the present is accomplished through 'the brief epochs, microseconds in duration, of thermonuclear time'.[109] The fortifications he encounters are the inverse of the ones painstakingly built by Robinson in that they expose Traven to, rather than shelter him from, the island's desolating realities. The blockhouses constructed around the test sites resemble the mythological structures of an unknown civilisation: 'One question in particular intrigued him: "What sort of people would inhabit this minimal concrete city?"'[110] Traven's wife and son died in a motor accident, and the island's military infrastructure merges with a landscape of motorways and urban infrastructure. These derelict spaces offer Traven a vision of technologically mediated mass death, an 'immense synthesis of the historical and psychic zero'.[111]

'The Terminal Beach' uses the concept of the 'spinal landscape', which Ballard deploys throughout *The Drowned World* (1963) and *The Atrocity Exhibition*. Traven regards the island's test sites as an exteriorisation of his internal states, but one where his routines, memories and organic needs are hollowed out and mechanised: 'he had become a creature of reflexes, kindled from levels above those of his existing nervous system (if the autonomic system was dominated by the past, Traven sensed, the cerebro-spinal reached towards the future)'.[112] In *The Atrocity Exhibition*, the spinal landscape is identified with both the austere concrete of motorways and the 'inhospitality of [the] mineral world, with its inorganic growths'.[113] The spinal landscape suggests the inorganic and mineral nature of human intelligence, the visual analogue for which is found in the contours of modern cities. Ballard's celebrated novels of the 1970s obsessively map this terrain, documenting it with an architectural precision but also searching out its hidden, often dangerous, libidinal investments. The spinal landscape detaches desire from the organism through the liberating power of technology, the car crash becoming the perfect figure of this dangerous collision of the libidinal and the technological. If for Enlightenment thinkers such as Fontenelle and Voltaire shipwreck is the unavoidable and necessary risk modernity must take, as Blumenberg argues, the car crash is for Ballard the spectacular object of a collective death instinct.

Crash is, of course, Ballard's most extensive and notorious engagement with this topic. *Concrete Island* shows him approaching it through the vantage of a Robinsonian desert island, which provides a certain degree of optimism that the former novel lacks. The wasteland beneath the motorway suggests an escape from the traumas of the road. The text begins with a car crash that maroons its protagonist on 'a small traffic island, some two hundred yards long and triangular in shape, that lay in the waste ground between three converging motorways'.[114] Maitland's initial attempts to gain the attention of a motorist in rush-hour traffic culminate in a broken leg received from the impact of a passing car. The steep embankments on all sides of the island, along with his injury, subsequently prevent his escape. He encounters a mentally impaired vagrant and a prostitute who conspire, initially, to keep him captive. Ultimately, however, Maitland refuses the offer of rescue and realises, much like Tournier's Robinson, that he doesn't want to leave the island. One of the key strands of Defoe's narrative that Ballard brings out is that the shipwreck/crash may have been secretly desired all along. Like Defoe's Robinson, Maitland recognises a self-destructiveness that leads him to his island:

> Why had he driven so fast? . . . His seat belt, rarely worn, hung from its pinion by his shoulder. As Maitland frankly recognized, he invariably drove well above the speed limit. Once inside a car some rogue gene, a strain of rashness, overran the rest of his usually cautious and clear-minded character.[115]

As he watches London's multitudes stream by him, he realises his own sense of alienation and a loathing for his fellow motorists, reminiscing that the happiest time in his life was spent as a child 'playing endlessly by himself in a long suburban garden surrounded by a high fence'.[116] There is an unexpected yet undeniable nostalgia for a lost England in the narrative. The waste ground of the island bears the traces of old Victorian streets and houses, and Maitland discovers an old air-raid shelter and a disused cinema whose posters of Fred Astaire and Ginger Rogers cause him to reminisce about 'sitting alone in the empty circles of huge suburban Odeons' during his adolescence.[117] The island also reminds him of his visits to La Grande Notte, a 'futuristic resort complex' with 'affectless architecture' and 'stylised concrete surfaces', 'the vast, empty parking lots laid down by the planners years before any tourist would arrive to park their cars, like a city abandoned in advance of itself'.[118] Ultimately, it is the possibilities of empty space, rather than any sense of alienation, that come to dominate Maitland's life on the island and lead him to stay there. The island becomes an extension, even a realisation, of his inner desolation, but it functions also as a release from the psychological pressures of his failed marriage and habitual infidelity.

Concrete Island quite presciently raised the question of the aesthetic value of derelict urban spaces. Since the late 1990s, geographers, urban planners and architects have become increasingly concerned with this issue. The architect Ignasi de Solà-Morales has used the French term 'terrain vague' – whose links, via Laforgue, to Eliot's 'vacant lot' I touched on briefly in the last chapter – to categorise such spaces. The French term, according to Solà-Morales, captures the sense of 'void, absence, yet also promise, the space of the possible, of expectation', a new kind of desert island feeling which springs from the interstices of social and economic regulation:

> In these apparently forgotten places, the memory of the past seems to predominate over the present. Here, only a few residual values survive, despite the total disaffection from the activity of the city. These strange places exist outside the city's effective circuits and productive structures. From the economic point of view, industrial areas, railway stations, ports, unsafe residential neighborhoods, and contaminated places are where the city is no longer.
>
> Unincorporated margins, interior islands void of activity, oversights, these areas are simply un-inhabited, un-safe, un-productive. In short, they are foreign to the urban system, mentally exterior in the physical interior of the city, its negative image, as much a critique as a possible alternative.[119]

Maitland's island is an architectural and economic void but the sense of promise that Solà-Morales describes is palpable in Ballard's text as Maitland, with an accompanying sense of personal revivification, gradually realises that the island is a site of possibility in which the distinction between waste and valuable space may be interrogated and broken down.[120]

These possibilities are not restricted, in Ballard's work, to traditional sites of dereliction and decline. His 1990 short story 'The Enormous Space' begins with a divorced banker named Ballantyne – no doubt a reference to the author of the famous imperial romance *The Coral Island* (1858) – taking the decision, one morning, not to leave his home in the London suburb of Croydon: 'To shut out the world, and solve all my difficulties at a stroke, I had the simplest of weapons – my own front door. I needed only to close it, and decide never to leave my house again.'[121] Like Maitland, Ballantyne identifies himself explicitly with Robinson Crusoe, but a Robinson committed to dissolving the world instead of recreating it: 'Crusoe wished to bring the Croydons of his own day to life again on his island. I want to expel them, and find in their place a far richer realm formed from the elements of light, time and space.'[122] The suffocating insularity of suburban life becomes an apparent means of escape into a utopian smooth space composed of intensities of light, duration and distance. Ballantyne exultantly burns his money, personal documents and all the mail he receives in pursuit of a spatio-temporal sensation detached from any form of selfhood or memory. He comes to occupy a depthless topological space: 'The house begins to resemble an advanced mathematical surface, a three-dimensional chessboard.'[123] As his food runs out, he discovers within the house a hitherto unexplored realm that grows larger the further he travels into it:

> Another door leads to a wide and silent corridor, clearly unentered for years. There is no staircase, but far away there are entrances to other rooms, filled with the sort of light that glows from X-ray viewing screens. Here and there an isolated chair sits against a wall, in one immense room there is nothing but a dressing table, in another the gleaming cabinet of a grandfather clock presides over the endlessly carpeted floor.[124]

Like Robinson, he defends his world without others from all intruders: he kills neighbourhood pets, and ultimately his human visitors, for nourishment, becoming Englishman and cannibal in one. As the spaces of the house grow to immense proportions, Ballantyne compares his discovery of them 'to Columbus's discovery of the new world'.[125] But the utopian promise quickly turns bad and what he finds is ultimately nothing more than the lure of death. His fascination with empty space is a mere dream of annihilation. At the very opening of the text, he notices a neighbour gazing up at a passing airliner and thinks: 'she is dreaming of Martinique or Mauritius, while I am dreaming of nothing'.[126] The dream of empty space turns murderous and the imperial romance becomes a nightmare, while the suburban home itself becomes *terra nullius*. Ballantyne spurns Robinson's careful recreation of provincial England but his own colonising efforts lead him to a final, deadly zero point rather than to any 'richer realm'. In the last lines of the story, he enters into the vast arctic waste of his freezer compartment, where he has stored the dead body of his former secretary, to occupy 'the still centre of the world'.[127]

DESERT DESIRE AND UTOPIA: LE GUIN, KIM STANLEY ROBINSON AND WORLD REDUCTION

For both Deleuze and Derrida, the Robinson Crusoe narrative is philosophically important because it brackets or suspends the world in order to consider its possible disappearance and reproduction. That the world can be lost and made has occupied much modern philosophy, and Defoe's novel can be said to anticipate the insights of Kant, the first philosopher to challenge the traditional metaphysics of world inherited from Plato and Aristotle.[128] Kant argued that we can have no possible experience of the world as a whole, and that therefore the world is – like other metaphysical entities such as God – a pure idea of reason for which no corresponding empirical concept can be found. Kant insisted that the idea of the world leads us inexorably into contradictions, or what he called 'antinomies'. Yet he also argued that we need such ideas as regulative principles: we must act *as if* the world exists, even though we have no possible experience of it as a totality.[129] This is exactly what Robinson does. Confronted with the catastrophe of the loss of the world as a given empirical reality, he decides to act *as if* it still existed, and this decision allows him to recreate it through his labours. The 'as if' is his central technological discovery on the island. This is the essence of the Robinson paradox. As Derrida points out, since the 'as if' constitutes the world as a structure in our everyday experience, the world is nothing but a shared pretence, 'a word, a vocable, a convenient and reassuring bit of chatter, the name of a life insurance policy for living beings losing their world'.[130] It is ultimately, then, on the desolate terrain of world loss that the question of the world is best posed. Despite Robinson's solitude this remains fundamentally a *political* question because if the shared pretence of the world is an insurance policy against losing it, then it is also a policing and a regulating of collective possibility.

In his work on Ursula Le Guin, Fredric Jameson has suggested the importance of what he calls 'world reduction', which he defines as a 'surgical excision of empirical reality, something like a process of ontological attenuation in which the sheer teeming multiplicity of what exists, of what we call reality, is deliberately thinned and weeded out through an operation of radical abstraction and simplification'.[131] If we can think of the utopian imagination as an impulse or *desire* – which is what Jameson, following Ernst Bloch, does – then it is one in which the *empirical plenitude of the world is reduced*. Reduction, here, can be understood in the phenomenological sense as the suspending of our 'natural attitude' towards the objective world. In Deleuzian terms, the working machines or organs that constitute the worldliness of the world are frozen by the desert of the body without organs. Utopia is a desert desire in this precise sense.[132] Although Jameson doesn't explicitly acknowledge the link, world reduction is also absolutely central to the robinsonade.

In Le Guin's *The Dispossessed* (1974) and Kim Stanley Robinson's *Red Mars* (1992), the desert island becomes the desert planet and the prospect of reproducing the world that has been lost becomes the speculative labour or imagining how the world could function differently in radically altered environmental and ecological contexts. In both novels, the desert becomes a utopian space. Le Guin's Anarres is a barren planet where very little grows and animal life is limited to fish, worms and insects. Anarres was settled 150 years prior to the beginning of the narrative by an anarchist group following the principles of a woman named Odo, a revolutionary who was persecuted on her home planet of Urras. Urras is a place, much like Earth, characterised by abundance, biodiversity, consumerism, militarist geopolitics, immense economic inequalities and deeply rooted patriarchal social organisation. Odo is imprisoned and dies without seeing her political ideas realised, but her followers are allowed to settle on Anarres with the agreement they never return. Odonian society has no state, private property, laws or prisons, and people there are apparently free to do as they wish. The very inhospitality of the desert lends to their ideals of collectivism an environmental necessity that is negotiated by the Odonians with stoic forbearance. All individualistic behaviour, or 'egoizing', is socially censured in a way that fosters conformism, but this latter fact is denied by the planet's official ideology. Anarres – which for the Urrasti is the 'moon' – is thus also a place of insularity, exile and displaced history, as if it were the negative image of the world it has left behind: 'the Settlers of Anarres had turned their backs on the Old World and its past, opted for the future only. But as surely as the future becomes the past, the past becomes the future'.[133] The relationship between the two planets – one Earthlike in its ecology, the other barren and lunar – allows Le Guin to explore the nature of the utopian impulse as deterritorialisation and desire for a new social and political foundation.[134] The desert planet is precisely where the future itself comes into being as abstraction or pure potentiality.

When a scientist named Shevek, a specialist in temporal physics, leaves Anarres for Urras in order to share his research it is the first direct contact between the two planets. The people he initially meets on Urras are the affluent and educated elite, but he soon learns the scale of the planet's economic inequalities. Shevek identifies the failings of Urrasti society with a consumerist desire for immediate gratification and self-enrichment and thus with an obsession with the present: 'there is nothing but the present, this Urras, the rich, real, stable present, the moment now. And you think that is something which can be possessed!'[135] Temporal flux and futurity are forms of *dis*possession: the smooth space of Anarres is the terrain of the dispossession of the present, the flux by which the present is emptied out to constitute a future. Shevek's hope, however, is to free his own society from the frozen futurity of a possible world that remains *only* possible, internally abstract and sterile, always awaiting realisation. Le Guin thus contrasts utopian possibility against historical reality, but the contrast is not simple.

Anarres is identified with the future but also appears petrified, frozen out of history, while Urras, for all its obsession with the present, is sunk in forms of historical turmoil that closely resemble Cold War geopolitics. Meanwhile, growth is equated with change, whereas Odonians are 'a people selected by a vision of freedom, and adapted to a barren world, a world of distances, silences, desolations'.[136] The environmental aesthetics of the desert allow Le Guin to portray her Odonians in terms of an ennobling burden of poverty that bears all the hallmarks of ascetic mysticism. The verdant forests on Urras remind Shevek of the extent to which his own society has insulated itself against change, and the text uses botanical imagery to critique this insularity. He has decided to go to Urras and share his research because 'it is of the nature of idea to be communicated: written, spoken, done. The idea is like grass. It craves light, likes crowds, thrives on crossbreeding, grows better for being stepped on'.[137] The novel's opposition of Urrasti consumerism and Anarresti anarcho-ascetic poverty constitutes for Jameson an antimony at the heart of its utopianism, but one that Shevek's scientific work is itself based around solving.[138]

In the Urrasti tradition, the two main branches of temporal physics are the Simultaneity and Sequency schools. Resolving their opposition means seeking a resolution between an eternal present and the transition between past and future. While the present is always empirically full, the transitional point is formal and empty. This has key moral and political dimensions amounting to a distinction between determinism on the one hand and an abstract or empty concept of freedom on the other. At a cocktail party on Urras, Shevek defends Simultaneity from the suggestion that it eradicates moral responsibility:

> That is the dilemma of determinism. You are quite right, it is implicit in Simultanist thinking. But Sequency thinking also has its dilemma. It is like this, to make a foolish little picture – you are throwing a rock at a tree, and if you are a Simultanist the rock has already hit the tree, and if you are a Sequentist it never can. So which do you choose? Maybe you prefer to throw rocks without thinking about it, no choice. I prefer to make things difficult, and choose both.[139]

Shevek's research seeks to resolve an antinomy in temporal physics and for this he is sought out by the warring governments of Urras, for whom his work has far-reaching technological applications. But his goals are ethico-political more than they are scientific. The static utopianism of Anarres needs the animating force of individual choice just as the Urrasti obsession with the present needs a sense of historical meaning. This is why Shevek sees contact with Urras as necessary, even if this makes him appear a traitor to his fellow Odonians.

The book ends by coming full circle: Shevek allies himself to socialist and anarchist factions on Urras, then returns to Anarres in the hope that his discoveries will lead to improvements on both worlds. Key to the narrative's latter half is the revelation that his research allows for the development of a device called an 'ansible', which allows instantaneous communication regardless of physical distance. Shevek's hope is that this technology will realise a utopian federation of worlds and eradicate the kind of insularity that plagues Anarres. A central component of the book's apparently happy ending is the action of Keng, an ambassador from Earth who helps Shevek escape from Urras and to whom Shevek reveals his plans for the ansible. She expresses her admiration for Urras and tells Shevek:

> My world, my Earth, is a ruin. A planet spoiled by the human species. We multiplied and gobbled and fought until there was nothing left, and then we died. We controlled neither appetite nor violence; we did not adapt. We destroyed ourselves. But we destroyed the world first. There are no forests left on my Earth. The air is grey, the sky is grey, it is always hot. It is habitable, it is still habitable, but not as this world is. This is a living world, a harmony. Mine is a discord. You Odonians chose a desert; we Terrans made a desert.... We survive there as you do. People are tough! There are nearly a half billion of us now. Once there were nine billion.[140]

Keng may be an apologist for the injustices of Urras, but her image of a desert Earth tempers the utopian enthusiasm Shevek manifests for the ansible. Instantaneous communication entails the dissolution of spatial and temporal difference in the dissemination of meaning. As Shevek himself suggests, the ansible does not 'transmit' anything, since transmission is a temporal process of sending and receiving across distances. Rather, it makes messages *simultaneous* to one another and thus reinvents language as a medium indifferent to spatial constraints. It is fitting that Keng is the one who expresses scepticism over the ansible's utopian promise. The space-time compression involved in globalisation is surely part of the process that has ruined her Earth. The abolition of geography is the very dream that has given us imperialism, capitalism and the ecological catastrophes of the Anthropocene. What the ansible promises is the perfection of technology as world-building, but the consequence is that 'Earth' in the Heideggerian sense of resistance to such technologies disappears entirely. Since Shevek feels that Odonian society has engineered its social relations all too efficiently and to the point of an unthinking conformism, his insistence on a technological solution to this problem can only strike us as unconvincing.

But what happens if technology becomes the *site* of the utopian struggle rather than the means of its ultimate realisation? Robinson's

Red Mars is the first novel in a trilogy telling the story of the human terraforming of Mars. The relationships between science, technology and labour presented by the text become the key means for imagining socio-political contestation. The technoscientific means of world-disclosure become the components of political allegory. Jameson argues that science fiction, particularly work from the 1940s and 1950s, often conveys a 'collective folk-dream' about the nature of scientific labour, according to which the scientist

> doesn't do real work (yet power is his and social status as well), his remuneration is not monetary or at the very least money seems no object, there is something fascinating about his laboratory (the home workshop magnified to institutional dimensions, a combination of factory and clinic), about the way he works nights (he isn't bound by routine or the eight-hour day).[141]

Jameson adds that 'none of this has anything to do with science itself, but is rather a distorted reflection of our own feelings and dreams about work alienated and nonalienated: it is a wish-fulfillment'.[142] Science fiction thus presents utopian desire mediated through technoscientific work. The idea is explicitly engaged by the scientists in *Red Mars*, who see in the task of terraforming the desert planet the possibility of non-alienated labour. Of the first group of one hundred scientists who initially land as colonisers, the Russian engineer Arkady Bogdanov – namesake of the Bolshevik scientist and author of the Martian science fiction novel *Red Star* (1908) – is the novel's main opponent of the private corporate interests that seek to take hold of the planet's resources. Near the end of the novel, he explains his vision to the American John Boone, first man on Mars:

> When we first arrived, and for twenty years after that, Mars was like Antarctica but even purer. We were outside the world, we didn't even own things ... This arrangement resembles the prehistoric way to live, and it therefore feels right to us, because our brains recognize it from three millions of years practicing it. ... It allows you to concentrate your attention on the real work, which means everything that is done to stay alive, or make things, or satisfy one's curiosity, or play. That is utopia, John.[143]

The utopianism of labour is one possible answer to the question Moretti asks about Defoe's Robinson on his island: why does he work so much?[144] Bogdanov argues that enclaves of scientific research, such as Arctic science stations, are 'islands', refuges in the vast ocean of transnational capital.[145] But whereas Robinson's work ethic emerged from a desire to reproduce the bourgeois world, Bogdanov's version is oriented towards an entirely new one, parasitic on capitalism but ultimately opposed to it, in which the divisions between manual and intellectual activity dissolve. As with Le Guin's Anarres, such a world can come into being on Mars because of environmental necessities. But as the scientists set about turning Mars into a new Earth and the old one suffers the ravages of climate change and over-population, the nature of the society being established by terraforming comes to be fiercely contested. The Bogdanovites, as they come to be called, are one of a number of different factions. The Reds, represented by the geologist Ann Clayborne, value the non-living landscape of pre-colonial Mars over all organic invaders, while the Greens, represented by the biologist Hiroko Ai, are a band of nature mystics seeking to spread life throughout the barrenness. The opposition, here, between geology and biology becomes an *ideological* opposition, as it does also in Le Guin. The physicist Sax Russell, meanwhile, pursues the goal of terraforming by any means necessary, but this pragmatic, non-ideologically aligned position is cast by Robinson as a pernicious subjective idealism by which science performs the duty of spreading consciousness – or what we might regard as the structure of world-disclosure as such – throughout the universe. For all of these factions, however, political struggle is ultimately identified with a struggle over the technologies of world-disclosure.

McKenzie Wark follows Jameson's suggestion that *Red Mars* may be read as a robinsonade. The habitat that the First Hundred build is removed from their spacecraft just as Robinson's is from the wrecked ship.[146] For Wark, *Robinson Crusoe* is the key precursor in literary history of 'capitalist realism', the idea that capitalism's economic realities are so inescapable that a convincing post-capitalist future is unthinkable.[147] Defoe's story 'lacks any transcendent leap towards the heavens or the future. It is as horizontal as a pipeline. It is about making something of this world, not transcending it in favor of another'.[148] It is strange, in this sense, to think that the robinsonade could be compatible with the utopian impulse, famously identified by Bloch with a future-oriented outlook, let alone be one of the main vehicles of it. As Wark remarks, following Moretti's reading, Robinson's labours are fundamentally *connective*: 'In Defoe, things can be useful in themselves. They are connectable only sideways, in networks of other things. With this you get that, with that you make this, and so on. Things are described in detail.'[149] In Defoe's attention to particulars, 'what is lost is the totality. The world dissolves into these particulars'.[150] This, as we have seen, is not strictly true: the loss of world that forces Robinson to attend so closely to the particulars of his island also reveals his remarkable ability to *presume the world as totality* even while recognising its absence. The Robinson paradox is nothing other than this presumption, and it is Robinson's central technological innovation. That Robinson does not resolve his paradox but rather *puts it to use* allows it to take on genuinely utopian potential in texts such as *Red Mars*.

In pursuing such a reading of Robinson's novel, however, we cannot avoid the unsettling idea that the Anthropocene itself may be a utopian concept. For most, of course, it is distinctly dystopian, but for others – 'optimists', as Heise calls them – the Anthropocene 'opens up the possibility of reimagining the nature of the future not as a return to the past or a realm apart from humans, but as a nature reshaped by humans'.[151] As geoengineering comes increasingly to seem a necessary part of any possible response to climate catastrophe, Earth itself becomes the desert island of which the robinsonade has for centuries dreamed. This raises the question of Robinson's solitude, which was always a solitude with some others. E. O. Wilson's concept of the Eremozoic or Eremocene as an alternative way of imagining the Anthropocene is relevant here: the *erēmos* that gives Wilson his coinage is etymologically tied not only to the desert but to solitude.[152] In the Bible, moreover, the *erēmos* denotes the place where sheep are abandoned by a shepherd: 'Which one of you, having a hundred sheep and losing one of them, does not leave the ninety-nine in the *erēmos* and go after the one that is lost until he finds it?'[153] To think of Earthly life as abandoned sheep suggests a new mode of pastoral, perhaps, but it may also suggest the disappearance of the shepherd's transcendent role as steward or guardian. Robinson needed to imagine his island as deserted precisely in order to unite *in himself* the world he had lost with the new land beneath his feet. But, as we've seen, this unity is broken by the very paradox on which it is founded. The paradox remains our own. To think of life in all its forms as 'alone together', collectively dispersed on a planet without a transcendence – human or divine – to guide it, is the challenge of our age.

NOTES

1. Mentz, *Shipwreck Modernity*, p. 2.
2. Ibid. p. xx.
3. Blumenberg, *Shipwreck with Spectator*, pp. 10–11.
4. Ibid. p. 29.
5. Moretti, *The Bourgeois*, pp. 26–8.
6. Deleuze and Guattari, *A Thousand Plateaus*, p. 377.
7. In the preface to the English translation of his second book on cinema, Deleuze explains, with reference to films by Rossellini, Antonioni and others, why cinema in postwar Europe changed fundamentally:

   > The fact is that, in Europe, the post-war period has greatly increased the situations which we no longer know how to react to, in spaces

which we no longer know how to describe. These were 'any spaces whatever', deserted but inhabited, disused warehouses, waste ground, cities in the course of demolition or reconstruction. And in these any-spaces-whatever a new race of characters was stirring, kind of mutant: they saw rather than acted, they were seers. Hence Rossellini's great trilogy, *Europe 51*, *Stromboli*, *Germany Year 0*: a child in the destroyed city, a foreign woman on the island, a bourgeoise woman who starts to 'see' what is around her. (*Cinema 2*, p. xi)

The volcanic island of Stromboli in Rossellini's film is, like the devastated spaces of postwar Europe generally, the site of a new perception. The deserts that feature in Antonioni's *Red Desert* (1964), *Zabriskie Point* (1970) and *The Passenger* (1975) have this same quality and serve similar functions. Antonioni's characters are isolated, damaged, exhausted or neurotic, but for precisely this reason they facilitate the emergence of a new set of sensations that are premised on this very devastation of bodily experience (Ibid. pp. 204–5). At the end of *Zabriskie Point*, an alienated couple travel to Death Valley and attempt to populate the desert with potential forms of sexual revivification. This film's desert orgy scene provides images of how we might understand what Deleuze means by 'populous solitude'.

8. For a philosophical account of modernity's historicity, see Peter Osborne's *The Politics of Time: Modernity and Avant-Garde* (1995). In seeking an immanent path to the understanding of history as totality, one is necessarily led to an 'end of history' position. Immanent universal history must inevitably (from Hegel onwards) have an eschatological component. As Osborne writes vis-à-vis Ricoeur on Heideggerian being-towards-death:

If there can be no 'temporalization of temporality' without the anticipation of death as index of the finitude of existence, so, by extension, there can be no temporalization of historical time, no historical temporality, without the anticipation of an equivalent kind of 'end' to history: no 'history' without the anticipation of an 'end to history'. If Dasein is being-towards-death, and history is the product of inscriptions of phenomenological time onto cosmological time, then we can define historical beings as beings-toward-the-end-of-history. This is the hidden logic of Ricoeur's reading of Heidegger. (p. 61)

9. Mentz, *Shipwreck Modernity*, p. 172.
10. Moretti, *The Bourgeois*, p. 45.
11. Darwin, *The Origin of Species*, pp. 350–1.
12. Deleuze, 'Desert Islands', in *Desert Islands and Other Texts*, p. 9.
13. Coleridge, *Specimens of the Table Talk of the Late Samuel Taylor Coleridge, Vol. II*, p. 338.
14. Coleridge, *The Rime of the Ancient Mariner*, in *Samuel Taylor Coleridge: The Major Works*, lines 598–600.

15. Deleuze, 'Desert Islands', p. 9.
16. Ibid. p. 9.
17. Ibid. p. 9.
18. Ibid. p. 10.
19. Ibid. p. 10.
20. For work on Deleuze and solitude, see Brusseau, *Isolated Experiences* and Pelbart, *Cartography of Exhaustion*.
21. Deleuze, 'Desert Islands', p. 13.
22. Ibid. p. 13.
23. Ibid. p. 13.
24. Marcel Griaule's anthropological work is Deleuze and Guattari's main source for Dogon cosmology (*Anti-Oedipus*, p. 154). For Griaule's discussion of the 'second genesis' of the world and the cosmic egg in Dogon mythology, and for the image of the Dogon egg which Deleuze and Guattari use for the body without organs chapter of *A Thousand Plateaus*, see Griaule, *The Pale Fox*, pp. 117–21.
25. Deleuze and Guattari, *Anti-Oedipus*, p. 158.
26. Deleuze, 'Desert Islands', p. 12.
27. As Ian Watt writes in his classic text, 'economic individualism explains much of Crusoe's character; economic specialization and its associated ideology help to account for the appeal of his adventures; but it is Puritan individualism which controls his spiritual being' (Watt, *The Rise of the Novel*, p. 74).
28. Joyce, 'Realism and Idealism in English Literature', p. 174.
29. Rousseau, *Emile*, p. 184.
30. Marx, *Grundrisse*, p. 83.
31. Ibid. p. 83.
32. Walcott, 'The Figure of Crusoe', p. 35.
33. Walcott, 'Crusoe's Journal', in *Collected Poems*, p. 92.
34. Deleuze and Guattari, *Anti-Oedipus*, p. 140.
35. Giddens, *The Consequences of Modernity*, p. 19.
36. Deleuze, 'Desert Islands', p. 12.
37. Ibid. p. 12.
38. Defoe, *Robinson Crusoe*, p. 49.
39. Deleuze and Guattari, *A Thousand Plateaus*, p. 164.
40. Schonhorn, *Defoe's Politics*, p. 144.
41. Deleuze, 'Desert Islands', p. 12.
42. Ibid. p. 12.
43. Derrida, *The Beast and the Sovereign, Volume II*, p. 21.
44. Ibid. p. 4.
45. Defoe, *Robinson Crusoe*, p. 108.
46. Derrida, *The Beast and the Sovereign, Volume II*, p. 77.
47. Ibid. p. 54.
48. Moretti, *The Bourgeois*, p. 30.
49. Derrida, *The Beast and the Sovereign, Volume II*, p. 48.

50. Ibid. p. 139.
51. Ibid. p. 84.
52. Ibid. p. 87.
53. Defoe, *Robinson Crusoe*, p. 12.
54. Mentz, *Shipwreck Modernity*, p. xvii.
55. Moore, *Capitalism in the Web of Life*, p. 10.
56. Sloterdijk, *In the World Interior of Capital*, p. 32.
57. The archaeologist Matt Edgeworth describes the humanly altered ground as the 'archaeosphere':

> The archaeosphere can be described as the sum of humanly modified deposits on the surface of the Earth. Occupation debris, landfill, urban artificial ground, quarried materials, ploughsoils, other cultivation soils, dumps of industrial waste, more ancient strata containing cultural material – all these together now form an enveloping and rapidly growing layer or set of layers over a large proportion of land surfaces in densely settled and cultivated parts of the world. Within these layers are novel materials unprecedented in the rest of nature – pottery, glass, concrete, plastics and so on – often in teeming profusion and variety of artefact form. Running through the deposits are service trenches containing vast networks of pipes, wires, fibre-optic cables. (Edgeworth, 'Grounded Objects', p. 107)

58. Heidegger, 'The Origin of the Work of Art', in *Poetry, Language, Thought*, p. 61.
59. Derrida, *The Beast and the Sovereign, Volume II*, pp. 78–9.
60. Defoe, *Robinson Crusoe*, p. 61.
61. Derrida, *The Beast and the Sovereign, Volume II*, pp. 77–8.
62. Derrida, 'Faith and Knowledge', p. 42.
63. Ibid. p. 43. For a wide-ranging discussion of the desert motif in Derrida's work, see Laurent Milesi's 'Thinking (Through) the Desert (la pensée du désert) With(in) Jacques Derrida'.
64. Derrida, 'Faith and Knowledge', pp. 57–8.
65. Ibid. p. 55.
66. Ibid. p. 43.
67. Naas, *Miracle and Machine*, p. 76.
68. Derrida, *The Beast and the Sovereign, Volume II*, p. 9.
69. Derrida, 'Rams', p. 140.
70. For a thorough account of Derrida's concept of world and the notion of the end of the world in the Derridean sense, see the last two chapters of Gaston's *The Concept of World from Kant to Derrida*.
71. Derrida, *The Beast and the Sovereign, Volume II*, p. 265.
72. Ibid. p. 265.
73. Deleuze, *The Logic of Sense*, p. 48.
74. Deleuze, 'How Do We Recognize Structuralism?', in *Desert Islands and Other Texts*, pp. 185–6.

75. Ibid. p. 186.
76. Lévi-Strauss writes:

> I see in *mana, wakan, orenda,* and other notions of the same type, the conscious expression of a *semantic function,* whose role is to enable symbolic thinking to operate despite the contradiction inherent in it. That explains the apparently insoluble antinomies attaching to the notion of *mana,* which struck ethnographers so forcibly, and on which Mauss shed light: force and action; quality and state; substantive, adjective and verb all at once; abstract and concrete; omnipresent and localised. And, indeed, *mana* is all those things together; but is that not precisely because it is none of those things, but a simple form, or to be more accurate, a symbol in its pure state, therefore liable to take on any symbolic content whatever? In the system of symbols which makes up any cosmology, it would just be a *zero symbolic value,* that is, a sign marking the necessity of a supplementary symbolic content over and above that which the signified already contains, which can be any value at all. (*Introduction to the Work of Marcel Mauss,* pp. 63–4)

Lacan remarks, in relation to this passage: 'it seems to me that what we are dealing with here is rather the signifier of the lack of this zero symbol' (*Écrits,* p. 243). The phallus is thus a signifier of lack. This grounds the Lacanian concept of desire in non-being, which Deleuze and Guattari fundamentally oppose. The Deleuzian zero is not lack but the minimal possible intensity, or the minimum of being. For a discussion of the zero in Lacanian psychoanalysis, see Eyers, *Post-Rationalism,* p. 25.
77. Deleuze, *The Logic of Sense,* p. 49.
78. Ibid. p. 48.
79. Levinas, 'The Transcendence of Worlds', p. 148.
80. Tournier, *Friday,* p. 51.
81. Ibid. p. 38.
82. Ibid. p. 55.
83. Ibid. p. 64.
84. Ibid. p. 67.
85. Abbey, *Desert Solitaire,* p. 32.
86. Tournier, *Friday,* p. 113.
87. Ibid. p. 198.
88. Deleuze, *The Logic of Sense,* p. 302.
89. Ibid. p. 303.
90. Lacan, *Écrits,* p. 43.
91. Eyers, *Lacan and the Concept of the 'Real',* p. 105.
92. Deleuze, *The Logic of Sense,* p. 304.
93. Ibid. p. 320.
94. Ibid. p. 311.
95. Tournier, *Friday,* p. 90.

96. Ibid. p. 211.
97. Burroughs, 'Preface', in J. G. Ballard, *The Atrocity Exhibition*, p. vii.
98. On the desert in Ballard's work, see Finkelstein, '"Deserts of Vast Eternity"' and Knowles, 'Aeolian Harps in the Desert'. Finkelstein's article discusses the relationship between Ballard and Smithson on the topic of entropy.
99. Ballard, *Concrete Island*, p. 32.
100. Ibid. p. 4.
101. Ballard, *The Drought*, p. 176.
102. Ibid. p. 154.
103. More, *Utopia*, p. 41.
104. Wells, *The Time Machine*, p. 99.
105. Ruddick, *Ultimate Island*, p. 87.
106. Ballard, 'The Terminal Beach', in *The Terminal Beach*, p. 136.
107. Ibid. p. 139.
108. Ibid. p. 140.
109. Ibid. p. 139.
110. Ibid. p. 137.
111. Ibid. pp. 138–9.
112. Ibid. p. 146.
113. Ballard, *The Atrocity Exhibition*, p. 41.
114. Ballard, *Concrete Island*, p. 11.
115. Ibid. p. 9.
116. Ibid. p. 27.
117. Ibid. p. 91.
118. Ibid. p. 65.
119. Solà-Morales, 'Terrain Vague', p. 26.
120. Paul Farley and Michael Symmons Roberts's book *Edgelands* (2012) evokes and celebrates the derelict, post-industrial spaces of northern England. The edgelands, much like the terrain vague of Sola-Moràles, form an unofficial wilderness in the cracks of modern cities: 'a Victorian factory knocked down, a business park newly built, a section of waste ground cleared and landscaped, a pre-war warehouse abandoned and open to the elements' (p. 6). Farley and Roberts evoke these places in a way that suggests a continuity rather than a break with the tradition of Coleridge and Wordsworth and the broader English environmental imagination, of which Ballard too is part.
121. Ballard, 'The Enormous Space', in *War Fever*, p. 118.
122. Ibid. p. 120.
123. Ibid. p. 121.
124. Ibid. p. 125.
125. Ibid. p. 127.
126. Ibid. p. 118.
127. Ibid. p. 129.
128. Gaston, *The Concept of World from Kant to Derrida*, p. 5.

129. Gaston writes that

> the Kantian regulative idea of the world, which suspends any claim to the world itself as a given or self-evident concept, is still the most radical concept of world in the history of philosophy. In insisting that one must act *as if* there is a given world, it invites the possibility of a philosophy without world. (*The Concept of World from Kant to Derrida*, p. 28)

130. Derrida, *The Beast and the Sovereign, Volume II*, p. 267.
131. Jameson, *Archaeologies of the Future*, p. 271.
132. For a fascinating synthesis of Deleuze and Jameson, see Ian Buchanan's book *Deleuzism: A Metacommentary* (2000).
133. Le Guin, *The Dispossessed*, p. 76.
134. Ursula Heise is critical of Jameson's reading of Le Guin because he appears to figure her reduced ecologies as mere metaphors for social relations rather than as descriptions of literal environmental conditions ('Reduced Ecologies', p. 101). However, this criticism presumes that an abstraction of the natural from the social is possible, while it is precisely the impossibility of doing this that characterises Odonian politics and economy. The Odonian ideal sees nature and society as entirely bound up with one another so that 'nature' as such does not appear as an ecology beyond social relations. It is only when Shevek goes to the green and verdant world of Urras, where the commodity form reigns, that he is able to distinguish between nature and society and himself formulate an environmentalist critique of Urrasti capitalism.
135. Le Guin, *The Dispossessed*, p. 287.
136. Ibid. p. 300.
137. Ibid. p. 62.
138. Jameson, *Archaeologies of the Future*, p. 157.
139. Le Guin, *The Dispossessed*, p. 187.
140. Ibid. p. 286.
141. Jameson, *Marxism and Form*, p. 405.
142. Ibid. p. 405.
143. Robinson, *Red Mars*, p. 402.
144. Moretti, *The Bourgeois*, p. 30.
145. Robinson, *Red Mars*, p. 403.
146. Jameson, *Archaeologies of the Future*, pp. 402–3.
147. Wark, *Molecular Red*, p. 183.
148. Ibid. pp. 183–4.
149. Ibid. p. 184.
150. Ibid. p. 184.
151. Heise, *Imagining Extinction*, p. 203.
152. Wilson, *Half-Earth*, p. 20.
153. Luke 15: 4.

5. Desert Polemologies

DEVASTATION, TERRITORY AND THE STATE

Environmental devastation involves a particular kind of violence that is hard to determine. For Heidegger, it is an ontological rather than an ontic violence which doesn't just destroy but 'blocks all future growth and prevents all building'.[1] For Deleuze and Guattari, the desert of the body without organs petrifies the desiring-machines, the components of world production, but this is necessary for desire to deterritorialise and begin anew. Devastation is not, then, simply destruction of the living. As Matthew Fuller and Olga Goriunova argue, today's 'complex devastational forms' should not be seen merely in terms of an attenuation or diminishment of life and biodiversity.[2] Devastation merges with the reproduction of capitalist society, and thus with life itself. Specific instances of the damage and risks associated with the Anthropocene – species extinction, habitat loss, soil degradation, disturbances in the oxygen and nitrogen cycles, eutrophication, oil spills, the extinguishing of peoples and cultures – fail to capture the kind, and not only the degree, of violence involved. Justin McBrien writes of capitalism's expansion as a generalised necrosis or 'becoming extinction'.[3] The problem is how to recognise environmental damage *as* damage once a regime of violence becomes structurally necessary for what we experience as normal or even desirable for the capitalist mode of production. As Heidegger argues, 'the devastation of the earth can easily go hand in hand with a guaranteed supreme living standard for man'.[4] This resonates with what Rob Nixon has called the 'slow violence' of environmental degradation, which operates on much larger timescales than those events which we usually code as violent.[5]

We can pursue these problems by considering how the relationships between space, politics and the state entail different forms of violence, and how the desert figures in polemological discourse (the discourse of war). I want to suggest that what Deleuze and Guattari call the 'war machine' can be considered a devastational form that combats the structural violence of the state. I understand the war machine in this chapter primarily as a set of affects, tied to desert landscapes, which are capable of registering devastation as both a subjective and environmental reality. The violence of devastation is both interlinked and contrasted with the violence of the state. Devastation ungrounds, but the state manifests a founding violence that marks out a territory or a world over which it has dominion. That is, the state *creates* a territory at the same time as it asserts power over it, in a way Deleuze and Guattari describe as 'magical'. As Hannah Arendt writes:

> All laws first create a space in which they are valid, and this space is the world in which we can move about in freedom. What lies outside this space is without law and, even more precisely, without world; as far as human community is concerned, it is a desert.[6]

The wars of annihilation made possible in the twentieth century are special in that what they destroy is 'more than the world of the vanquished foe; it is above all the in-between, the space that lies between the warring parties and their peoples, the territory that, taken as a whole, forms the world on earth'.[7] The desert in this sense is the erasure of the territorial differences that allow worlds and states to be made and unmade. The Cold War can be understood on the basis of the ability to calculate these differences as elements of strategy. The desert, then, as Arendt understands it, becomes the object of technological wars of annihilation, but we have seen Heidegger argue that the technological imperialism of the modern age also functions in this way to create a desert. Put otherwise, for capitalism to realise itself as global, it needs to imagine the Earth as essentially a worldwide smooth space where the territorial divisions of states become uncertain or dissolve entirely.[8]

As we have seen, for Deleuze and Guattari the state corresponds to the striated space of the *polis* in contrast to the smooth space of the *nomos*. They argue that the *nomos* in its original ancient Greek usage meant an area adjacent to the city (the backcountry or mountainside) in which people and animals are distributed in a different way than in the city or striated agricultural spaces. Their critique of the state-form is thus based on an assertion of the irreducibly political nature of space. The work of Carl Schmitt provides a useful point of comparison here because it deploys a different conception of the *nomos* in an attempt to ground an understanding of international law.[9] In *The* Nomos *of the Earth* (1950), written during the final years of the Second World War,

Schmitt argued that the 'Eurocentric' era, the era of European colonialism, had come to an end and with it the ways in which modern states legitimated their authority as international political actors. This crisis of legitimacy could be addressed by returning to the ancient concept of *nomos*, a term that became synonymous with 'law' but which originally meant a relationship with the land. Schmitt insists upon a foundational connection between orientation in space and order in the political sense: '*Nomos* comes from *nemein* – a [Greek] word that means both "to divide" and "to pasture". Thus, nomos is the immediate form in which the political and social order of a people becomes spatially visible – the initial measure and division of pastureland.'[10] In Schmitt's interpretation, the *nomos* grounds the legitimacy of state authority in an original and founding claim to the land, and legal order is derived from how land is appropriated, divided up, enclosed and measured. Deleuze and Guattari interpret *nomos* in a way that inverts Schmitt's claims while retaining his insistence on the political primacy of space. Drawing on a work by Emmanuel Laroche that Schmitt also uses, they insist on a fundamental 'alternative between the city, or *polis*, ruled by laws, and the outskirts as the place of the *nomos*'.[11] The *nomos*, as primary relationship to the land, is *resistant* to state appropriation, not foundational for it. They suggest a whole environmental aesthetics of the desert, a *sensorium*, by which to think the *nomos* as a space of political resistance:

> The same terms are used to describe ice deserts as sand deserts: there is no line separating earth and sky; there is no intermediate distance, no perspective or contour; visibility is limited; and yet there is an extraordinarily fine topology that relies not on points or objects but rather on haecceities, on sets of relations (winds, undulations of snow or sand, the song of the sand or the creaking of ice, the tactile qualities of both). It is a tactile space, or rather 'haptic,' a sonorous much more than a visual space.[12]

The *nomos* is not primarily a physical space but an aesthetico-conceptual topology, a *spatium* that allows us to think power beyond the state-form by which law is grounded on the division and measurement of land. Shifting sands can inspire counter-state affects, even in those working for the state.[13] The state-form codes and overcodes space while the *nomos* produces it as deterritorialised. We can attempt either to master space with fixed lines, points and other representations, or we can compose it nomadically through itinerant occupations and movements.

This distinction between striated and smooth is not a strict opposition but a complex interrelation. The state emerged through intimate contact with smooth spaces. Deracination and clearing are involved in

European forms of agriculture more than other forms.[14] What we call 'civilisation' developed in the smooth spaces of the deserts and steppes of central Asia, which also facilitated the growth of global trade networks from the fifteenth century onwards.[15] Virilio has frequently emphasised the role of the desert frontier or glacis, the no-man's-land surrounding the empire, which becomes the object of the emperor's gaze as a field of military vision.[16] Stuart Elden writes that cartographic techniques became particularly important politically from the seventeenth century onwards because of the need to map 'mountainous regions' and 'deserts or tundra', and to create abstract divisions of 'unknown places in the colonized world'.[17]

States, then, do not rely solely on the striated spaces under their direct control but need the smooth spaces of sea, steppe and desert as well as those of the air and telecommunications. In the case of naval power, states not only exert dominance by means of the sea by occupying its surface but come to rely on the economic and other kinds of flows that can only operate by way of it. The same could be said for the topologies of telecommunications today.[18] The state *needs smooth spaces to stratify*; it thus 'reimparts' elements that exceed its control in order to widen its 'apparatus of capture'.[19] The colonisation of the New World functioned precisely in this way and was crucial to how European states legitimated their authority. By confronting European power with forms of smooth space that were entirely novel, the New World accelerated the development of a homogeneous representational space by which the Western mind mapped the globe. Robert Sack writes that charters for seventeenth-century English settlements in Virginia and elsewhere 'described territorial claims abstractly and geometrically and, in conjunction with conceptually and then actually clearing the land of Indians, the geometric lines of territorial authority became sweeping space-clearing and maintaining devices for territorially instituting communities'.[20] Likewise, the United States Geological Survey originated from the expansionist necessity to map the terrain acquired through the Louisiana Purchase and the Mexican–American War in the first half of the nineteenth century. The gaze of a surveyor such as John Charles Frémont was also the 'gaze of the conqueror', as Rebecca Solnit puts it.[21]

THE WAR MACHINE AND THE GROWING DESERT

The condition of modern spatiality is thus one in which a Eurocentric striated space encounters, appropriates and extends spatial alterity as a condition of its expansion. To the extent that striated space abstracts from the physical in order to measure and divide it, it spreads a *desert of abstraction*, suggesting an uncanny affinity with the physical deserts encountered by European colonialism. This is described in Pynchon's novel *Gravity's Rainbow* (1973) by Dominus Blicero, a maniacal SS officer and V-2 rocket commander who, in the last days of the war, dreams of an apocalyptic synthesis of power and technology through sadomasochistic sex. Blicero is a reincarnation of Weissmann, who featured as a marginal figure in the southwest Africa episode in *V*. His reappearance in the later novel underscores a continuity Pynchon sees between colonisation, the Nazi project and postwar America. As Blicero maintains to his sacrificial victim Gottfried:

> America *was* the edge of the World. A message for Europe, continent-sized, inescapable. Europe had found the site for its Kingdom of Death, that special Death the West had invented. Savages had their waste regions, Kalaharis, lakes so misty they could not see the other side. But Europe had gone deeper ... In Africa, Asia, Amerindia, Oceania, Europe came and established its order of Analysis and Death. What it could not use, it killed or altered. In time the death-colonies grew strong enough to break away. But the impulse to empire, the mission to propagate death, the structure of it, kept on. Now we are in the last phase. American Death has come to occupy Europe. It has learned empire from its old metropolis. But now we have *only* the structure left us. ... Is the cycle over now, and a new one ready to begin? Will our new Edge, our new Deathkingdom, be the Moon?[22]

Europe's colonial movement west is part of a planetary death instinct. Claims to the legitimate exercise of power made by European states depended upon the existence of an exterior domain in which it could pursue its 'civilising mission'. This involved not just physical violence but the violence of 'analysis', the reconstitution of space as a set of functions, movements and limits that can be abstractly described – the arc of a rocket's trajectory becomes frozen into a parabola. What Schmitt calls 'global linear thinking' is the condition of the Deathkingdom.[23] When the centre of Western power moves from Europe to America in the twentieth century, the 'old' exterior of the non-European, uncivilised or half-civilised world disappears, but the will to empire remains, Blicero insists, as sheer 'structure' or impulse 'to propagate death' in the form of a technological warfare. This is embodied in the Nazi and then American Rocket-State.[24]

For Deleuze and Guattari, as for Hegel, the question of the state leads us beyond political philosophy in the strict sense to questions about subjectivity, ethics, desire and thought itself.[25] Hegel's theory of the state maintained that it is the self-realisation, in history, of an ethical Idea, with constitutional monarchy being the 'infinite form' of the Idea.[26] The state is, like reason, self-grounding, producer of its own legitimating conditions or 'mystical foundations of authority', as Derrida would say.[27] But it must also channel the will and energies of citizens and render these 'rational'. Hegel writes that the state 'is ethical spirit as the substantial will manifest and clear to itself, knowing and thinking itself, accomplishing what it knows and insofar as it knows it'.[28] Deleuze and Guattari agree that the state is self-grounding in this way and that it has not only served to legitimate certain forms of power but, more importantly, ways of thinking, feeling, desiring and producing. The state is both pure Idea *and* material reality. Precisely *as* an Idea, it marshals will, desire and material resources; it is a kind of machine, or assemblage of machines arranged around a central point distributing relative interior and exterior domains. Subjectivity, as psychoanalysis has shown, can be produced on the basis of an internalised model of the law of the father. Deleuze and Guattari's war machine is thus offered not simply as a model of militant resistance to the state but, more importantly, as a means of conceiving a subjectivity beyond the state-form. If subjectivity is determined by the state-form as an interiority submitted to an external, law-giving transcendence, then the war machine is a way of thinking an utterly different assemblage of thought, desire and affect, *a subjectivity of the absolute outside as opposed to a subjectivity of interiority/exteriority*. Deleuze and Guattari go so far as to suggest that the war machine grants 'another justice, another space-time'.[29] The absolute outside is the desert, and the war machine's primary purpose, they tell us, is to 'make the desert, the steppe, grow'.[30] The desert of nihilism or state violence is countered by the desert of the nomad, who is 'there, on the land, wherever there forms a smooth space that gnaws, and tends to grow, in all directions. The nomads inhabit these places; they remain in them, and they themselves make them grow'.[31] The term 'nomad' does not refer so much to actual nomadic peoples as to 'an abstraction, an Idea' offered in response to the Idea of the state.[32] At the same time, a simple opposition of state and war machine is insufficient because the state *appropriates* a war machine in the form of an army, even if it will always mistrust the military institutions it creates in order to do so.[33] Additionally, as we've seen, the state must itself reimpart and incorporate smooth spaces in various ways, giving rise to a global assemblage of war, technology and capital that can be considered a devastational megamachine.[34]

Georges Dumézil's work on Indo-European myth is Deleuze and Guattari's main source for the relationship between the state and war. Dumézil argues that throughout various mythological and theological traditions, sovereignty is represented by means of a pairing of gods, one corresponding to the figure of jurist-organiser and the other to the figure of magician-creator:

> Sovereignty aligns itself on two planes, at once antithetical and complementary, necessary to each other and consequently without hostility, with no mythology of conflict.... These planes ... are those of juridical sovereignty, near to man, luminous, reassuring, etc., and magical sovereignty, far from man, dark, terrible, etc.[35]

Dumézil argues that the mythic figure of the warrior remains external to and autonomous from this two-headed sovereignty, and as a result appears 'disturbing ... for the social order and the order of the cosmos'.[36] Warriors had to be appropriated, '[redeployed] in the service of the good religion ... to preserve their force and valor while depriving them of their autonomy'.[37] In the history of the state, the war machine is caught between magical and juridical capture, between the magic of signs and the bonds of law. But this appropriation remains fundamentally unstable. As Deleuze and Guattari write: 'each time there is an operation against the State – insubordination, rioting, guerrilla warfare, or revolution as act – it can be said that a war machine has revived, that a new nomadic potential has appeared, accompanied by the reconstitution of a smooth space'.[38] While the examples they give here are directly political and historical, their main concern is to understand how counter-state phenomena manifest in the realms of science, art, philosophy, and even at the level of desire and affect. The state in transcendence bears upon the body, giving it a certain organisation (work becomes discipline as opposed to play, for example), but the war machine suggests an alternative subjective model: 'the regime of the war machine is ... that *of affects*, which relate only to the moving body in itself'.[39] Affects may become the 'weapons' of a war machine, a way of fending off the state-form at the level of desire and the aesthetic. This is attested to in nomad arts such as jewellery-making, but also 'in the *chanson de geste*, and the chivalric novel or novel of courtly love'.[40]

The war machine is allied to conceptions of material flux and hydraulic models of matter. The atomism of Democritus and Lucretius and the geometry of Archimedes are antithetical to the 'royal or imperial sciences' of the state-form.[41] The war machine thus conceptualises an *ontology of force* beyond the self-grounding violence of the state. Given this ontological dimension, the war machine can be compared with Heidegger's reading of the Greek notion of *polemos* as found in the fragments of Heraclitus. With respect to the fragment that states 'war (*polemos*) is the father of all and king of all', Heidegger in a seminar from 1934–5 argues that battle [*Kampf*] is the power that creates beings, . . . battle also and precisely preserves and governs beings in their essential subsistence. Battle is indeed creator, yet also ruler. Wherever battle ceases as a power of preservation, standstill begins: a leveling out, mediocrity, harmlessness, atrophy, and decline.[42]

Heidegger contrasts two regimes of violence here. *Polemos* (rendered here as *Kampf*) is a generative violence that preserves and creates. This is the essence of Heraclitean flux:

> 'everything flows.' This does not mean that everything is continually in a process of change and without subsistence, but rather that you cannot take up position on any one side alone, but will be carried, through strife as conflict, to the opposite side.[43]

This conflictual becoming is contrasted to the other regime of violence, that of atrophy and decline. The latter regime is precisely the kind of damage Heidegger associates with the desert and devastation.

In what is his best-known deployment of the concept of *polemos*, Heidegger argues that art works express historical truth through a 'strife' (*Streit*) of Earth and world:

> In setting up a world and setting forth the earth, the work is an instigating of this striving. This does not happen so that the work should at the same time settle and put an end to the conflict in an insipid agreement, but so that the strife may remain a strife.[44]

The disjunction between Earth and world appears via *polemos* as a generative violence. As Kelly Oliver puts it, while 'the technological worldview threatens earth and world [with] annihilation, [Heidegger] also deploys an alternative conception of war as polemos that takes us beyond warring nation states toward a more primordial force of the earth itself'.[45] The spread of nihilism across the planet is manifest precisely in the *cessation* of *polemos* and the establishment of a global regime of violence that is all the more insidious for being a kind of peace. For Deleuze and Guattari, the regime of violence particular to the state is self-grounding, operating not only through the transparency of laws but through a magical inscription of its authority. In order for the state to emerge, the exterior elements it needs – citizens, property, material resources and so on – must *already* be at its disposal, such that the 'capture' effected by the state must also generate *what* it captures, as if by magic.[46] This *structural violence* may in fact lead to a kind of peace more terrifying than war.[47] Where Deleuze and Guattari differ from Heidegger is in their contention that the violence of the war machine may operate against the insipid terror of state capture while actively spreading the desert of a smooth space.

The growing desert is thus ambiguous because it is located precisely at the intersection of the structural violence of the state and the rupturing force of the Earth. Deleuze and Guattari recognise that in the late twentieth century the war machine begins to constitute a new, post-fascist global militarism, a 'new nomadism' in which states appear as mere cogs in a transnational, military-industrial machine.[48] For them, this was best exemplified by the Cold War nuclear stand-off. For us today, it is exemplified by how the geopolitics of Western imperialism are articulated with climate and fossil fuels. We must consequently admit that 'smooth space and the form of exteriority do not have an irresistible revolutionary calling'.[49] Nevertheless, global smooth space remains the conceptual topology by which the question of what lies beyond the state-form can most effectively be posed. This has obvious eschatological dimensions, but eschatology here can involve a subjective transformation of desire and affect. In this way, the forces of the Earth and the idea of a new Earth constitute the post-capitalist horizon. The literature of the last hundred years provides us with important demonstrations of how war, the desert and subjectivity intersect, so it is to this literary polemology of the desert that we will now turn our attention.

VAPOROUS SUBJECTIVITY: T. E. LAWRENCE AND PEOPLE'S WAR

Seven Pillars of Wisdom: A Triumph (1926), T. E. Lawrence's autobiographical account of the Arab Revolt during the First World War, offers an example of how the war machine, as an assemblage moving between the poles of the nomad (the Bedouins) and the state (the British Army and Empire), functions at a literary level. The desert plays a key role in the text as both an optical and affective space in which a vaporous subjectivity is distributed according to the movements of guerrilla warfare. Lawrence perceives the war in the desert not simply through an optical aesthetics of haze and mirage but itself as a vaporous collective subject, a hypersubject, distinct from the solidity usually attributed to armies and individual fighters. While considering how his Bedouin forces might counter the greater numbers of the Turkish army, he writes:

> suppose we were (as we might be) an influence, an idea, a thing intangible, invulnerable, without front or back, drifting about like a gas? Armies were like plants, immobile, firm-rooted, nourished through long stems to the head. We might be a vapour, blowing where we listed. Our kingdoms lay in each man's mind; and as we wanted nothing material to live on, so we might offer nothing material to the killing. It seemed a regular soldier might

be helpless without a target, owning only what he sat on, and subjugating only what, by order, he could poke his rifle at.[50]

Guerrilla war is conceived here in terms of a metaphysics of smooth space and is informed by Carl von Clausewitz's account of people's war, as I will show in a moment. But in its aesthetics of evaporation, this passage demonstrates how Lawrence's self-portrait is rendered as a campaign against the solidity of his embodied self. Existing accounts of the book have often drawn on psychoanalysis to understand Lawrence's experience of the war as an existential ordeal. Kaja Silverman, for example, has argued that '*Seven Pillars* was written under the sign of fantasy, as is clearly indicated by its obsessive lingering over masochistic and homosexual detail.'[51] Biographical material on Lawrence's sexuality backs up such an interpretation, but it is his scenography that Silverman focuses on: he portrays the sufferings and degradations of his body in a way that makes the desert a *stage* for celibate, ascetic homosexual desire. The desert is sterile and thus clean, in opposition to the 'unhygienic' process of sexual reproduction.[52] Psychoanalysis can only bring us so far, however, since Lawrence's specific form of desert desire moves beyond the individual or biographical level towards a group subjectivity organised around the poles of nomad and state.

Seven Pillars is ostensibly a memoir documenting Lawrence's involvement in the revolt against the Ottoman Empire begun by Sharif Hussein ibn Ali, Emir of Mecca in June of 1916. Lawrence's academic research on Crusader castles brought him to the Middle East in 1909 and with the outbreak of the war he served as an intelligence officer for the British Army in Cairo. As a proponent of the Arab revolt, he was selected to go to the Hejaz (modern-day Saudi Arabia) to help coordinate British assistance to the Bedouins. With the help of Hussein's sons (notably Feisal, subsequent king of Iraq) and a large number of nomadic fighters, Lawrence participated in a guerrilla war against Turkish and German forces, prosecuted largely through demolition of the railways connecting Turkey and Arabia. The narrative begins with a dedicatory poem to Salim Ahmed, Lawrence's companion before the campaign, and culminates, after a long trek through the desert, with the establishment of an Arab government in Damascus amid the foetor of corpses in an army hospital.

The text often proceeds in a self-aware epic style – Lawrence carries the *Morte d'Arthur* in his saddlebags – and describes a huge number of participants and places, raids and demolitions, in great detail. While Doughty's *Travels in Arabia Deserta* (1888) provided Lawrence with a literary model, the former's epic mode was nostalgic and antiquarian while the latter's was distinctly modern and ironic. This is apparent when, for example, Lawrence considers the heroism of men such as the Bedouin leader Auda Abu-Tayeh in contrast to his own 'diffuse' self:

> I had had one craving all my life – for the power of self-expression in some imaginative form – but had been too diffuse ever to acquire a technique. At last accident, with perverted humour, in casting me as a man of action had given me place in the Arab Revolt, a theme ready and epic to a direct eye and hand, thus offering me an outlet in literature, the technique-less art. Whereupon I became excited only over mechanism. The epic mode was alien to me, as to my generation. Memory gave me no clue to the heroic, so that I could not feel such men as Auda in myself. He seemed fantastic as the hills of Rumm, old as Mallory.[53]

Too much Lawrence scholarship has been devoted to attempts to separate fact from fiction in his account, but the style of *Seven Pillars* deliberately and successfully resists such efforts. The narrative is aware of its own evasiveness, as when Lawrence writes in the initially suppressed introductory chapter that 'my proper share [in the campaign] was a minor one, but because of a fluent pen, a free speech, and a certain adroitness of brain, I took upon myself, as I describe it, a mock primacy'.[54] Even as Lawrence exalts himself as a modern-day knight errant, he remains tormented by feelings of fraud. *This* is the true ordeal he documents. Like Eliot's, it is one of a modern condition unsure of its links to past traditions.[55]

What distinguishes Lawrence from precursors such as Doughty and Gertrude Bell is the way in which his record of the conflict serves an analysis of selfhood and desire. Lawrence regards the desert as a space in which he is physically and spiritually hollowed out: 'The abstraction of the desert landscape cleansed me, and rendered my mind vacant with its superfluous greatness.'[56] While the language he uses often borrows from religion, his ordeal was essentially a libidinal and affective one involving a devastation of his inner life. Feelings of shame and self-loathing predominate, partly due to the political circumstances of imperialism. Lawrence is aware that British promises to recognise Arab independence after the war are likely to be betrayed:

> The Arab Revolt had begun on false pretences. To gain the Sherif's help our Cabinet had offered, through Sir Henry McMahon, to support the establishment of native governments in parts of Syria and Mesopotamia, 'saving the interests of our ally, France'. The last modest clause concealed a treaty (kept secret, till too late, from McMahon, and therefore from the Sherif) by which France, England and Russia agreed to annex some of these promised areas, and to establish their respective spheres of influence over all the rest.[57]

The book is dominated by feelings of shame, but the reasons for this go beyond the matter of McMahon's hollow pledge. Lawrence's desert is *simulacral*, such that the relationships between the fraudulent and the authentic tend to collapse altogether: 'I began to wonder if all established reputations were founded, like mine, on fraud.'[58] As with the deserts of the American southwest in Van Dyke and Abbey, Lawrence's desert becomes a realm of pure appearances. This is why the dreamlike and the fantastical pervade the text to the extent they do, but standard psychoanalytical notions of fantasy do not properly capture this. The desert becomes a stage on which the body's degradation is played out, as in a masochistic fantasy. But the libidinal investment in this degradation produces a simulacral body, a living mirage, that is beyond psychoanalytic subjectivity: 'The body was too coarse to feel the utmost of our sorrows and of our joys. Therefore, we abandoned it as rubbish: we left it below us to march forward, a breathing simulacrum.'[59] While Lawrence sometimes asserts a dualistic conflict of mind and body (which he describes as central to Islam), he ultimately sides with a *molecular monism* in order to describe his ordeal in terms of becoming and process:

> The conception of antithetical mind and matter, which was basic in the Arab self-surrender, helped me not at all. I achieved surrender (so far as I did achieve it) by the very opposite road, through my notion that mental and physical were inseparably one: that our bodies, the universe, our thoughts and tactilities were conceived in and of the molecular sludge of matter, the universal element through which form drifted as clots and patterns of varying density.[60]

Lawrence's self-analysis thus follows a gradient between solid matter and vaporous immateriality. If the guerrilla war of the Bedouins is a vapour, then the regular army under the control of the state is a solid body. Following the capture of Damascus and the arrival of British and other soldiers at the end of the book, Lawrence remarks on 'how the secret of uniform was to make a crowd solid, dignified, impersonal. . . . This death's livery which walled its bearers from ordinary life, was sign that they had sold their wills and bodies to the State.'[61]

In his essay on Lawrence, Deleuze emphasises the optical significance of vapour by referring to Goethe's argument in *The Theory of Colours* (1810) that light is transmitted by a transparent medium 'of the nature of air and gas'.[62] Deleuze defines light in this sense not as the illumination of space but as the opening *to* space: '[light is] a pure transparency, invisible, colorless, unformed, untouchable. It is the Idea, the God of the Arabs. But the Idea, or the abstract, has no transcendence . . . Light is the opening that creates space'.[63] Light is an initial *immanent* occupation of space, a pure transparency which is itself visible, Goethe argued, as white. Lawrence's descriptions of locations such as the Rumm Valley and the gorge of Wadi Jizil use a colour palette reminiscent of Van Dyke:

> The walls each side were of regular bands of sandstone, streaked red in many shades. The union of dark cliffs, pink floors, and pale green shrubbery was beautiful to eyes sated with months of sunlight and sooty shadow. When evening came, the declining sun crimsoned one side of the valley with its glow, leaving the other in purple gloom.[64]

Such rhapsodic use of colour often appears when Lawrence feels himself to be walking in the steps of earlier travellers such as Doughty and Bell, but he more often appears tortured by the blinding white of the desert's surfaces, and in these moments the picturesque and sublime modes fall away. While crossing 'monotonous, glittering sand' and white 'polished mud', Lawrence feels like a man drowning in light.[65] The light of the desert then becomes a medium of self-dissolution.

What Deleuze does not address is how Lawrence's conception of the Arab Revolt as vapour was directly inspired by Clausewitz, who moved beyond the physics of solid bodies in order to theorise war anew in the nineteenth century. His conception of 'People's War' stemmed from his analysis of the Spanish resistance to Napoleon, which proceeded through guerrilla tactics. People's War, Clausewitz writes, is like 'the process of evaporation: it depends on how much surface is exposed. The greater the surface and the area of contact between it and the enemy forces, the thinner the latter have to be spread, the greater the effect of a general uprising'.[66] People's War must resist massing into a solid body, must remain molecular and cloudlike: 'A general uprising, as we see it, should be nebulous and elusive; its resistance should never materialize as a concrete body.'[67] Howard Caygill has shown how Clausewitz provides an *elemental* theory of war in response to the French Revolution and the breakdown of the state's monopoly on violence. If war is fire, as it is for Clausewitz, then its intensity follows a gradient according to which it is materialised as a solid (earth), a liquid (water) or a vapour (air).[68] The war machine as appropriated by the state is a solid body, in its revolutionary form it is a liquid, but as resistance or People's War, whether revolutionary or counter-revolutionary, it is *vapour*.

The desert thus displays its characteristic ambiguity: it can ground the solidity of monuments but also be the site of their disintegration. While considering the logistics of a demolition near the ancient Roman ruins of Um el Jemal, Lawrence writes of time and human finitude in a way reminiscent of the broken statue of Ozymandias: 'such incongruous buildings, in what was then and now a desert cockpit, accused their builders of insensitiveness; almost of a vulgar assertion of man's right (Roman right) to live unchanged in all his estate'.[69] As Stephen Tabachnick argues, the emphasis Lawrence places on the ruin motif gives the very title of his book a contradictory quality: 'Instead of indicating a complete structure ... this title now conjures up a broken temple or palace without walls or roof lying somewhere in the East.'[70] Lines from the dedicatory poem confirm such an interpretation: 'Men prayed me that I set our work, the inviolate house, as a memory to you. / But for fit monument I shattered it, unfinished.'[71] Lawrence figured his own self-demolition in a similar way. In 1925, while seeking refuge from his newfound fame as an enlisted man in the ranks of the RAF, Lawrence wrote to Charlotte Shaw, asking: 'do you know what it is when you see, suddenly, that your life is all a ruin?'.[72] As Tabachnick puts it, Lawrence 'records his fragmentation rather than wholeness, and never managed to form a consistent intellectual synthesis of his experiences'.[73] Following the notorious scene, almost certainly fictional, in which he is beaten and raped by a Turkish Bey and his guards in Deraa, Lawrence writes that 'the citadel of my integrity had been irrevocably lost'.[74] Later, he casts the relationships between mind and body, intellect and action using these very same terms, which also echo the dedicatory poem: 'the eagerness to overhear and oversee myself was my assault upon my own inviolate citadel'.[75]

His self-portrait is thus inextricable from an assault upon his self that leaves only a ruin as record or monument. Deleuze argues that 'Lawrence's undertaking is a cold and concerted destruction of the ego, carried to its limit'.[76] The ruination of the self is necessary for the production of 'a subjectivity of the revolutionary group'.[77] This collective subject is *fabulated* in the desert's optical space:

> [Lawrence has] a tendency to project into things, into reality, into the future, and even into the sky an image of himself and others so intense that it has a life of its own: an image that is always stitched together, patched up, continually growing along the way, to the point where it becomes fabulous.[78]

This is achieved not only through an assault on the self's 'citadel', since mere disintegration is not enough to produce it; it is possible rather only through the Arabs and the collective energy they provide Lawrence. This is an energy of deterritorialisation: in his imitation of the Arabs – felt by him so often as a kind of fraud – he loses the moorings of his Englishness. The role of exhaustion is key here:

> the effort for these years to live in the dress of Arabs, and to imitate their mental foundation, quitted me of my English self, and let me look at the West and its conventions with new eyes: they destroyed it all for me. ...

I had dropped one form and not taken on the other ... Such detachment came at times to a man exhausted by prolonged physical effort and isolation. His body plodded on mechanically, while his reasonable mind left him, and from without looked down critically on him, wondering what that futile lumber did and why.[79]

The exhausted body is a self without identity, refined down to its sheer materiality like a desert ruin. The Arabs themselves are felt by Lawrence to embody this state by their very nature. Said, critiquing Lawrence as an exemplar of the British Orientalist tradition, picks out a passage from a letter from 1918 in which Lawrence explains that

> the Arab appealed to my imagination. It is the old, old civilisation, which has refined itself clear of household gods, and half the trappings which ours hastens to assume. The gospel of bareness in materials is a good one, and it involves apparently a sort of moral bareness too. ... In part it is a mental and moral fatigue, a race trained out, and to avoid difficulties they have to jettison so much that we think honorable and grave.[80]

The Arab for Lawrence is, as Said argues, 'exhausted ... in his very temporal persistence', and the individual life stories of particular Arabs are thus refined out of existence.[81] This reduces the complexities of the Arab world down to a primitive materiality or 'bareness' surveyed by an Orientalist gaze. When Lawrence, at the very end of *Seven Pillars*, dreams of a 'new Asia',[82] Said argues that this signals how, from the perspective of the West, the First World War marked a crisis in which the Orient had to be wrested from its passive materiality in order to 'enter history'.[83] The Orient in the twentieth century could not remain an inert matter; rather, the Orientalist himself had to *become the Orient* in order to stimulate it into life. Said's critique of Lawrence, then, is that 'all the events putatively ascribed to the historical Arab Revolt are reduced finally to Lawrence's experiences on its behalf'.[84] Lawrence 'embodies' the Orient by pursuing a libidinal and affective fusion with the desert.

To the extent that Lawrence's desert ordeal staged an encounter between the West and the East, we can perhaps read it less in terms of an assertion of imperial dominance, as Said does, than of a crisis of Western subjectivity. Certainly, Lawrence remains through it all, and despite his passionate defence of Arab independence, a British imperial agent. He ultimately reterritorialises on the British Army towards the end of the book when troops arrive with their Rolls Royce armoured cars to assist the final stages of the revolt. He writes, in a way suggestive of a picturesque Orientalism, of how 'it was the men who looked real and the background which became scene-painting. Their newness and certainty (the Definiteness of British troops in uniform) did Azrak greater honour than plain loneliness'.[85] We can even read the ruin motif as itself a site of reterritorialisation since it is a solid body and, by Lawrence's own account, the surviving trace of state sovereignty. *The Mint* (1936), the book that Lawrence wrote after *Seven Pillars* documenting his life as an enlisted man in the RAF under the name of Ross, suggests how his investment in the collective revolutionary subject of the revolt was followed by an investment in the British military as a corporate body. The anonymity of military life became a means for him to sustain, for a time at least, his process of identity loss while reterritorialising on the state pole. It is thus possible to say that Said, for whom Lawrence is an arch-Orientalist, and Deleuze, who views him in terms of revolutionary subjectivity, are both correct since they point to different aspects of the same thing. Lawrence's desert ordeal staged an encounter between West and East in which the collapse of what Schmitt called the Eurocentric global order is documented as a subjective process of devastation. The Orientalist view of 'the Arab' as an artefact of desert bareness appealed to Lawrence precisely because it reflected a sense of the crisis of Western subjectivity, a loss of everything 'honorable and grave' in the Western sense of self at the dawn of the twentieth century.

DEATHKINGDOMS: THE APOCALYPTIC WEST IN MCCARTHY AND BURROUGHS

Cormac McCarthy's *Blood Meridian* (1985) and William Burroughs's *The Place of Dead Roads* (1983) are apocalyptic westerns written under the shadow of Vietnam and nuclear war. The desert features in both texts as a stage on which the history of American militarism can be re-enacted and retold as eschatology. There is a carnivalesque quality to both texts, a linking of violence to ceremony, magic and ritual, and a corresponding sense that the desert functions well as a stage precisely because it lies beyond the laws of authoritative secular histories. These are counter-mythologies that recast the iconography of the American frontier in terms of violence and atrocity, but there is also in these works an awareness of space as the primary medium of power. If Lawrence saw the smooth spaces of the Arabian desert in terms of the ruination of a certain form of Western selfhood and of the fraudulence of imperial narratives, then McCarthy and Burroughs confront a new kind of imperium whose spatiality seems to elude narrative description altogether.

We can locate the western as McCarthy and Burroughs practise it in these texts in relation to the geopolitical entity called 'the West'.

Deleuze and Guattari suggest that the relationship between Europe and its Eastern others that so concerned Lawrence is recapitulated in the American context:

> directions in America are different: the search for arborescence and the return to the Old World occur in the East. But there is the rhizomatic West, with its Indians without ancestry, its ever-receding limit, its shifting and displaced frontiers. There is a whole American 'map' in the West, where even the trees form rhizomes. America reversed the directions: it put its Orient in the West, as if it were precisely in America that the earth came full circle; its West is the edge of the East.[86]

The West, as a schema of European power, becomes properly *global* only through America's recommencement of it in a new spatial context. However, the reversal of directions suggests that America marks both an extension *and* a disruption of Western power. The geographical element is key: when the West as a political project establishes itself in the New World, it discovers something of its own destiny in the western regions of the American continent, where material conditions were least suited to a resumption of European cultural and agricultural life. As Frederick Jackson Turner maintained in his 'frontier thesis' of 1893, it was precisely the encounter with what was then called the 'Great American Desert' – the regions west of the hundredth meridian and the Mississippi river – that helped forge myths of manifest destiny through quasi-religious visions of clearing and cultivating the wilderness.[87] The dream of reclaiming the desert through agriculture appears, with ecologically disastrous effects, with figures such as scientist and Mormon theologian John A. Widtsoe, who proclaimed a religiously inflected pseudoscience of 'dry farming', maintaining that intense cultivation of the land conserved moisture. But what Deleuze and Guattari argue is that if the American imperium relies on the older imperialism of the East–West binary, it also disturbs it with *rhizomatic* movements that preclude European notions of grounding, roots and foundations. The West thus appears to undermine itself through the very process by which it globalises itself.[88]

Deleuze and Guattari are informed by Leslie Fiedler's conception of the West as not only a geographical but an *imaginary* dimension. As Fiedler writes in a classic text from 1968: 'before a single White man had set foot on American soil, the whole continent had been dreamed by Europe as "the West": a legendary place beyond or under the ocean wave, a land of the dead or those who rise from the dead'.[89] The European imagination had long considered the fourth direction of the compass a mythological space: '[the West] could not possibly be a territory inhabited or inhabitable by those for whom Christ had died, but only a watery waste banned to all but spirits'.[90] The West has been the location of the Fortunate Isles, Elysium and Paradise; in Irish legend, it is where Tír na nÓg, the underworld and land of perpetual youth, is found. To try to go into the West, to follow the sun to the land without people, was not only ill-omened and fatal, but 'mad', since it is madness to try 'to live in a dream'.[91] When Europeans realise the West is not only real but peopled, the 'American' is born and the West becomes the subject of the new mythology of the frontier, Manifest Destiny and American Exceptionalism.

The western as genre or archetype, then, tells of what happens when a transplanted white Anglo-Saxon Protestant (WASP) encounters a 'radically alien other', the Indian. This encounter is followed either by the subsequent metamorphosis of the WASP into something 'neither White nor Red', or the annihilation of the Indian. In the first scenario, writes Fiedler, 'possibilities are opened up for another kind of Western, a secondary Western dealing with the adventures of that New Man, the American *tertium quid*'. In the second scenario, 'our home-grown final solution – the Western disappears as a living form, for the West has, in effect, been made into an East'.[92] *Blood Meridian* is a Western of the second type: it is not a 'new' western but an anti-western, since it shows how the myth of the West both realises *and* extinguishes itself in the bloodshed of settler colonial conquest. *The Place of Dead Roads* – a work Fiedler himself anticipates[93] – is of the first type, since it not only presents the American as a 'New Man' but as a post- or superhuman being, capable of surviving death itself and entering the realm of spirits.

McCarthy's novel follows a character known only as 'the kid', born in 1833 in Tennessee with little familial ties or roots. Like Melville's Ishmael, he is the American as orphan. The narrative tracks his movements westward across Texas and northern Mexico to California in the years after the Mexican–American War. After a failed filibuster mission in Mexico, the kid joins a gang of scalp-hunters led by a man named Glanton but presided over by the mysterious villain Judge Holden. The Glanton gang have been contracted by the governor of Chihuahua to kill Apaches and provide their scalps. Most of the narrative follows the Glanton gang's murderous itinerary and eventual fragmentation. While McCarthy drew on real events and historical sources such as Samuel Chamberlain's memoir *My Confession: Recollections of a Rogue* (written in 1850), in which figures named Glanton and Holden appear, he is clearly not presenting a historical fiction in any normal sense.[94] Nor is he working in the mythological mode by which America has so often, in fiction and beyond, narrated its past. Rather, he presents what we might call an inverted or nihilist mythology. The novel's desert southwest appears biblical to the extent that it suggests, as it would have done for the frontier settlers, a landscape forsaken by God, a 'terra damnata': 'Bone palings ruled the small and dusty purlieus here and death seemed the most prevalent feature of the landscape.'[95] But where the frontier myth sees in such a wilderness the possibility of redemption, the aimlessness of the kid's journeys and the sheer gratuitousness of the slaughter in which he participates portrays westward expansion as a movement of pure devastation. The novel ends with the kid in his fifties, near the close of the western era, continuing his rootless existence in a Texas countryside now dotted with buffalo carcasses. In this landscape of extinction, he is murdered by Judge Holden, who dances naked and sings of his triumph on the stage of a saloon. McCarthy's nihilist mythology, then, gives us a final judgement, an apocalypse, but one without revelation. As the judge himself puts it, 'the mystery is that there is no mystery'.[96]

A key recurring feature of McCarthy's deserts is their astronomical and sidereal character, their alignment with the heavenly bodies. The barrenness of the terrain gives a sense of terrestrial space as groundless, of the planet as set into a surrounding void towards which everything is propelled. In a scene in which the Glanton gang encounter a travelling circus and the judge performs a tarot reading, we find the gang huddled around a campfire:

> the ragged flames fled down the wind as if sucked by some maelstrom out there in the void, some vortex in that waste apposite to which man's transit and his reckonings alike lay abrogate. As if beyond will or fate he and his beasts and his trappings moved both in card and in substance under consignment to some third and other destiny.[97]

Beyond will and fate is the inertia of astronomical bodies relative to others: a dry lake bed is seen 'shimmering like the mare imbrium', the latter a lava plain on the moon.[98] It is the sheer *cosmic fact of space* distinct from what might make it a habitable world that evokes terror, and McCarthy's language draws its incantatory, propulsive power precisely from the confrontation with such worldless space.

McCarthy's desert suggests an ontological politics: it is an immanent terrain whose 'optical democracy' entails a 'neuter austerity' where 'all phenomena were bequeathed a strange equality and no one thing nor spider nor stone nor blade of grass could put forth claim to precedence'.[99] The judge becomes a spokesman for the ontological regime underpinning McCarthy's remarkable prose.[100] Challenging the Christian cosmology of the other gang members, the judge avers that God does not speak in scripture but in the immanent monism of matter, 'in stones and trees, the bones of things'.[101] He is aligned with the tarot not because he is a diviner of secrets but because he is a master of signs and thus a kind of magician, who performs tricks.[102] He is constantly copying things into his notebooks, much to the confusion of Glanton, who wishes only to take things by force. He is also a fiddler and a dancer, a creature of *refrains*.[103] The violent progress of Glanton's gang is marked by the chanting of the circus woman during the tarot reading, the howling of wolves, the drumming of rain, the sounds of dogs, owls and buzzards, the revelry of the gang at Governor Trias's palace with the judge's quadrille and the blind harpist, and so on. It is through something ceremonial or ritualistic, and not just through force, that the judge asserts his 'claim' to the land: 'The judge placed his hands on the ground. He looked at his inquisitor. This is my claim, he said.'[104] But McCarthy's narrative also presents Glanton's gang as *autochthons*, part of the landscape themselves. Their territory is less northern Mexico and the Texan border than the primal deserted unity of the continents, the original non-ground on which all subsequent grounding or worlding takes place:

> Deployed upon that plain they moved in a constant elision, ordained agents of the actual dividing out the world which they encountered and leaving what had been and what would never be alike extinguished on the ground behind them. Spectre horsemen, pale with dust, anonymous in the crenellated heat. Above all else they appeared wholly at venture, primal, provisional, devoid of order. Like beings provoked out of the absolute rock and set nameless and at no remove from their own loomings to wander ravenous and doomed and mute as gorgons shambling the brutal wastes of Gondwanaland in a time before nomenclature was and each was all.[105]

The American, McCarthy seems to be saying, emerges not from European genealogies but appears rootless out of the land itself, a being of rock and dust.

The figure of the judge is crucial to understanding the novel. He is a grim caricature of Enlightenment knowledge, delivering orotund speeches on geology, archaeology and other subjects and claiming the absolute authority of a 'suzerain' over the Earth.[106] He nevertheless disparages religious notions of transcendence that would insist on something beyond appearances. The desert is *pure surface*, rendering everything accessible in an optical democracy. His proper terrain is the desert as a field of immanence in which words and things are subject not to a transcendent scheme but to tactics and forces. He makes this point in his Heraclitean disquisition on war. War, he insists, is a game, but far from trivialising war, this raises it to the level of cosmology and ontology: 'all games aspire to the condition of war for here that which is wagered swallows up game, player, all . . . War is the ultimate game because war is at last a forcing of the unity of existence. War is god'.[107] In this way, the judge appears to be asserting the pre-eminence of a war machine. How are we to resolve this with the fact that he also seems to embody both heads (juridical and magical) of state sovereignty? The war machine can, as we've seen, either resist the striated space of the state in a revolutionary fashion or be appropriated by the state. But Deleuze and Guattari suggest a *third* possibility: the war machine may itself take over a state and subjugate it to an aim that is purely destructive. The state in this sense becomes 'suicidal', 'a pure, cold line of abolition' embodying a passion for death.[108] This is Deleuze and Guattari's definition of fascism, but it was also a major part of the Cold War's eschatological militarism, embodied in what Pynchon called the Deathkingdom. The judge does not claim the authority of a state, but of something more terrible: a war machine that has *become* a state and is not simply appropriated by one.

McCarthy's nihilist mythology leaves us no escape route. But what of the western's central mythological component, according to Fiedler, the 'new man' born in the confrontation of white European subjectivity with the radically other? In Burroughs, the white man becomes the white shaman. The death of the Indians is acknowledged as final, but the otherness of the landscape of the West retains a transformative power. *The Place of Dead Roads* is the second part of a late trilogy of works in which Burroughs's personal search for redemption is mapped onto visions of a global war between forces of control and liberation. The first instalment, *Cities of the Red Night* (1981), is (among many other things) a retelling of the European colonisation of the New World and how the chance to build a utopian society on anti-authoritarian principles was lost. The final instalment, *The Western Lands* (1987), borrows its main themes from ancient Egyptian cosmology: the title of the book designates the desert region west of the Nile, the location of the Land of the Dead, the domain of gods and spirits. The trilogy aligns American history with Burroughs's own personal mythology, at whose heart is a search for immortality.

He presents the path to liberation as a combat against the human organism itself: biological finitude is a barrier to human evolutionary destiny. The obscure agents of control mobilise organic needs of every kind to maintain their authority. Burroughs imagines all society to be based on control and regulation of the organism, while a distinct body – what Deleuze and Guattari would call the body without organs but what Burroughs calls 'the astral or dream body' – is demanded as a matter of the utmost urgency.[109] The organic body is for Burroughs a 'human artifact' (or 'H.A.') because it is – like Indian arrowheads or flintlock rifles – obsolete with respect to the deterritorialising forces of history and technology. In this way, he links the obsolescence of the human in its present biological state with an apocalyptic sense of history while calling for an inorganic subjectivity capable of realising human evolutionary destiny, which for Burroughs entails the exploration of space:

> the first step toward space exploration is to examine the human artifact with *biologic* alterations in mind that will render our H.A. more suitable for space conditions and space travel. . . . We are like water creatures looking up at the land and air and wondering how we can survive in that alien medium. The water we live in is Time. That alien medium we glimpse beyond time is Space. And that is where we are going.[110]

Space in the astronomical or science fictional sense is linked here with the discovery of *spatiality itself*.

The protagonist of *Dead Roads* is Kim Carsons, a name recalling Kit Carson, the legendary nineteenth-century American frontiersman. At the outset of the book, 'Kim decides to go west and become a shootist'.[111] He becomes involved in establishing an underground network called the Johnson Family, whose purpose is to combat the agents of control. Knowledge of the war and its stakes 'passes from Johnson to Johnson, in freight cars and jails, in seedy rooming houses and precarious compounds, in hop joints and rafts floating down the great rivers of South America, in guerrilla camps and desert tents'.[112] Burroughs's narrative, while jumping back and forth in time, evokes the period covering the end of the western era and the emergence of twentieth-century industrial society. The forms of spatiality evoked both by the notion of guerrilla war and by the western setting are not incidental to Burroughs's project since it is precisely the conquest of space that is at issue: the 'habitations' of the Johnsons and their allies are 'the desolate places, the lands between the lands, the cities between the cities'.[113]

The familiar landscape elements of the formulaic western – mesas, mountains and dusty frontier towns – provide Burroughs with the scenography of a war against control, whose chief manifestation at the level of social institutions is Christianity.[114] For Burroughs, religion tends to monopolise access to immortality through a transcendent power structure or 'One God universe'.[115] His model of control, meanwhile, is the virus or parasite: an alien element takes over a host. To this extent, all organic life is the result of an extra-terrestrial invasion. This gives rise to a cosmology every bit as brutal and unforgiving as Judge Holden's: 'Planet Earth is by its nature and function a battlefield.'[116] Language is the most insidious and sophisticated mechanism of control: 'their most potent tool of manipulation is the word'.[117] One of Burroughs's most far-reaching ideas is that words are viral replicators, *territorial refrains* that hold desire in place, while writing is a constant struggle over the deterritorialised spaces of a psychosexual and psychobiological frontier. Burroughs explored the possibilities of hackneyed and conventional forms, and his texts are often a tissue of appropriated stock figures and phrases strung together like motifs in a musical theme. Burroughs treats *all* language as second-hand and worn-out but in this way seeks to subvert the control mechanism at the heart of the word 'virus'.

This relates to his notorious experiences as a drug addict: opiates or 'junk' drive the addict into an absurdly nightmarish world but may also reveal the entirety of human habits to be a nightmare of need and control. *Naked Lunch* (1959), his most well-known book, is composed of fragmentary set-pieces and elaborate sketches, 'routines' (as Burroughs called them) which in turn reveal a terrifying routinisation and mechanisation of behaviour. In works such as *Naked Lunch* and *The Soft Machine* (1961), he presents visions of deserts, wastelands, derelict zones and other excremental, abject landscapes as constituting a terrain of drug use and homosexual desire. The vacant lots that charmed and racked the mind of the young Eliot feature frequently in Burroughs's work to evoke a sterile sexuality and forms of desire trapped in their own barren routines of fulfilment:

> Out of junk in East St. Louis sick dawn he threw himself across the washbasin pressing his stomach against the cool porcelain. I draped myself over his body laughing. His shorts dissolved in rectal mucus and carbolic soap. summer dawn smells from a vacant lot.[118]

Drug addiction and homosexuality are seen to correlate with entropic landscapes of various kinds. Need, as a mechanism of control, *exhausts* the body but also its environments. Some of Burroughs's most evocative writing comes from his attempts to portray desire and landscape as succumbing to the same exhaustion:

> a scream shoots down a white hospital corridor . . . out along a wide dusty street between palm trees, whistles out across the desert like a bullet (vulture wings husk in the dry air), a thousand boys come at once in outhouses, bleak public school toilets, attics, basements, treehouses, Ferris wheels, deserted houses, limestone caves, rowboats, garages, barns, rubbly windy city outskirts behind mud walls (smell of dried excrement).[119]

In *Dead Roads*, the generic conventions of the western allow Burroughs to explore these concerns via the homoeroticism which, as Fiedler argues, has long been a feature of American literature's constructions of wilderness.[120] The path to the western lands, the desert paradise where the organism is dissolved and the alien invaders dispelled, is to be reached via an abolition of sexual difference and sexual reproduction. To the extent that sexual difference establishes the organism on dimorphism, consciousness is captured by the control virus. As one character puts it in *Cities of the Red Night*, 'the whole quality of human consciousness, as expressed in male and female, is basically a virus mechanism'.[121] Burroughs counsels an apocalyptic male homosexuality by way of response: 'The Old Man's route is sex between males. Sex forms the matrix of a dualistic and therefore solid and real universe. It is therefore possible to resolve the dualistic conflict in a sex act, where dualism need not exist.'[122] Through redoubling, identity can triumph over difference, and Burroughs's utopian re-engineering of the human artefact thus succumbs to a very old misogynistic dream, which is also the ascetic dream of Christianity: 'The Western Lands is the natural, uncorrupted state of all male humans. We have been seduced from our biologic and spiritual destiny by the Sex Enemy.'[123] What Burroughs presents as an overcoming of the organism's perilous sexual dimorphism is, in fact, a sexual fantasy and a dream of the annihilation of difference. Instead of coming from an encounter between white man and red, as Fielder would have it, Burroughs's 'new man' of the American West stems from a phallocentric white shamanism all too reminiscent of D. H. Lawrence's *The Plumed Serpent*.

DESOLATIONS OF THE PHALLUS: CARTER, OEDIPUS AND THE SEXUAL POLITICS OF THE DESERT

The apocalyptic sexuality of Burroughs and D. H. Lawrence fails because of its phallocentrism, which effectively reinstates the One God universe, or – what is the same thing – the state-form within an immanent smooth space. We can turn by way of comparison to Angela Carter, an author profoundly influenced by Burroughs, who presents a feminist critique of apocalyptic sexuality in her novel *The Passion of New Eve* (1982). Carter's narrative follows a male chauvinist literary intellectual named Evelyn who travels from England to New York and becomes swept up in a civil war breaking out along racial and gender lines. When he arrives in the city, fragments of graffiti suggest a feminist revolt is underway: 'Were the blacks responsible, or the Women? The Women? What did they mean? Seeing my stranger's bewilderment, a cop pointed out to me, inscribed on a wall, the female circle – thus: ♀ with, inside it, a set of bared teeth.'[124] As the revolt intensifies and the 'entropic city' sinks into chaos, Evelyn enters into a relationship with and then rapes a black nightclub dancer named Leilah, leaving her for dead. Evelyn then flees the city as if fleeing reproductive life itself: 'I reached the desert, the abode of enforced sterility, the dehydrated sea of fertility, the post-menopausal part of the earth.'[125] In the desert, he is captured by a group of militant one-breasted women and taken to their underground headquarters, Beulah. There he meets Mother, a monstrous fertility goddess and figurehead of the militant group. She performs a surgical procedure on Evelyn, castrating him and turning him into the 'ideal' woman, the New Eve of the book's title.

The Passion of New Eve is a critique of the mythological power of sex and gender and a meditation on the violence involved in the production of feminine subjects. Carter herself described the novel as 'antimythic', but it draws exuberantly on a great range of mythico-religious ideas about sexuality and sexual difference from the ancient Phrygians to Christianity and Hollywood. On one level, this is done to parody the cosmic sexuality found not only in the phallocentrism of Lawrence and Burroughs but in certain strands of feminism. Beneath the layers of satire and parody, however, is the serious point that *images* of sex and gender have inescapably material, technological and often violent origins. Carter's New Eve, like Villers's Future Eve, is a non-natural being, carved by Mother's scalpel, 'the first child of her manufactory'.[126] Mother herself, we learn, was once a Los Angeles plastic surgeon, and fashioned her monstrous body herself. Carter's strategy, then, is to demythologise but also denaturalise femininity, to sever its links to reproductive life. The desert, as a space of violence and fantasy, is central to this as it is, in Carter's description, a place of sterility and infertility, a topos where the relationships between desire, sexuality and life may be called into question.

In her non-fiction book *The Sadeian Woman* (1979), Carter insists that the taboo on explicit violent pornography of the kind Sade practised is so strong because of the implicit violence at work in the production of femininity in Western culture at large.[127] Marilyn Monroe is a pop culture Justine: 'their dazzling fair skins are of such a delicate texture that they look as if they will bruise at a touch, carrying the exciting stigmata of sexual violence for a long time, and that is why gentlemen prefer blondes'.[128] Carter's polemic is that Sade's pornographic imagination manifests not simply misogyny but a revolt against 'the whole metaphysic of sexual differences' and the crude naturalisation of the phallic and the feminine that has long been at the root of Western society and subjectivity.[129] The crudity of sexual differentiation is visible in pornography but also in redemptive notions of sexuality's mythological and religious foundations: 'all the mythic versions of women, from the myth of the redeeming purity of the virgin to that of the healing, reconciling mother, are consolatory nonsenses'.[130] At the end of *New Eve*, even Mother herself has a 'nervous breakdown' and becomes supplementary to the revolution for which she was once godhead.[131]

The novel's main target, then, is less phallocentrism itself than the function of naturalisation at work in representations of sexual difference. Such representations have crucial environmental and agricultural underpinnings because they imply

> a system of relations between the partners that equates the woman to the passive receptivity of the soil, to the richness and fecundity of the earth. A whole range of images poeticises, kitschifies, departicularises intercourse, such as wind beating down corn, rain driving against bending trees, towers falling, all tributes to the freedom and strength of the roving, fecundating, irresistible male principle and the heavy, downward, equally irresistible gravity of the receptive soil. The soil that is, good heavens, myself. It is a most self-enhancing notion; I have almost seduced myself with it.[132]

The desert provides Carter with an anti-fecund terrain on which images of sex and gender are both invoked and shattered. The American context is crucial, since this was the paradise, the garden site of a new Adam, imagined for so long by Europeans. The images that drove the initial colonisation of the continent were of the kind Carter here describes. At the end of the sixteenth century, Sir Walter Raleigh described the Guyanas to his investors as 'a country that hath yet her Maydenhead'.[133] If the paradisal garden naturalises images of sexuality by rooting them in some grounding mimetic relationship to reproductive life, then the desert foregrounds their artificiality. Carter's desert, then, is an *iconoclastic* one, where images and likenesses are broken. As Régis Debray puts it in his discussion of the Old Testament: 'urban folk worship statues; along come the people of the desert and hack them to pieces – whether it be Moses, Calvin and his sectarians, who decapitated stone virgins and saints with axes, or the last of the Taliban'.[134] To this extent, Carter's desert remains the desert of a monotheistic passion rather than the desert of the war machine of the one-breasted militants, from whose revolutionary goals the novel maintains a distance.

The text opens on an image already bearing the marks of disintegration. On his last night in London, Evelyn goes to see a film starring Tristessa de St Ange, an actress from Hollywood's Golden Age whom he adores as an archetype of femininity. The cinematic image suggests the desolation to come: 'the film stock was old and scratched, as if the desolating passage of time were made visible in the rain upon the screen, audible in the worn stuttering of the sound track, yet these erosions of temporality only enhanced your luminous presence'.[135] Evelyn ejaculates to this eroded image thanks to the fellatio performed on him by a woman whose name he cannot remember, but it is essentially a masturbatory act. Once Evelyn becomes Eve and is pressed into the harem of the one-eyed, one-legged cult leader Zero, it is revealed that Tristessa, who has retired to the deserts of southern California, is a male transvestite. The idealisation of femininity embodied in Tristessa, then, is shown to be a result of the 'vicious circle' and 'dead end' of male narcissistic fantasy.[136]

The relation between image or symbol and flesh is the central preoccupation of the book and the issue around which its sexual politics revolve. Carter does not dismiss fantasy as an empty play of images, but asks where fantasy's power comes from and how desire becomes immanent in images. The background of the novel is America at the end of the 1960s, a point when the hopes of that decade were turning into nightmares. The gun-loving Zero embodies at once the desert messianism of Charles Manson and the militaristic patriotism of the Vietnam War. The legacy of Vietnam is suggested in places in Carter's text, such as the scene in which Eve is captured by a Christian boy militia. After escaping Zero on his helicopter, a dying Tristessa impregnates Eve on top of a cushion bearing the American flag:

> Flesh is a function of enchantment. It uncreates the world . . . How can I find words the equivalent of this mute speech of flesh as we folded ourselves within a single self in the desert, under our dappled canopy, on our bed of filthy cushions? Alone, quite alone, in the heart of that gigantic metaphor for sterility, where our child was conceived on the star-spangled-banner, yet we peopled this immemorial loneliness with all we had been, or might be, or had dreamed of being.[137]

At the very point the relation between flesh and fantasy seems to secure itself in 'the great Platonic hermaphrodite' and 'the self-created eternity of lovers', the apocalyptic unity shatters: 'I beat down upon you mercilessly, with atavistic relish, but the glass woman I saw beneath me smashed under my passion and the splinters scattered and recomposed themselves into a man who overwhelmed me.'[138] Apocalyptic sexuality shatters into the violence of male narcissism and the self-annihilating passion for images. Carter seems to hesitate between the lure of cosmic sexuality and an iconoclastic critique of the male narcissistic imaginary, but her concern may be said to lie with the *desolations of the image* itself. In America, there is nothing rooting images or fantasies to historical reality, there is only an endless optical space. In Tristessa's face, Eve discerns 'all the desolation of America'.[139] Tristessa's enchantment is the abyssal enchantment of a society without history: 'The abyss on which her eyes open, ah! it is the abyss of myself, of emptiness, of inward void. I, she, we are outside history.'[140] The image sustains desire in a self-moving artificiality. When Eve discovers that Tristessa is a man, the abstraction of desire from being is only intensified. The revelation of Tristessa's maleness only confirms what was at the root of her seductiveness all along: 'Tristessa had ... no ontological status, only an iconographic one.'[141] The 'mineral eradication of being' found in the desert is thus extended by Tristessa's existence as *pure image*.[142]

Carter here anticipates some aspects of Baudrillard's account of postmodernism in his travelogue *America* (1986), his search for 'the America of desert speed, of motels and mineral surfaces'.[143] For Baudrillard, America fascinates because its culture is precisely the death of European culture and the end of history: 'the form that dominates the American West, and doubtless all of American culture, is a seismic form: a fractal, interstitial culture, born of a rift with the Old World, a tactile, fragile, mobile, superficial culture'.[144] The hyperreal or simulacral images of film, television and advertising are the spectacular form of culture's disappearance: 'things seem to be made of a more unreal substance; they seem to turn and move in a void as if by a special lighting effect, a fine membrane you pass through without noticing it'.[145] It is in this sense that cinema idols are 'the last great myth of our modernity ... *They embody one single passion only: the passion for images*, and the immanence of desire in the image'.[146] When desire becomes immanent in the image, it moves beyond time and history in what Baudrillard elsewhere, famously, called 'the desert of the real'.[147] This is the outcome of denaturalisation, but it doesn't necessarily spell the end of myth. Rather, Carter and Baudrillard display both anxiety and enthusiasm about the fact that America is a place where myths are reborn without history.

Carter shares with Burroughs a preoccupation with spatiality and mortality. Following Evelyn's transformation into Eve, the desert matriarchs at Beulah announce that 'time is a man, space is a woman ... kill time and live forever'.[148] This may help us to understand why Carter distances herself from the militants' goals. This is the oedipal ambition – to kill the father and have sex with the mother is to try to halt the historical cycle of generations. The phallic law of the father is time itself, but oedipal desire is the passion of the phallus trying to overcome itself, to abolish time through an absolute possession of enjoyment as primary agent of fecundation. As the matriarchs explain:

> [Oedipus] had a sensible desire to murder his father, who dragged him from the womb in complicity with historicity ... But Oedipus botched the job. In complicity with phallocentricity, he concluded his trajectory a blind old

man, wandering by the seashore ... Man lives in historicity; his phallic projectory takes him onwards and upwards – but to where? Where but to the barren sea of infertility, the craters of the moon![149]

Phallic history exhausts itself in the space of the desert. What it discovers there is not the realisation of the oedipal fantasy but the passion of pure annihilation, a deathkingdom. Mother's plan is to fertilise Eve with the sperm collected from Evelyn prior to his transformation, but Mother botches the job as much as Oedipus does when Eve escapes and copulates with Tristessa. In this sense, *New Eve* is a recasting of the Oedipus narrative, or at least a traversal of its logic. Mother, the sterile technocratic goddess of fertility, surgically fashions Eve with the intention of repopulating a devastated postwar continent. But her plans are thwarted by the phallocratic yet infertile Zero, the mad poet and cult leader, who captures Eve and makes her his wife. One-eyed and one-legged, Zero is an Oedipus figure in whom power and impotence are combined: 'I am Zero ... the lowest point; vanishing point; nullity. I am the freezing point in Centigrade and my wives experience the flame of my frigidity as passion.'[150] Like Judge Holden, he is a dancer, and prefers to howl his poems rather than write them down.[151] His phallic power is an 'avenging fire' directed against all women and Tristessa in particular, since Zero blames his infertility on her screen presence: 'Tristessa had magicked away his reproductive capacity via the medium of the cinema screen.'[152]

In Sade's texts, Carter tells us, the phallus 'is a mechanical device, an engine or an instrument of warfare, a weapon'.[153] Orgasm for Sade's libertines requires 'enormous expenditures of energy' and takes on an increasingly suicidal and annihilating force, such that the libertines end up just as captive as their victims.[154] If phallic desire is a kind of 'despotism' based on the triumph of the ego, then it is not enough for the partner of the sadist to simply submit, they must be annihilated.[155] But in such a world without others, the despotic phallus – desire's state-form – must work harder and harder at the elaboration of fantasies intended to realise its triumph over the other. The fecundity of the imagination is grounded on an annihilating agency that ultimately severs the image from a practical relation to anything outside it, rendering it both impotent and omnipotent at once and collapsing imaginary and real into the desolations of hyperreality.

This is the situation Baudrillard describes in his travels through the deserts of America's west and southwest, but for Carter the situation relates directly to the politics of sexual difference and liberation. Mother's plan to succeed where Oedipus had failed is shown to be futile. Her nervous breakdown, we are told at the end of the narrative, stemmed from her realisation that 'she could not make time stand still'.[156] Mother is depicted as an old woman sitting by the shore, like Oedipus after his banishment. The war of liberation continues, but Carter's novel is ultimately less interested in articulating a liberatory sexual politics than in exploring the capture of desire by images in postmodern culture. There is violence in the production and propagation of gendered identity that ideas of sexual difference, even in their revolutionary forms, often fail to grasp. Images sustain a libidinal economy, but the passion for images becomes all the more violent and troubling when they are shorn from their historical referents. This violence cannot be resolved through traversing the oedipal fantasy, whose metaphysic of sexual difference is intended to reconcile us to history. The conclusion we are led to is that the deadlock of Oedipus leaves us all in the position of Sade's libertines, requiring ever greater expenditures of energy for the production of images that annihilate their referents.

OMEGA: DELILLO, NEGARESTANI AND IRAQ

Carter's text suggests that simulacral images take on a new strategic importance in the politics of the post-Vietnam era. This is echoed in Virilio's analysis of the new American militarism as displayed for the first time by the build-up to the Iraq War in 1990.[157] Observing the mobilisations of Operation Desert Storm, Virilio argues that the image constitutes a new mode of strategy, a new way of occupying ground: 'to deploy, here and there, an invincible armada no longer has any meaning outside the express condition of strategically occupying the screen (live coverage), the image prevailing over that of which it is nevertheless only the image'.[158] Electronic communications and teletechnology, including mass media, radar and automated weapons systems, constitute a 'fourth front' in addition to land, sea and air.[159] Postmodern war institutes a new *nomos* in this way. Communications technologies effectively eliminate the element of time and seem to realise ancient dreams of religious salvation and absolute power to which the spatiality of the desert was central: 'photosensitive inductor, the desert ... is linked in every case to liberation from time: divine eternity for the Anchorite, State eternity for Caesar dreaming of turning the frontiers of his empire into a vast desert'.[160] But such dreams are ultimately just ways of making the desert of nihilism grow, since the ubiquity of the image brings about an asceticism or 'apatheia', a term Virilio takes from the Desert Fathers themselves:

> We're still here in the domain of cinematic illusion, of the mirage of information precipitated on the computer screen – what is given is exactly the information but not the sensation; it is *apatheia*, this scientific impassibility

which makes it so that the more informed man is the more the desert of the world expands around him.[161]

The technoscientific 'mirage' of contemporary warfare realises what Nietzsche identified through his notion of the ascetic ideal as the self-annihilating tendency of life. One effect of this situation, however, is that war and thought come to occupy the same space. Thought is a kind of asceticism. It is not only, as Virilio observes, that the man of war is no longer the soldier but the thinker, but that thought itself may acquire the praxis of a war machine.[162] The desert of nihilism offers thought, and also art, new strategies beyond the aims of the bellicose state.

DeLillo's novel *Point Omega* (2010), a meditation on the 2003 invasion of Iraq set in 2006, can be read in terms of these ideas. The novel's focus is the seventy-three-year-old Richard Elster, an academic who has worked as a consultant to the American government. He is the new man of war that Virilio identifies: 'He was there to conceptualise, his word, in quotes, to apply overarching ideas and principles to such matters as troop deployment and counterinsurgency.'[163] Elster, a twenty-first-century anchorite, has retreated to a clapboard house in Anza-Borrego Desert State Park in southern California, a landscape characterised not only by its remoteness but by its fossils and geological record. It is a landscape of extinction. He has gone there to seek peace but also a liberation from time: 'I feel the landscape more than I see it. I never know what day it is. I never know if a minute has passed or an hour. I don't get old here.'[164] His solitude is broken by a filmmaker, Jim Finley, who has come to make a documentary about Elster's involvement in the war, and by his daughter Jessie, who has arrived to escape the unwanted advances of a disturbed man named Dennis.

Through Finley's narrative and Elster's testimony, the text's austere style approaches something like a minimalist prose poetry. For Finley, the desert is a place of affects and intensities that collapse distinctions between the visible and the thinkable: 'Heat, space, stillness, distance. They've become visual states of mind. I'm not sure what that means. I keep seeing figures in isolation, I see past physical dimension.'[165] Finley has made one previous film, an avant-garde collage of comedian Jerry Lewis's appearances on 1950s television. Finley describes the footage as 'resembling some deviant technological lifeform struggling out of the irradiated dust of the atomic age'.[166] For Elster, meanwhile, the hyper-real or simulacral image is the very essence of war:

> Lying is necessary. The state has to lie. There is no lie in war or in preparation for war that can't be defended. We went beyond this. We tried to create new realities overnight, careful sets of words that resemble advertising

slogans in memorability and repeatability. These were words that would yield pictures eventually and then become three-dimensional.¹⁶⁷

What makes the image strategically efficacious is not that it is a deception but that it creates a reality over which it can have absolute power. It is not that the image is manipulated by the state in order mask the truth of war but that images have an annihilatory power greater than physical destructiveness. Twenty-first-century American imperialism is *in excess* of the state-form, since the deployment of this power constitutes not a political but an *eschatological* horizon. Elster makes some attempts to justify his position through vague references to American exceptionalism, but he is driven ultimately by a passion for annihilation. Prior to his time in government, he delivered a series of lectures 'on what he called the dream of extinction'.¹⁶⁸ He has an awareness of the extinct species fossilised in Anza-Borrego's geological strata, and articulates the very process that Freud identified with the death instinct: 'Matter wants to lose its self-consciousness. We're the mind and heart that matter has become. Time to close it down. This is what drives us now . . . We want to be the dead matter we used to be.'¹⁶⁹ The desert is where time seems both to extinguish itself and be solidified as the deep time of extinctions:

> 'Time falling away. That's what I feel here,' he said. 'Time becoming slowly older. Enormously old. Not day by day. This is deep time, epochal time. Our lives receding into the long past. That's what's out there. The Pleistocene desert, the rule of extinction.'¹⁷⁰

Elster is a student of the Jesuit philosopher Pierre Teilhard de Chardin, whose concept of the 'omega point' gives the novel its title. Teilhard defined the omega point as a movement of consciousness towards cosmic singularity. Consciousness is for Teilhard a form of 'spiritualised energy' constituting what he calls a 'noosphere', an extended consciousness overlaying the biosphere. He conceives of consciousness and morality as *forces* comparable to those marshalled by war, writing that 'when the spirit of discovery absorbs the whole vital force contained in the spirit of war' – that is, when energy is channelled into thought instead of destructiveness – 'then an irresistible tide of free energies will advance into the most progressive tracts of the noosphere'.¹⁷¹ The omega as principle of universal synthesis is nothing other than love, for Teilhard, but for Elster it remains ambiguously tied to the prospect of devastation or annihilation: 'Paroxysm. Either a sublime transformation of mind and soul or some worldly convulsion. We want it to happen.'¹⁷²

The novel's ending, however, undercuts Elster's high-flown rhetoric.

When his daughter is stabbed to death by Dennis, Elster's view of war's eschatological sublimity falls away. Finley's narrative acknowledges this as they make their way out of the desert: 'The omega point has narrowed, here and now, to the point of a knife as it enters a body. All the man's grand themes funnelled down to local grief.'[173] Dennis's motives are left unclear, but he is shown to be obsessed with Scottish artist Douglas Gordon's installation piece 24 Hour Psycho (1993), which shows the original Hitchcock movie slowed to a twenty-four-hour running time. His total absorption in the images, explored in the book's opening and closing sections, takes on the same profundity that Elster invests in the hyperreal images of war: 'The film had the same relationship to the original movie that the original movie had to real lived experience. This was the departure from the departure. The original movie was fiction, this was real.'[174] For Elster and Dennis, the exaltation of the image suggests a sublime liberation from the referent but in each case the promise of liberation gives way to a simple murderous reality. The guilt Elster refuses to acknowledge for his part in the Iraq invasion returns as an unbearable personal loss.

DeLillo's reference to Teilhard suggests that the central issue regarding America's military interventions in the Middle East is energy conceived in the broadest terms, not just in terms of the strategic pursuit of oil that has been central to American foreign policy since the Carter administration.[175] The desert setting, meanwhile, suggests an eschatological scenario of absolute depletion, a zero point against which all our conceptions of energy must be set. Negarestani's *Cyclonopedia: Complicity with Anonymous Materials* (2008) offers a very interesting comparison to DeLillo's text. *Cyclonopedia* is a remarkable, unclassifiable mix of theoretical discourse, ancient Persian history and Lovecraftian speculative horror presented as a reconstruction and interpretation of the fragmentary research notes, as they pass through various hands, of Hamid Parsani, a fictional professor of archaeology at Tehran University.[176] Parsani's central idea is that the Middle East is an autonomous living entity leading history towards apocalyptic singularity, or what Negarestani – in a curious anticipation of DeLillo – calls 'Tellurian Omega' (tellurian, from the Latin *tellus*, means 'of the Earth').[177] The 'life' of the Middle East is not social or organic but *cyclonic*, a vortex in which politics, religion, fossil fuels, climate and geography amplify one another as forces in a cyclone. Nick Land, a key influence on Negarestani, writes that 'cyclones are atmospheric machines that transform latent energy into angular momentum in a feed-back process of potentially catastrophic consequence'.[178] The politics of the Middle East, the Iraq War, the War on Terror and Islamic

Jihad are to be grasped not according to history or politics but according to an energetics of forces, a *vicious circle*, whose main terms are the desert and oil:

> Both the technocapitalist process of desertification in War on Terror and the radical monotheistic ethos for the desert converge upon oil as an object of production, a pivot of terror, a fuel, a politico-economic lubricant and an entity whose life is directly connected to earth. While for western technocapitalism, the desert gives rise to the oiliness of war machines and the hyper-consumption of capitalism en route to singularity, for Jihad oil is a catalyst to speed the rise of the Kingdom, the desert. . . . Oil lubes the whole desert expedition toward Tellurian Omega (either as the Desert of God or the host of singularity, the New Earth).[179]

The omega points of both DeLillo and Negarestani *invert* the usually divine or transcendent orientation of apocalypse by presenting it as an apocalypse consummated in the deep time of geology, an ancientness 'without tradition', as Negarestani puts it.[180] The 'end of history', in other words, is coeval with the geocosmic temporality of the Earth, whose reality the Anthropocene forces us to reckon with.[181]

In Parsani's account, the key link between history and deep time is oil, the latter figured not as an inert resource but as a geohistorical agent in its own right, a 'being' along the lines of Lovecraft's Cthulhu or the occultural entities of ancient Persian religion, whose unearthing has fatal consequences. The war between Western technocapitalist interests and Islamic Jihad is a surface narrative, a cypher for a deeper story, while oil is a 'lubricant' causing both narratives to approach one another. Wahhabism is drawn to the desert because the latter possesses a 'militant horizontality'; it is a site where idols are levelled and where an absolute submission to the divine can be accomplished.[182] American war machines, on the other hand, possess a 'desertifying' or devastational overwhelming force, a power of annihilation that was first practised in the jungles of Vietnam. An American colonel in Iraq named Jackson West acquires some of Parsani's writings and becomes a convert to the apocalypticism of the Tellurian Omega:

> This is not Vietnam, this is not the jungle; the desert is always ready to subvert all human thoughts, to suck warmachines dry. If we sprayed their boonies with Agent Orange to deprive the Vietnamese of their food and shelter, here the enemy fights alongside us to liberate the desert: this, rather than our defeat, is the ultimate goal they try to reach.[183]

American war machines have been programmed with the logic of the desert and thus serve to liberate forces of devastation that belong to the Earth as body without organs. The target of the war machine in this sense is the *polis* or state-form rather than any identifiable enemy. In the urban warfare of the Middle East, a passion for the desert causes American militarism and terrorist insurgency to converge:

> [America's] tactics and extra-terminating weaponries have been programmed to make deserts of cities, disassembling anything erected cell by cell, atom by atom with a nonhuman passion . . . this is how they become as one with their Wahhabi adversaries in levelling anything erected, eradicating all manifestations of idolatry.[184]

Negarestani, drawing on Bataille's notion of solar economy, argues that the war machines of American militarism and Islamist terrorism are only the means to realise a greater planetary transformation in which the hegemony of the Sun, the energy source of all organic systems, is overturned. The militarised demand for oil, then, is a cypher for another tendency or another *polemos*, a planetary death instinct in which organic life extinguishes itself in its own energy source. The molten core of the Earth seeks immanent unity with the Sun. The desert is where these two narratives – the surface narrative of human history and the geologic or cosmic narratives of deep time – are played out in a cyclonic embrace that turns the Middle East into a plane of immanence. Islamist terrorism and American militarism are complicit not only in the asymmetric escalation of each other's war machines but in elaborating a deeper planetary and geological story, written in the strata and porous insides of the Earth. The surface apocalyptics of religion, war and energy are to be read as components of this other story in which Earth's depths are terminally fused with the Sun as energy source. This fusion is an insurgency against the verticality of state, God and the Sun's hegemony.

Negarestani emphasises the 'holey spaces' of ruin and decay as potential alternatives to this apocalyptic terminus, however. Deleuze and Guattari write that between smooth and striated space lies an intermediary holey space, where the solidity of bodies is punctured and undermined.[185] They draw on an image from Eisenstein's film *Strike* (1925), in which figures emerge out of holes in the ground. Holes undermine depth's ability to play the role of ground while occupying an ambiguous position between surface and depth. Mining and bombing create holes, but Negarestani – in a manner that may remind us of Lawrence and the ruined imperial self – emphasises a general ruination that can be grasped as dust and decay. The Middle East itself can be seen as a holey space of ruined solids. But where Lawrence tended to see the ruin as a vestige of the solid body of the state, Negarestani sees it in truly nomadic terms as a process of *decay without annihilation*:

> By undermining the ground upon which power can be effectuated and lines of destruction mobilized, decay misdirects – in the sense of a permanent

derailing – the processes of terminus. If the social, economic and political definition of power is determined by its formation, and the formation itself is decided by its ground, then decay's peaceful (non-annihilative) assault on the ground of power formations is effectuated as a concrete sabotage against the very definition of power.[186]

Parsani writes that dust or 'dustism' is the medium of the New Earth's approach: 'Dustism is the middle-eastern way of renewing and becoming new for the Earth.'[187] Dust is a kind of becoming that does not reterritorialise on a ruined body or suggest an annihilative terminal point. While Elster cannot think of the omega point without dreaming of extinction, Parsani thinks of it as 'a limitrophic process through which the object shrinks progressively toward zero without eventuating the act of annihilation'.[188] Dust itself is a kind of war machine, an affective arrangement that causes the solidity of conventional warfare and tactics to corrode in a non-annihilative (peaceful) approach to zero.

DeLillo and Negarestani, then, use the desert to present eschatological narratives that invert the terms of traditional apocalyptic, directing our attention downwards into the Earth conceived as a zero point instead of upwards towards a transcendent terminus. Eschatology in this way becomes continuous with deep time, while singularity becomes a katabatic or downward moving convergence of human temporality with the temporalities of geology and mass extinction. We can read DeLillo and Negarestani in this way as offering powerful speculative fictions for the Anthropocene that can be placed alongside texts such as Atwood's *MaddAddam* trilogy and other works recognised as exemplars of climate fiction. In *Point Omega* and *Cyclonopedia*, the desert is a metaphysical mediator between surface and depth in which these two dimensions – the key dimensions of Earthly life – are collapsed into one another in a speculative search for a new dimensionality, or a new spacetime.

NOTES

1. Heidegger, *What Is Called Thinking?*, p. 29.
2. Fuller and Goriunova, 'Devastation', p. 324.
3. McBrien, 'Accumulating Extinction', p. 116.
4. Heidegger, *What Is Called Thinking?*, p. 30.
5. Nixon, *Slow Violence and the Environmentalism of the Poor*, p. 13.
6. Arendt, 'Introduction *into* Politics', p. 190.
7. Ibid. p. 190.
8. Wendy Brown provides an analysis of the proliferation of walls and fences in twenty-first-century regimes across the world in terms of the decline of the modern (Westphalian) state:

> What is also striking about these new barriers is that even as they limn or attempt to define nation-state boundaries, they are not built as defenses against potential attacks by other sovereigns, as fortresses against invading armies, or even as shields against weapons launched in interstate wars. Rather, while the particular danger may vary, these walls target nonstate transnational actors – individuals, groups, movements, organizations, and industries. They react to transnational, rather than international relations and respond to persistent, but often informal or subterranean powers, rather than to military undertakings. The migration, smuggling, crime, terror, and even political purposes that walls would interdict are rarely state sponsored, nor, for the most part, are they incited by national interests. Rather, they take shape apart from conventions of Westphalian international order in which sovereign nation-states are the dominant political actors. As such, they appear as signs of a post-Westphalian world. (*Walled States, Waning Sovereignty*, p. 21)

The decline of Westphalian sovereignty is manifest as the attempted striation of an increasingly worldwide network of counter-state forces operating in the smooth spaces beyond direct state control. On the relationships between state, territory and war, see Stuart Elden's books *Terror and Territory* and *The Birth of Territory*.

9. For work on the links between Schmitt and Deleuze, see Rae, 'Violence, Territorialization, and Signification', Simons, 'Carl Schmitt's Spatial Rhetoric', and the chapter 'Nomadology' in Sibertin-Blanc's *State and Politics*.
10. Schmitt, *The Nomos of the Earth*, p. 70.
11. Deleuze and Guattari, *A Thousand Plateaus*, p. 557.
12. Ibid. p. 382.
13. As Marijn Nieuwenhuis writes: 'sand's haecceity is characterised by a mode of material fluidity and shaped by a perpetual process of becoming rather than rooted being' ('A Grain of Sand Against a World of Territory', p. 20). Nieuwenhuis points to *The Physics of Blown Sand and Desert Dunes* (1941) by Ralph Alger Bagnold, the British desert explorer and geologist who served as a commander during the Second World War, as a key source that allowed to the British Army to develop a strategic awareness of sand.
14. Deleuze and Guattari, *A Thousand Plateaus*, p. 384.
15. Cunliffe, *By Steppe, Desert, and Ocean*, p. 25.
16. Virilio, *Speed and Politics*, p. 94.
17. Elden, *The Birth of Territory*, pp. 325–6.
18. Keller Easterling has coined the term 'extrastatecraft' to describe the management of infrastructure spaces beyond the direct control of the state. Telecommunications form a large part of this extra-state domain, exerting huge influence over the design of cities. Once urban spaces can

be treated as parts of information flows, they can more easily be integrated into global networks of capital and technology. Extrastatecraft, then, denotes the political techniques required to govern these entanglements of *polis* and *nomos*.
19. Deleuze and Guattari, *A Thousand Plateaus*, p. 387.
20. Sack, *Human Territoriality*, p. 134.
21. Solnit, *As Eve Said to the Serpent*, p. 70.
22. Pynchon, *Gravity's Rainbow*, pp. 856–7.
23. Schmitt, *The Nomos of the Earth*, p. 87.
24. The state, as it features in Pynchon's text, is not a nation-state but an international cartel state, operating across territories. It is a transcendent point whose core remains withdrawn and concealed, while his main characters (and readers) are placed within a general, immanent field of exteriority determined by the paranoiac attraction exerted by the state's form of interiority. On the state in *Gravity's Rainbow*, see Malpas and Taylor, *Thomas Pynchon*, p. 116.
25. On the vexed question of Deleuze's relationship to Hegel, see Somers-Hall, *Hegel, Deleuze, and the Critique of Representation*, and Widder, 'Deleuze and Guattari's "War Machine" as a Critique of Hegel's Political Philosophy'.
26. Hegel, *Outlines of the Philosophy of Right*, p. 259.
27. Derrida, 'Force of Law, p. 242.
28. Hegel, *Outlines of the Philosophy of Right*, p. 228.
29. Deleuze and Guattari, *A Thousand Plateaus*, pp. 353–4.
30. Ibid. p. 417.
31. Ibid. p. 382.
32. Ibid. p. 420.
33. Ibid. p. 355.
34. The term 'megamachine' comes from Lewis Mumford. In his prologue to the first volume of *The Myth of the Machine* from 1967, he describes the megamachine in the following way:

> The study of the Pyramid Age I made in preparation for writing 'The City in History' unexpectedly revealed that a close parallel existed between the first authoritarian civilizations in the Near East and our own, though most of our contemporaries still regard modem technics, not only as the highest point in man's intellectual development, but as an entirely new phenomenon. On the contrary, I found that what economists lately termed the Machine Age or the Power Age, had its origin, not in the so-called Industrial Revolution of the eighteenth century, but at the very outset in the organization of an archetypal machine composed of human parts. . . . Such order, such collective security and abundance, such stimulating cultural mixtures were first achieved in Mesopotamia and Egypt, and later in India, China, Persia, and in the Andean and Mayan cultures: and they were never surpassed

until the megamachine was reconstituted in a new form in our own time. (*The Myth of the Machine*, pp. 11–12)

The megamachine was made possible by the idea of divine kingship, which facilitated the mechanisation of people and the constitution of the first molar masses in the ancient empires. Modern technics, on the other hand, came to be defined by the impersonal bureaucratic order of the counting house and the discipline of the monastery: 'The new bureaucracy devoted to managerial organization and coordination again became a necessary adjunct to all large-scale, longdistance enterprises: book-keeping and record-keeping set the pace, in standardized uniformity, for all the other parts of the machine' (p. 278).

35. Dumézil, *The Destiny of the Warrior*, p. 55.
36. Ibid. pp. 63–4.
37. Ibid. p. 116.
38. Deleuze and Guattari, *A Thousand Plateaus*, p. 386.
39. Ibid. p. 400.
40. Ibid. p. 400.
41. Ibid. pp. 361–2.
42. Heidegger, *Hölderlin's Hymns "Germania" and "The Rhine"*, p. 112.
43. Ibid. p. 113.
44. Heidegger, 'The Origin of the Work of Art', in *Poetry, Language, Thought*, p. 48.
45. Oliver, *Earth and World*, p. 11.
46. Deleuze and Guattari, *A Thousand Plateaus*, pp. 447–8.
47. Ibid. pp. 421, 448.
48. Ibid. p. 387.
49. Ibid. p. 387.
50. Lawrence, *Seven Pillars of Wisdom*, p. 182.
51. Silverman, *Male Subjectivity at the Margins*, p. 303.
52. Lawrence, *Seven Pillars of Wisdom*, p. 338.
53. Ibid. p. 545.
54. Ibid. p. 6.
55. It is this sense of the epic mode as something alien yet necessary that aligns Lawrence with his modernist contemporaries. On Lawrence, modernism and epic, see Dentith, *Epic and Empire in Nineteenth-Century Britain*, and Paris, 'T. E. Lawrence's *Seven Pillars of Wisdom* and the Erotics of Literary History'. At the end of 1925, while correcting the proofs of *Seven Pillars*, Lawrence wrote in a letter regarding Eliot's *Poems 1909–1925*: 'It's odd, you know, to be reading these poems, so full of the future, so far ahead of our time; and then back to my book, whose prose stinks of coffins and ancestors & armorial hatchments' (*The Letters of T. E. Lawrence*, p. 488). It is, however, the awareness of the past as a place of death and ruination that situates

Lawrence closer to Eliot than he recognises. For both, the desert is synonymous with ruin, while the past becomes accessible through an eroding temporality.

56. Lawrence, *Seven Pillars of Wisdom*, p. 506.
57. Ibid. p. 266.
58. Ibid. p. 559.
59. Ibid. p. 12.
60. Ibid. p. 459.
61. Ibid. p. 638.
62. Goethe, *Theory of Colours*, p. 60.
63. Deleuze, *Essays Critical and Clinical*, p. 115.
64. Lawrence, *Seven Pillars of Wisdom*, p. 227.
65. Ibid. pp. 241–2.
66. Clausewitz, *On War*, p. 480.
67. Ibid. p. 481.
68. Caygill, *On Resistance*, p. 25.
69. Lawrence, *Seven Pillars of Wisdom*, p. 586.
70. Tabachnick, 'The Waste Land in *Seven Pillars of Wisdom*', p. 120.
71. Lawrence, *Seven Pillars of Wisdom*, p. 1.
72. Lawrence, quoted in Tabachnick, 'The Waste Land in *Seven Pillars of Wisdom*', p. 123.
73. Ibid. p. 14.
74. Lawrence, *Seven Pillars of Wisdom*, p. 438.
75. Ibid. p. 560.
76. Deleuze, *Essays Critical and Clinical*, p. 117.
77. Ibid. p. 118.
78. Ibid. pp. 117–18.
79. Lawrence, *Seven Pillars of Wisdom*, p. 14.
80. Lawrence, quoted in Said, *Orientalism*, pp. 228–9.
81. Said, *Orientalism*, p. 230. For a comparative reading of Said and Deleuze on Lawrence, see the fourth chapter of Mutman, *The Politics of Writing Islam*.
82. Lawrence, *Seven Pillars of Wisdom*, p. 657.
83. Said, *Orientalism*, p. 240.
84. Ibid. p. 243.
85. Lawrence, *Seven Pillars of Wisdom*, pp. 555–6.
86. Deleuze and Guattari, *A Thousand Plateaus*, p. 19.
87. Limerick, *Desert Passages*, pp. 165–6.
88. For an excellent analysis of this contradiction, see Walker, 'The Schema of the West and the Apparatus of Capture'.
89. Fiedler, *The Return of the Vanishing American*, p. 24.
90. Ibid. pp. 27–8.
91. Ibid. p. 33.
92. Ibid. pp. 22–3.
93. Ibid. p. 13.

94. For a comprehensive investigation into McCarthy's sources, see Sepich, *Notes on* Blood Meridian.
95. McCarthy, *Blood Meridian*, p. 50.
96. Ibid. p. 266.
97. Ibid. p. 102.
98. Ibid. p. 112.
99. Ibid. p. 261.
100. Steven Shaviro acknowledges the link between McCarthy's prose and the judge's declamatory, stentorian voice:

> For McCarthy as for the judge, writing is inevitably an act of war: deracination, divinatory affirmation, the composition and conduction of dangerous forces, and the production of an active counter-memory. Writing, like war, is a ceremonial and sacrificial act; and *Blood Meridian* is a novel written in blood, awash in blood' ('The Very Life of the Darkness', p. 19)

101. McCarthy, *Blood Meridian*, p. 124.
102. Ibid. p. 259.
103. Ibid. p. 349.
104. Ibid. p. 209.
105. Ibid. p. 182.
106. Ibid. p. 209.
107. Ibid. pp. 262–3.
108. Deleuze and Guattari, *A Thousand Plateaus*, p. 230.
109. Burroughs, *The Place of Dead Roads*, p. 41.
110. Ibid. pp. 40–1.
111. Ibid. p. 46.
112. Ibid. p. 105.
113. Ibid. p. 93.
114. Ibid. p. 33.
115. Burroughs, *The Western Lands*, pp. 111–13.
116. Burroughs, *The Place of Dead Roads*, p. 117.
117. Ibid. p. 97.
118. Burroughs, *The Soft Machine*, p. 5.
119. Burroughs, *Naked Lunch*, p. 79.
120. Fiedler, *Love and Death in the American Novel*, p. 347.
121. Burroughs, *Cities of the Red Night*, p. 25.
122. Burroughs, *The Place of Dead Roads*, p. 172.
123. Burroughs, *The Western Lands*, p. 75.
124. Carter, *The Passion of New Eve*, p. 11.
125. Ibid. p. 40.
126. Ibid. p. 50.
127. Carter, *The Sadeian Woman*, p. 23.
128. Ibid. p. 63.
129. Ibid. p. 4.

130. Ibid. p. 5.
131. Carter, *The Passion of New Eve*, p. 174.
132. Carter, *The Sadeian Woman*, p. 8.
133. Raleigh, quoted in Kolodny, *The Land Before Her*, p. 3.
134. Debray, *God*, p. 51.
135. Carter, *The Passion of New Eve*, p. 5.
136. Ibid. p. 173.
137. Ibid. p. 148.
138. Ibid. p. 149.
139. Ibid. p. 121.
140. Ibid. p. 125.
141. Ibid. p. 129.
142. Ibid. p. 47.
143. Baudrillard, *America*, p. 5.
144. Ibid. p. 11.
145. Ibid. p. 29.
146. Ibid. p. 59.
147. Baudrillard, *Simulacra and Simulation*, p. 1.
148. Carter, *The Passion of New Eve*, p. 53.
149. Ibid. p. 53.
150. Ibid. p. 102.
151. Ibid. pp. 103–4.
152. Ibid. p. 104.
153. Carter, *The Sadeian Woman*, p. 72.
154. Ibid. pp. 148–9.
155. Ibid. pp. 142–3.
156. Carter, *The Passion of New Eve*, p. 174.
157. Andrew Bacevich suggests how a new militarism took shape in America after Vietnam and argues that the 1990 Iraq War marks a key point in this transformation. He detects an aesthetic transformation of war in this new American militarism:

> The old twentieth-century aesthetic of armed conflict as barbarism, brutality, ugliness, and sheer waste grew out of World War I, as depicted by writers such as Ernest Hemingway, Erich Maria Remarque, and Robert Graves. World War II, Korea, and Vietnam reaffirmed that aesthetic, in the latter case with films like *Apocalypse Now*, *Platoon*, and *Full Metal Jacket*. . . . But by the turn of the twenty-first century, a new image of war had emerged, if not fully displacing the old one at least serving as a counterweight. To many observers, events of the 1990s suggested that war's very nature was undergoing a profound change. The era of mass armies, going back to the time of Napoleon, and of mechanized warfare, an offshoot of industrialization, was coming to an end. A new era of high-tech warfare, waged by highly skilled professionals equipped with 'smart' weapons, had commenced.

Describing the result inspired the creation of a new lexicon of military terms: war was becoming surgical, frictionless, postmodern, even abstract or virtual. (*The New American Militarism*, p. 20)

158. Virilio, *Desert Screen*, p. 16.
159. Ibid. p. 85.
160. Virilio, *The Aesthetics of Disappearance*, p. 28.
161. Ibid. p. 46.
162. Virilio, *Desert Screen*, p. 98.
163. DeLillo, *Point Omega*, pp. 23–4.
164. Ibid. p. 30.
165. Ibid. p. 24.
166. Ibid. p. 32.
167. Ibid. p. 36.
168. Ibid. p. 45.
169. Ibid. p. 64.
170. Ibid. p. 91.
171. De Chardin, *Human Energy*, p. 136.
172. DeLillo, *Point Omega*, p. 91.
173. Ibid. p. 124.
174. Ibid. p. 17.
175. Bacevich, *The New American Militarism*, p. 182.
176. The role of the desert in Negarestani's text suggests links with broader Arabic traditions of desert writing. Rob Nixon notes, with respect to Saudi novelist Abdelrahman Munif's 1984 text *'al-Tih* (meaning 'lost in the wilderness', but translated into English as *Cities of Salt*), that

    Arabic literature boasts an immense tradition of wilderness literature in which the desert figures variously as a place of obliteration, threat, derangement, prophecy, and purifying promise. Yet the narrative arc of *'al-Tih* – from wadi to refinery town – disturbs any straightforward opposition between oasis civilization and desert barbarism. The most threatening desert marauders, the barbarians out there, are by implication imperialism's primitive accumulators. The full force of the novel's titular bewilderment is felt when the Bedouin characters are thrust into the high-speed, unintelligible chaos of the company town – the urban wilderness that is petromodernity's cultural creation. (*Slow Violence and the Environmentalism of the Poor*, p. 90)

    These links between the desert as place of derangement and purification with the devastations of petromodernity are central to *Cyclonopedia*.
177. Negarestani, *Cyclonopedia*, p. 17.
178. Land, *The Thirst for Annihilation*, p. 106.
179. Negarestani, *Cyclonopedia*, p. 19.
180. Ibid. p. 96.

181. As Bradley Fest suggests, DeLillo and Negarestani's texts can be considered properly post-postmodern in that the eschatologies of both authors 'stage bold encounters with different ways of making meaning ungrounded from modernity's sense of perpetual crisis and postmodernity's "end of history"' ('Geologies of Finitude', p. 567).
182. Negarestani, *Cyclonopedia*, p. 18.
183. Ibid. p. 132.
184. Ibid. p. 141.
185. Deleuze and Guattari, *A Thousand Plateaus*, p. 415.
186. Negarestani, *Cyclonopedia*, p. 183.
187. Ibid. p. 92.
188. Ibid. p. 185.

Conclusion:
Beyond the Carbon Imaginary

The desert is an object of speculative desire in modern art and thought. As a space where images and representations are broken, it facilitates a far-reaching critique of representation. This is at the heart of modernism's wasteland aesthetics. For modernism, the desert, wasteland or *Wüste* was not just the image of a world in pieces but the site of a breaking of likenesses. Eliot's vacant lots were first of all a means of transgressing aesthetic laws and embracing the terrain vague of decoded space. In his Suprematist manifesto, the Russian painter Kazimir Malevich called for a 'non-objectivist' art by which the objects of the phenomenal world would be nullified in a release of pure feeling and an impoverishment of perception: 'No more "likenesses of reality", no idealistic images – nothing but a desert!'[1] His famous painting of a white square on a white background expresses the strange coexistence of impoverishment and intensity, as if the smallest degree of difference could function to liberate a new subjectivity beyond the representational consciousness that correlates it with an object. This is what I have tentatively termed a hypersubject. In the late 1960s, Robert Smithson referenced Malevich's desert in his own attempts to articulate a new conception of space by means of the entropic landscapes that he saw embodied in the monumental sculptures of Donald Judd and Sol LeWitt, the glass boxes of Park Avenue architecture, and New Jersey's suburban wastelands.[2] Smithson, along with his contemporaries Michael Heizer and Walter de Maria, set out for the deserts of California, Nevada and Utah to construct their site-specific art in the arid landscape. The goal was not simply to move beyond the gallery space or artist's studio but beyond what Smithson called 'the biological metaphor', the aesthetic tendency, as he saw it, to model all being on the organic processes of life, growth, degradation and death.[3] As with the Desert Fathers of late antiquity, the desert was a space in which both nature and *polis* could be eliminated in favour of a third term beyond the organic. As Smithson writes,

> the desert is less 'nature' than concept, a place that swallows up boundaries. When the artist goes to the desert he enriches his absence and burns off the water (paint) on his brain. The slush of the city evaporates from the artist's mind as he installs his art. Heizer's 'dry lakes' become mental maps that contain the vacancy of Thanatos.[4]

What unites modernists and postmodernists is the feeling that the desert is the topos of a subjectivity in need of new models, new cognitive maps, a subject on the brink of abandoning the entire of project of dwelling. To this extent, Malevich and Smithson are of a piece with Nietzsche, Eliot and D. H. Lawrence, all of whom saw the approach and onset of the twentieth century by way of a fundamental spatial disturbance in which notions of place, home and *oikos* were becoming increasingly important but also increasingly obscure and terrible. Lawrence, we will recall, discussed his idea of the 'spirit of place' in terms of the geographical displacements of the New World, the genocide of its Native populations and the resultant 'demon of the continent'.[5] As Heidegger demonstrates, in the epoch of modern technology, the *oikos* can only be conceived through the devastation that menaces it. The project of dwelling, if it is to be sustained, can only proceed on a ground that seems to be disappearing.

From our contemporary perspective, we must recognise that the crisis of Western subjectivity for which the desert and wasteland have so often furnished key symbols has become a crisis of planetary life itself and no longer simply the existential ordeal of the artist or philosopher. Smithson's biological metaphor has become what Povinelli calls the 'Carbon Imaginary', the aesthetic mode by which late capitalism envisages the 'gap' or 'scarred region' between life and non-life and thus comes to correlate and unify – we might say *overcode* – these two terms.[6] Iain Hamilton Grant identifies something similar in the 'cognitive-industrial carbon despotism' of modern capitalist states, the philosophical avatar of which is Kantianism.[7] The state-form today is still biopolitical and produces the life of its citizens on the basis of a sovereign decision about where the difference between life and non-life lies. But as the line between the two becomes uncertain, and as the fate of carbon-based lifeforms becomes perilously intertwined with unsustainable demands for carbon-based fuels, we see more clearly that biopower – the governance of life – is subtended by geontopower – the governance of life in relation to what is not life.[8] As Alan Stoekl has observed in his book on Bataille, the death of God and the religious crisis this installs in the heart of Western subjectivity is fundamentally an energy crisis:

> God would be inseparable from the very movement and finitude of matter itself, from the violent agitation of its atoms. And without God the primacy and integrity of the human ... would also be at risk. And no more Man as well; no more agency that could simply control energy, and for whom energy is always available, mastered.[9]

The desert, as the geological form of entropy and space of the difference between *bios* and *geos*, is where the crisis of subjectivity is played out. The Anthropocene is the epoch in which Man comes to recognise his own metaphysical depletion in the strata of an Earth he has tried to make in his own likeness. Agamben writes that '*Homo sapiens* ... is neither a clearly defined species nor a substance; it is, rather, a machine or device for producing the recognition of the human.'[10] Man is the being that recognises himself as such, but the Anthropocene marks the point at which the anthropological machine freezes in the body without organs of an unrecognisable Earth.

In Freud's theory of the death instinct, the energetics of libido are such that the organism can only maintain itself through 'binding' and ultimately depleting the quantities of free energy in the psyche. Freud suggests that the reason why nightmare images of the battlefields of the First World War would replay over and over in the minds of traumatised survivors, despite his insistence that dreams are wish fulfilments, is that such imagery provides an occasion to attain retroactive binding of traumatic stimuli.[11] The psyche attempts, in other words, to dissolve the fear of death through a libidinal fixation on the event of death itself as replayed in the imagination, suturing death to life via the spectacle of the nightmare. Freud comes to express this, in one of his most famous pronouncements, through the assertion of a general entropic tendency by which all life is driven 'to return to the quiescence of the inorganic world'.[12] The binding of life is thus only a preparation for an extinction that ultimately effaces the distinction between living and non-living by uniting them. The Carbon Imaginary would seem to be late capitalism's own way of binding the free energies of capital and asserting the correlation of life and non-life. The gap between these terms grounds the sovereignty of a biopolitical decision about where the boundary between the two lies. But the Carbon Imaginary is also manifest in spectacles of annihilation and eschatological visions where, as Deleuze and Guattari would put it, the energy liberated by capitalism's decoding of space flows freely over an absolutely deterritorialised Earth. Capitalism is the 'nightmare' of all other social formations, the universal negative image of human society as such.[13] What all other societies warded off through social codes or maintained as an apocalyptic or mythical terminus, capitalism builds into its own mode of production, into its very desiring-machines. Capitalism's desert is immanent to it, but, as we've seen, it needs the sovereignty of a state to maintain transcendence as an archaism with a current function, a memory of the God or the father that has been toppled into the dust like a desert ruin. This is why Nietzsche's growing desert is so riven with ambiguity, why it is at once the domain of the libido and the ascetic ideal by which life extinguishes itself.

In a philosophical tradition that has passed from Heidegger to Blanchot, Levinas and Derrida to Deleuze and Guattari over the course of the twentieth century, the desert has remained a soteriological terrain, a place of potential salvation where man overcomes himself. This overcoming, Nietzsche declared, is nothing other than 'the meaning of the earth' itself.[14] We need to understand the legacy of these philosophers in terms of our present environmental condition while also trying to think of life and non-life beyond the geontopolitics of the state-form. The philosophies of difference that dominated the twentieth century used images of the desert to construct a conceptual topology where difference could be subjected to transformative critique. It was only through a confrontation with the stark indifference of space as finite but unlimited extension that difference in itself, without a conceptual model that would relate it to identity or recognition, could possibly be saved. The Anthropocene itself suggests an epoch of indifference where the identity of Man or the Anthropos is stamped onto the Earth's history with devastating effect. The loss of biodiversity is the violence of a terrifying homogenisation before which we stand aghast by our own footprint, like Robinson before his. Questions of difference and indifference are thus being raised on planetary and environmental scales, which is why geophilosophy offers an important path.

It is on this basis that we should assert that it is only by *losing* the world that we stand any hope of generating an *ethos* and an ethics of the Earth, or what Kelly Oliver calls 'terraphilia'.[15] As strange as it may sound, topophilia – the love of place – stands in the way of an Earth ethics. It is insufficient to assert that the *oikos* is the means by which we should save difference from the homogenisation of the global. Rather, it behoves us to apprehend the absolute *in* the local, as Deleuze and Guattari insist only a nomadically distributed hypersubjectivity, a subjectivity that does not try to recognise itself as a being-in-place, is capable of doing. What Heidegger calls desertification or devastation is key here: devastation razes territories and ungrounds worlds. He identifies this with the technological worldview, but as a violence more uncanny than destruction it may also be construed along the lines of Deleuze and Guattari's war machine as that which counters the structurally necessary violence by which worlds are delimited and enclosed in a *polis*. The capitalist world system or world interior to which we are so captive today maintains and normalises itself as a regime of environmental damage the nature of whose violence remains scarcely thinkable. Technology facilitates this, of course, but in its unintended devastating effects it unleashes those primordial forces of the Earth that Heidegger called *polemos*.

It is thus a matter of articulating the link between the structurally necessary violence of capitalist production on the one hand and the violence to the planet that we understand in terms of catastrophic climate change, habitat loss and mass extinction on the other. At the causal level, the two are the same thing. But we generally imagine the effects of climate change in terms of a spectacular collapse, that is, in terms of the Carbon Imaginary's own fantasies of destruction, without relating this to the slow violence of the everyday reproduction of society. It is curious how easy it is and how willing we are to imagine spectacles of environmental catastrophe, almost as if our ideas of the environment as a surrounding world were premised on an apprehension of a fundamental worldlessness. There is nevertheless something reassuring about such spectacles, as if in the very act of witnessing them we also imagine ourselves surviving them.

The Carbon Imaginary thrives on the idea of extinction. We should for this reason be somewhat suspect of the explosion of climate fiction in literature and film over the past twenty years. The deserts of the American southwest feature in recent 'cli-fi' novels such as Paolo Bacigalupi's *The Water Knife* (2015) and Claire Vaye Watkins's *Gold Fame Citrus* (2015) in the form of dystopian and post-historical landscapes where water has become the key scarce resource. In Bacigalupi's science fiction thriller, high-tech arcologies save the wealthy while the rest perish amid dust storms and social disintegration in a near-future Arizona suffering from severe drought. Watkins's very different novel, resounding with Atwoodian humour and surrealism, suggests the persistence of the figure of the desert messiah and the nomadic thrill of redemption that the West has for so long represented in the American imagination. Desertification in both texts presents a crisis of internal displacement in which the borders between states become militarised, racialised and difficult or impossible to cross. In *Gold Fame Citrus*, a couple and their adopted daughter flee a decaying Los Angeles only to become lost in the Amargosa Dune Sea, a vast moving desert of sand that has swallowed much of California and Nevada and subsumed the entire Mojave Desert. Within the Dune Sea, moving within its drifting ecology, live a band of refugees led by a fraudulent water douser and messiah figure named Levi Zabriskie. *The Water Knife* follows the pursuit of a set of ancient and thus highly valuable rights to the water of the Colorado River, which are hidden inside a first edition copy of Marc Reisner's *Cadillac Desert*. The rights originate with the Hohokam, who thrived in Arizona's Phoenix basin until about 1400 when they mysteriously disappeared, despite having advanced irrigation and canal systems. The Pima Indians claim the Hohokam as ancestors, and the word 'Hohokam' is itself a Pima word meaning vanished or extinct. As bleak as Bacigalupi's Phoenix is, the arcologies that rise out of the dust and squalor gleam with the promise of technological salvation. While both novels evoke the devastations of a twenty-first-century Dust Bowl, then, they also maintain a belief in the desert as a potentially redemptive space where faith or ingenuity may come to our rescue, where American myths of religious and technological salvation may still remain active even in the face of extinction. The desert is where cultures die but are also reborn.

While we can and should be wary of such messages, deserts are undeniably filled with imaginative potentials that can help us rethink the relationships between life and non-life beyond our contemporary political and semiotic regimes. It becomes a question, as Negarestani would say, of derailing the processes of terminus that have now gripped us, of extracting from the Carbon Imaginary's self-reinforcing fantasies of extinction a non-annihilative approach to the omega where a new imaginary of Earthly life can assert itself. The task is to think our annihilation without willing it, to imagine it without believing that by doing so we have somehow survived it. The desert of nihilism grows, certainly, but as it does so it converges on other deserts, on unrecognisable terrains in a future where questions of life can be posed anew.

NOTES

1. Malevich, *The Non-Objective World*, p. 68.
2. Smithson, *The Collected Writings*, p. 14.
3. Ibid. p. 35.
4. Ibid. pp. 109–10.
5. Lawrence, *Classic Studies in American Literature*, pp. 42–3.
6. Povinelli, *Geontologies*, p. 38.
7. Hamilton Grant, '"At the Mountains of Madness"', pp. 99–100.
8. Povinelli, *Geontologies*, p. 172.

9. Stoekl, *Bataille's Peak*, p. 8.
10. Agamben, *The Open*, p. 26.
11. Freud, 'Beyond the Pleasure Principle', in *The Standard Edition*, Vol. *XVIII*, pp. 31–2.
12. Ibid. p. 62.
13. Deleuze and Guattari, *Anti-Oedipus*, p. 153.
14. Nietzsche, *Thus Spoke Zarathustra*, p. 6.
15. Oliver, *Earth and World*, p. 208.

Bibliography

Abbey, Edward, *Desert Solitaire: A Season in the Wilderness* (New York: Ballantine Books, 1968).
Adams, Henry, *The Degradation of the Democratic Dogma* (New York: Macmillan, 1919).
Adams, Henry, *The Education of Henry Adams: An Autobiography*, ed. Ira B. Nadel (Oxford: Oxford University Press, 1999).
Agamben, Giorgio, *The Open: Man and Animal*, trans. Kevin Attell (Stanford: Stanford University Press, 2004).
Arce, María Laura, *Paul Auster and the Influence of Maurice Blanchot* (Jefferson, NC: McFarland & Company, 2016).
Arendt, Hannah, 'Introduction *into* Politics', in Jerome Kohn (ed.), *The Promise of Politics*, trans. John E. Woods (New York: Schocken Books, 2005), pp. 93–200.
Armstrong, Tim, *Modernism, Technology, and the Body: A Cultural Study* (Cambridge: Cambridge University Press, 1998).
Arnalds, Olafur, 'Desertification: An Appeal for a Broader Perspective', in Olafar Arnalds and Steve Archer (eds), *Rangeland Desertification* (Dordrecht: Kluwer Academic Publications, 2000), pp. 5–15.
Artaud, Antonin, *Antonin Artaud: Selected Writings*, ed. Susan Sontag, trans. Helen Weaver (New York: Farrar, Straus and Giroux, 1976).
Atwood, Margaret, 'Time Capsule Found on the Dead Planet', in Mark Martin (ed.), *I'm With the Bears: Short Stories for a Damaged Planet* (London: Verso, 2011), pp. 191–3.
Auden, W. H., *The Enchafèd Flood: Or, The Romantic Iconography of the Sea* (New York: Vintage, 1967).
Auster, Paul, *Collected Poems* (London: Faber and Faber, 2007).
Auster, Paul, *In the Country of Last Things* (London: Faber and Faber, 1987).
Auster, Paul, *The Art of Hunger: Essays, Prefaces, Interviews* (New York: Penguin, 1997).
Austin, Mary, *The American Rhythm: Studies and Reëxpressions of Amerindian Songs*, facsimile of 1930 edn (Santa Fe: Sunstone Press, 2007).
Bacevich, Andrew, *The New American Militarism: How Americans are Seduced by War* (New York: Oxford, 2005).

Bachelard, Gaston, *The Dialectic of Duration*, trans. Mary McAllester Jones (Manchester: Clinamen Press, 2000).
Bacigalupi, Paolo, *The Water Knife* (London: Orbit, 2015).
Ballard, J. G., *Concrete Island* (London: Vintage, 1994).
Ballard, J. G., *Crash* (London: Jonathan Cape, 1973).
Ballard, J. G., *The Atrocity Exhibition* (London: Flamingo, 1993).
Ballard, J. G., *The Drought* (London: Flamingo, 1993).
Ballard, J. G., *The Drowned World* (London: Gollancz, 1963).
Ballard, J. G., *The Terminal Beach* (Harmondsworth: Penguin, 1964).
Ballard, J. G., *War Fever* (London: Paladin, 1991).
Bambach, Charles, *Heidegger's Roots: Nietzsche, National Socialism, and the Greeks* (Ithaca: Cornell University Press, 2003).
Banham, Peter Reyner, *Scenes in America Deserta* (Cambridge, MA: MIT Press, 1989).
Barrell, John, *The Idea of Landscape and the Sense of Place, 1730–1840: An Approach to the Poetry of John Clare* (Cambridge: Cambridge University Press, 1972).
Barrow, John, *Travels into the Interior of Southern Africa, Vol. 1*, 2nd edn (London: Cadell and Davies, 1806).
Bate, Jonathan, *Romantic Ecology: Wordsworth and the Environmental Tradition* (London: Routledge, 1991).
Bate, Jonathan, *The Song of the Earth* (Cambridge, MA: Harvard University Press, 2000).
Baudrillard, Jean, *America*, trans. Chris Turner (New York and London: Verso, 1988).
Baudrillard, Jean, *Simulacra and Simulation*, trans. Sheila Faria Glaser (Ann Arbor: University of Michigan Press, 1994).
Beaulieu, Alain, 'Deleuze and Guattari's Geodynamism and Husserl's Geostatism: Two Cosmological Perspectives', in Dorothea Olkowski and Eftichis Pirovolakis (eds), *Deleuze and Guattari's Philosophy of Freedom: Freedom's Refrains* (New York and London: Routledge, 2019), pp. 169–77.
Beck, John, 'Without Form and Void: The American Desert as Trope and Terrain', *Nepantla: Views from South*, 2.1 (2001), 63–83.
Benjaminsen, Tor A., and Gunnvor Berge, 'Myths of Timbuktu: From African El Dorado to Desertification', *International Journal of Political Economy*, 34.1 (2004), 31–59.
Berger, Alan, *Drosscape: Wasting Land in Urban America* (New York: Princeton Architectural Press, 2006).
Berger, John, *About Looking* (New York: Pantheon, 1980).
Berman, Marshall, *All That Is Solid Melts Into Air: The Experience of Modernity* (London and New York: Verso, 1982).
Bevis, Richard, *The Road to Egdon Heath: Aesthetics of the Great in Nature* (Montreal and Kingston: McGill-Queen's University Press, 1999).
Biermann, Frank, *Earth System Governance: World Politics in the Anthropocene* (Cambridge, MA: MIT Press, 2014).

Blanchot, Maurice, *The Book to Come*, trans. Charlotte Mandell (Stanford: Stanford University Press, 2003).

Blanchot, Maurice, *The Space of Literature*, trans. Ann Smock (Lincoln and London: University of Nebraska Press, 1982).

Blumenberg, Hans, *Shipwreck with Spectator: Paradigm of a Metaphor for Existence*, trans. Steven Rendall (Cambridge, MA: MIT Press, 1997).

Bonneuil, Christophe, 'The Geological Turn: Narratives of the Anthropocene', in Clive Hamilton, Christophe Bonneuil and François Gemenne (eds), *The Anthropocene and the Global Environmental Crisis: Rethinking Modernity in a New Epoch* (London and New York: Routledge, 2015), pp. 17–31.

Bowles, Paul, *Travels: Collected Writings, 1950–93*, ed. Mark Ellingham (London: Sort of Books, 2010).

Braidotti, Rosi, and Simone Bignall (eds), *Posthuman Ecologies: Complexity and Process After Deleuze* (London: Rowman & Littlefield, 2019).

Breuer, Josef, and Sigmund Freud, 'Studies on Hysteria', in *The Standard Edition of the Complete Psychological Works of Sigmund Freud, Vol. II*, ed. and trans. James Strachey (London: The Hogarth Press, 1955).

Brown, Charles S., and Ted Toadvine (eds), *Eco-Phenomenology: Back to the Earth Itself* (Albany: State University of New York Press, 2003).

Brown, Peter, *The Body and Society: Men, Women, and Sexual Renunciation in Early Christianity* (London: Faber and Faber, 1989).

Brown, Wendy, *Walled States, Waning Sovereignty* (New York: Zone Books, 2010).

Brusseau, James, *Isolated Experiences: Gilles Deleuze and the Solitudes of Reversed Platonism* (Albany: State University of New York Press, 1998).

Buchanan, Brett, *Onto-Ethologies: The Animal Environments of Uexküll, Heidegger, Merleau-Ponty, and Deleuze* (Albany: State University of New York Press, 2008).

Buchanan, Ian, *Deleuzism: A Metacommentary* (Edinburgh: Edinburgh University Press, 2000).

Bunyan, John, *The Pilgrim's Progress*, ed. W. R. Owens (Oxford: Oxford University Press, 2003).

Burke, Edmund, *A Philosophical Enquiry into the Origin of Our Ideas of the Sublime and Beautiful*, ed. Paul Guyer (Oxford: Oxford University Press, 2015).

Burroughs, William S., *Cities of the Red Night* (London: Penguin, 1981).

Burroughs, William S., *Naked Lunch: The Restored Text*, ed. James Grauerholtz and Barry Miles (New York: Grove Press, 2001).

Burroughs, William S., 'Preface', in J. G. Ballard, *The Atrocity Exhibition* (London: Flamingo, 1993), pp. vii–viii.

Burroughs, William S., *The Place of Dead Roads* (London: Penguin, 1983).

Burroughs, William S., *The Soft Machine*, revised edn (London: Calder and Boyars, 1968).

Burroughs, William S., *The Western Lands* (London: Picador, 1988).

Burroughs, William S., and Brion Gysin, *The Third Mind* (New York: Viking, 1978).
Butler, Octavia E., *Parable of the Sower* (New York and Boston: Grand Central, 1993).
Canavan, Gerry, 'Introduction: If This Goes On', in Gerry Canavan and Kim Stanley Robinson (eds), *Green Planets: Ecology and Science Fiction* (Middletown, CT: Wesleyan University Press, 2014), pp. 1–21.
Carlson, Colin, Kevin R. Burgio, Eric R. Dougherty, Anna J. Phillips, Veronica M. Bueno, Christopher F. Clements, Giovanni Castaldo, Tad A. Dallas, Carrie A. Cizauskas, Graeme S. Cumming, Jorge Doña, Nyeema C. Harris, Roger Jovani, Sergey Mironov, Oliver C. Muellerklein, Heather C. Proctor and Wayne M. Getz, 'Parasite Biodiversity Faces Extinction and Redistribution in a Changing Climate', *Science Advance*s, 3.9 (2017).
Carter, Angela, *The Passion of New Eve* (London: Virago, 1982).
Carter, Angela, *The Sadeian Woman: An Exercise in Cultural History* (Harmondsworth: Penguin, 1979).
Casey, Edward S., *Getting Back into Place: Toward a Renewed Understanding of the Place-World* (Bloomington: University of Indiana Press, 1993).
Casey, Edward S., *The Fate of Place: A Philosophical History* (Berkeley: University of California Press, 1997).
Cassuto, David N., *Dripping Dry: Literature, Politics, and Water in the Desert Southwest* (Ann Arbor: University of Michigan Press, 2001).
Caygill, Howard, *On Resistance: A Philosophy of Defiance* (London: Bloomsbury, 2013).
Childs, Donald J., *Modernism and Eugenics: Woolf, Eliot, Yeats, and the Culture of Degeneration* (Cambridge: Cambridge University Press, 2001).
Clausewitz, Carl von, *On War*, indexed edn, ed. and trans. Michael Howard and Peter Paret (Princeton: Princeton University Press, 1984).
Cohen, Jeffrey Jerome, 'Introduction: Ecology's Rainbow', in Jeffrey Jerome Cohen (ed.), *Prismatic Ecology: Ecotheory Beyond Green* (Minneapolis: University of Minnesota Press, 2013), pp. xv–xxxv.
Cohen, Josh, 'Desertions: Paul Auster, Edmond Jabès, and the Writing of Auschwitz', *Journal of the Midwest Modern Language Association*, 33.3 (2000), 94–107.
Colebrook, Claire, *Death of the PostHuman: Essays on Extinction, Vol. 1* (Ann Arbor: Open Humanities Press/University of Michigan Press, 2014).
Coleridge, Samuel Taylor, *Samuel Taylor Coleridge: The Major Works*, ed. H. J. Jackson (Oxford: Oxford University Press, 1985).
Coleridge, Samuel Taylor, *Specimens of the Table Talk of the Late Samuel Taylor Coleridge, Vol. II* (London: John Murray, 1835).
Crawford, Robert, *The Savage and the City in the Work of T. S. Eliot* (Oxford: Clarendon Press, 1987).
Crockett, Clayton, and Jeffrey W. Robbins, *Religion, Politics, and the Earth: The New Materialism* (New York: Palgrave Macmillan, 2012).
Crutzen, Paul J., 'Geology of Mankind', *Nature*, 415 (2002), 23.

Cunliffe, Barry, *By Steppe, Desert, and Ocean: The Birth of Eurasia* (Oxford: Oxford University Press, 2015).

Darwin, Charles, *The Origin of Species By Means of Natural Selection; or, the Preservation of Favoured Races in the Struggle for Life* (Cambridge: Cambridge University Press, 2009).

Davis, Diana K., 'Desert "Wastes" of the Maghreb: Desertification Narratives in French Colonial Environmental History of North Africa', *Cultural Geographies*, 11.4 (2004), 359–87.

Davis, Heather, and Etienne Turpin, 'Art & Death: Lives Between the Fifth Assessment & the Sixth Extinction', in Heather Davis and Etienne Turpin (eds), *Art in the Anthropocene: Encounters Among Aesthetics, Politics, Environments and Epistemologies* (London: Open Humanities Press, 2015), pp. 3–29.

Debray, Régis, *God: An Itinerary*, trans. Jeffrey Mehlman (London: Verso, 2004).

Defoe, Daniel, *Robinson Crusoe*, 2nd edn, ed. Michael Shinagel (New York: W. W. Norton, 1994).

DeLanda, Manuel, *A Thousand Years of Nonlinear History* (New York: Zone Books, 1997).

DeLanda, Manuel, *Intensive Science and Virtual Philosophy* (London and New York: Continuum, 2002).

Deleuze, Gilles, *Cinema 2: The Time-Image*, trans. Hugh Tomlinson and Robert Galeta (Minneapolis: University of Minnesota Press, 1989).

Deleuze, Gilles, *Desert Islands and Other Texts, 1953–1974*, ed. David Lapoujade, trans. Michael Taormina (New York: Semiotext(e), 2004).

Deleuze, Gilles, *Difference and Repetition*, trans. Paul Patton (New York: Columbia University Press, 1994).

Deleuze, Gilles, *Essays Critical and Clinical*, trans. Daniel W. Smith and Michael A. Greco (Minneapolis: University of Minnesota Press, 1997).

Deleuze, Gilles, *Lectures on Leibniz*, 1980, trans. Charles J. Stivale, https://www.webdeleuze.com/textes/130 (last accessed 29 November 2019).

Deleuze, Gilles, *Nietzsche and Philosophy*, trans. Hugh Tomlinson (London: Continuum, 2002).

Deleuze, Gilles, *Spinoza: Practical Philosophy*, trans. Robert Hurley (San Francisco: City Lights, 1988).

Deleuze, Gilles, *The Logic of Sense*, ed. Constantin V. Boundas, trans. Mark Lester with Charles Stivale (New York: Columbia University Press, 1990).

Deleuze, Gilles, *What is Grounding?*, from transcripted notes taken by Pierre Lefebvre, ed. Tony Yanick, Jason Adams and Mohammad Salemy, trans. Arjen Kleinherenbrink (Grand Rapids: &&& Publishing, 2015).

Deleuze, Gilles, and Félix Guattari, *Anti-Oedipus: Capitalism and Schizophrenia*, trans. Robert Hurley, Mark Seem and Helen R. Lane (Minneapolis: University of Minnesota Press, 1983).

Deleuze, Gilles, and Félix Guattari, *A Thousand Plateaus: Capitalism and*

Schizophrenia, trans. Brian Massumi (Minneapolis: University of Minnesota Press, 1987).

Deleuze, Gilles, and Félix Guattari, *What Is Philosophy?*, trans. Hugh Tomlinson and Graham Burchell (New York: Columbia University Press, 1994).

DeLillo, Don, *Point Omega* (London: Picador, 2010).

Dentith, Simon, *Epic and Empire in Nineteenth-Century Britain* (Cambridge: Cambridge University Press, 2006).

Derrida, Jacques, *Edmund Husserl's Origin of Geometry: An Introduction*, trans. John P. Leavy Jr. (Lincoln and London: University of Nebraska Press, 1989).

Derrida, Jacques, 'Faith and Knowledge: The Two Sources of "Religion" at the Limits of Reason Alone', in Gil Anidjar (ed.), *Acts of Religion*, trans. Mary Quaintance (New York and London: Routledge, 2002), pp. 228–98.

Derrida, Jacques, 'Force of Law: The "Mystical Foundation of Authority"', in Gil Anidjar (ed.), *Acts of Religion*, trans. Samuel Weber (New York and London: Routledge, 2002), pp. 40–101.

Derrida, Jacques, *On the Name*, ed. Thomas Dutoit, trans. David Wood, John P. Leavey, Jr and Ian McLeod (Stanford: Stanford University Press, 1995).

Derrida, Jacques, 'Rams: Uninterrupted Dialogue – Between Two Infinities', in Jacques Derrida, *Sovereignties in Question: The Poetics of Paul Celan*, ed. Thomas Dutoit and Outi Pasanen, trans. Thomas Dutoit and Philippe Romanski (New York: Fordham University Press, 2005), pp. 135–63.

Derrida, Jacques, *The Beast and the Sovereign, Vol. II*, ed. Michel Lisse, Marie-Louise Mallet and Ginette Michaud, trans. Geoffrey Bennington (Chicago and London: University of Chicago Press, 2011).

Di Cesare, Donatella, *Heidegger and the Jews: The Black Notebooks*, trans. Murtha Baca (Cambridge: Polity, 2018).

Di Palma, Vittoria, *Wasteland: A History* (New Haven, CT and New York: Yale University Press, 2014).

Dodds, Joseph, *Psychoanalysis and Ecology at the Edge of Chaos: Complexity Theory, Deleuze\Guattari and Psychoanalysis for a Climate in Crisis* (London and New York: Routledge, 2011).

Doughty, Charles M., *Travels in Arabia Deserta* (London: Jonathan Cape, 1921).

Duffy, Cian, *Landscapes of the Sublime, 1700–1830: Classic Ground* (London: Palgrave Macmillan, 2013).

Dumézil, Georges, *The Destiny of the Warrior*, trans. Alf Hiltebeitel (Chicago: University of Chicago Press, 1970).

Easterling, Keller, *Extrastatecraft: The Power of Infrastructure Space* (London: Verso, 2014).6

Eberhardt, Isabelle, *In the Shadow of Islam*, trans. Sharon Bangert (London and Chicago: Peter Owen, 2003).

Economides, Louise, *The Ecology of Wonder in Romantic and Postmodern Literature* (New York: Palgrave Macmillan, 2016).

Edensor, Tim, *Industrial Ruins: Space, Aesthetics, and Materiality* (New York: Berg, 2005).
Edgeworth, Matt, 'Grounded Objects: Archaeology and Speculative Realism', *Archaeological Dialogues*, 23.1 (2016), 93–113.
Elden, Stuart, *Terror and Territory: The Spatial Extent of Sovereignty* (Minneapolis: University of Minnesota Press, 2009).
Elden, Stuart, *The Birth of Territory* (Chicago and London: University of Chicago Press, 2013).
Eliot, T. S., *After Strange Gods: A Primer of Modern Heresy* (London: Faber and Faber, 1933).
Eliot, T. S., *Christianity and Culture: The Idea of a Christian Society and Notes Towards the Definition of Culture* (San Diego: Harcourt Brace, 1976).
Eliot, T. S., 'London Letter: September, 1921', in Anthony Cuda and Ronald Schuchard (eds), *The Complete Prose of T. S. Eliot, the Critical Edition*, Vol. 2: *The Perfect Critic, 1919–1926* (London: Faber and Faber; Baltimore: Johns Hopkins University Press, 2014), pp. 369–74.
Eliot, T. S., *The Poems of T. S. Eliot*, Vol. 1: *Collected and Uncollected Poems*, ed. Christopher Ricks and Jim McCue (London: Faber and Faber, 2015).
Eliot, T. S., *To Criticize the Critic and Other Writings* (London: Faber and Faber, 1978).
Eyers, Tom, *Lacan and the Concept of the 'Real'* (Basingstoke: Palgrave Macmillan, 2012).
Eyers, Tom, *Post-Rationalism: Psychoanalysis, Epistemology, and Marxism in Post-War France* (London: Bloomsbury, 2013).
Farley, Paul and Michael Symmons Roberts, *Edgelands: Journey's into England's True Wilderness* (London: Vintage, 2012).
Fest, Bradley, 'Geologies of Finitude: The Deep Time of Twenty-First-Century Catastrophe in Don DeLillo's *Point Omega* and Reza Negarestani's *Cyclonopedia*', *Critique: Studies in Contemporary Fiction*, 57.5 (2016), 565–78.
Fiedler, Leslie A., *Love and Death in the American Novel* (New York: Criterion, 1960).
Fiedler, Leslie A., *The Return of the Vanishing American* (London: Paladin, 1968).
Finkelstein, Haim, '"Deserts of Vast Eternity": J. G. Ballard and Robert Smithson', *Foundation*, 39 (1987), 50–62.
Flaxman, Gregory, *Gilles Deleuze and the Fabulation of Philosophy: Powers of the False*, Vol. 1 (Minneapolis: University of Minnesota Press, 2012).
Foucault, Michel, 'Of Other Spaces', trans. Jay Miskowiec, *Diacritics*, 16.1 (1986), 22–7.
Freud, Sigmund, *The Standard Edition of the Complete Psychological Works of Sigmund Freud*, Vol. XII, trans. James Strachey (London: Hogarth Press, 1958).
Freud, Sigmund, *The Standard Edition of the Complete Psychological Works of Sigmund Freud*, Vol. XVIII, trans. James Strachey (London: Hogarth Press, 1955).

Freud, Sigmund, *The Standard Edition of the Complete Psychological Works of Sigmund Freud*, Vol. XIV, trans. James Strachey (London: Hogarth Press, 1957).

Freud, Sigmund, *The Standard Edition of the Complete Psychological Works of Sigmund Freud*, Vol. XV, trans. James Strachey (London: Hogarth Press, 1961).

Fromentin, Eugène, *Between Sea and Sahara: An Orientalist Adventure*, trans. Blake Robinson (London: Tauris Parke, 2004).

Frost, Laura, *Sex Drives: Fantasies of Fascism in Literary Modernism* (Ithaca and London: Cornell University Press, 2002).

Fuller, Matthew, and Olga Goriunova, 'Devastation', in Erich Hörl and James Burton (eds), *General Ecology: The New Ecological Paradigm* (London: Bloomsbury Academic, 2017), pp. 323–44.

Garrard, Greg, 'Heidegger Nazism Ecocriticism', *Interdisciplinary Studies in Literature and Environment*, 17.2 (2010), 251–71.

Gasché, Rodolphe, *Geophilosophy: On Gilles Deleuze and Félix Guattari's What Is Philosophy?* (Evanston: Northwestern University Press, 2014).

Gaston, Sean, *The Concept of World from Kant to Derrida* (London: Rowman & Littlefield, 2013).

Gersdorf, Catrin, 'America/Deserta: Postmodernism and the Poetics of Space', *Anglia*, 126.2 (2008), 241–57.

Gersdorf, Catrin, *The Poetics and Politics of the Desert: Landscape and the Construction of America* (Amsterdam and New York: Rodopi, 2009).

Giddens, Anthony, *The Consequences of Modernity* (Cambridge: Polity, 1991).

Glotfelty, Cheryll, and Harold Fromm (eds), *The Ecocriticism Reader: Landmarks in Literary Ecology* (Athens and London: University of Georgia Press, 1996).

Goethe, Johann Wolfgang Von, *Theory of Colours*, trans. Charles Lock Eastlake (Cambridge, MA: MIT Press, 1970).

Goldsmith, Oliver, *Poems and Plays*, ed. Tom Davis (London: Dent, 1975).

Gott, Henry Michael, *Ascetic Modernism in the Work of T. S. Eliot and Gustave Flaubert* (London and New York: Routledge, 2013).

Graulund, Rune, 'Contrasts: A Defence of Desert Writings', *Nordic Journal of English Studies*, 2.2 (2003), 345–61.

Griaule, Marcel, *The Pale Fox*, trans. Stephen C. Infantino (Chino Valley, AZ: Continuum Foundation, 1986).

Grumberg, Karen, *Place and Ideology in Contemporary Hebrew Literature* (New York: Syracuse University Press, 2011).

Grundlehner, Philip (ed.), *The Poetry of Friedrich Nietzsche*, trans. Philip Grundlehner (New York and Oxford: Oxford University Press, 1986).

Hallward, Peter, *Out of This World: Deleuze and the Philosophy of Creation* (London: Verso, 2006).

Halsey, Mark, *Deleuze and Environmental Damage: Violence of the Text* (Aldershot: Ashgate, 2006).

Hamilton Grant, Iain, '"At the Mountains of Madness": The Demonology of the New Earth and the Politics of Becoming', in Keith Ansell Pearson (ed.), *Deleuze and Philosophy: The Difference Engineer* (London: Routledge, 1997), pp. 93–114.

Hamilton Grant, Iain, *Philosophies of Nature After Schelling* (London: Continuum, 2006).

Haraway, Donna, *Staying with the Trouble: Making Kin in the Chthulucene* (Durham, NC and London: Duke University Press, 2016).

Hardy, Thomas, *The Return of the Native*, ed. George Woodcock (London: Penguin, 1978).

Haynes, Roslynn D., *Desert: Nature and Culture* (London: Reaktion Books, 2013).

Hegel, Georg Wilhelm Friedrich, *Outlines of the Philosophy of Right*, ed. Stephen Houlgate, trans. T. M. Knox (Oxford: Oxford University Press, 2008).

Heidegger, Martin, *An Introduction to Metaphysics*, trans. Ralph Manheim (New Haven and London: Yale University Press, 1959).

Heidegger, Martin, *Being and Time*, trans. John Macquarrie and Edward Robinson (Oxford: Blackwell, 1962).

Heidegger, Martin, *Country Path Conversations*, trans. Bret W. Davis (Bloomington and Indianapolis: Indiana University Press, 2010).

Heidegger, Martin, *Hölderlin's Hymns "Germania" and "The Rhine"*, trans. William McNeill and Julia Ireland (Bloomington and Indianapolis: Indiana University Press, 2014).

Heidegger, Martin, 'Letter on Humanism', in David Farrell Krell (ed.), *Martin Heidegger: Basic Writings*, trans. Frank A. Capuzzi with J. Glenn Gray and David Farrell Krell (San Francisco: HarperCollins, 1993), pp. 213–65.

Heidegger, Martin, *Nature, History, State: 1933–1934*, ed. and trans. Gregory Fried and Richard Polt (London: Bloomsbury, 2013).

Heidegger, Martin, *Poetry, Language, Thought*, trans. Albert Hofstadter (New York: Harper and Row, 1971).

Heidegger, Martin, *The End of Philosophy*, trans. Joan Stambaugh (Chicago: Chicago University Press, 2003).

Heidegger, Martin, *The Fundamental Concepts of Metaphysics: World, Finitude, Solitude*, trans. William McNeill and Nicholas Walker (Bloomington and Indianapolis: Indiana University Press, 1995).

Heidegger, Martin, *What Is Called Thinking?* trans. J. Glenn Gray (New York: Harper and Row, 1968).

Heise, Ursula K., *Imagining Extinction: The Cultural Meanings of Endangered Species* (Chicago and London: University of Chicago Press, 2016).

Heise, Ursula K., 'Reduced Ecologies: Science Fiction and the Meanings of Biological Scarcity', *European Journal of English Studies*, 16.2 (2012), 99–112.

Heise, Ursula K., *Sense of Place and Sense of Planet: The Environmental Imagination of the Global* (Oxford: Oxford University Press, 2008).

Hell, Julia, and Andreas Schönle (eds), *Ruins of Modernity* (Durham, NC and London: Duke University Press, 2010).
Herzogenrath, Bernd (ed.), *An [Un]Likely Alliance: Thinking Environment[s] with Deleuze/Guattari* (Newcastle upon Tyne: Cambridge Scholars, 2008).
Herzogenrath, Bernd (ed.), *Deleuze/Guattari & Ecology* (London: Palgrave Macmillan, 2009).
Hetherington, Kevin, *The Badlands of Modernity: Heterotopia and Social Ordering* (London and New York: Routledge, 1997).
Hinlicky, Paul R., and Brent Adkins, *Rethinking Philosophy and Theology with Deleuze: A New Cartography* (London: Bloomsbury, 2013).
Hill, Christopher, *The World Turned Upside Down: Radical Ideas During the English* Revolution (London: Penguin, 1975).
Holleman, Hannah, *Dust Bowls of Empire: Imperialism, Environmental Politics, and the Injustice of "Green" Capitalism* (New Haven and London: Yale University Press, 2018).
Hörl, Erich, and James Burton (eds), *General Ecology: The New Ecological Paradigm* (London: Bloomsbury, 2017).
Hume, Kathryn, 'William S. Burroughs's Phantasmic Geography', *Contemporary Literature*, 40.1 (1999), 111–35.
Humma, John B., *Metaphor and Meaning in D.H. Lawrence's Later Novels* (Columbia: University of Missouri Press, 1990).
Husserl, Edmund, 'Foundational Investigations of the Phenomenological Origin of the Spatiality of Nature', in Peter McCormick and Frederick Elliston (eds), *Husserl: Shorter Works*, trans. Fred Kersten (Notre Dame: University of Notre Dame Press, 1981), pp. 222–33.
Husserl, Edmund, *The Crisis of European Sciences and Transcendental Phenomenology: An Introduction to Phenomenological Philosophy*, trans. David Carr (Evanston: Northwestern University Press, 1970).
Jameson, Fredric, *Archaeologies of the Future: The Desire Called Utopia and Other Science Fictions* (London: Verso, 2005).
Jameson, Fredric, *Marxism and Form: Twentieth-Century Dialectical Theories of Literature* (Princeton: Princeton University Press, 1971).
Jasper, David, *The Sacred Desert: Religion, Literature, Art, and Culture* (Oxford: Blackwell, 2004).
Jefferies, Richard, *After London; or Wild England*, ed. Mark Frost (Edinburgh: Edinburgh University Press, 2017).
Jellis, Thomas, Joe Gerlach and J. D. Dewsbury (eds), *Why Guattari? A Liberation of Cartographies, Ecologies and Politics* (New York and London: Routledge, 2019).
Johnson, Andrew Tyler, 'A Critique of the Husserlian and Heideggerian Concepts of Earth: Toward a Transcendental Earth that Accords with the Experience of Life', *Journal of the British Society for Phenomenology*, 45.3 (2014), 220–38.
Joyce, James, 'Realism and Idealism in English Literature (Daniel Defoe – William

Blake)', in Kevin Barry (ed.), *Occasional, Critical, and Political Writing*, trans. Conor Deane (Oxford: Oxford University Press, 2000), pp. 163–82.

Kant, Immanuel, *Critique of Judgment*, trans. Werner S. Pluhar (Indianapolis and Cambridge: Hackett, 1987).

Kant, Immanuel, *Critique of Pure Reason*, trans. Paul Guyer and Allen W. Wood (Cambridge: Cambridge University Press, 1998).

Kerslake, Christian, *Immanence and the Vertigo of Philosophy: From Kant to Deleuze* (Edinburgh: Edinburgh University Press, 2009).

Kleinherenbrink, Arjen, 'Territory and Ritornello: Deleuze and Guattari on Thinking Living Beings', *Deleuze Studies*, 9.2 (2015), 208–30.

Knowles, Thomas, 'Aeolian Harps in the Desert: Romanticism and *Vermillion Sands*', in Richard Brown, Christopher Duffy and Elizabeth Stainforth (eds), *J. G. Ballard: Landscapes of Tomorrow* (Leiden and Boston: Brill Rodopi, 2016), pp. 23–39.

Kolbert, Elizabeth, *The Sixth Extinction: An Unnatural History* (London: Bloomsbury 2014).

Kolodny, Annette, *The Land Before Her: Fantasy an Experience of the American Frontiers, 1630–1860* (Chapel Hill and London: University of North Carolina Press, 1984).

Koolhaas, Rem, 'Junkspace', *October*, 100 (2002), 175–90.

Lacan, Jacques, *Autres écrits* (Paris: Éditions du Seuil, 2001).

Lacan, Jacques, *Écrits: A Selection*, trans. Alan Sheridan (London and New York: Routledge/Tavistock, 1977).

Lacan, Jacques, *The Seminar of Jacques Lacan: Book III. The Psychoses, 1955–1956*, ed. Jacques Alain-Miller, trans. Russell Grigg (New York and London: Norton, 1993).

Lacarrière, Jacques, *Men Possessed by God: The Story of the Desert Monks of Ancient Christendom*, trans. Roy Monkcom (Garden City, NY: Doubleday, 1964).

Lambert, Gregg, *Who's Afraid of Deleuze and Guattari?* (London: Continuum, 2006).

Land, Nick, *The Thirst for Annihilation: Georges Bataille and Virulent Nihilism (an Essay in Atheistic Religion)* (London: Routledge, 1992).

Latour, Bruno, *Down to Earth: Politics in the New Climatic Regime*, trans. Catherine Porter (Cambridge: Polity, 2018).

Latour, Bruno, *Facing Gaia: Eight Lectures on the New Climatic Regime*, trans. Catherine Porter (Cambridge: Polity, 2017).

Latour, Bruno, 'Love Your Monsters: Why We Must Care for our Technologies as We Do for Our Children', *Breakthrough Journal*, 2 (2011), 19–27.

Lawrence, D. H., *Apocalypse and the Writings on Revelation*, ed. Mara Kalnins (London: Penguin, 1995).

Lawrence, D. H., *Classic Studies in American Literature*, ed. Ezra Greenspan, Lindeth Vasey and John Worthen (Cambridge: Cambridge University Press, 2003).

Lawrence, D. H., *Mornings in Mexico* (London: I. B. Tauris, 2009).
Lawrence, D. H., *The Plumed Serpent* (New York: Vintage, 1992).
Lawrence, T. E., 'Introduction', in Charles M. Doughty, *Travels in Arabia Deserta*, new edn (London: Jonathan Cape, 1921), pp. xvii–xxvii.
Lawrence, T. E., *Seven Pillars of Wisdom* (Ware: Wordsworth, 1997).
Lawrence, T. E., *The Letters of T. E. Lawrence*, ed. David Garnett (London: Jonathan Cape, 1938).
Lawrence, T. E., *The Mint* (London: Penguin, 1978).
Leavis, F. R., *New Bearings in English Poetry: A Study of the Contemporary Situation* (Harmondsworth: Penguin, 1963).
Lefebvre, Henri, *The Production of Space*, trans. Donald Nicholson-Smith (Oxford: Blackwell, 1991).
Le Goff, Jacques, *The Medieval Imagination*, trans. Arthur Goldhammer (Chicago and London: University of Chicago Press, 1988).
Le Guin, Ursula K., *The Dispossessed* (London: HarperCollins, 1974).
Levinas, Emmanuel, *Existence and Existents*, trans. Alphonso Lingis (Dordrecht: Kluwer Academic Publishing, 1988).
Levinas, Emmanuel, *Otherwise than Being or Beyond Essence*, trans. Alphonso Lingis (Pittsburgh: Duquesne University Press, 1998).
Levinas, Emmanuel, *Proper Names*, trans. Michael B. Smith (Stanford: Stanford University Press, 1996).
Levinas, Emmanuel, 'The Transcendence of Worlds', in *The Levinas Reader*, ed. and trans. Seán Hand (Oxford: Basil Blackwell, 1989), pp. 144–9.
Lévi-Strauss, Claude, *Introduction to the Work of Marcel Mauss*, trans. Felicity Baker (London: Routledge & Kegan Paul, 1987).
Lewis, Simon L., and Mark A. Maslin, *The Human Planet: How We Created the Anthropocene* (London: Penguin, 2018).
Limerick, Patricia Nelson, *Desert Passages: Encounters with the American Deserts* (Albuquerque: University of New Mexico Press, 1985).
Lindqvist, Sven, *Desert Divers*, trans. Joan Tate (London: Granta, 2000).
Lukács, Georg, *The Theory of the Novel: A Historico-Philosophical Essay on the Forms of Great Epic Literature*, trans. Anna Bostock (Cambridge, MA: MIT Press, 1971).
Lynch, Tom, *Xerophilia: Ecocritical Explorations in Southwestern Literature* (Lubbock: Texas Tech University Press, 2008).
Malevich, Kasimir, *The Non-Objective World: The Manifesto of Suprematism*, trans. Howard Dearstyne (Mineola, NY: Dover Publications, 2003).
Malpas, Jeff, *Heidegger and the Thinking of Place: Explorations in the Topology of Being* (Cambridge, MA: MIT Press, 2012).
Malpas, Jeff, *Heidegger's Topology: Being, Place, World* (Cambridge, MA: MIT Press, 2006).
Malpas, Simon, and Andrew Taylor, *Thomas Pynchon* (Manchester and New York: Manchester University Press, 2013).
Marsh, John, 'Hired Men and Hired Women: Modern American Poetry and the Labor Problem', in Cary Nelson (ed.), *The Oxford Handbook of*

Modern and Contemporary American Poetry (Oxford: Oxford University Press, 2012), pp. 120–42.

Marx, Karl, *Grundrisse: Foundations of the Critique of Political Economy (Rough Draft)*, trans. Martin Nicolaus (London: Penguin, 1973).

McBrien, Justin, 'Accumulating Extinction: Planetary Catastrophism in the Necrocene', in Jason W. Moore (ed.), *Anthropocene or Capitalocene?: Nature, History, and the Crisis of Capitalism* (Oakland: PM Press, 2016), pp. 116–37.

McCarthy, Cormac, *Blood Meridian, or, The Evening Redness in the West* (London: Picador, 1985).

McCormack, Derek P., *Refrains for Moving Bodies: Experience and Experiment in Affective Spaces* (Durham, NC: Duke University Press, 2013).

McNamee, Gregory (ed.), *The Desert Reader: A Literary Companion* (Albuquerque: University of New Mexico Press, 1995).

Meillassoux, Quentin, *After Finitude: An Essay on the Necessity of Contingency*, trans. Ray Brassier (London: Continuum, 2008).

Mentz, Steve, *Shipwreck Modernity: Ecologies of Globalization, 1550–1719* (Minneapolis: University of Minnesota Press, 2015).

Miles, Malcolm, *Eco-Aesthetics: Art, Literature and Architecture in a Period of Climate Change* (London: Bloomsbury, 2014).

Milesi, Laurent, 'Thinking (Through) the Desert (la pensée du désert) With(in) Jacques Derrida', in Martin McQuillan (ed.), *The Politics of Deconstruction: Jacques Derrida and the Other of Philosophy* (London: Pluto Press, 2007), pp. 173–92.

Millet, Kate, *Sexual Politics* (New York: Columbia University Press, 2016).

Mole, Gary D., *Lévinas, Blanchot, Jabès: Figures of Estrangement* (Gainesville: University of Florida Press, 1997).

Moore, Jason W., *Capitalism in the Web of Life: Ecology and the Accumulation of Capital* (London and New York: Verso, 2015).

More, Thomas, *Utopia*, revised edn, ed. George M. Logan and Robert M. Adams (Cambridge: Cambridge University Press, 2002).

Moretti, Franco, *The Bourgeois: Between History and Literature* (London and New York: Verso, 2013).

Morton, Timothy, *Being Ecological* (London: Penguin, 2018).

Morton, Timothy, 'Coexistence and Coexistents: Ecology without a World', in Axel Goodbody and Kate Rigby (eds), *Ecocritical Theory: New European Approaches* (Charlottesville and London: University of Virginia Press, 2011), pp. 168–80.

Morton, Timothy, *Ecology without Nature: Rethinking Environmental Aesthetics* (Cambridge, MA and London: Harvard University Press, 2007).

Morton, Timothy, *Humankind: Solidarity with Nonhuman People* (London: Verso, 2019).

Morton, Timothy, *Hyperobjects: Philosophy and Ecology After the End of the World* (Minneapolis and London: University of Minnesota Press, 2013).

Morton, Timothy, *Shelley and the Revolution of Taste: The Body and the Natural World* (Cambridge: Cambridge University Press, 1994).
Morton, Timothy, *The Poetics of Spice: Romantic Consumerism and the Exotic* (Cambridge: Cambridge University Press, 2000).
Müller Chris, 'Style and Arrogance: The Ethics of Heidegger's Style', in Ivan Callus, James Corby and Gloria Lauri-Lucente (eds), *Style in Theory: Between Literature and Philosophy* (London: Bloomsbury, 2013), pp. 141–62.
Mumford, Lewis, *The Myth of the Machine: Technics and Human Development* (New York: Harcourt Brace Jovanovich, 1967).
Murphy, Peter, and David Roberts, *Dialectic of Romanticism: A Critique of Modernism* (London: Continuum, 2004).
Mutman, Mahmut, *The Politics of Writing Islam: Voicing Difference* (London: Bloomsbury, 2014).
Naas, Michael, *Miracle and Machine: Jacques Derrida and the Two Sources of Religion, Science, and the Media* (New York: Fordham University Press, 2012).
Nancy, Jean-Luc, *The Inoperative Community*, ed. Peter Connor, trans. Peter Connor, Lisa Garbus, Michael Holland and Simona Sawhney (Minneapolis and Oxford: University of Minnesota Press, 1991).
Negarestani, Reza, *Cyclonopedia: Complicity with Anonymous Materials* (Melbourne: re.press, 2008).
Neher, André, *The Exile of the Word: From the Silence of the Bible to the Silence of Auschwitz*, trans. David Maisel (Philadelphia: The Jewish Publication Society of America, 1981).
Nichols, Ashton, *Beyond Romantic Ecocriticism: Toward Urbanatural Roosting* (New York: Palgrave Macmillan, 2011).
Nietzsche, Friedrich, *On the Genealogy of Morality*, trans. Carol Diethe (Cambridge: Cambridge University Press, 2006).
Nietzsche, Friedrich, *Philosophy in the Tragic Age of the Greeks*, trans. Marianne Cowan (Washington, DC: Regnery Publishing, 1962).
Nietzsche, Friedrich, *The Gay Science: With a Prelude in German Rhymes and an Appendix of Songs*, ed. Bernard Williams, trans. Josefine Nauckhoff, poems trans. Adrian Del Caro (Cambridge: Cambridge University Press, 2001).
Nietzsche, Friedrich, *The Peacock and the Buffalo: The Poetry of Nietzsche*, trans. James Luchte (London: Continuum, 2010).
Nietzsche, Friedrich, *The Will to Power*, trans. Walter Kaufmann and R. J. Hollingdale (New York: Vintage, 1967).
Nietzsche, Friedrich, *Thus Spoke Zarathustra: A Book for All and None*, ed. Adrian Del Caro and Robert B. Pippin, trans. Adrian Del Caro (Cambridge: Cambridge University Press, 2006).
Nieuwenhuis, Marijn, 'A Grain of Sand Against a World of Territory: Experiences of Sand and Sandscapes in China', in Kimberley Peters, Philip Steinberg and Elaine Stratford (eds), *Territory Beyond Terra* (London and New York: Rowman & Littlefield, 2018), pp. 19–34.

Nixon, Rob, *Slow Violence and the Environmentalism of the Poor* (Cambridge, MA: Harvard University Press, 2011).
Oh, Eunyoung, *D. H. Lawrence's Border Crossing: Colonialism in His Travel Writings and "Leadership" Novels* (New York and London: Routledge, 2014).
Oliver, Kelly, *Earth and World: Philosophy After the Apollo Missions* (New York: Columbia University Press, 2015).
Ondaatje, Michael, *The English Patient* (New York: Alfred A. Knopf, 1992).
Osborne, Peter, *The Politics of Time: Modernity and Avant-Garde* (London: Verso, 1995).
Otto, Rudolf, *The Idea of the Holy: An Inquiry into the Non-Rational Factor in the Idea of the Divine and Its Relation to the Rational*, 2nd edn, trans. John W. Harvey (London: Oxford University Press, 1923).
Ottum, Lisa, and Seth T. Reno, 'Introduction: Recovering Ecology's Affects', in Lisa Ottum and Seth T. Reno (eds), *Wordsworth and the Green Romantics: Affect and Ecology in the Nineteenth Century* (Durham: University of New Hampshire Press, 2016), pp. 1–27.
Paris, Vaclav, 'T. E. Lawrence's *Seven Pillars of Wisdom* and the Erotics of Literary History: Straddling Epic', *English Literature in Transition*, 60.1 (2017), 16–35.
Park, Mungo, *Travels in the Interior of Africa* (Edinburgh: Adam and Charles Black, 1858).
Patey, Caroline, 'Whose Tradition? T. S. Eliot and the Text of Anthropology', in Giovanni Cianci and Jason Harding (eds), *T. S. Eliot and the Concept of Tradition* (Cambridge: Cambridge University Press, 2007), pp. 161–73.
Pelbart, Peter Pàl, *Cartography of Exhaustion: Nihilism Inside Out*, trans. John Laudenberger and Felix Rebolledo Palazuclos (Minneapolis: Univocal, 2015).
Pite, Ralph, 'How Green Were the Romantics?', *Studies in Romanticism*, 35.3 (1996), 357–73.
Plotnitsky, Arkady, 'Manifolds: On the Concept of Space in Riemann and Deleuze', in Simon Duffy (ed.), *Virtual Mathematics: The Logic of Difference* (Manchester: Clinamen, 2006), pp. 187–208.
Pound, Ezra, *Antheil and the Treatise on Harmony, with Supplementary Notes* (Chicago: Pascal Covici, 1927).
Pound, Ezra, 'A Retrospect', in T. S. Eliot (ed.), *Literary Essays of Ezra Pound* (New York: New Directions, 1968), pp. 3–14.
Povinelli, Elizabeth, *Geontologies: A Requiem to Late Capitalism* (Durham, NC and London: Duke University Press, 2016).
Protevi, John, 'The Organism as the Judgement of God: Aristotle, Kant and Deleuze on Nature (that is, on Biology, Theology and Politics)', in Mary Bryden (ed.), *Deleuze and Religion* (London and New York: Routledge, 2001), pp. 30–41.
Pynchon, Thomas, *Gravity's Rainbow* (London: Vintage, 1973).
Pynchon, Thomas, *Slow Learner: Early Stories* (New York: Back Bay, 1984).

Pynchon, Thomas, *The Crying of Lot 49* (New York: Vintage, 2000).
Pynchon, Thomas, *V.* (London: Vintage, 1995).
Rae, Gavin, *Ontology in Heidegger and Deleuze: A Comparative Analysis* (Basingstoke: Palgrave Macmillan, 2014).
Rae, Gavin, 'Violence, Territorialization, and Signification: The Political from Carl Schmitt and Gilles Deleuze', *Theoria and Praxis*, 1.1 (2013), 1–17.
Raine, Craig, *T. S. Eliot* (Oxford: Oxford University Press, 2006).
Rainey, Lawrence (ed.), *Modernism: An Anthology* (Malden, MA: Blackwell, 2005).
Reisner, Marc, *Cadillac Desert: The American West and Its Disappearing Water* (New York: Viking, 1986).
Relph, Edward, *Place and Placelessness* (London: Pion, 1976).
Rigby, Kate, *Topographies of the Sacred: The Poetics of Place in European Romanticism* (Charlottesville and London: University of Virginia Press, 2004).
Robinson, Kim Stanley, *Red Mars* (London: HarperCollins, 1992).
Romm, Joseph, 'The Next Dust Bowl', *Nature*, 478 (2011), 450–1.
Rousseau, Jean-Jacques, *Emile, or On Education*, trans. Allan Bloom (New York: Basic Books, 1979).
Ruddick, Nicholas, *Ultimate Island: On the Nature of British Science Fiction* (Westport, CT: Greenwood Press, 1993).
Sack, Robert David, *Human Territoriality: Its Theory and History* (Cambridge: Cambridge University Press, 1986).
Said, Edward W., *Orientalism* (New York: Vintage, 1978).
Saint-Exupéry, Antoine de, *Wind, Sand and Stars*, trans. William Rees (London: Penguin, 1995).
Saldanha, Arun, and Hannah Stark (eds), *Deleuze and Guattari in the Anthropocene: Special Issue of Deleuze Studies*, 10.4 (2016).
Santner, Eric L., *My Own Private Germany: Daniel Paul Schreber's Secret History of Modernity* (Princeton: Princeton University Press, 1996).
Sass, Louis A., *Madness and Modernism: Insanity in the Light of Modern Art, Literature, and Thought* (New York: Basic Books, 1992).
Schellnhuber, Hans Joachim, '"Earth System" Analysis and the Second Copernican Revolution', *Nature*, 402 (1999), 19–23.
Schmitt, Carl, *The Nomos of the Earth in the International Law of the Jus Publicum Europaeum*, trans. G. L. Ulmen (New York: Telos, 2003).
Schneidau, Herbert N., *Sacred Discontent: The Bible and Western Tradition* (Berkeley and Los Angeles: University of California Press, 1976).
Schonhorn, Manuel, *Defoe's Politics: Parliament, Power, Kingship and Robinson Crusoe* (Cambridge: Cambridge University Press, 1991).
Schreber, Daniel Paul, *Memoirs of My Nervous Illness*, ed. and trans. Ida Macalpine and Richard A. Hunter (New York: New York Review, 2000).
Seed, David, *The Fictional Labyrinths of Thomas Pynchon* (Basingstoke: Macmillan, 1988).

Sepich, John, *Notes on Blood Meridian*, revised and expanded edn (Austin: University of Texas Press, 2008).

Shaviro, Steven, '"The Very Life of the Darkness": A Reading of *Blood Meridian*', in Harold Bloom (ed.), *Bloom's Modern Critical Views: Cormac McCarthy*, new edn (New York: Bloom's Literary Criticism, 2009), pp. 9–21.

Shelley, Percy Bysshe, *The Major Works*, ed. Zachary Leader and Michael O'Neill (Oxford: Oxford University Press, 2003).

Shepard, Paul, *Nature and Madness* (Athens and London: University of Georgia Press, 1982).

Sholtz, Janae, *The Invention of a People: Heidegger and Deleuze on Art and the Political* (Edinburgh: Edinburgh University Press, 2015).

Sibertin-Blanc, Guillaume, *State and Politics: Deleuze and Guattari on Marx*, trans. Ames Hodges (South Pasadena: Semiotext(e), 2016).

Silverman, Kaja, *Male Subjectivity at the Margins* (London: Routledge, 1992).

Simons, Oliver, 'Carl Schmitt's Spatial Rhetoric', in Jens Meierhenrich and Oliver Simons (eds), *The Oxford Handbook of Carl Schmitt* (New York: Oxford University Press, 2016), pp. 776–99.

Sloterdijk, Peter, *In the World Interior of Capital: For a Philosophical Theory of Globalization*, trans. Wieland Hoban (Cambridge: Polity, 2013).

Smithson, Robert, *The Collected Writings*, ed. Jack Flam (Berkeley and Los Angeles: University of California Press, 1996).

Solà-Morales, Ignasi de, 'Terrain Vague', in Manuela Mariani and Patrick Barron (eds), *Terrain Vague: Interstices at the Edge of the Pale* (London and New York: Routledge, 2014), pp. 24–30.

Solnit, Rebecca, *As Eve Said to the Serpent: On Landscape, Gender, and Art* (Athens: University of Georgia Press, 2001).

Solnit, Rebecca, *Savage Dreams: A Journey into the Hidden Wars of the American West* (Berkeley and Los Angeles: University of California Press, 2014).

Somers-Hall, Henry, *Hegel, Deleuze, and the Critique of Representation: Dialectics of Negation and Difference* (Albany: State University of New York Press, 2012).

Steffen, Will, Paul J. Crutzen and John R. McNeill, 'The Anthropocene: Are Humans Now Overwhelming the Great Forces of Nature?', *AMBIO: A Journal of the Human Environment*, 36.8 (2007), 614–21.

Steffen, Will, Jacques Grinevald, Paul Crutzen and John McNeill, 'The Anthropocene: Conceptual and Historical Perspectives', *Philosophical Transactions of the Royal Society A*, 369 (2011), pp. 842–67.

Stengers, Isabelle, *In Catastrophic Times: Resisting the Coming Barbarism*, trans. Andrew Goffey (London: Open Humanities Press/Meson Press, 2015).

Stoekl, Allan, *Bataille's Peak: Energy, Religion, and Postsustainability* (Minneapolis: University of Minnesota Press, 2007).

Sullivan, Sian, and Katherine Homewood, 'On Non-equilibrium and Nomadism: Knowledge, Diversity and Global Modernity in Drylands (and

Beyond ...)', *CSGR Working Paper*, 122.3 (2003), https://warwick.ac.uk/fac/soc/pais/research/researchcentres/csgr/papers/workingpapers/2003/wp12203.pdf (last accessed on 29 November 2019).

Tabachnick, Stephen E., 'The Waste Land in *Seven Pillars of Wisdom*', in Stephen E. Tabachnick (ed.), *The T. E. Lawrence Puzzle* (Athens: University of Georgia Press, 1984), pp. 115–23.

Tally Jr., Robert T., and Christine M. Battista (eds), *Ecocriticism and Geocriticism: Overlapping Territories in Environmental and Spatial Literary Studies* (New York: Palgrave Macmillan, 2016).

Tanner, Tony, *City of Words: American Fiction 1950–1970* (London: Jonathan Cape, 1971).

Teague, David W., *The Southwest in American Literature and Art: The Rise of a Desert Aesthetic* (Tucson: University of Arizona Press, 1997).

Teilhard de Chardin, Pierre, *Human Energy*, trans. J. M. Cohen (London: Collins, 1969).

Tennyson, Alfred Lord, *Tennyson: A Selected Edition*, ed. Christopher Ricks (London and New York: Routledge, 2014).

Terblanche, Etienne, *T. S. Eliot, Poetry, and the Earth: The Name of the Lotos Rose* (Lanham, MD: Lexington Books, 2016).

Thomas, David S. G., and Nicholas J. Middleton, *Desertification: Exploding the Myth* (Chichester: John Wiley, 1994).

Tournier, Michel, *Friday*, trans. Norman Denny (New York: Pantheon Books, 1969).

Tynan, Aidan, 'Ballard, Smithson and the Biophilosophy of the Crystal', *Green Letters*, 22.4 (2018), 398–411.

Uexküll, Jakob von, *A Foray into the Worlds of Animals and Humans* with *A Theory of Meaning*, trans. Joseph D. O'Neil (Minneapolis: University of Minnesota Press, 2010).

Van Dyke, John C., *The Desert: Further Studies in Natural Appearances* (Baltimore and London: Johns Hopkins University Press, 1999).

Van Wyck, Peter C., *Primitives in the Wilderness: Deep Ecology and the Missing Human Subject* (Albany: State University of New York, 1997).

Vickery, John B., '*The Plumed Serpent* and the Reviving God', *Journal of Modern Literature*, 2.4 (1972), 505–32.

Vince, Gaia, *Adventures in the Anthropocene: A Journey to the Heart of the Planet We Made* (London: Chatto and Windus, 2014).

Viney, William, *Waste: A Philosophy of Things* (London and New York: Bloomsbury, 2015).

Virilio, Paul, *Desert Screen: War at the Speed of Light*, trans. Michael Degener (London: Continuum, 2002).

Virilio, Paul, *Speed and Politics*, trans. Marc Polizzotti (Los Angeles: Semiotext(e), 2006).

Virilio, Paul, *The Aesthetics of Disappearance*, trans. Philip Beitchman (New York: Semiotext(e), 1991).

Walcott, Derek, *Collected Poems: 1948–1984* (London: Faber and Faber, 1986).
Walcott, Derek, 'The Figure of Crusoe', in Robert D. Hamner (ed.), *Critical Perspectives on Derek Walcott* (Boulder, CO and London: Lynne Rienner, 1996), pp. 33–40.
Walker, Gavin, 'The Schema of the West and the Apparatus of Capture: Variations on Deleuze and Guattari', *Deleuze and Guattari Studies*, 12.2 (2018), 210–35.
Wark, McKenzie, *Molecular Red: Theory for the Anthropocene* (London: Verso, 2015).
Watkins, Claire Vaye, *Gold Fame Citrus* (London: Quercus, 2015).
Watt, Ian, *The Rise of the Novel: Studies in Defoe, Richardson and Fielding* (Berkeley and Los Angeles: University of California Press, 1957).
Welland, Michael, *The Desert: Lands of Lost Borders* (London: Reaktion Books, 2015).
Wells, H. G., *The Time Machine* (London: Macmillan, 2017).
Westphal, Bernard, *Geocriticism: Real and Fictional Spaces*, trans. Robert T. Tally, Jr (New York: Palgrave Macmillan, 2011).
Whitworth, Michael H., *Reading Modernist Poetry* (Malden, MA: Wiley-Blackwell, 2010).
Whyte, Ian D., *A Dictionary of Environmental History* (London and New York: I. B. Tauris, 2013).
Widder, Nathan, 'Deleuze and Guattari's "War Machine" as a Critique of Hegel's Political Philosophy', *Hegel Bulletin*, 39.2 (2018), 304–25.
Wiener, Norbert, *The Human Use of Human Beings: Cybernetics and Society* (London: Free Association Books, 1989).
Wild, Peter, *Desert Literature: The Modern Period* (Boise, ID: Boise State University, 2000).
Williams, Raymond, *Culture and Materialism: Selected Essays* (London: Verso, 2005).
Williams, Raymond, *The Country and the City* (London: Chatto and Windus, 1973).
Williams, Terry Tempest, *Red: Passion and Patience in the Desert* (New York: Random House, 2001).
Wilson, Edward O., *Consilience: The Unity of Knowledge* (New York: Vintage, 1998).
Wilson, Edward O., *Half-Earth: Our Planet's Fight for Survival* (New York: Liveright Publishing, 2016).
Wordsworth, William, *William Wordsworth: The Major Works*, ed. Stephen Gill (Oxford: Oxford University Press, 2000).
Yovel, Yirmiyahu, 'Nietzsche and Spinoza: *Amor Fati* and *Amor Dei*', in Yirmiyahu Yovel (ed.), *Nietzsche as Affirmative Thinker* (Dordrecht: Martinus Nijhoff, 1986), pp. 183–203.
Zalasiewicz, Jan, Colin N. Waters, Mark Williams, Anthony D. Barnosky, Alejandro Cearreta, Paul Crutzen, Erle Ellis, Michael A. Ellis, Ian J. Fairchild,

Jacques Grinevald, Peter K. Haff, Irka Hajdas, Reinhold Leinfelder, John McNeill, Eric O. Odada, Clément Poirier, Daniel Richter, Will Steffen, Colin Summerhayes, James P. M. Syvitski, Davor Vidas, Michael Wagreich, Scott L. Wing, Alexander P. Wolfe, Zhisheng An and Naomi Oreskes, 'When did the Anthropocene begin? A Mid-Twentieth Century Boundary Level is Stratigraphically Optimal', *Quaternary International*, 383 (2015), 196–203.

Žižek, Slavoj, *Welcome to the Desert of the Real!: Five Essays on September 11 and Related Dates* (London: Verso 2002).

Index

Abbey, Edward, 18, 19, 24, 35, 105, 154, 188
absolute outside, 30, 32, 60, 182
accidia, *akēdeia*, 113
Adams, Henry, 124, 127
Adkins, Brent, 90n76
aesthetics, 6–7, 8, 12, 14–16, 25–6, 27–8, 31, 36–7, 40, 42, 46n39, 80–2, 86–7, 94, 96, 98, 99–102, 104–6, 108, 112–13, 123–4, 162, 179, 185–6, 218n157
  of wasteland, 3, 4, 85, 97, 112, 123, 128, 139, 221
Agamben, Giorgio, 223
age of deserts, 26–7, 96; *see also* Eremozoic, Eremocene
agriculture, 23, 36, 74, 75, 100–1, 145, 178, 180, 193, 202; *see also* land enclosures
American southwest, 24, 28, 41–2, 122, 188, 194–5, 205, 221, 225–6
Anthropocene, 4–5, 12–16, 26, 27, 30, 33, 42, 52, 71, 95, 96, 138, 147–8, 167, 170, 177, 210, 212, 223, 224; *see also* Eremozoic, Eremocene; geology
anti-Semitism, 44n18; *see also* Holocaust; Second World War
Antonioni, Michelangelo, 170n7
apocalypse, 4, 10, 15, 27, 55–6, 77–8, 80, 82, 103, 110, 116, 120–1, 133n32, 157–8, 181, 192, 195, 198, 200, 203, 209, 210–12, 224; *see also* eschatology
aporia, aporetic space (Derridean concept), 11, 149
Arendt, Hannah, 7, 178
aridity, 19, 22, 24, 64, 99, 103, 104, 110, 111, 116, 221; *see also* dust, Dust Bowl, dust-bowlification

Aristotle, 39, 58, 65, 163
Artaud, Antonin, 58
asceticism, 22, 24–5, 27, 34, 62, 63, 77–80, 85, 113, 166, 186, 200, 206–7, 224
atopia, 29, 31, 39–40, 61, 109–10; *see also* placelessness
Attic peninsula, 64
Atwood, Margaret, 27, 133n32, 212, 225
Auden, W. H., 18, 38, 104
Auster, Paul, 5, 8, 41, 97, 128–30
Austin, Mary, 36, 122–3

Bachelard, Gaston, 132n15
Bacigalupi, Paolo, 225–6
Ballard, J. G., 5, 8, 10, 41, 156–63
Banham, Peter Reyner, 3, 124
Barrow, John, 101, 102, 105
Bataille, Georges, 82, 211, 222
Baudrillard, Jean, 7, 21, 24–5, 47n71, 48n81, 124, 204, 205
Beaulieu, Alain, 89n36
Berger, Alan, 74
Berger, John, 82
Berman, Marshall, 9
Bevis, Richard W., 17, 19, 100
biopolitics, biopower, 10, 53, 222, 223
Blanchot, Maurice, 7, 31–2, 43n18, 53, 60, 89n37, 98, 99, 129, 224
Blumenberg, Hans, 138, 160
body without organs (Deleuzian concept), 35, 58–60, 61, 66, 72, 76, 80, 81, 142, 149, 152, 172n24, 177, 197, 210
  Anthropocene and, 223
  desert island and, 139
  desert of, 35, 72, 164, 177
  literature and, 109
  utopia and, 164

248

Bowles, Paul, 62–3
Brown, Peter, 47n69
Brown, Wendy, 212n8
Buchanan, Ian, 176n132
built environment, 18, 25, 38, 73–4, 102, 109–10, 112–13, 126, 130, 156, 159, 160–2, 173n57, 175n120, 213n18, 219n176; *see also* suburbia; urban wastelands
Bunyan, John, 107–8
Burke, Edmund, 101–2
Burroughs, William S., 5, 8, 40–1, 51n139, 114, 125, 127, 192, 197–200, 201, 204
Byron, George Gordon, Lord, 7

capitalism, 5, 8–9, 15, 23, 34, 36, 37, 52–3, 55–7, 69, 77, 96, 105–9, 128, 131, 142–3, 147–8, 153, 168–9, 177, 178, 222–5
  biopower and, 10–11
  death instinct and, 28, 223
  desert and, 21, 31, 53, 80, 84, 210, 224
  schizophrenia and, 56, 58
  shipwreck and, 138–9
  spatiality and, 72–6
carbon imaginary, 11, 222–5; *see also* energy, energetics
Carlos Williams, William, 110
Carter, Angela, 5, 8, 21, 41, 200–6
Casey, Edward, 23, 29, 39, 49n89, 61
Cassuto, David, 19, 134n53
Caygill, Howard, 189
Celan, Paul, 150
central Asia, 180
Chateaubriand, François-René de, 103
Chirico, Giorgio de, 81
Christianity, 21, 24, 63, 77–8, 102–3, 107, 111, 116, 120–1, 123, 134n60, 150, 156, 195, 198, 200, 201, 203
cinema, cinematic image, 42, 170n7, 202, 204, 205, 206–7
Clare, John, 106
Clausewitz, Carl von, 189
climate change, 10, 13, 23, 57, 109, 131n1, 169, 170, 185, 225
climate fiction, 212, 225
Cohen, Jeffrey Jerome, 20
Cohen, Josh, 129
Colebrook, Claire, 45n34
Coleridge, Samuel Taylor, 24, 140

colonialism, 9, 23, 101, 118, 125–6, 143–4, 180, 181, 194, 197, 202
Crawford, Robert, 117
Crockett, Clayton, 21
Crutzen, Paul, 12, 13
cyclone, 209

Darwin, Charles, 140
death instinct, 11, 28, 79, 157, 160, 181, 208, 211, 223
death of God, 2, 7, 21, 33, 53, 70, 77, 86, 222
Debray, Régis, 107, 134n60, 202
Defoe, Daniel, 145, 146, 147, 154, 169
deforestation, 23, 75, 105, 111
DeLanda, Manuel, 52, 85
Deleuze, Gilles, 34, 38, 40, 52, 64–5, 66, 69–70, 71, 77, 82, 84–5, 90n39, 91n82, 91n93, 120, 139–45, 147, 148, 151–3, 154–6, 163, 170n7, 176n132, 188–90, 192, 213n9, 214n25, 216n81
  and Guattari, Félix, 2, 3, 5, 7, 9, 11, 12, 16, 22, 34–5, 38–9, 41, 44n22, 50n111, 52–5, 57–62, 63, 64, 66, 69, 72–5, 76, 77, 80–3, 86–7, 88n28, 89n36, 95, 97–9, 110, 132n15, 132n18, 134n74, 142, 152, 174n76, 177–9, 181–5, 193, 197, 211, 223–5
DeLillo, Don, 2, 5, 8, 21, 41, 42, 207–10, 212, 220n181
demonology, demons, 21, 70–1, 91n87, 116, 222
Derrida, Jacques, 5, 7, 11, 21, 33–4, 53, 89n36, 145–50, 152, 163–4, 173n63, 173n70, 182, 224
desert, etymology of, 22–3
Desert Fathers, 21, 22, 24, 113, 206, 221
desert islands, 5, 34, 131, 139–46, 148–9, 151–62, 163–4, 168–70, 170n7
desert of abstraction, 24, 34, 61–2, 149, 165, 180–2, 187
desert of *jouissance*, 79
desert of the real, 21, 25, 47n71, 48n81, 204; *see also* simulacrum
desert ordeal, 33–5, 55, 62–3, 77, 79, 86, 109, 116, 117, 128, 152, 157, 186–8, 191–2
desertification, 5, 23, 32, 46n60, 47n64, 48n77, 83, 225
desertum-civitas, 24–5

desire, 3, 7, 9, 22, 27, 34–5, 54, 55, 57–8, 60, 62, 63, 72, 79–81, 86, 115, 129, 141, 146–7, 154–6, 159, 160, 164, 168, 174n76, 177, 181–3, 185, 186, 187, 199, 201, 203–6, 221; *see also* sexuality
deterritorialisation (Deleuzian concept), 2, 11, 16, 35, 39–40, 47n71, 53–4, 57, 61–2, 67–9, 72–3, 79, 86–7, 89n36, 94–6, 98–9, 109, 114, 119, 125, 143, 165, 179, 190, 199, 223
devastation (Heideggerian concept), 7, 12, 15, 23, 26–7, 31–3, 35, 47n77, 53–6, 61, 80, 83–4, 94, 96–7, 108, 116, 127, 129–30, 131n1, 143, 158–9, 171n7, 177–8, 182, 184, 187, 192, 195, 205, 208, 210, 219n176, 222, 224–6
Di Palma, Vittoria, 24, 107–8
Don Juan, 76
Doughty, Charles, 27, 29, 186, 187, 189
drosscape, 74, 76
Duffy, Cian, 100
Dumézil, Georges, 182–3
dust, Dust Bowl, dust-bowlification, 23, 47n63, 111, 118, 130, 196, 207, 211–12, 225–6
dwelling (Heideggerian concept), 8, 11–12, 15–16, 29–31, 38–40, 44n18, 49n89, 61, 67, 68, 80–1, 83–4, 87, 94–9, 222

Earth (philosophical concept), 2, 7, 12, 14–16, 22, 30–3, 38–9, 45n34, 45n36, 54–7, 59, 63–4, 66–8, 70–7, 80–1, 84–7, 88n15, 89n36, 92n123, 93n145, 95–6, 98–9, 116–17, 140–2, 145, 147–8, 150, 154, 167, 170, 177–8, 184–5, 210–12, 223–5; *see also* new Earth
Eberhardt, Isabelle, 23
ecocriticism, 2, 6, 8, 12, 18–20, 33, 35–6, 42n1, 44n22, 52, 94–5, 112, 132n5
ecophenomenology, 29–30, 49n88, 89n36
ecopoetics, 40, 95–6
edgelands, 9, 175n120
Edgeworth, Matt, 173n57
Egypt, 22, 33, 75, 100, 103, 125, 129, 197, 214n34
Eisenstein, Sergei, 211
Elden, Stuart, 180, 213n8

Eliot, T. S., 4, 5, 7, 19, 21, 39–40, 51n139, 97, 109–17, 123, 124, 125, 128, 134n73, 162, 187, 199, 215n55, 221, 222
energy, energetics, 5, 9–10, 21–2, 25–6, 35, 40, 42, 54, 55–8, 69, 72, 81–2, 84–5, 97, 109, 116, 123, 125, 127, 139, 144, 151–2, 205–6, 208–11, 223
entropy, entropic landscape, 22, 25, 28, 35, 36–7, 40, 47n74, 79, 82, 84–5, 97, 110, 125–9, 130, 134n73, 199, 201, 221, 223
environmental damage, 5, 6, 177, 225; *see also* devastation
Eremozoic, Eremocene, 26–7, 42, 170; *see also* age of deserts
eschatology, 5, 7, 15, 27, 42, 53, 82, 86, 97, 124, 126, 130–1, 139, 143, 159–60, 171n8, 185, 192, 197, 208–9, 212, 223; *see also* apocalypse
exhaustion, 1, 3, 5, 14, 21, 25–6, 28, 34–5, 37, 40–1, 78–9, 82, 103, 116, 121, 124, 155, 171n7, 190–1, 199
extinction, 10, 12, 14, 26, 109, 177, 195, 207–8, 212, 223, 225–6
Eyers, Tom, 155

Farley, Paul, 175n120
fascism, 44n18, 49n89, 95, 99, 119–20, 126, 181, 185, 197
Fiedler, Leslie, 193–4, 197, 199; *see also* western (genre)
First World War, 8, 110, 113, 116, 185–7, 191, 218n157, 223
Flaxman, Gregory, 64, 68
Foucault, Michel, 8, 28–9
Freud, Sigmund, 5, 11, 28, 34, 54, 55–6, 60, 72, 79, 154, 208, 223; *see also* psychoanalysis
Fromentin, Eugène, 104–5
Fuller, Matthew, 177

geocentrism, 5, 54, 59, 80
geocriticism, 44n22
geology, 10–11, 12–14, 25, 52, 54–5, 66, 70–2, 80, 86, 91n82, 116–17, 119, 141, 160, 169, 196, 207, 208, 210–12, 223; *see also* Anthropocene; libidinal geology
geophilosophy, 3, 4, 12, 14, 22, 34–5, 38, 42, 52, 54, 59, 63, 66, 69, 89n36, 95, 118, 139, 148, 224

Gersdorf, Catrin, 19, 41, 124
Giddens, Anthony, 144
Goethe, Johann Wolfgang von, 9, 78, 103, 188–9
Goldsmith, Oliver, 36–7, 108–9, 111, 113
Gordon, Douglas, 209
Gordon, Lyndall, 112
Goriunova, Olga, 177
Graulund, Rune, 19
Great American Desert, 193
green literary analysis, 20, 43n1, 112; *see also* ecocriticism
Griaule, Marcel, 172n24
ground, grounding, 2, 12, 16, 22, 39, 54–5, 57, 59–60, 62, 63, 64–73, 75–6, 79, 86–7, 92n123, 94–5, 129, 131, 141, 147, 150, 173n57, 178–9, 181–4, 189, 193, 195–6, 211–12, 222–4
growing desert (Nietzschean concept), 5, 23, 31–3, 35, 53, 76–8, 80, 82–4, 87, 108, 110, 125, 182, 185, 206, 224, 226; *see also* nihilism

Haeckel, Ernst, 14
Hamilton Grant, Iain, 91n82, 91n87, 222
Haraway, Donna, 4, 14, 95
Hardy, Thomas, 17, 18, 40, 100
Hegel, Georg Wilhelm Friedrich, 22, 58, 65, 73, 181–2
Heidegger, Martin, 5, 7, 11–12, 15–16, 26–7, 29–33, 35, 39–40, 44n18, 45n34, 46n41, 47n77, 49n89, 53, 61, 64, 69, 73, 80, 82–3, 85, 87, 89n36, 91n76, 94–6, 98, 143, 145, 147–8, 149, 150, 167, 171n8, 177, 178, 183–4, 222, 224–5
Heise, Ursula K., 131n1, 170, 176n134
Heizer, Michael, 221
Herbert, Frank, 19
heterotopia (Foucauldian concept), 8
Hetherington, Kevin, 8
Hinlicky, Paul, 90n76
history, 13, 18, 19, 23, 24, 26–8, 31, 33, 37, 41, 52, 72, 77, 79–80, 87, 110–11, 114, 124, 127–31, 134n60, 138–9, 143, 165–6, 168, 169, 170, 171n8, 181, 191, 192–3, 198, 203–6, 209–11, 224–5
Hölderlin, Johann Christian Friedrich von, 31, 95
Holleman, Hannah, 23, 47n63

Holocaust, 126, 129; *see also* anti-Semitism; Second World War
Husserl, Edmund, 5, 59, 69, 89n36
hypersubject, 57, 62, 185, 221, 224; *see also* subjectivity

immanence, 22, 53, 60–1, 62, 64, 66–73, 75–6, 78–80, 129–31, 139, 171n8, 188, 195–6, 200, 203–4, 211, 224; *see also* transcendence
intensity (Deleuzian concept), 73, 81–2, 84–6, 87
Iraq War, 42, 206–7, 209–11, 218n157
Islam, 188, 209–11

Jabès, Edmond, 129
Jameson, Fredric, 164, 166, 168–9, 176n132, 176n134
Jasper, David, 21
Jaspers, Karl, 55
Johnson, Andrew Tyler, 89n36
Joyce, James, 142
Judaism, 77, 107, 120, 128–30; *see also* anti-Semitism
junk time, 110, 114, 199
junkspace, 73–4, 76, 91n93

Kafka, Franz, 21, 31, 129
Kant, Immanuel, 34, 54, 58, 64, 68–71, 86, 90n76, 149, 163–4, 176n129, 222
Kerslake, Christian, 64
Klossowski, Pierre, 82
Kolbert, Elizabeth, 12
Koolhaas, Rem, 73; *see also* junkspace

Lacan, Jacques, 48n81, 50n111, 55, 79, 151, 154–5, 174n76; *see also* psychoanalysis
Lacarrierè, Jacques, 24, 63
Laforgue, Jules, 112, 162
Lambert, Gregg, 52
Land, Nick, 209
land enclosures, 106, 108
Latour, Bruno, 15, 29, 45n36, 87, 92n123, 93n145, 131n1
Lawrence, D. H. 5, 7, 97, 110, 116–23, 124, 125, 200, 201, 222
Lawrence, T. E., 5, 8, 41, 103, 185–92, 193, 211, 215n55
Le Goff, Jacques, 24
Le Guin, Ursula, 5, 164–7, 169, 176n134

Le Vaillant, François, 101, 102, 105
Leavis, F. R., 113
Lefebvre, Henri, 28–9, 48n83
Levinas, Emmanuel, 7, 11–12, 30, 32–3, 43n18, 53, 98, 152, 224
Lévi-Strauss, Claude, 151, 174n76
Lewis, Simon, 13
libidinal geology, 80, 116; see also desire; sexuality
Limerick, Patricia Nelson, 19
Lindqvist, Sven, 18, 104
Lukács, Georg, 11
Luther, Martin, 79
Lynch, Tom, 19

Malevich, Kazimir, 221–2
Manson, Charles, 203
Marx, Karl, 57, 143
Marxism, 15, 28, 53, 143
Maslin, Mark, 13
McBrien, Justin, 177
McCarthy, Cormac, 4, 5, 21, 192, 194–7, 217n100
McCormack, Derek, 97
McNamee, Gregory, 19
McNeill, John R., 13
Meillassoux, Quentin, 29
Mentz, Steve, 138, 147
messianism, 107, 203, 225, 226
metaphysics, 1, 3, 7, 14, 31, 53, 61, 64, 68–70, 72, 75–7, 82, 84, 103, 142, 163–4, 201, 223
  desert and, 79, 80, 212
  of self, 3, 103
  of space, 28–9, 39, 48n83, 73, 75, 84, 127, 186
Mexico, 41, 76, 116–19, 121–2, 180, 194, 196
Middle East, 100, 102, 107, 186, 209–12
Middleton, Nicholas, 23
Millet, Kate, 120
modernism, 4, 5, 8, 18–19, 21, 26, 39, 81, 85, 94, 97, 99, 110–11, 123, 128, 215n55, 221–2
monotheism, 33, 61, 76, 202, 210
Monroe, Marilyn, 201
Moore, Jason W., 13, 15, 147
More, Thomas, 159
Moretti, Franco, 146, 168, 169
Morton, Timothy, 4, 6–7, 14–16, 24, 30, 38–9, 43n1, 57, 88n27, 96, 100–1
Moses, 66, 202

Müller, Chris, 93n134
Munif, Abdelrahman, 219n176

Naas, Michael, 149
National Socialism see fascism
Native Americans, 105, 116–18, 122–3, 126, 180, 193, 194, 197–8, 222, 226
Negarestani, Reza, 5, 209–12, 226
Neher, André, 129
new Earth (Deleuzian concept), 80, 86, 93n145, 169, 185, 210, 212; see also Earth; geophilosophy
Nicholas Ruddick, 159
Nietzsche, Friedrich, 1, 2, 4, 5, 7, 30–1, 33, 53–4, 64, 68, 69, 77–80, 82–3, 97, 103, 110, 116, 118–19, 120, 207, 222, 224
nihilism, 2, 31, 77, 79, 80, 83, 119, 120, 182, 184, 195, 197
  desert of, 53, 182, 206–7, 226
  see also death of God
Nixon, Rob, 177, 219n176
noise, 99, 110, 114–15, 126, 127–8
nomad, nomadism, 11, 16, 23, 32, 33, 34, 39–41, 43n18, 54, 57, 61, 62, 63, 67, 68, 74, 79, 84, 87, 98–9, 107, 124, 128, 179, 182–3, 185–6, 211, 224, 225
north Africa, 10, 23, 24, 41, 125
nuclear war, 7, 13, 42, 158–9, 185, 192, 207

Oedipus complex, 34, 60–1, 62, 72, 76, 77, 156, 204–6; see also psychoanalysis
Oliver, Kelly, 7, 184, 224
Ondaatje, Michael, 16
Operation Desert Storm, 206; see also Iraq War
orientalism, 78, 103, 104, 191–2
Osborne, Peter, 171n8
Otto, Rudolph, 33

Park, Mungo, 101, 102, 105
people to come (Deleuzian concept), 63, 119, 121, 139
perversion, 154–5, 157
phallus, 72, 117–18, 120, 122–3, 151, 174n76, 200–2, 204–5
placelessness, 11, 29, 33, 39–40, 61, 109–11, 116, 117, 119
Plato, 58, 64, 149, 163
Pococke, Richard, 100

postmodernism, 5, 7, 8, 18, 19, 21, 24–5, 26, 28, 39, 41, 52, 85, 94, 97, 99, 123–4, 204, 206, 220n181, 222
Pound, Ezra, 113, 135n92
Povinelli, Elizabeth A., 10–11, 13n1, 222
Protevi, John, 58
psychoanalysis, 5, 9, 22, 34–5, 50n111, 55, 61, 72, 154–5, 174n76, 182, 186, 188; *see also* desire; sexuality
Pynchon, Thomas, 5, 8, 41, 97, 114, 124–9, 134n73, 181, 197, 214n24

Raine, Craig, 111
refrain, ritornello (Deleuzian concept), 5, 16, 32, 40, 83, 86, 97–9, 110, 114–15, 117, 121, 122–3, 124, 125, 128, 132n15, 132n18, 196, 199
Renan, Ernst, 33
representational consciousness, 32, 35, 53, 55, 65, 69, 70–1, 73, 80–3, 86, 91n76, 95, 98, 111, 221
rhizome (Deleuzian concept), 75, 134n74, 193
Rigby, Kate, 20, 43n1, 97, 106
Robbins, Jeffrey W., 21
Robinson, Kim Stanley, 5, 19, 164, 167–70
Robinson Crusoe myth, 5, 9, 34, 139–48, 152–3, 154, 156–7
Romanticism, Romantic period, 2–7, 11, 17, 18, 33, 35, 37–9, 42n1, 86–7, 94, 96–7, 99–100, 103, 108–9, 111
Rossellini, Roberto, 171n7
ruins, 9, 38, 43n10, 74, 100, 102–3, 107, 110, 114, 189–92, 211–12

Sack, Robert, 180
Sade, Marquis de, 201, 205–6
Sahara, 18, 32, 62–3, 100–1, 104
Said, Edward, 103, 191–2, 216n81
Santner, Eric, 56
Sass, Louis A., 80–1
Schelling, Friedrich Wilhelm Joseph, 54, 91n82
schizophrenia, 34–5, 54–9, 61–3, 65, 80–2, 88n28, 151
Schmitt, Carl, 178–9, 181, 192, 213n9
Schneidau, Herbert, 75–6
Schonhorn, Manuel, 145
Schreber, Daniel Paul, 55–6
Second World War, 26, 30, 124–5, 130, 178, 213n13, 218n157

sexuality, 11, 34, 40, 60, 78, 113, 115, 116, 117–18, 127, 146, 154–5, 156, 157, 171n7, 181, 186, 199–206; *see also* desire; psychoanalysis
Shakespeare, William, 9, 159
Shelley, Percy Bysshe, 2, 5, 19, 38–40, 100–1, 103, 110–11, 133n32
Shepard, Paul, 75, 85
shipwreck, 5, 138–9, 141, 145, 156, 160–1
signs, semiosis, 2, 3, 5, 11, 25, 38, 40, 49n83, 60, 84, 86, 87, 94, 97–8, 99–102, 109, 110, 114–16, 123–4, 125, 129, 142, 151–2, 174n76, 183, 186, 188, 196, 226
silence, 31, 99, 100, 101, 115, 128–30, 166
Silverman, Kaja, 186
simulacrum, 21, 25, 47n71, 188, 204, 206–7
Sloterdijk, Peter, 15, 73, 96, 147
Smithson, Robert, 9, 25, 47n74, 221–2
Solà-Morales, Ignasi de, 162, 175n120
solitude, loneliness, 7, 22, 24, 26, 63, 118, 139, 141, 145, 146, 150, 152, 156, 164, 170, 172n20, 203; *see also* Eremozoic, Eremocene
Solnit, Rebecca, 180
space, 2–3, 5, 7, 11, 15, 16, 23–5, 27, 28–31, 40–2, 53–4, 59–63, 84–5, 94, 96–7, 99, 102, 104, 112, 118, 123, 129, 132n15, 139–40, 155, 156–7, 165, 170n7, 175n120, 177–80, 187, 188–90, 198, 200, 201, 203, 204, 211, 213n18, 221, 224
  decoded, 57, 109–10, 128, 143, 221, 223
  disenchanted, 3, 48n83, 159, 181
  empty, 33, 39, 40, 125, 144, 151, 157, 161–3
  Euclidean, 85
  place and, 8, 11–12, 28–30, 61–2, 89n37, 94, 116–17, 149, 222, 224
  production of, 86, 141–2
  smooth and striated, 39, 73–5, 91n93, 100–1, 104, 106, 119, 127, 178, 180, 182–6, 192, 200, 211
  spatium and, 61–3, 71–3, 85, 144, 179
  unworlded, 5, 11, 30, 81, 94, 131, 139, 152, 154, 195

state, 5, 49n89, 53, 61, 69, 73–4, 76, 99, 177–85, 188, 192, 197, 200, 207–8, 211, 213n18, 214n24, 222, 224
Steffen, Will, 13
Stengers, Isabelle, 15, 45n36
Stoekl, Alan, 222
subjectivity, 1–3, 5, 6, 22, 29, 34–5, 54–5, 57, 60–5, 69–70, 80, 83, 102–3, 128, 155–6, 181–3, 185–6, 188, 190–2, 197–8, 201, 221–4
sublime, 3, 9, 17, 20, 40, 100–2, 108, 189, 209
suburbia, 20, 25, 112, 156–8, 161–3, 221; see also built environment
surface/depth relationship, 18, 60–1, 65–6, 71–2, 140, 153–4, 160, 211–12
Symmons Roberts, Michael, 175n120

Tabachnick, Stephen, 190
Tanner, Tony, 125
Teilhard de Chardin, Pierre, 208–9
Tennyson, Alfred Lord, 71
terrain vague, 112, 162, 175n120, 221
theology, 21, 31, 33, 42, 56, 58, 102, 107–8, 129, 149
Thomas, David, 23
time, 18, 23, 28, 70, 84, 89n37, 97–8, 110, 114–15, 146, 158–60, 168, 171n8, 177, 189, 198, 202, 204, 206, 207–8, 210–12; *see also* history
topology, topological space, 1, 53, 60–2, 71, 77, 85, 149, 163, 179, 180, 185, 224
Tournier, Michel, 5, 147, 152–6, 161
transcendence, 2, 33, 53, 58, 60–1, 66, 69, 71–2, 75–6, 79, 86, 106, 127, 129, 130, 143, 148, 169–70, 182–3, 188, 196, 198, 210, 212, 214n24, 224; *see also* immanence
transcendental homelessness, 11, 12, 14
Turner, Frederick Jackson, 193
Turner, Joseph Mallord William, 82

Uexküll, Jakob von, 14, 95, 98, 132n8
urban wastelands, 9; *see also* built environment; suburbia
utopia, 8, 20, 39, 103, 139, 141, 143, 153, 155, 156, 159, 162, 163, 164–70, 197, 200

vacant lot motif, 40–1, 112–13, 116, 162, 199, 221
Van Dyke, John C., 17, 105, 133n48, 133n53, 188–9
Van Wyck, Peter C., 14
vapour, 185, 189
Vernant, Jean-Pierre, 64
Vietnam War, 192, 203, 206, 210, 218n157
Viney, William, 9, 40
violence, 5, 32–3, 127, 156–7, 177–8, 181–5, 189, 192, 196, 201, 206, 219n176, 224–5; *see also* devastation; environmental damage; war
Virilio, Paul, 7, 41, 180, 206–7

Walcott, Derek, 143
war, 4, 5, 7–8, 11, 41–2, 74–5, 110, 113, 116–17, 123–5, 130, 159, 170n7, 178, 180–92, 194, 196–8, 202, 203, 205, 206–12, 213n8, 217n100, 218n157, 223
war machine (Deleuzian concept), 41, 74, 178, 182–5, 197, 202, 207, 210–12, 225
Wark, Mackenzie, 169
wasteland, 1, 3, 4, 9, 10, 17, 18, 19, 22, 24, 26, 28, 31–2, 37, 40, 48n77, 70, 83, 106–8, 110, 111–14, 117–18, 123, 128, 130, 161, 222
Watkins, Claire Vaye, 225
Watt, Ian, 172n27
Welland, Michael, 20, 22
Wells, H. G., 159
Western (genre), 192–5, 197–200
Wiener, Norbert, 127, 134n73
Wild, Peter, 133n53
Williams, Raymond, 36–7, 106, 108–9
Wilson, E. O., 26, 27, 170
Wordsworth, William, 6, 19, 103, 109
worldlessness, 4, 5, 11, 15, 29–30, 44n18, 131, 145, 150, 195, 225

Yeats, W. B., 4, 21, 110
Yovel, Yirmiyahu, 79

zero point, zero intensity, 9–11, 18, 26–7, 58–9, 66, 82, 85, 89n36, 139, 143–4, 151–2, 155, 160, 163, 174n76, 209, 212
Žižek, Slavoj, 28, 48n81

EU representative:
Easy Access System Europe
Mustamäe tee 50, 10621 Tallinn, Estonia
Gpsr.requests@easproject.com

www.ingramcontent.com/pod-product-compliance
Lightning Source LLC
Chambersburg PA
CBHW070323240426
43671CB00013BA/2342